Hearths of Darkness

HEARTHS OF DARKNESS

The Family in the American Horror Film

Updated Edition

Tony Williams

University Press of Mississippi / Jackson

www.upress.state.ms.us

The University Press of Mississippi is a member
of the Association of American University Presses.

First edition published 1996 by Fairleigh Dickinson University Press
New edition copyright © 2014 by Tony Williams
All rights reserved
Manufactured in the United States of America

First printing 2014

∞

Library of Congress Cataloging-in-Publication Data

Williams, Tony, 1946 January 11–
Hearths of darkness : the family in the American horror film / Tony Wil-
liams. — New edition.
pages cm
Includes bibliographical references and index.
ISBN 978-1-62846-190-9 (cloth : alk. paper) — ISBN 978-1-62846-107-7
(pbk. : alk. paper) — ISBN 978-1-62846-108-4 (ebook) 1. Horror films—
United States—History and criticism. 2. Families in motion pictures. I. Title.
PN1995.9.H6W46 2014
791.43'61640973—dc23   2014014294

British Library Cataloging-in-Publication Data available

TO THE UNHOLY TRINITY OF HORROR FILM CRITICISM

Reynold Humphries   Christopher Sharrett

and the Memory of Robin Wood (1931–2009)

Contents

Contents

Acknowledgments

This work has undergone a long, but necessary, transformation since its beginning some eighteen years ago. I wish to thank the following people, and I apologize for any omissions. I'd like to begin by thanking Robin Wood for his kindness, generosity, and humanity in encouraging me during the early stages, as well as for inviting me to participate in the 1979 Toronto Festival of Festivals Horror Film Retrospective he organized with Richard Lippe. Acknowledgments are also due to Christopher Sharrett for many valuable suggestions. I'd also like to thank Douglas Winter for many stimulating suggestions made in correspondence and conversation. Special acknowledgments to Bryon Kluesner, Elizabeth Stinson, Robert Benson, Chris Sislak, and Lisa Abernathy of Varsity Video, Carbondale, Illinois, for guidance in terms of renting videos for this project. Tom Weisser of Video Search of Miami also supplied some rare material. Gratitude is also due to Beverly Fitzgerald and Cindy Grant of the Department of Cinema and Photography, Southern Illinois University at Carbondale, for secretarial assistance. Thanks to copyeditor Diane Burke, production editor Paul Rieder, as well as suggestions made by an anonymous reviewer. Finally, last (but certainly not least), special thanks to Kathleen Ensor for much patience, understanding, and support over the last few years.

◆ ◆ ◆

I feel very honored that the University Press of Mississippi has graciously allowed the appearance of a second edition of this book. My gratitude to Leila Salisbury, whose innovative work as a publisher in bringing out new work in the field of film studies, as well as updated versions of other important books, is immense. I also wish to thank Valerie Jones for her enormous help with my second book for this press, as well as Peter Tonguette for his meticulous role in going through the manuscript. I'm also honored by the fact that David

Roche has found much value in excavating past work from a very different historical era and understanding that the findings of several decades ago still echo today. Finally, I have gained much from the continuing critical support of friends such as Reynold Humphries and Christopher Sharrett and hope to learn more from certain members of a younger generation who are treating this subject matter with much more seriousness than others today.

Hearths of Darkness

Introduction to the New Edition

Hearths of Darkness first appeared in 1996 during an era in which the horror film definitively exhibited its present stage of terminal decline that endured into the early years of the twenty-first century as most examples of Hollywood (and even Southeast Asian cinema) reveal. The bleak succession of decades characterized by the presidencies of Clinton, Bush, and Obama, each much worse than their predecessor, witnessed an even deeper sense of cultural and historical crisis than was the case in the 1980s and 1990s. Far worse has been the collapse of any viable oppositional movements engaged in active critical mobilization against the status quo since the 1960s. Changes seemed possible then. They appear impossible now though one must never give up hope since history reveals that reversals are always possible at the most unlikely of times as the Bolshevik Revolution and the victory of the Vietnamese against a powerful and ruthless aggressor reveal.

The family still remains powerfully entrenched within popular consciousness, and even celebrated by former oppositional groups, such as gays and lesbians, who now eagerly embrace an institution that once opposed their very existence. Yet if there is one thing that history can teach us it is the powerful role of ideology and conservative political strategies that yield ground whenever necessary to encompass formerly opposing elements into a new amoeba-blob formation while real changes necessary for a fair and just society remain inactive due to denial forming mechanisms manufactured by powerful business and media interests. Like 1905 in Russia, progressive ideas appear on the retreat but they are by no means extinct.

As in the first edition, an important point needs emphasis. This book is not about families in general but rather the ideologically imposed version that denies any alternatives to its rule in human society. Whenever individuals are forced into continuing an institution that caused them great personal unhappiness, one in which they were born into and had no escape from at a vulnerable age, then great pathological damage can occur. This book continues

3

to document American cinematic examples of a dysfunctional institution. Undoubtedly, happy families may exist but this is no reason for the socially imposed continuation of an institution remaining dominant to the exclusion of any other viable alternatives. One of the ironies of the contemporary situation involves groups that once had an opportunity to change society for the better embracing those very mechanisms that once characterized them as outsiders. However, acceptance and economic incentives always provide key incentives for those eager to "take the money and run" back into the arms of the very social system that once condemned them.

Currently, the family still remains as a dominant unit in society, as much a part of the status quo as it was in the time Engels wrote his powerful 1884 essay, "The Origins of the Family, Private Property, and the State." The institution still remains stubbornly intact despite high increases in divorce and physical and mental abuse within its walls documented beyond any shadow of a doubt over the past several decades. It is an institution that may suit some but not others, and its rigid presence is still the cause of great unhappiness for those trapped within its domain. The family horror films of the 1970s represented an important movement within a genre that then had the potential of operating as a powerful cultural counterforce influence to suggest the necessity for fundamental change in human society. Unfortunately, despite the existence of many important talents whose careers began operating within this genre such as Larry Cohen, Wes Craven, Brian De Palma, Tobe Hooper, and others, it soon declined due to the encroaching control of corporations who subjected any diverse and oppositional type of creativity to the conditions of the marketplace. This phenomenon, which also characterized social institutions such as health and education, soon extended itself into other areas of human existence, hoping to instill into its victims mindless conformity and consumerism. That it did not entirely succeed owed much to the remnants of natural human resilience, the existence of several oppositional groups, and the contrapuntal thoughts of many who would not "go willingly into the dark night" of capitalist society.

One such talent who remained resilient in the face of overwhelming odds is Larry Cohen. Despite the fact that he did not direct as frequently as he did in previous decades, he continued to work as a screenwriter, often writing imaginative treatments that the Hollywood industry did not respect or understand. One such screenplay was *Uncle Sam* (1997). Directed by William Lustig (with whom Cohen had collaborated on the *Maniac Cop* films), *Uncle Sam* related the grim moral tale of a soldier who dies from friendly fire during the first Gulf War in Kuwait. He returns from the dead to take revenge on an unpatriotic America that includes the suitor of his widow and dumb kids, as well as those who deserve to get it. Although the narrative has several connections with Bob Clark's *Dead of Night* (1972), Cohen wrote one of his most ironic and sophisticated screenplays in which the veteran who punishes corrupt politicians, lawyers, and irreverent flag-burning teenagers is also shown to have abused his younger sister in early life and grew up to be a bullying adult who found the military an ideal cover for his aggressive tendencies. The film starred Isaac Hayes as a disabled Korean War veteran who blames himself for creating a monster by filling a violent male with visions of military glory, glory which Sam uses in life and beyond the grave to trap his young nephew into following in his footsteps. *Uncle Sam* has an apocalyptic conclusion where Hayes's character, Sam's nephew, and a disabled boy (the victim of Fourth of July fireworks) form a new defensive family to destroy this patriarchal monster. It is one characterized by the conspicuous absence of any traditional father or mother figure. They may form a new society. The film ends on a positive note with the nephew burning his war toys as his very relieved mother watches. Sam's nephew may now embrace another type of family rather than the military represented by his violent uncle and the current American business and military establishment. Despite its sophisticated premises, *Uncle Sam*, unfortunately, changed nothing: the horror genre continued its decline, one celebrated by an uncritical new generation.

Keen to embrace any changes in critical fashion, certain members of the current era's academic establishment engage in embracing ahistorical trends, justifying "torture porn," and the dying embers of postmodernism while capitalism engulfs in flames those less fortunate than themselves. I exclude from this category scholars such as David Bordwell, whose devotion to the meticulous study of film form and poetics is nothing less than sincere and whose work serves as a challenge to us all, no matter how much we may diverge from his type of critical approach. I've often felt that a deep study of his work may make us better makers of meaning, though not in the sense he would necessarily approve of. I reserve my disagreements for those who actively deny the role of the horror film as having an active social meaning. At its best, the horror genre calls on the spectator to engage with the narrative to see whether whatever excesses it generates are relevant. Are they actually responses to the context rather than a means of providing gratuitous displays of gore and special effects? Does the violence have a significant meaning or is it there as a result of self-indulgence on the part of the director pandering to an audience s/he regards as shallow and stupid? Such issues bring into play the question of responsibility, one affecting both director and spectator. Unfortunately, from the late 1970s onwards, the horror film mostly became self-indulgent exercises in gore and special effects. Recent remakes of earlier disposable products, such as *Friday the 13th* and *Nightmare on Elm Street*, and the deliberate gutting of key social themes within earlier versions of films such as *The Texas Chain Saw Massacre*, *The Hills have Eyes*, *The Last House on the Left*, and *Dawn of the Dead* speak for themselves.[1] No matter how much the apologists for what has been correctly defined as "torture porn" attempt to argue for the supposed importance of such work, they are little better than neoconservative and neoliberal groupies for an industry (and now a government) that engages in life imitating artifact. I will not dignify these films with the term "art."[2] Furthermore, the loss of Robin Wood (1931–2009), who wrote the first key essay on the horror film that influenced us all, is a case in point since he recognized the beginning of our current ideological malaise and condemned the decline of a genre he initially championed in the 1970s, one in which the reactionary horror film eventually gained ascendency over more progressive examples.[3] Fortunately, there are a few critics left who operate in their particular ways according to the important critical tradition of humanitarian responsibility he pioneered in the realm of film study. I include Reynold Humphries, Christopher Sharrett, David Greven, David Roche, Annalee Newitz, Linnie Blake, and Brad Stevens in this category, and I hope there may be others that I have unjustifiably overlooked.[4]

When first written, *Hearths of Darkness* was not envisaged as just a historical document limited to any one particular era but as a record of a significant moment in cinema which suggested the necessity of future change and the beginning of what would become a new type of society in the future that would eliminate vestiges of the old (including the need for horror films). Such an optimism for social change also occurred in the early years of the new Soviet society, as Leon Trotsky's short collection of essays, *Problems of Everyday Life* (1924), documented hopes for change in the relationships between human beings, especially in the family at a time when utopian hopes for a new society would possibly result in positive changes in human behavior. We now know that such desires never achieved realization due to both the stubborn continuation of old patterns of thought within Soviet society and the developing bureaucracy and totalitarian control developed by Trotsky's rival Stalin that gave the very idea of "communism," let alone socialism, a bad name from which it has never recovered. (It is also in the interests of the establishment to promote that bad name continually.) Yet utopian hopes for a better world do exist. Despite the fact that pioneers such as Marx never described the future in detail and engaged in generalities, it is also important to acclaim any movement that does describe a system much better than the one we live in because it may provide a model for future changes. One little-known example of this continuing pattern of utopian thought appears in the works of Chinese educator and philosopher Kang Youwei (1858–1927).

Those familiar with Zhu Shilin's *Sorrows of the Forbidden City* (1948) and Li Han-siang's two films about the Dowager Empress, *The Empress Dowager* (1975) and *The Last Tempest* (1976), will recall hearing the name of Kang Youwei and seeing his presence in Li's second film where he, along with the emperor, attempts to institute reforms in late nineteenth-century China during the Hundred Days movement of 1898 against powerful establishment interests. His most well-known book is *Da Tong shu*.[5] Begun in 1884 and not published in its entirety until 1935, it envisaged a future utopian society inspired by Confucius that would be ruled by one central government and be free from all political and racial boundaries. Like many utopian projections about the future, it contains both progressive ideas and negative ones that belong to the context in which the author lived. For this study, however, the key aspect of Kang's work is conceiving of a world in which marriage is not a lifelong contract but one only valid for a year that can be renewed at the non-coerced wish of either partner. Conceiving of the first era of his historical overview as a "World of Disorder" involving the presence of political and national boundaries and inequality between men and women, Kang thought of a future time when the sexes would be equal and that gay relationships (including marriage) would not be condemned but regarded as a normal part of human existence in that final "Age of Complete Peace and Equality When One World has been Achieved."[6]

What is really remarkable about Kang's work is not just the idea of the eventual abolition of the State and private property but also the destruction of the very institution of the family. In Book Two, Part Six of *Datong*, Kang engages in a detailed argument as to the necessity of abolishing the family to attain that utopian One World of Complete Peace and Equality. He sees the institution as placing great strain on both the parents and children leading to inequality tension. In one section he provides a logical argument against the current right-wing tendency of homeschooling: "For, if people do the teaching themselves, and if the family itself is a school, then confusion and narrowness are already extreme, and we cannot have breadth, lofty intelligence and purity."[7] The character of Stuart in Samuel Fuller's *Shock Corridor* (1962) is one emotional casualty of such a situation. Nurturing and all stages of education will be public and not private affairs. Kang's solution may not appeal to everyone and, like all ideas, would need adaptation and modification. But his aim is to avoid the psychological dissonances and tensions that occur in most families. He aims at a solution that benefits everyone. Nurturing will be a public task through all ages of life. It is remarkable to read a work that envisages not just free public education but also free healthcare and care of the aged. All these aspects go together in a world that will have no class, family, and national divisions. "The parents will not have the toil of nurturing and caring for the children, or the expense of educating them. Moreover, the children will be cut off from the father and the mother and will not see them very often, for being removed to distant places. Yet again (because of) moving about, they will not be acquainted with each other. This is not to leave the family, but to be naturally without the family. Having neither given favours nor received favours, there will naturally be no ingratitude. To carry this out will be very easy; its result will be great contentment."[8]

Eliminating the family is part of the goal of abolishing the conditions that produce competition. Once that is done the competitive drive can be rechanneled into cooperative and constructive action. In *Datong*, Kang describes the new society in detail absent in Marx, believing that the new age of peace and harmony will bring equality and contentment in a world free from the stresses and struggles we encounter today. Debate still continues as to whether traditional Chinese ideals or Western thought inspired his socialist ideas. Since the Datong concept appears to have evolved over a long period of time, it is probably a mixture of both. Yet what is important is his constant reference to the Confucian ideal of *ren* or *humanity* throughout his thought; Kang would have regarded the concepts of the dictatorship of the proletariat or the Great Leader syndrome with horror and another bad example of the Leadership element he aimed to abolish in his New Society.[9]

As he outlines in the concluding pages of *Datong*, Kang is adamant that the abolition of the family is a key plank in ensuring the One World of Complete Peace and Equality, which still eludes us.

"There will be no husbands and wives, and so there will be no fighting over sexual desire, no provisions against sexual immorality, no repressive regulations of bearing of grievances, no resentment or hatred, no divorces, no miseries of punishment and killing. There will be no family relationships, and so there will be no need to support (one's family members), no compulsion to do the right thing (by them), no wrangling over (property shares). There will be no nobility, and so there will be no depending upon intimidation or coercion, no oppression, no grabbling, no intriguing for position, no toadying. There will be no private property . . . There will be no class divisions, and so there will be no mistreatment or oppressive laws (on the part of the superior class) and their violation and opposition (by the inferior classes)."[10]

Whether we reach the goal of complete equality—where everyone will be at peace with no need of any form of punishment, capital or otherwise—is still doubtful since we are more deeply within an Age of Disorder than ever before. Warning signs certainly exist. The family horror film is still one of them, sounding like a warning bell of disturbing features and echoing the wider world outside. Although it may not be as dominant as it once was, it still maintains its role as a symbolic alarm bell of our era's internal and external problems. Like any flexible subgenre, it will adapt and change as new cultural and historical factors emerge responding in whatever manner necessary. The family still remains but it is under siege more than ever before—both in everyday life and cultural representations. Until social conditions change for the better, the family will still remain a *hearth of darkness*, with its associated imagery becoming more and more disturbing.

As Samuel Fuller wrote at the end of *Run of the Arrow*: "The end of this story can only be written by you."

1

Introduction: Family Assault in the American Horror Film

During the 1970s an unusual event affected Hollywood's representation of the American family. Generally revered as a positive icon of "normal" human society, the institution underwent severe assault. The antagonist was no external force such as the Frankenstein monster, Count Dracula, or Cat Woman; instead the threat came from within. In *Night of the Living Dead* (1968), a young girl cannibalizes her father and hacks her mother to death. In *Rosemary's Baby* (1968) Satan decides to reverse two thousand years of Christian hegemony by sending his messiah to destroy American society from within. Polanski's film anticipates an assault that continues in *The Exorcist* (1973) and *The Omen* (1976). An androgynous alien embarks on inverting the Christ legend in *God Told Me To* (1976). Mutant babies emerge from typical American families in *It's Alive* (1973) and *It Lives Again* (1978). In *The Last House on the Left* (1972), *The Texas Chain Saw Massacre* (1974), and *The Hills Have Eyes* (1977), typical American families encounter their monstrous counterparts, undergo (or perpetuate) brutal violence, and eventually survive with full knowledge of their kinship to their monstrous counterparts. All these depictions contradict normal idealized family images in mainstream American film and television. They disrupt the ideological norms of family sitcoms such *as Father Knows Best, I Love Lucy, Ozzie and Harriet, The Donna Reed Show, The Life of Riley*, and *Leave It to Beaver*.

This study intends to examine cinematic treatments of this assault from Universal Studios in the 1930s to the present day. It aims to analyze a specific movement within the horror genre by tracing its origins in American culture and society. Opposing critics who regard family horror as a nonexistent or negligible factor within the genre, *Hearths of Darkness* argues that it is a fundamental structure of Hollywood cinema. Rather than attempt any comprehensive overview, this work examines specific films that deal with the family as a material cause of horrific events.[1]

Far from providing a *Masterpiece Theatre* survey of familiar works by distinguished names, *Hearths of Darkness* concentrates upon comparatively obscure and underappreciated films such as *Grave of the Vampire*; *Jack's Wife*; *Martin*; *Alice, Sweet Alice*; *Flowers in the Attic*; and *Manhunter*, in addition to such well-known works as the Frankenstein and Val Lewton series. There is a particular reason for this strategy: neglected works more insightfully examine family horror than better known examples. As Larry Cohen and George Romero films demonstrate, low budget, independent features often contain more dynamic interpretations than those from major studios, and underappreciated works may offer viewers more complex meanings than widely distributed films. The type of radical argument presented in any film far outweighs prestigious canonical definitions involving studio and authorship.[2] Neglected films are more crucial in this respect. They are more important than big budget works that often dilute material to gain appropriate ratings and wider market distribution.

Far from being innovatory, family horror belongs to an American cultural tradition whose literary roots influenced a cinematic tradition developing from Universal, Val Lewton, Hitchcock, and other films into a definable 1970s subgenre. It did not wither away in the eighties but affected several so-called "slasher films" such as the *Friday the 13th, Halloween*, and the *Nightmare on Elm Street* series. Certain directors did achieve significant results but not in isolation from relevant cultural and cinematic parameters. Hitchcock's achievements in the 1950s belong to a context that also generated such films as *The Bad Seed, Homicidal*, and *Lady in a Cage*. They are all part of the same social era and represent different responses to it. Recently neglected works such as *Manhunter* and *Day of the Dead* are also more innovative than overacclaimed and overrated films such as *The Silence of the Lambs*.

The family plays a significant role in any society determining everyone's psychic and social formation according to changing historical, political, and ideological dimensions. Families may be complex entities, good or bad, depending on particular circumstances. As an institutional prop of bourgeois capitalism, producing colonized subjects and reproducing ideological values, the family is extremely dangerous. A case may be made for abolishing it entirely. But this argument is too rigidly dogmatic. It avoids more challenging dialectic and dialogic approaches to understanding families as contradictory entities containing good and bad features. Despite existing within capitalism, some families attempt alternative strategies by nurturing their children's talents and inspiring oppositional thought; other families brutally reproduce oppressive structures within their own spheres of influence, literally becoming "hearths of darkness." Filmic representations often depict traumatic disturbances by using formal codes of supernatural horror and spectacular violence. As Michael Lerner points out, "For most people, 'family' is a code word that expresses their hopes for a long-term loving and committed relationship. It is this that people yearn for, and this yearning represents a positive and hopeful fact."[3] Institutional structures pervert this yearning. Using physical and mental instruments of torture, they turn vulnerable individuals into neurotic conformists, psychotically disturbed victims, or even serial killers avenging former humiliations upon a new generation of surrogate victims.

This work examines cinematic representations of dangerous family situations. Although connections exist between dysfunctional real-life families and their cinematic counterparts, the relationship is often indirect and complex. Meanings occur—often contradicting the manifest level of textual operations. Films are narrative devices, operating within fictional and ideological contexts ultimately determined by material factors within society in a complex manner.

Hearths of Darkness also examines cinematic representations of contradictions and psychotic breakdown. It uses psychoanalytic perspectives by understanding family horror as the return of the repressed within a specific cinematic context. Sigmund Freud's original formulations, supplemented by recent clinical evidence and sociological perspectives, still provide valuable insights into understanding the dangerous nature of pathologic social formations.[4] As Freud recognized, civilization relies on repression, often molding individuals in ways detrimental to their individual potentials. But repression never totally succeeds. Repressed factors return in distorted forms, often violently reacting against agents of repression such as state or family. Certain films show a crisis situation depicting this return. Universal (1930s) and RKO (1940s) representations depict Frankenstein monsters and Cat People as family victims in an indirect, allegorical manner. Films from *Psycho* onward often present the monster as originating within the family, a dysfunctional and traumatic product of internal tension.[5]

Freud's definition of an Oedipus complex, generated within a family situation, still usefully explains psychic mechanisms operating within an exploitative patriarchal capitalist system. The family is the ideal launching pad for producing gendered beings. It has a specific social and psychic function, policing desire, social relationships, and artistic expression. According to Freud's scenario the male child must relinquish identification with the pre-Oedipal feminine maternal realm to gain access to the Law of the Father. Females must accept a subordinate status. Children must suitably fit into work and home. Despite social changes since Freud's time, the Oedipus complex still symbolically depicts a status quo operating within western patriarchal society.

However, this process is neither as universal as Freud believed nor is it devoid of outside influence. If we substitute the role of parents as active social agents, complicit in their children's oppression (as well as their own) for Freud's universal, unconscious discourse, a different picture emerges. The Oedipal trajectory is not a natural course of individual development. It results from social manipulation. In a discarded aside in *Introductory Lectures on Psychoanalysis*, Freud discerned that the child learns the particular gendered direction society expects from normal family values.[6] What appears as instinctual actually results from an oppressive behavioral pattern within bourgeois society. It may take psychopathologic directions when parents rigidly force offspring into dangerous conformist patterns. They may punish children as surrogate victims for their own social frustrations and inability to live up to patriarchal family values. Psychotically submitting to patriarchal rules, the father may become a monster who sexually and violently dominates his family, compensating for his lack of ideologically defined capitalist success outside the home. The mother may unthinkingly reproduce ideologic dictates by forcing children into conformist patterns, abusing them, or even turning a blind eye to her husband's psychotic activities. A circular pattern may result. Traumatically abused victims may become future victimizers, continuing the dark punitive Law of the Father like Jerry Blake of *The Stepfather*.

The family horror film demonstrates this process. But it belongs to a genre neither inherently progressive nor reactionary. Any text combines both features, especially one belonging to a genre implicated in formal psychic mechanisms that display violent aggression and special effects. Robin Wood regards certain horror films as containing utopian aspirations that represent attempts to resolve tensions emerging from everyday lives "in more radical ways than our consciousness can allow." Other critics differ.[7] Christine Gledhill believes that the horror film "simply offers a fetishistic feast in acknowledgement and perpetuation of the perversity on which patriarchy is founded, the simultaneous fascination with, and disavowal of female sexuality."[8] Retreats into fantasy may take conservative as well as radical directions in works such as *Fatal Attraction* (1987), *Parenthood* (1989), *Presumed Innocent* (1990), *Regarding Henry* (1991), *The Hand That Rocks the Cradle*, and *Single White Female* (both 1992) show. Films often contain conflicting meanings involving hegemonic contests that reflect social contradictions.[9] A supposedly progressive work such as Jonathan Demme's *Philadelphia* (1993) safely contains its AIDS narrative within Capraesque, ideologic, overdetermined images of family life. Conversely even a despised *Friday the 13th film* may reveal meanings the text wishes desperately to repress. Films reflect social contradictions. They never, in themselves, change society, but they may reveal tensions forming the basis for future movements. What actually counts is not the text or aligned genre but the degree of contradiction involved in each particular film that suggests the necessity for progressive alternatives to be realized in a world outside the cinema.

Family horror films attempt this. But they suffer from enclosure within a formal structure often antithetical to radical meanings. Recent investigations into the horror genre concentrate upon formal mechanisms and often ignore relevant textual meanings. The genre's very form may attempt to repress revolutionary insights. As Freud pointed out in *Jokes and Their Relation to the Unconscious*, the very nature a repressed outlet takes allows the "safe" expression of ideas in a socially safe manner. As a never taken seriously genre, the horror film lends itself to such recuperation within formal boundaries. However, although examples from the seventies revealed some significant radical overtones, recent counterparts attempt to deny this, relying on special effects devices inherent within the genre's very nature. But the final texts are not always monolithically conservative. Form does not totally dictate content. However, examining the horror genre's formal mechanisms becomes essential toward understanding ideologic repressive blockages.

Like melodrama with its hysterical overtones, the horror film is a genre of excess with a particular style and content. Formal attributes do not mark any genre as "progressive." As Laura Mulvey and Jackie Byars note, certain melodramas function conservatively, employing stylistic and thematic devices to conceal, rather than reveal, contradictions.[10] But sometimes significant contradictions appear within each text's particular content. The melodrama is a sister genre to family horror because it has a specific relationship to it in terms of depicting family trauma. Within melodramas excessive elements often appear at the moment of extreme family tension and breakdown. These features parallel the excessive special effects that occur at specific moments within the horror genre. Both devices attempt to distract audiences away from what is really happening.

Andrew Tudor rejects any idea of a definable family horror film. Like "body horror" in the eighties, *he* regards it as one feature in the genre's vision of a morally and physically disordered universe.[11] Noting the family's importance as a "basic ordering structure in the genre's social setting," he sees the attack on the family as due to the development of a "paranoid horror," peculiar to the 1970s and 1980s, where the family becomes "the most obvious and easily represented social analogue to the threatened mind or body of the modern genre."[12]

By contrast I not only wish to argue for the validity of a family trajectory within horror itself but also suggest the genre's very form has an intrinsic relationship with family situations. Paranoia and threat are not inseparable from families. Psychoanalytic findings reveal that vulnerable children acquire these feelings in early family life. The family is a key component in many representations ranging from Freud's own family romance to art, literature, and cinema itself. Both Wood and Wes Craven regard the family as the major structuring device in Hollywood cinema.[13] Contemporary horror's formal and paranoid aspects are fundamental components of family horror.

Freudian psychoanalytic concepts emerge from clinical case histories all involving the nuclear family. They did not fall ill in isolation from this structure. Freudian psychoanalysis analyzes victims of malfunctioning family structures. As applied to the horror film, the Freudian paradigm is family related. Thus, all horror films are really family horror films containing psychic mechanisms that are derived from clinical cases associated with dysfunctional families. Some films express this connection better than others—particularly the family horror film.

Cinema is also a social institution closely aligned with psychic mechanisms that attempt to regulate subjectivity in particular ways similar to traditional families. Film genres may function as a part of society's mental machinery. As Christian Metz states, "The cinematic institution is not just the cinema industry (which works to fill cinemas, not to empty them), it is also the mental machinery—another industry—which spectators 'accustomed to the cinema' have internalized historically and which have adapted them to the consumption of film."[14] Relevant cultural factors influence an audience's acceptance of particular artistic forms within any historical era. On their basic levels, genres operate according to repetition and difference patterns. A horror film reveals social equilibrium affected by a disequilibrium often caused by monsters. The monster is a feature of most horror films, but it sometimes has connections with a normality to which it is supposedly opposed.

Steve Neale understands the monster's body as expressing a fundamental signifier of the horror genre.[15] Voyeuristically fascinated by the monster's strange appearance, audiences become attracted to spectacular and exhibitionist mechanisms operating within the horror genre. This fascination usually ends with the spectacle of the monster's destruction. Neale regards such exhibitionistic overtones as having fetishistic associations. A fetish involves a denial of something by placing a substitutionary mechanism in its place. In Freudian terms this involves disavowal of sexual difference. But this does not prevent us from also noting relevant historical and cultural factors behind such forms of disavowal as Laura Mulvey recently argues.[16] A horror film may attempt to disavow a repressive family situation by displaying excessive formal elements to distract audiences.

If we understand disavowal in Lacanian terms (a perfectly legitimate procedure as long as we understand this to denote a particular, nonuniversal, conservative mode of control), it insightfully describes the *attempted* operations of patriarchal psychic mechanisms. After encountering traumatic castration disrupting a pre-Oedipal relationship to the mother's body, the child disavows "lack" (or difference) by engaging in a fetishistic process whereby substitutionary operations attempt to deny the original trauma. This condition continues throughout the rest of the child's life, affecting meaning and representation. As far as cinema is concerned, representations and genres are rooted within this unconscious dilemma. Imaginary representations occur. They not only attempt to deny an original castration trauma involving the child's relationship to the mother but also try combating other contradictions to the status quo whether social or artistic. Fetishism is one mechanism involved in producing substitutionary deceptive imaginary representations.

Neale sees fetishism as fundamental to the horror genre. It is designed to suspend inquiry into what is really behind imaginary representations. The monster's body is a familiar fetishistic device. It generates (and is the source of) the special effects inherent to the genre. Trapping the spectator's gaze in voyeuristic fascination, films use the monster's body as a spectacular fetish effect operating in a disavowing function. Horror films may embody a manufactured trauma by denying not just the original castration trauma but also any contradictory, antisocial tendencies. Historically speaking it is not surprising that many works of horror of the seventies reveal a balance between the genre's formal mechanics and radical meanings within the text. By contrast the majority of work in the eighties and nineties, emerging from an era of conservative reaction and artistic impoverishment, overemphasized spectacular fetishistic formal elements within the horror genre, particularly in slasher films. The spectator's gaze may become fascinated by a particular film's stylistic overinvestment, a factor common to both *Friday the 13th* and the films of David Lynch. Alternatively Tim Hunter's *The River's Edge* interrogates voyeuristic tendencies inherent within the gaze, leading viewer's to question the social formations that cause such individual dilemmas. Hunter's film presents a bleak, nihilistic vision of Reagan-era youth who are living within a spiritually bankrupt wasteland devoid of radical alternatives, justifiably critical of a failed, narcissistically inclined sixties generation.[17] As reader-reception theories show, viewers may not succumb to textual one-dimensional readings.[18] They may choose to read "against the grain," bypassing spectacular violent mechanisms within slasher films to privilege neglected thematic motifs within the text and discern what exactly suffers repression. Viewers have the potential of reading beyond deceptive formal devices.

Disavowing mechanisms do not always totally succeed. Neale also notes the horror film as being "concerned so centrally not only with curiosity, knowledge and belief, but also, and crucially, with their transgressive and 'forbidden forms' and with the establishment of the terms and consequences to which such forms are to be understood."[19] A genre's formal operations may not entirely overpower these transgressive elements. Conflicting voices may struggle for expression within every film. This is particularly so if certain horror films contain contradictions opposing ideologic attempts to impose acceptable normality. These contradictions may suggest alternative patterns opposing rigid family values.

Recently defined features of "body horror" and textual "horrality" appear to contradict this. As Pete Boss notes, "it is difficult to integrate readings of political progressivity with the fantasies of physical degradation and vulnerability" featured within recent works.[20] But what relevant social factors cause such excessive features of signifying excess? Right-wing reaction, AIDS, pollution, unemployment, homelessness, the destruction of the ozone layer, and personal insecurity within everyday life may generate apocalyptic manifestations of bodily destruction in such cases, seeking to deny relevant material causes by concentrating upon formal displays of spectacular destruction. But it is possible to bypass these formal voyeuristic attractions and engage in alternative interpretations. Other explanations may clarify the excessive appearance of body horror. Patriarchal hysteria over masculinity's contemporary dysfunctional condition may influence various representations of decaying and dissolving male subjects in Cronenberg's *The Brood* (1979), *Videodrome* (1983), and John Carpenter's *The Thing* (1982).

Although the Reagan era attempted to restore family values by attacking feminism and restoring male hegemony, it also saw the massive destruction of male-dominated heavy industries, resulting in high unemployment and the creation of low-income "feminine" service jobs and the destabilization of patriarchal family foundations. Gender roles fell into crisis. Families broke up, family farms were foreclosed accompanied by frequent cases of suicide, teenagers distrusted their parents more than before, and reports of dysfunctional and abusive families became common. The right reaction did not go uncontested. Minority groups actively fought back. Despite its conservative agenda, the Reagan-Bush ideology did not totally succeed. Although slasher films presented the younger generation as surrogate victims of patriarchal executioners, most revealed victims fighting back and, in certain cases, winning as in the later *Friday the 13th* and *Nightmare on Elm Street* series. But, despite gratuitous violent imagery, one thing was certain—the traditional family was finished. The very virulent nature of slasher films reveals an unconscious patriarchal hysteria trying to hold back contradictory tensions, especially those involving changing gender roles.

Neale notes interesting relationships between horror films and gender.[21] The monster's very nature questions the Oedipal trajectory's gender norms. As various Frankenstein and "Mad Scientist" films show, monsters do not usually follow normal patterns of family reproduction. But neither are they totally nonhuman. They possess human traits whether they are two-legged Frankenstein creatures, mutant babies, or gormandizing Blobs! As diffuse and heterogenous constructions, monsters often challenge patriarchal family norms. Monsters must remain "monsters" with no explicit relationship to everyday life. Socially conditioned psychic mechanisms rally to turn dangerous pleasures into unpleasure.[22] But this process is not rigidly monolithic.

Some feminist critics see significant relationships between monsters and heroines within the genre. Linda Williams notes certain horror films involve parallels between the woman's look and monsters that query patriarchal gender definitions. Both female and monster potentially threaten a socially defined male order of things, depending on the family as an agent for social reproduction.[23]

Jacqueline Rose's analysis of *The Birds* highlights the role of woman as monster within the traditional family. It also associates the family with the paranoia Tudor separates from family horror. Rose associates the family with paranoia and aggression. She refers to Melanie Klein's descriptions of paranoid mechanisms affecting the child's early ego development and the aggressive drives involved within its problematic subjective development in patriarchal society. A direct connection exists between the winged aggressive attack against Melanie Daniels and Mrs. Brenner's paranoid fears of losing Mitch to Melanie.[24] Like Marion Crane in *Psycho*, Melanie threatens Mrs. Brenner's incestuously perverse family structure. The film contrasts a mother fearful of abandonment by her son and a daughter abandoned by her mother years before. At the climax Melanie becomes Mrs. Brenner's ideal daughter, safely recuperating within the family and no longer a sexual threat to her domain. The birds have reduced Melanie to a state of infantile dependence. They externally symbolize Mrs. Brenner's paranoid-aggressive drives against a figure she regards as a "monster." The effect is a lesser, but nonetheless violent, version of Mrs. Bates's disciplinary and punitive function in *Psycho*. It also echoes motifs in *I Walked with a Zombie*.

As Rose recognizes, "The effect of the aggression is therefore revelatory of its source."[25] Like *Psycho*, *The Birds* reveals the horror genre's characteristic use of spectacularly violent aggression. However, these fetishistic formal operations attempt to conceal material origins responsible for their manifestation. As Rose shows it is possible to interrogate the text by psychoanalytic means and analyze the particular mechanisms at work. Viewers may thus discover relevant material factors within a generic monstrous guise. A psychopathologic family structure, defining woman as monster and subjecting her to patriarchally motivated paranoid-aggressive drives, emerges from such analysis.

Barbara Creed also sees intrinsic connections between horror and gender. Referring to Freud's essays "On Fetishism" and "Medusa's Head," she notes significant parallels between formal features of horror films and a particular patriarchal mental imagery. Programmed by "castration anxiety," male spectators may interpret feminine difference as a monstrous result from a cultural conditioning that defines women as inferior and unclean. Noting associations between horror films and birth-imagery involving blood, bodily waste, and fluidity, Creed cites Julia Kristeva's ideas concerning traditional definitions of women. Patriarchy often views females as "other" and "abject" beings.[26] In both historical and contemporary manifestations, the "abject" does not "respect borders, positions, rules."[27] Seeing parallels between culturally produced anxieties involving blood, decay, death, dismemberment, bodily deterioration, and incest, and horror films containing these features, Creed notes a common origin. Both territories involve competing tensions between the prepatriarchal maternal realm and a patriarchal domain of order and shame. Horror films thus parallel religion's historic role in defining boundaries. Neale also notes that horror film discourses are "so frequently saturated with religion, while critical discourses accompanying the genre are rooted in mysticism and other forms of irrationalism," which he regards as a particular form of disavowal.[28]

Both Neale and Creed see the horror film as displaying mechanisms of psychic control that defend the patriarchal order from anything threatening its stability. Emphasizing the genre's formal effects, they provide valuable insights into relevant psychic operations. Patriarchy depends on a particular "order of things," that is, an institutional psychic structure needing the family to process subjects into accepting rigid rules concerning gender and social reproduction. These psychic operations necessitate a patriarchal family structure, but they are not always totally successful. The repressed always returns in one form or another. Although theoretical and formal descriptions are valuable, they are only part of the story. Family horror manifests itself differently in each particular text. A close analysis of content is necessary in any serious study of this phenomenon.

The family horror film is no isolated entity. It echoes important patterns within the national psyche that appear within literature, theater, history, and other cinematic genres. David Rabe's radical Vietnam-era play, *Sticks and Bones*, is an indispensable text for understanding Vietnam family horror films whose characters often deny disturbing events. Historically American society similarly attempted to ignore the trauma of Vietnam until it was too late. Such associations have cultural and historical connections. They parallel Raymond Williams's definition of a cultural materialism involving "a continuous interaction between ideology and the material forces of history," in which a field of mutually if also "unevenly determining forces" establishes each society's tendencies and contradictions.[29] Such interactions also characterize cinema. Wood warns of dangers facing any attempts to separate cinematic genres from each other. They really represent "different strategies for dealing with the same ideological tensions," particularly those involving monogamy, civilization, and family structures.[30] The family horror film excessively depicts factors appearing in other Hollywood genres as Wood recognizes.

"The concept of Family—a motif that cuts across all genres in the Hollywood cinema, informing and structuring westerns, musicals, comedies, gangster films, melodramas alike—is obviously basic to American ideology, and in the American film the Child has his full meaning only in relation to it.[31]

John Cawelti believes the western speaks to adolescent male fears concerning adulthood and its accompanying tensions.[32] Several Hollywood westerns reveal tensions between family values and independence also occurring in family horror. Raymond Bellour regards the Hollywood western as structured toward negotiating male desire and forming a monogamous family couple.[33] But sometimes the machinery breaks down. In her analysis of two classic Hollywood westerns—*Duel in the Sun* and *The Man Who Shot Liberty Valance*—Laura Mulvey analyzes the presence of psychic mechanisms disrupting Bellour's ideal of a happy Hollywood family ending. Originating from pre-Oedipal desires, they oppose the family's institutional role in manufacturing conformist personalities.[34] Like the horror film and melodrama, even the male-orientated western genre attempts to negotiate tensions depicting nonrecuperable characters as antisocial or "monstrous." The "look" Linda Williams describes in the horror film also exists in the western, a look destabilizing acceptable family gender definitions. Neale and Paul Willeman note certain auto-erotic scopophiliac mechanisms, operating in certain westerns, that reveal masculine pleasure at the sight of a male body.[35] Like the horror genre the western has its own stylistic codes (such as landscape, costume, and Indians) that attempt to disavow homoerotic features. Neale explains the frequent active and violent nature of certain westerns in terms of such disavowals. Understanding the fluid nature of cinematic genres explains why many horror films are hybrid formations using motifs found in other Hollywood genres. Both *The Texas Chain Saw Massacre* and *Race with the Devil* have affinities to the western. The Tobin family in Anthony Mann's *Man of the West* (1958) predate Hooper's slaughterhouse kin.[36] Both American literature and cinema feature dark families opposing normal communities functioning as their repressed counterparts. This trait is both historical and cultural. The Ishmael Bush clan in J. Fenimore Cooper's *The Prairie* have cinematic descendants such as the Clantons of John Ford's *My Darling Clementine* (1946), the Cleggs of *Wagonmaster* (1950), and the Hammonds of Sam Peckinpah's *Ride the High Country* (1962).

Several westerns depict Indians as demonic monsters from the id, a feature present within violent frontier imagery from Puritan times onward.[37] Whether in the Puritan Captivity Myth or the Hunter Narrative, Indians appear as "abject" beings or monsters. The rigid Puritan community projected their repressed sexual and violent tendencies onto their Indian neighbors. Cooper's Leatherstocking aims at a state of physical and moral purity, fearing to become too much like his Indian brother Chingachgook with his "unacceptable" sexual and violent associations. These fears appear in certain films. Ford's *Drums Along the Mohawk* (1939) introduces Blue Back with an expressionist lighting that makes him resemble a sexually threatening Frankenstein monster when he approaches the heroine. Like Elizabeth in *Frankenstein* (1931), she collapses in the bedroom. In Val Lewton's *Apache Drums* (1950), Indians suddenly appear from the darkness like horror film monsters. In Ford's *The Searchers* (1956), Scar appears like a monster from Ethan Edwards's id, destroying the family and carrying away its females—actions the white hero unconsciously desires.

Monsters also appear in gangster films. As portrayed by Cagney, Robinson, and Muni, the tough guys of *Public Enemy* (1931), *Little Caesar* (1930), and *Scarface* (1932) violently overcompensate for deep masculine insecurities by reacting against the family and feminine "soft" values. Cagney's later performance in *White Heat* (1948) reveals a mother's role that nurtures his psychosis. Later *Godfather II* (1974) depicts Michael Corleone as a monster created by family and social circumstances determining his destiny even before birth.[38]

Melodrama's hysterical nature as a genre of excess parallels horror,[39] especially in depicting victims created by patriarchal family values. Unlike sacrificing mothers in maternal melodramas such as *Stella Dallas* (1925/1937), Laura Hope Crews's suffocating mother in *The Silver Cord* (1933) manipulatively conspires to keep her adult sons in a state of infantile dependence. She deliberately destroys their sexual relationships, anticipating Mrs. Bates of *Psycho*. Like Norman Bates, Kyle Hadley of *Written on the Wind* (1957) is a monster created within a traditional family. Kyle also parallels another hysterically weak son—Dave Waggoner in Mann's *The Man from Laramie* (1955)—who cannot live up to a masculine ideal dictated by patriarchy. Dave is a family victim; his condition is generated by the family antagonism between an overbearing father and a suffocating mother. Dave hysterically overcompensates by engaging in excessive violence to prove his manhood. He acts like a rampaging horror film monster throughout this film.

Similar family tensions affect Pearl in *Duel in the Sun*, revealing key associations between western, melodrama, and horror film. And in Mann's earlier, aptly titled *The Furies* (1950), Barbara Stanwyck's masculine daughter-figure incestuously desires her father by wanting to inherit his property like a first-born son. After scarring his mistress she becomes an outcast from her home, designated monstrous by patriarchal law. Many Mann films contain dysfunctional families with angst-ridden children contradicting normal family values.

"Weak" son figures also appear in epic works such as *El Cid* (1961) and *The Fall of the Roman Empire* (1964) whereas Hollywood musicals such as *Meet Me in St. Louis* (1944), *Yolanda and the Thief* (1945), and *Oklahoma* (1956) contain significant nightmare sequences opposing family normality. Even *Frankenstein Meets the Wolf Man* (1943) contains a musical number well before *The Rocky Horror Show* (1975) united horror film and musical: Adia Kuznetoff's Tyrolean song—*Faro-la, faro li!* After this sequence wolf man Lawrence Talbot resembles melodramatic male hysterics such as Dave Waggoman and Kyle Hadley. In *Meet Me in St. Louis*, young Tootie demolishes snow people, which releases her aggressive feelings against her family.[40] Her act anticipates the more direct methods of Karen and Regan in *Night of the Living Dead* (1968) and *The Exorcist* (1973). *Yolanda and the Thief* also contains a dream sequence depicting the hero's neurotic fears over monogamy and family. *Oklahoma*'s dark dream sequence reveals Laurie's secret desires for sexual assault by Judd, who represents Curly's monster from the id.

Even *Citizen Kane* (1941) contains family horror motifs. The opening shots abound in gloomy expressionistic horror film signifiers with a dark Gothic castle dominating the bleak landscape. Although Kane is no Dracula or Frankenstein, he is a symbolic monster in personal and professional life, a victim of capitalist avarice who soon becomes an oppressor. Welles hints that young Charles comes from a dysfunctional family: his mother appears cold and never exhibits warmth towards her son whereas Charles's father is much older and lacks family authority. Mrs. Kane may wish to send Charles away from home to protect him from an abusive father. Inheriting a large fortune Charles overcompensates for traumatic early separation. He is trapped within Freud's anal stage, acquiring both people and possessions and yearning for a control he never had in his early life. He eventually dies longing for "Rosebud," a maternal symbol of a lost family relationship that was never ideal. Like trauma victims and *Psycho's* Norman Bates, Charles unconsciously represses the reality of a morbid family situation. By engaging in idyllic reminiscences of a mother (whose persona is ambiguous in the flashback sequence), Charles exhibits tendencies present in other monstrous sons in *Psycho*, *Don't Go into the House* (1979), and *Maniac* (1980).

Released in the same year, *Keeper of the Flame* displays similar features. Newspaperman Spencer Tracy uncovers the real character of a deceased military hero (loosely modeled on General McArthur), discovering a fascist streak beneath an idyllic patriotic mask. He traces the origins to a repressive mother who lives in a Gothic house. *Keeper of the Flame* is an interesting work, linking family upbringing, capitalism, and society, that is suggestive of Wilhelm Reich's thesis of families as the breeding ground for fascism in *The Mass Psychology of Fascism*. Repressive mothers feature in films such as *Now Voyager* (1942) and *The Baby* (1972) and in TV movies such as *The Killer Bees* (1974). By submitting to patriarchal norms, they overcompensate for victimization by sacrificially destroying their children. Every June Cleaver has a Ma Barker or Ma Grissom. In *Bloody Mama* (1970) the former controls her violent, male children by manipulative incestuous bonds of mother love. Her methods parallel Mrs. Halyard's in *Lady in a Cage* (1964). *The Grissom Gang's* Ma Grissom (1971) is a cinematic descendant of Puritan Captivity Myth monstrous mother, Hannah P. Dustin, condemned by Leslie A. Fielder in *The Return of the Vanishing American* for her treacherously murderous deeds.

Of all genres the family horror film is the one emphasizing these particular features. But it must never be viewed in isolation. Like Hollywood cinema, it represents a response to cultural discourses within American literature.

American literature contains many examples of tensions between the family and individual freedom. Huck Finn "lights off" for the territory and travels down the river with Jim, his Negro companion. Huck also is an abused child—he is brutalized by his drunken father. In *Moby Dick*, Ishmael joins the Pequod for some undisclosed family reason and forms a strong friendship with Queequeg, as Natty Bumppo did with Chingachgook. The opening chapters of *Pierre* reveal a suffocating family situation. Mrs. Glendenning uses her son to mirror her own desires, living her life through his, like the mother in *The Silver Cord* and Oliver Reed in *Curse of the Cat People* (1944). Melville's semiautobiographical "I and My Chimney" depicts symbolic male castration and domestic conflict. The highly subversive "The Tartarus of Maids" shows a radical awareness of female exploitation within capitalism.[41] Jack London's male and female heroines venture into Klondike and South Sea wildernesses away from civilized constraint. The revolt is not always totally male-orientated.[42] And Emily Dickinson's white "angel of destruction" spins her yarn of pearl in a poetic feminist protest.[43]

One early novel anticipating family horror themes is Robert Montgomery Bird's *Nick of the Woods* (1837). As a work of paranoia, it is a generic hybrid, fusing western and horror motifs later found in works such as *The Texas Chain Saw Massacre* (1973) and *Race with the Devil* (1975). Like Blue Back in *Drums Along the Mohawk*, Nathan Slaughter's opening appearance evokes images of a horror film monster. He is "a figure stalking through the woods at a distance, looking as tall and gigantic in the growing twilight, as the airy demon of the Brocken or the equally colossal spectres seen on the wild summits of the Peruvian Andes."[44] Nathan is a dark version of the Hunter of the Puritan Captivity Myth, stalking an Indian foe and decimating any tribes he encounters. He also resembles the Indian hater of Melville's *The Confidence Man*. The once pacifist Quaker conceals a dark secret—savage Indians murdered his family after he handed them his weapons. Although consciously doing this as an act of good faith, the novel suggestively implies he secretly desired the Indians to destroy his family. Unable to come to terms with this wish, he engages in an individual odyssey by slaughtering any Indian he encounters. Like Ethan Edwards, Indians become scapegoats for his repressed paranoia. This tradition reappears in *It's Alive* when Frank Davies becomes a twentieth-century Indian hater, initially denying his close affinity with his mutant son.

The family horror film belongs to this important American cultural tradition of protest against domestic constraint.[45] It has roots within a Gothic tradition that links such figures as Nathaniel Hawthorne, Edgar Allan Poe, Ambrose Bierce, and H. P. Lovecraft. Explicitly described by Lovecraft as a "scion of antique Salem and great-grandson of the bloodiest of the old witchcraft judges,"[46] a morbid Puritan background of claustrophobic family associations haunts Hawthorne's writings. *The House of Seven Gables* contains two family horror motifs: Colonel Pyncheon's ancestral portrait, which embodies a dark family curse, and the house itself. The latter represents claustrophobic family dominance, that is, the past's hold upon the present. *Curse of the Cat People, Meet Me in St. Louis*, and *Psycho* all feature Gothic houses. In *The Scarlet Letter*, Roger Chillingworth (ancestor of *Rosemary's Baby's* Roman Castavet), returns from a Satanically defined wilderness. He represents the repressed side of Dimmesdale, who conceals his sexual sin from the community. But Pearl, the love-child of Dimmesdale and Hester Prynne, is the most interesting character in the novel. She anticipates the demonic children of such Satanic films as *The Exorcist* and *The Omen*. The Puritan community regards this hyperactive child as Satanic because her behavior affronts rigid family defined norms of social control.[47] Haunted by his family associations with the Salem witch trial judges, Hawthorne understands Pearl's motivations. She not only reacts against a family situation based upon lies but is also an heir to children of the witch trial period. These young girls, aged between eleven and twenty, usually accused middle-aged females between the ages of forty-one to sixty.[48] Obviously they resented repressive family practices by projecting their discontent onto maternal figures who were responsible for maintaining family discipline. Misunderstanding the nature of their resentment, they expressed their anger in mystifying language, using Satan as a code for their discontent. Their activities not only represented a form of disavowing fetishism, they also echoed later explanations used in films such as *Rosemary's Baby*, *The Exorcist*, and *The Omen*.

Puritan witchfinders believed demonic possession influenced childish aggressiveness. Cotton Mather saw this as a motivating factor behind the Goodwin children's disobedience toward both their parents and the minister who prayed for their soul.[49] Some Puritan children anticipated Karen's actions in *Night of the Living Dead*. Ministering to Elizabeth Knapp during traumatic fits, the Reverend Samuel Willard noted that Satan "urged upon her constant temptations to murder her parents, her neighbors, or children . . . or even make away with herself."[50] These features really represent childish reactions against repressive family situations.

Derived from Puritan traditions, Gothic motifs find their way into American literature. In Hawthorne's "Young Goodman Brown," the title character travels into a dark forest. He projects paranoid tendencies onto this landscape that originate from his unwillingness to acknowledge his wife's sexual desires. This mode of repression parallels similar psychic mechanisms within westerns and horror films whereby the wilderness functions as a displacement mechanism.

"Alice Doan's Appeal" is another return of the repressed narrative. Derived from Puritan traditions and anticipating *Race with the Devil*, the tale involves a nightmare situation whereby the heroine encounters Salem's revered dead who appear in blasphemous incarnations that contradict earthly pious family associations.[51]

Edgar Allan Poe explored the dark side of family normality in various writings. Marriage tales such as "Eleonora," "Berenice," "Morella," and "Ligea" depict revealing motifs of suffocating relationships, incest, and necrophilia within monogamous family relationships.[52] "The Fall of the House of Usher" tells of a decaying house whose very structure reflects an incestuous, necrophiliac, dark family secret between brother and sister.

Similar family relationships appear in Ambrose Bierce's tales. They usually involve a parental figure's grisly death in relation to a dysfunctional family.[53] "The Death of Halpin Fraser" depicts a dying man's last days as he becomes haunted by memories of an incestuous relationship with an avenging mother, and "The Spook House" anticipates motifs in *The Texas Chain Saw Massacre* and *The Hills Have Eyes*.

H. P. Lovecraft's fiction has a strong relationship to family horror. His Cthulhu Mythos not only anticipates the body horror themes of 1980s cinema, with composite human-monster figures such as Wilbur Whately of "The Dunwich Horror," it also reflects the author's own situation as an abused child.[54] Certain tales depict paranoid male heroes threatened by an ancestral curse. *The Case of Charles Dexter Ward* deals with a paternal ancestor who psychically and physically devours his descendant. "The Rats in the Walls" features a Gothic house, cannibalism, blasphemous hints of humanity's foul origins, and a degenerate ancestral possession that eventually destroys the hero. "The Thing on the Doorstep" is Lovecraft's Gothic rendering of child abuse: a father's spirit possesses his daughter's body; she dominates her lover thereby causing his eventual physical dissolution.

◆ ◆ ◆

Family horror films continue this important cultural tradition. This book examines the most important examples. The following chapter, "Classical Shapes of Rage: Universal and Beyond," traces family horror within *Frankenstein* and other Universal films. Despite regarding horror as an external threat, the films cannot entirely disguise the fact that it actually emanates internally from the family. Chapter 3, "Lewton or 'The Ambiguities,'" reveals the producer's sympathetic understanding of all too-human monsters created by oppressive patriarchal family normality. Chapter 4, "To *Psycho* and Beyond: The Hitchcock Connection," concentrates on *Shadow of a Doubt* and *Psycho* in relationship to later treatments of family horror. Although Hitchcock's treatments are superior, they also belong to a historical context temporarily divesting the genre of supernatural associations that reveal families as the real source of horror. Minor works such as *The Bad Seed*, *Homicidal*, *The Strangler*, and *Lady in a Cage* also reflect similar, if less accomplished, understandings by showing Hitchcock's relationship to a particular cultural context. Unfortunately, most horror films exhibited a reluctance to carry examinations of the 1950s to their logical conclusions. Chapter 5, "Return of the Native: The Satanic Assaults," examines the satanist cycle as examples of recourse to deceptive supernatural explanations. Despite this several films in this series contain contradictory features that reveal the Satanic threat as really emanating from family trauma. The widely condemned *Exorcist II—The Heretic* actually attempts progressive directions to escape from the genre's conservative premises. Chapter 6, "Far from Vietnam: The Family at War," reveals the Vietnam War's effect on family horror. David Rabe's *Sticks and Bones* reveals family denial mechanisms present in films such as *The Hills Have Eyes*. Chapter 7, "Sacrificial Victims," examines lesser known horror films such as *Grave of the Vampire, Jack's Wife, Martin,* and *Alice, Sweet Alice,* and the films of Larry Cohen, which reveal suggestive material motifs within supernatural horror. Chapter 8, "Chain Saw Massacres: The Apocalyptic Dimension," analyzes family trauma as an example of contemporary crisis cinema. Chapter 9, "The Return of Kronos," argues that family horror themes actually occur within conservative treatments in the *Friday the 13th* and *Halloween* series. Chapter 10, "*Poltergeist* and Freddy's Nightmares" continues this argument by stating family horror themes are still featured in films of the eighties but in a different manner from their predecessors. Chapter 11, "The King Adaptations," examines cinematic treatments of Stephen King's work as a continuation of family horror themes within his literary output. Chapter 12, "Into the Nineties," examines neglected examples of recent family horror films such as the *Child's Play* series, *Manhunter,* the *Stepfather* films, *Parents, Psycho IV, Flowers in the Attic,* and *Day of the Dead* as more appropriately and genuinely realizing tensions within the genre rather than overpraised works like *The Silence of the Lambs.*

The family horror film belongs to a definable historical context. As it develops it reveals associations the genre's formal mechanisms attempt to repress. Such associations really began in the Universal films, a body of work that attempted to externalize a horror that really originated from within the family.

2

Classical Shapes of Rage: Universal and Beyond

Universal's Baron Frankenstein originates from nineteenth-century literary motifs documented in *Love and Death in the American Novel*. Instead of fleeing into the wilderness with a male companion, Frankenstein retreats into his laboratory to create a monster. He seeks refuge from familial obligations to engage in an act that is contrary to civilized morality. The scientist gives birth, producing a creature who represents his repressed alter ego. Its clumsy physical movements parallel those of a child prior to its induction into society's rigid behavioral and educational patterns. Count Dracula breaks every social taboo by violating both males and females; Larry Talbot's wolf man is a tragic family victim. These so-called monsters embody alternatives that society rejects. Denied expression they channel their energies into violence. Family and society destroy supposedly external threats that really originate internally.

Superficially the family appears as irrelevant plot distractions within the Universal series. Ivan Butler criticizes the "stiff dullness in the 'normal' scenes and characters" and the "abysmal plunge into the inanities of the wedding preparations and the rest of the village nonsense" in *Frankenstein*.[1] They are, however, really fundamental to the narrative. As family representations they statically oppose the dynamic nature of the monster's assault on social taboos. As a flowing entity, emerging into life from the charnel house of death, the creature is an "abject" violent embodiment of everything society refuses to face. Embodying the cannibalistic and aggressive elements within Freud's oral and anal stages in his "Three Essays on Sexuality," the monster's very nature offends his civilized antagonists.[2] Although the monster represents

29

everything the family wishes to repress, it also violently incarnates their thwarted desires—the monster is not merely a monster.

Colin Clive's Henry Frankenstein flees from his pallid sweetheart and stuffy, aristocratic father to produce the real "heir to the house of Frankenstein." In *The Bride of Frankenstein* (1935), male and female monsters represent the other sides of their respective creators, Henry Frankenstein and Mary Shelley. *Son of Frankenstein* (1939) depicts Henry's son, Wolf, falling under the spell of father's portrait and retreating from his dull family to revive a being Ygor describes as his own "brother." Both Ygor and the creature are socially created monsters that merge at the climax of *The Ghost of Frankenstein* (1940). In *Dracula* (1931) and *Dracula's Daughter* (1936), father and daughter embody socially unacceptable bisexual, oral-aggressive components that threaten civilization's rigid gender structures. Lawrence Talbot's lycanthropic condition originates within a repressive family institution.

All these monsters are family creations. Henry Frankenstein artificially creates a monster; his successor of the 1970s, Frank Davies, procreates one in *It's Alive* (1974). Although severely wounded at the climax, Frank Langella's Count manages to devastate patriarchal institutions in John Badham's *Dracula* (1979), and the Andy Warhol *Frankenstein* (1974) presents an already corrupt family institution. Its director Paul Morrissey's excessive visceral displays reveal the impossibility of drawing any fine line between family and monsters.

There is an important difference between the thirties and later decades. The Universal series imagines the family threatened by outside forces according to each text's manifest level. However, close examination reveals that monsters articulate deep tensions already within the family. Later decades will understand the impossibility of such blatant, external projections, but Universal's representations were part of an isolationist America retreating from foreign landscapes, securing its "City on a Hill," and developing apartheid mechanisms against "unwholesome" influences. Hollywood produced such regular guys as Clark Gable, James Stewart, John Wayne, and Fred Astaire for America. Villains were suspicious foreigners like Bela Lugosi, Boris Karloff, and the various gigolos in RKO's popular Astaire/Rogers series. If not dangerous, they were either untouchable, gentlemanly figures like Ronald Colman or stuffy, neurotic, highly strung types like Colin Clive.

The Great Depression and its isolationist tendencies continued earlier American mythic patterns. Although Nathaniel Hawthorne and Henry James praised Europe as the cradle of civilization, the majority opinion, represented by Ralph Waldo Emerson, Walt Whitman, and William Carlos Williams, hailed America as the new vine, free of her progenitor's corrupting soil.

Whitman extended the analogy to extreme proportions: Europe was a rotting corpse; its decomposing aroma threatened American vitality and immediate burial was essential.

Despite Woodrow Wilson's efforts, World War I's aftermath revived isolationism. Warren Harding's anti—League of Nations platform struck receptive chords within American nativist feelings. With the onset of a Republican administration foreshadowing Reaganite laissez-faire, Harding's Red Raids, the crushing of American socialism, the smearing of labor movements as foreign inspired, and the development of a culture of consumption and materialism (whose debilitating effects appear in the last two books of John Dos Passos's *U.S.A.* trilogy), xenophobia became a national characteristic. The Wall Street crash led to attacks on "foreign" Jewish bankers who were held responsible for engineering the collapse. Europe became the ideal scapegoat, and Bela Lugosi embodied an appropriate incarnation. Representing a decadent, class-ridden order, this suave aristocrat exerted a powerful charm on unsuspecting females by draining them of their vitality similar to the economic machinations of European financiers during that fatal Black Friday of 1929. The Old World became a "blasted heath"; its landscape threatened American ideals. In *The Werewolf of London* (1935), a foreign trip leads to the deadly infection that contaminates Henry Hull. Bela Lugosi's sinister overseer uses European feudal methods in a Haiti devoid of any awkward American associations in *White Zombie* (1932).[3]

This paranoid strain had cultural and psychoanalytic features that were derived from Puritan scapegoat mechanisms. Universal's supernatural motifs contain definable psychic patterns. Freud's 1919 essay, "The Uncanny," explains relevant associations in the Frankenstein series.

Noting the ambivalent nature of the uncanny (*unheimlich*) and its opposite (*heimlich*), Freud argued that the former's supposed "strangeness" results from a repression process, defamiliarizing something initially familiar, to the subject under analysis. What was once acceptable becomes unacceptable or (using Kristeva's term) "abject." Freud linked the *unheimlich* to the womb.[4] As noted above these motifs derive from the role of the patriarchal family in disavowing the significance of the feminine and other oppositional features.

Freud also analyzed a "double" motif, one occurring in both literary and cinematic fantasies. He traced the development of this idea from Egyptian funerary practices. The "double" was a duplicate of the immortal soul. It functioned as an insurance policy guarding against the soul's possible destruction. Originally stemming from an erotic investment in the self at a very early age, the "double" eventually becomes something hated and feared, often functioning as a ghostly harbinger of death. Defensive feelings concerning narcissistic overattachment to one's own self become projected on to a hated and feared double. Noting parallels between cinematography and the dream-world after viewing the 1925 German expressionist film version of Poe's "William Wilson," *The Student of Prague*, Otto Rank made several key observations in his classic work, *The Double*. Recognizing connections between narcissism and paranoia in certain literary representations, he wrote that the most common symptom resulting from the subject's inner division and projection is "a powerful consciousness of guilt which forces the hero no longer to accept the responsibility for certain actions of his ego, but to place it upon another ego, a double, who is either personified by the devil himself or is created by making a diabolical pact."[5] The double represents a powerful narcissistic form of self-preservation, often depicted in a negative form. Freud also states that the "double" motif may receive fresh meanings from later stages of ego development.[6] Although the double originally personifies narcissistic self-love, it may appear in a hostile form.[7] Henry Frankenstein's monster certainly represents "a wish-defense (in Otto Rank's *The Double*) against a dreaded eternal destruction"—marriage and family, a suffocating floral chain he unconsciously reacts against. His monster violates all the social norms he dare not, finally confronting his creator as a "messenger of death" in a burning mill. The rejected creature faces a twin who refuses to acknowledge the implications of his creative process. Universal's first three *Frankenstein* films are really Gothic family romances.

This motif appears within the original novel. According to Ellen Moers, Mary Shelly was fully aware of its psychosexual and family elements. The novel contains aspects of both "awakening sexuality" and a "horror story of Maternity."[8] Mary Shelley studied her own family history, knew of her mother's pioneering feminist writings and their condemnation as the works of a "monster," and deeply felt the pain of paternal rejection when she became involved with Shelley. In *The Madwoman in the Attic*, Sandra M. Gilbert and Susan Gubar note the operations of gender-blurring techniques in the novel as well as incestuous associations. Reading *Frankenstein* as Mary Shelley's inversion of Milton's patriarchal *Paradise Lost*, they see a deliberate ambivalence in the constant role duplications and reduplications such as creator/creature, God/Satan, victimized monster/avenging monster. Traditional gender categories such as mother/daughter, orphans/beggars, and monsters/creators are inherent within the novel.[9] Working inside a filthy workshop with obscene sexual associations, Victor creates a being, but in so doing, he discovers he is neither God nor Adam but Eve, author of a monster.[10]

Frankenstein is thus a work of sublimated female rage, protesting at an unjust "order of things" founded upon artificial categorizations of human life within rigid family gender formations. Recognizing the presence of "abject" birth imagery, Gilbert and Gubar see the book echoing Adrienne Rich's twentieth-century description of female figurative monstrosity, "a woman in the shape of a monster / A monster in the shape of a woman."[11] Monstrosity also applies to all humans forced into restrictive family mediated gender roles. In that sense we are all monsters.

The cast list concluding the credit sequence is significant. Karloff's name is omitted—instead there is a question mark. Although concluding credits mention his name, this initial lack is important. Learning that early dramatizations placed a blank line next to the name of the actor playing the monster, Mary Shelley commented, "This nameless mode of naming the unnameable is rather good."[12] But as Gilbert and Gubar comment, this reply was disingenuous because names, as well as family trees, haunted Mary throughout her life. Mother of an illegitimate and prematurely born baby and sister of the illegitimate Fanny Imlay, she knew all too well the constricting nature of the family institution.[13]

The film version emphasizes what Henry reacts against. In the opening scenes a family group (grandparents, mother, child, and other relatives) mourns the death of one of its members. An initial shot reveals a hand lowering the coffin with a rope. This hand motif occurs frequently throughout the film, emphasizing the member both as a means of creation and destruction. The camera tilts up, tracking past the mother who holds her son's hand. Presumably they all mourn his father's death. When the group leaves, Henry and Fritz (Dwight Frye) disinter the body. Two prominent statues dominate the graveyard, articulating the film's duality motif. A hooded death figure leans on its sword, tilting toward the right; opposite is a crucified Christ. Unearthing the coffin Henry leans against it in close-shot. His hand rests, smoothing it like a lover comforting his sweetheart. He exclaims, "He is just resting, waiting for a new life to come."

Henry obviously wishes to reclaim a deceased father from the family institution by reconstituting the body and restoring life in his own parody of the birth process. Henry opposes the family from the very beginning—his proposed creation will not be "of woman born." As he later says to Dr. Waldman (Edward Van Sloan), "That body is not dead. It has never lived! I created it!"

The next sequence reveals the world from which Henry wishes to escape. It opens with a photograph of Henry. The frame's confines symbolize social entrapment. From what we have already seen, Henry is clearly not suited to the role his society wishes for him. He is isolated, socially and physically, from this domain of normality. Even the image reveals a significant tension. A candle appears to the right of the photograph. Its flame anticipates many oppositions—Henry's Promethean revolt, the lightning that animates the creature, and the fire that eventually consumes it.

Elizabeth (Mae Clarke) tells Victor (John Boles) of Henry's three-month isolation. In close-shot she speaks the following lines, intimating that Henry's "experiments" are really unconscious reactions to his future family entrapment: "The very day we announced our engagement he told me of his experiments. He said he was on the verge of a discovery so terrific that he doubted his own sanity. There was a strange look in his eyes—some mystery—his words carried me right away."

Henry's cynical, crusty father, Baron Frankenstein (Frederick Kerr), is suspicious. Stuffy, haughty, overbearing, taking a sadistic delight in humiliating the Burgomeister, treating servants and villagers condescendingly, he snorts, "I understand pretty well—huh!—there is another woman, and you're afraid to tell me. Pretty sort of experiments these must be! Huh!" Although correctly sensing sexual associations, the old fart inaccurately surmises Henry's real intentions. The sequence ends with the Baron storming away, intending to drag Henry into his marital obligations. "There is another woman and I'm going to find her."

Henry and Fritz labor successfully, birthing their creation despite family intrusion. At first sight Karloff's creature appears forbidding. Tall, alien, a stitched mixture of various body parts, it represents life's originally diffuse nature before emerging from the womb into identity and social training. But the creature initially seems confused and not dangerous. It appears curious, uneasy with his surroundings, obediently performing actions in response to Henry's commands; it is an untrained and unsocialized infant.

After the creation Henry appears as at ease as if he has just achieved orgasm. And so he has by giving "birth."[14] Henry's mentor, Waldman, opposes Henry's scientific idealism; he wishes to steer him into more socially acceptable channels and regards the creature as a blasphemous monster. When it reaches in innocence and curiosity for the light, Waldman cries, "Shut out the light"! Henry unthinkingly follows his older mentor, abandoning his creation to Fritz's sadistic tortures. Chained inside a dark dungeon, the creature winces in pain when provoked with a burning torch. Light now becomes a tormenting object.

By heeding Waldman's command, Henry submits to dominant social norms. Waldman wishes to bring Henry back into normal scientific channels. The Baron wishes to trap his son into performing his required social duties—of marrying and siring an "heir to the house of Frankenstein"—clearly ignoring the psychological damage this will cause his son. Waldman, the Baron, Elizabeth, and Victor are complicit agents in the social order. By immersing

Henry into the family, they stifle his energies, making him a normal husband and father, an acceptable social being similar to the one buried in the film's opening scenes.

The creature embodies Henry's double, his repressed alter ego, suggestive of a new world of gods and monsters. However, Henry cannot consciously accept the implications of his act, that is, the father abandons his child. Lacking nurture and positive directions, the creature turns violent. Its savage behavior results from social alienation and abandonment. Finding no acceptable outlet for potential energies, confined to a dark cellar, and tormented physically and mentally like an abused child, the creature moves toward violence. It turns on his creator like an angry child against a negligent father. Henry does not help the situation. He uses Fritz's torture object, the lighted torch, against his creation. The supposedly rational Henry ignores a confused being's helpless situation. Waldman subdues the creature. Reviving Henry, Waldman urges the creature's destruction. Totally oblivious of the real motives behind Waldman's request, as well as his own negligence for allowing Fritz's behavior, Henry agrees.

The next sequence reveals the pernicious alliance between family and social institutions. It also links Henry and his creature. In the laboratory Elizabeth urges Henry to return home and forget his experiments. They are both in mid-shot. Elizabeth is at the right of the screen while Henry's head is to the left. A row of surgeon's gowns appears behind them. Submitting to her desire, he falls into unconsciousness, his head reclining on the sofa. The image fades to black. The next scene is a high-angle shot of the unconscious creature on the operating table. Its head is to the left frame, paralleling Henry's position in the previous scene. Dr. Waldman examines the body before dissection. He stands over the creature in approximately the same position as Elizabeth did in the previous scene. The row of surgeons' gowns appears behind them. Waldman's attempt at physical castration duplicates Elizabeth's subtle moves which aim at Henry's symbolic castration.

However, the creature does not submit so easily. Feeling the knife penetrating its body, it awakes and strangles Waldman, subsequently escaping to wander through the countryside. The sequence concludes with a scene of Henry and Elizabeth in an idyllic rural setting. Their positions echo their former placement within the laboratory as well as doubling those of the creature and Waldman. Henry and Elizabeth comment on their Edenic environment's "heavenly" parallels. But Elizabeth is a socially seductive serpent. By repressing Henry's real desires she duplicates Waldman's destructive activity.

The creature is not totally dangerous. It only acts in self-defense against social and family institutional violence. Wandering through the countryside, it encounters little Maria. The little girl has no prejudice. But a tragic accident occurs: believing Maria will float on the lake like the flowers they throw in, the creature accidentally drowns her. Viewing restored footage sixty years later, the full scene shows the creature's perplexed reaction to its mistaken action.[15] Far from revealing sadistic pleasure, its face exhibits confusion and anxiety. It stumbles off into the countryside. Although dangerous the creature is not malicious (despite the criminal brain "explanation" which Whale ignores). It is a social victim, an oversized, confused adult/child abandoned by its father, as confused as John Steinbeck's Lenny in *Of Mice and Men*. Despite little Maria's tragic demise, Maria's father is really responsible for leaving his daughter to play, unsupervised, near a dangerous lake.

The House of Frankenstein learns of the tragedy immediately before Henry's marriage. A prominent close-up shows a miniature of a bridal pair representing Henry and Elizabeth. An orange-blossom circle entraps the two small figures, a flower representing three generations of Frankenstein family weddings. Baron Frankenstein makes a toast to the real reason for the nuptials—"an heir to the house of Frankenstein"—another member of a social class the family has to produce to maintain power. But the real heir is already in the house. While Henry weakens, the monster violently carries Henry's revolt to its ultimate conclusions. The creature intuitively returns to his other "home."

Henry locks Elizabeth in her bedroom as a safety measure. But Whale emphasizes what really lies behind this action by stressing a close-up of Henry's hand locking the door. He leaves her vulnerable, secretly wishing for the creature to enact his repressed desires. When the guests break down the door, Elizabeth's body lies across the bed, suggesting sexual violation. The creature thereby prevents a ceremony that Henry has struggled to avoid. But Henry never admits his responsibility—he desires his "child's" death at the hands of avenging villagers who are depicted like an angry lynch mob in a western.

Despite Henry's disavowal he does not escape filial retribution. The creature confronts and overpowers him, carrying him to a nearby windmill. Surrounded by the villagers, the creature throws him to the ground. The villagers set the mill alight, and the creature perishes in the flames, tormented to the last. A long-shot showing the blazing mill, its vane tilted to the right like the hooded death figure of the graveyard in the film's opening shot, concludes the sequence. The film ideally could conclude here.

But it does not. Universal studios desired a "happy ending, even a clumsy one."[16] Realistically Henry could not have survived his fall. When the villagers view his body, a hastily postdubbed voice on the soundtrack states he still lives. Henry exits the film like a corpse; he never recovers. The final scene is a weak coda. As the Baron toasts the future heir to the house of Frankenstein, we see no expected close-up of Henry and Elizabeth. Instead we view two background figures who could be substitutes (and probably are). Everything is conveniently forgotten as the family indulges in denial mechanisms by pretending nothing has really happened.

◆ ◆ ◆

The Bride of Frankenstein contains motifs involving the twofold, satirical treatment of religious institutions and of sexual desires within supposedly objective scientific experiments. Whale mediated these subversive ideas under the guise of black humor and succeeded in distracting studio executives and Hays Office officials.

The prologue associates Romanticism's leading lights (the Shelleys and Lord Byron) with dark irrational forces. *The Bride of Frankenstein* opens with a long-shot of a Gothic castle during a stormy night. As the camera tracks in, we see the castle on a hill which dominates the surrounding landscape, paralleling Frankenstein's laboratory in the earlier film. Inside Byron speaks about the storm in Promethean terms.

> How beautifully dramatic. . . . The crudest savage exhibition of Nature at her worst without—and we three, we elegant three within. I should like to think that an irate Jehovah was pointing those arrows of lightning directly at my head—the unbowed head of George Gordon, Lord Byron—England's greatest sinner.

The storm reminds the audience of the creature's birth in the first film. Conversing with Shelley, Byron speaks of Mary, "She is an angel." The camera position changes to a medium close-up of her. Working at her embroidery, she replies in a knowingly sweet voice, "You think so?" Byron compares Mary's fear of the storm with her recently written novel. "Can you believe that bland and lovely brow conceived a Frankenstein—a monster created from cadavers out of rifled graves?"

The lines significantly blur masculine and feminine creative boundaries. Although Mary writes and Frankenstein acts, both participate in a symbiotic birth process. Whale's visual style hints at the real meaning of the fantasy. During Byron's speech the shots privilege Mary and Byron. As husband Shelley's presence is perfunctory. Although we never return to these characters after the prologue, their presence haunts the film. Elsa Lanchester's Mary becomes the Bride of Frankenstein in the concluding scenes. Even though the others do not reappear, two later characters do—the creature and

Frankenstein. The creature's very presence represents a transgression of the natural order as did the real "Bad Lord Byron." After birthing the creature in her novel, Mary becomes a monster; Percy Shelley, her husband, parallels Henry Frankenstein. Contemporary criticisms of the trio's lifestyle in Switzerland referred to "unholy" practices involving marital violations. Whale concludes the sequence with visual associations that link sexuality and the Gothic, which culminate at the film's conclusion.

In *Frankenstein*, Whale visually links Henry and the creature by close-ups of their hands. When Henry acclaims the creature's birth—"It's Alive!"—its hand is the first object moving on the operating table. The mute creature can only gesture with its hands. In the disinterment sequence, a close-shot privileges Henry's hand stroking the coffin. Similar parallels occur in *The Bride of Frankenstein*. Admiring Mary's creative process, Byron moves toward her, "It was these fragile, white fingers that wrote the nightmare." Touching her hand, she pricks her finger with an embroidery needle. The flow of blood causes Mary consternation. This action anticipates the creature's attempt to stroke his bride's hands toward the end of the film, an action that leads to rejection. As Mary begins her tale, resurrecting the creature, Byron and Shelley sit at the left and right of her. Their positions anticipate Frankenstein, the creature, and his bride in the film's concluding laboratory sequence.

A montage of scenes from the original film follows. Henry is believed dead. Villagers carry him to the castle. Meanwhile little Maria's parents search for the creature's remains in the ashes of the ruined mill. Despite his wife's premonitions—"Maria drowned to death and you burned. What shall I do then?"—he obsessively searches the ashes and falls through the floor into a flooded cellar. His wife faints. Hans's obsessive search represents his guilt feelings for little Maria's death. His dark alter ego revives to confront him. In the waterlogged cellar a close-up reveals the creature's hand slowly emerging. Rising from the depths, it begins attacking a family unit. After drowning Hans, it throws his wife into the pit after she mistakenly helps it ascend.

A reign of terror begins. Further assaults on the family follow. Chased by the villagers, the creature's eventual capture parodies the crucifixion as the mob lifts its bound body above them. The creature is a demonic redeemer that opposes all institutions that deem it abnormal and "abject." Thus the creature first attacks the family that stimulates such aggressive feelings toward it. When the creature later escapes from jail, the camera follows a terrified mother searching for her child. She discovers the body in a churchyard. Because the creature naturally gravitates toward unsocialized, little children who parallel its own feelings of helpless vulnerability (*Frankenstein*, *The Son of Frankenstein*, *The Ghost of Frankenstein*), this act appears uncharacteristic.

However, there is no real evidence that the creature actually committed the deed. Another scene shows villagers discovering the murdered Neumann family. A bloodstained axe appears beside the father's body. Mother's body is significantly out of camera range in the upstairs bedroom.[17] The creature does terrify a gypsy family; by then, it regards any human society as unfriendly. These violent rampages are not unmotivated. They occur immediately after the creature's violent pursuit and humiliation by the jeering townspeople. The creature's violent actions follow continual rejection. It responds like a raging child who violently reacts to parental and social abuse—it is not responsible for its actions. Dr. Pretorius correctly blames Henry for the murders. "You know, do you not, that it is you, really, who is responsible for all those murders?" Pretorious recognizes that *father does not know best.*

The Bride of Frankenstein develops the relationship between Henry and his creature. When the villagers place Henry's body on the castle hall table, it resembles his creature's position on the laboratory table in the previous film. Appropriately Minnie's (Una O'Connor)[18] terrified cries of the creature's resurrection—"It's Alive! It's Alive"—coincide with the arrival of Henry's supposedly dead body at the castle. While Elizabeth (Valerie Hobson) believes Henry dead—"I was told of this. I was told on our wedding night"—Henry's hand drops down from the table. Its movement resembles the creature's first sign of life in *Frankenstein*, and Minnie's cries resemble Henry's orgasmic joy after his successful creation in the earlier film. These parallels are by no means coincidental.

During his recovery Elizabeth attempts to make Henry forget but he cannot. As he muses over the past, his expression begins to take on the demeanor associated with his original creative act. Obsessive, intense, excited, he breathlessly contrasts his blasphemous activities with its other, suppressed potentials.

> I've been cursed for looking into the mysteries of life. Perhaps death is sacred and I've profaned it. Oh, what a wonderful vision it was. I dreamed of giving to the world the secret God was so jealous of, the secret of life itself. Think of the power. I created a man. I could have bred a race.... In time I could have given eternal life.

Perturbed by thoughts of an alternative universe where women's traditional role has no place, Elizabeth reacts in fear, alarmed at Henry's aim to appropriate childbirth; she finally faints from fear when Dr. Pretorius (Ernest Thesiger) enters.

Pretorius is Henry's elderly alter ego replete with revealing effeminate associations; he is a solitary scientist outside social and familial constraints.

He calls on Henry to follow his original convictions. Henry attempts retreat into domesticity, "I'll have no more of this hell spawn. As soon as I'm well again I'm going to get married." Pretorius, however, forces Henry to visit his house to show him his own birthing activities.

Pretorius's creations are miniature homunculi—a queen, bishop, libidinous Henry VIII, and a devil figure with whom he identifies. Although Henry initially regards this as "black magic,"[19] Pretorius invokes the old biblical injunction, "Be fruitful and multiply." He plans to create a manmade race, and toasting the advent of a new world order, he tempts Henry into creating a female to match his creature. The sequence concludes with Pretorius's toast, "To a new world of Gods and Monsters."

Set in a society of conformist burgomeisters, families, and old maidservants, *The Bride of Frankenstein* reveals an incestuously debilitated social structure threatened by monsters. Yet the monstrous is never really monstrous. It becomes so by social hysteria. Despite oversentimental treatment, the misunderstood creature in *The Bride of Frankenstein* is potentially recuperable. But the system will never allow this as the hermit episode demonstrates. The hermit does not regard the creature as a threat. Representative of a weak but sincere Christianity, he adopts the creature and treats it with loving paternal care. As the hermit puts the creature to bed, like a father with a little child, the sequence concludes with "Ave Maria" prominently on the soundtrack. The hermit thanks God for bringing him a companion to share his loneliness. It is a poignant sequence. Blind and aged the old hermit lives outside the town as a useless senior citizen. Society rejects him. Both he and the creature are outside normal institutional structures. The hermit's simple Christianity has positive connotations that anticipate *Exorcist II*'s union of opposites, which lead toward a new social order. The arrival of two hunters destroys this potential, leaving the creature alone again and abandoned.

The creature intuitively returns to the graveyard of the earlier film, its original burial place. Discovering a vault entrance it descends, in actions inversely paralleling the legend of Christ's Descent into Hell. Rejected by a society that has ruined its one chance of redemption, it encounters Dr. Pretorius, a Satanic counterpart to the hermit, who nurtures the rage of this traumatized adult child. It now becomes a dangerous social threat. Prior to meeting Pretorius, the creature found a young girl's open coffin. Touching her head affectionately, he murmurs "friend." Like a seductive father, Pretorius manipulates his newly found child's vulnerable desires.

Kidnapping Elizabeth, Pretorius and the creature force Henry to create the monster's mate. Personified by Elsa Lanchester, Mary Shelley returns as a monster. Her white shroud symbolizes both marital bridal gown and burial garment, an ironic critique of bourgeois marriage. However, she rejects the creature and turns to Henry. Realizing the Bride's feelings of repulsion toward him, the creature falls into a destructive emotional rage. But, touched at Elizabeth's loyalty to her mate, it allows them to leave before destroying the laboratory.

Like the earlier film, *The Bride of Frankenstein* concludes with a perfunctory shot: Henry and Elizabeth look at the ruined laboratory. Both are free to return to everyday normality. The shot appears unconvincing. Staged and stylized it attempts to disavow still remaining tensions.[20]

◆ ◆ ◆

Son of Frankenstein is a complete contrast. Rowland V. Lee's direction is more sober, and Jack Otterson's stark set designs, visual lighting pools, and tortuous shadows appropriately depict expressionistically tormented thoughts.[21] As soon as the American Frankenstein family leave their small railway carriage, they enter a diseased landscape and dominating Gothic castle that contrasts American innocence with overpowering images of European decay and disease.

Son of Frankenstein begins with a long shot of the castle. A gate separates it from the village. In the next scene the camera pans up to the gate, revealing a sign, "Eingang Verboten," with Frankenstein's name above. The camera then pans down to the right, revealing some villagers pushing a cart. A group of boys think of throwing stones at the window, but after seeing Ygor (Bela Lugosi), they flee in terror. The imagery anticipates opening scenes in *Citizen Kane*.

A negative ancestral environment and family curse threaten Wolf. Before his arrival a village councillor remarks ominously, "It's in the blood I tell you! Another Frankenstein! Just as bad as his father who created a monster in the devil's own image, his father's son." The village is a superstitious, conservative institution that rigidly categorizes individuals with family origins, unyielding and inflexible in its oppressive formalities. It tolerates neither criminals (Ygor), monsters, or those who oppose its conformist attitudes. Wolf is damned as Frankenstein's son. He is also a monster, symbiotically linked to his father's creation. Frankenstein, the creature, and the village exist in a morbid association. Every negative social order requires convenient scapegoats.

Approaching the station Wolf reveals the real "family" ties behind the dark Frankenstein story. "Nine out of ten people call that misshapen monster of my father's experiment" (slight pause before the guard's announcement of the train's destination complements Wolf's attempt at finishing his sentence)—"Frankenstein." The villagers are more hostile to the Frankenstein family in this film. As Inspector Krogh (Lionel Atwill) states, Wolf suffers from a "virulent poison." He will never change it. A family curse contaminates him in the community's eyes, "You're poisoned by your name alone." Krogh bears the mark of the creature's rage. Many years ago, it tore out his arm. He urges Wolf to return to America, "You can change the name but not the brand." In the eyes of society, Wolf and the creature belong to the same family.

Castle Frankenstein's interior reveals Wolf's repressed mental turmoil. Giant staircase and spacious hall dominate, rendering human potential and control insignificant. Like H. P. Lovecraft's Charles Dexter Ward, Wolf faces an ancestral inheritance and strange environment that threatens to suffocate his individual personality. His stirring, albeit unconscious, feelings coincide with the creature's reanimation.

Visiting his father's ruined laboratory the next morning, Wolf encounters another representative of the dead—Ygor—sentenced to hang by the village court. Ygor's escape, even with a broken neck, beat impossible odds, and like the creature he survives. Feeling a strong affinity with a fellow outcast, Ygor looks after his "brother." Their relationship is a bond "between men" that threatens family and society. Ygor leads Wolf to the family vault where the creature lies in state like a Frankenstein family member. He tells Wolf about the creature, "No. He cannot be destroyed, cannot die. Your father made him for always. Now he's sick. Make him well, Frankenstein. Your father made him and Heinrich Frankenstein was your father too."

Ygor's claim astounds and excites Wolf. He decides to follow his father and usurp the normal family birthing process. Before leaving the vault Wolf changes the graffiti on his father's coffin from "Maker of Monsters" to "Maker of Men." He uses a lighted torch, reminding us of the "maternal" lightning in the original film.

Wolf's relationship to his "brother" visually emerges in one remarkable scene. Learning of the creature's revival, he rushes to his laboratory and confronts a dark sibling. The creature studies Wolf's face and recognizes some common bond. Conscious of its abnormality, it stretches out its hand to Wolf, inarticulately protesting the physique that separates it from his more "normal" brother. The creature leads Wolf to a mirror which reflects them both within the same frame. Only a hanging rope divides them. (Perhaps it is the same rope Wolf will finally use to destroy his brother.) The sequence ends with the creature touching Wolf's face; it wishes to articulate their indissoluble natures. It snarls, turning aside, perplexed, gesturing to Wolf with its hands. Wolf and the creature are brothers who inhabit different skins. Unfortunately, Wolf never comprehends this, never identifies with his repressed "other."

Ygor and the creature see Peter von Frankenstein as a potential recruit to their alienated world. Despite Donnie Dunagan's excruciating performance, his role is important. He represents another being, like little Maria, toward whom the creature feels an intuitive bond. As a small child not yet fully "socialized" by family conditioning, he is not biased toward beings society labels "abject." Peter has not yet undergone the Oedipal trajectory. He is unprejudiced toward an alternative realm of gods and monsters. *Son of Frankenstein* emphasizes that the creature intends no real harm against Peter. Peter calls it a "nice giant" who visits him in his playroom, an act his parents regard as an imaginative representation of *Jack the Giant Killer*. The creature attempts friendly over-tures as it did to little Maria. Although the creature later intends to avenge Ygor's death by throwing Peter into the sulphur pit, it hesitates. It places Peter on a nearby ladder, perhaps intending to adopt him as Ygor's replacement. The adult world intrudes. Wolf and Krogh automatically attack the creature. They do not understand (nor even wish to consider) the creature's possibly benevo-lent intentions. When Krogh fires his gun, the creature places Peter under its foot, wanting to protect him from stray bullets. Frightened by the bullets and the tearing out of Krogh's artificial arm, Peter calls to Wolf. Wolf swings against the creature on a rope and knocks it into the sulphur pit. The family classifies the creature as monstrous, violent, and unredeemable.

As with previous versions the final scene of *Son of Frankenstein* attempts a "happy ending." Despite earlier animosity the villagers congregate at the sta-tion to bid farewell to the Frankenstein family on their return to America. But Peter appears significantly unhappy. This may be a four-year-old's acting inexperience, but another interpretation is possible: Peter realizes what has really happened. He has lost his chance to participate in an alternative world of gods and monsters. He intuitively recognizes the truth behind social dis-courses of monstrous representations. He had discovered a "monster" who merely wished to play with him. Peter then faces an American normality which will make him forget and train him into conformity.

◆ ◆ ◆

The Ghost of Frankenstein resembles an assembly line production by mov-ing from one spectacular set-piece to another in sixty-seven minutes.[22] Yet it contains many haunting scenes. Surviving his shooting at Wolf's hands, Ygor crouches before the sulphur pit (now congealed) playing his flute, hoping for the creature's resurrection. Although they exist outside society in the ruined laboratory, the mere thought of that existence is too much for the villagers. They decide to destroy Castle Frankenstein completely.

The castle's demolition results in the creature's revival. Ygor aids the sul-phur-caked creature (Lon Chaney, Jr.) to emerge. They travel to the nearby village of Vasaria to seek aid from Henry's second son, Ludwig (Cedric Hardwicke). In Vasaria the creature watches a group of village boys bully a little girl, Cloestine. Seeing parallels to its own situation, it tries to help her. The creature's presence agitates the crowd, and the villagers physically assault it and carry it to jail. Borrowing from *The Golem*, this sequence continues the idea of the creature's original childlike status in *Frankenstein* and his betrayal by the adult world. Feeling an affinity with the similarly persecuted Cloestine, the creature sees her as another alienated, lonely being to whom family and society offer neither security nor happiness.

Ygor blackmails Ludwig into aiding his plans to cure the creature. Facing it in court, Ludwig denies any family relationship. Rejected again by a Frankenstein, the creature escapes. Despite his daughter's protestations, Ludwig decides to give the creature a new brain. Henry Frankenstein's ghost (or paternal influence) stimulates him into following the family tradition.

Like a sensitive child within an authoritarian family, the creature becomes a manipulated object for adult desires. It has no control over either destiny or body. Ludwig, his jealous assistant Dr. Bohmer (Lionel Atwill), and even Ygor use the creature for their own ends. The creature finds itself in the position of a vulnerable child, victimized by institutional forces. It also resembles a helpless victim of child abuse. Ygor wishes to leave his crippled body and transplant his brain into the creature's body. He changes from fellow outcast to jealous father-figure. His desires inversely echo those of the Frankenstein family by claiming authority over the creature's body. The Frankensteins blindly refuse to recognize the creature's individual desires. If it has no place in their family plans, they reject it like an unwanted child. Like its counterparts in dysfunctional family situations, the creature reacts traumatically. It violently rages against those responsible for its torment. The creature realizes that its only mode of entry into a rejecting family institution is via destructive conformity. It faces surgical lobotomy involving the insertion of either a normal brain (Dr. Kettering) or a cunning, manipulative figure (Ygor).

Possessing limited powers of rationality, the creature sees Cloestine as the only person whose brain it wants in its body. By kidnapping her it instinctively reacts against institutional forces. Suspicious of Ludwig's desire to give it "normal" intelligence and Ygor's egocentric ambitions to use its body for his own purposes, the creature prefers Cloestine's childlike innocence. It has no wish to comply with the adult world's selfish desires. Learning of Ygor's wishes, "You will have the brain of your friend Ygor! ... Tonight, Ygor will die for you," the creature violently reacts by throwing him against the wall and (accidentally) crushing his body. Ironically Ygor betrays the creature as Wolf Frankenstein betrayed him in the earlier film.

The megalomaniac Ygor deceitfully obtains his desires. With Boehmer's aid he manages to get his brain inside the creature's body and thereby defeats Ludwig's plans of restoring the family name and achieving worldwide scientific acclaim. Although Cloestine escapes, the creature is not so lucky. Ygor possesses its body. His dreams of power parallel Ludwig's, but they are short-lived. Boehmer discovers that the monster's blood cannot feed the sensory nerves surrounding Ygor's brain. Ygor suffers blindness from psychosomatic overload. Normality and the id cannot comfortably coexist. Ygor moves from companion to dominating father-figure. He changes sides, identifying himself with a controlling patriarchal ego and aligning himself with one of the family's main functions: control over the child's body. The scheme fails. The conscious mind cannot confront "monsters from the id." Psychological malfunction results. Ygor finds out what the cost of playing the enemy's game involves. Joining the other side causes self-destruction.

◆ ◆ ◆

Directed by George Waggner, with set Jack Otterson, *The Wolf Man*'s opening five minutes reveal the real causes behind Larry Talbot's lyncanthropic condition. Larry returns from America to the Welsh Talbot estate after an eighteen-year absence. A rigid English feudal structure dominates everyone. Enjoying his first sight of the three-hundred-year-old Gothic Talbot Castle, Larry enters the family home and is reunited with his father, Sir John (Claude Rains). A family portrait, which resembles an elder version of Larry, dominates a large fireplace. According to the Talbot family tradition, the elder brother, "next-in-line—is considered in everything." Resenting this unequal position, the younger brother generally leaves home. Larry and Sir John are together after a long absence following the heir-apparent's death in a hunting accident. Sir John admits his fault in exiling Larry. The Talbot family is a "stiff-necked, undemonstrative type and frequently this has been carried to unhappy extremes." Larry smiles genially, ironically replying "Don't I know that?" Although he appears likeable and forgiving, Larry undoubtedly harbors deep resentment against family rejection. Accepting Sir John's assurance that there will "be no more such reserve," he shakes hands. Larry's openness and genuine sincerity contrast with his father's reserved demeanor. Chaney's Talbot resembles an adult child, victimized by a traumatic family past.

Negative familial influences cause Larry's lycanthropy.[23] Although *The Wolf Man* attributes this to foreign (gypsy) contamination, the Talbot household is really responsible. The Talbot family has a reputation in the village. Gamekeeper Frank Andrews (Patric Knowles) warns his fiancée, Gwen

Conliffe (Evelyn Ankers), about Larry being the "son of Sir John Talbot." Although his apparent reasons are vague, Frank hints at the family's historical exercise of "lord of the manor" rights. The Talbots represent a rigid, patriarchal order that has no surviving wife or sisters.

Helping Sir John set up a telescope, Larry looks through it and spies on Gwen. His look has definite voyeuristic associations. Although Sir John states his "look" sees only a street scene, Larry obviously follows the paternal gaze to its logical consequences. Like a predatory wolf, Sir John may often spy on the village's unaware females. Larry looks on under his father's dominating and patriarchal eye. His voyeuristic desires soon develop sadistic overtones and become manifested in his lycanthropic transformation. This telescope sequence, with its sexually voyeuristic elements, precedes the events that lead to the first appearance of the wolf man. The Talbot family gaze has possessive and violent features.

Although Sir John approves of Larry getting to know the villagers, he cannot be totally blind about its consequences. He does not tell Larry that Gwen is already engaged to his own gamekeeper. He believes his new heir-apparent has every right to go on the prowl. After all, wasn't Larry's deceased brother "considered in everything," including things and people?

Despite turning down Larry's suggestion of a date, Gwen presents herself as available. As she leaves her shop, Larry stalks her behind a corner, a movement foreshadowing his later lycanthropic tendencies. Because Gwen knows about the Talbot family, she asks her friend Jenny Williams (Fay Helm) to accompany them towards a gypsy encampment.

The gypsy camp represents a different family system to the Talbots. Headed by Maleva (Maria Ouspenskaya), this outsider community is more caring and sympathetic. Widowed Maleva cares for her lycanthropically afflicted son, Bela. Unlike Sir John she never resorts to denial mechanisms and tries to protect the community from her son. Sir John never connects lycanthropy with his family's dysfunctional structure. He constantly ignores Larry's pleas for help. Sir John's callousness later appears when he abandons Larry to participate in the community "hunt" for the wolf. He cruelly ties Larry up in a chair by the window, providing him with a front row seat.

Larry becomes an ideal scapegoat. Attempting to visit church the Sunday after his first nocturnal excursion, he cannot join the community. Tracking down the aisle, the camera reveals everyone turning round to gaze at him suspiciously. The camera movement finishes with Sir John in the front of the church before his social allies Dr. Lloyd (Warren William) and Chief Constable Montford (Ralph Bellamy). The community is founded on family regulated sexual hypocrisy and denial, which is also evident in the prohibitive figure of Mrs. Williams who eagerly blames Gwen and Larry for her daughter's death.

Larry's attempt to confess before state and medical representatives falls on deaf ears. Although Dr. Lloyd is more aware of the environmental dangers to Larry's mental health, Sir John ignores him. Dr. Lloyd discerns the real reasons for Sir John's stubbornness, "Does the prestige of your family name mean more to you than his mental health?" Sir John insists Larry stay inside the family home. Despite his earlier offer to drop the Talbot family reserve of the "stiff necked, undemonstrable type," he exhibits the same quality when he refuses to stay with Larry on the night of the hunt. Larry's plea to his father, the first and final time he will call him by an affectionate name, is the most poignant in classic horror films. "Dad. Take the cane with you." He makes his father take his silver-headed wolf cane which he used to kill Bela. Larry sacrificially complies in his own execution.

Before this happens, Talbot encounters Maleva in the wood. He has left the hunt and is on his own. The shrewd woman knows his reasons. "You don't believe the witches' tales, do you? Were you hurrying back to the castle, did you have a moment's doubt? Were you hurrying to make sure he was all right?" A gunshot interrupts Sir John's reply. By now it is too late. He rushes to the final confrontation. As Larry attacks Gwen, he kills him with the silver-headed cane. Larry's peace only comes in death. The sorrowful Maleva pronounces the same benediction she uttered over her deceased son. "Your suffering is over. Now you will find peace for eternity." But two intercut shots of Sir John reveal the real nature of the "thorny" path that afflicted Larry in life.

Others soon arrive. As Frank embraces Gwen, Montford immediately utters the official version. "The wolf must have attacked her and Larry came to the rescue. I'm sorry Sir John." The status quo supports family denial mechanisms.

$$\blacklozenge \quad \blacklozenge \quad \blacklozenge$$

Later versions of the Frankenstein legend contain few developments, but other Universal films are notable. Bela Lugosi's Count Dracula is the Frankenstein creature's dark brother. Foreign born, aristocratic, and of ambiguous sexuality, he presents a direct threat against the family. Only Dr. Van Helsing's menacing patriarchal figure (Edward Van Sloan) can finally dispatch him. Although Dr. Waldman perishes at the hands of the creature, his counterpart survives in *Dracula* (1931).[24] Dracula is a bisexual being. Not only has he three "wives," but he also vampirizes Renfield (Dwight Frye). He manifests a transgressive sexuality beyond family boundaries, which aims at contaminating the pride of New England womanhood. Count Dracula is Frank McConnell's "Roger Chillingworth of Lend-Lease," who operates within a "profoundly Americanized mental landscape," transgressing sexual as well as historical insularity.[25]

In *Dracula's Daughter* (1936), his offspring uses her artistic background to gain access to susceptible female victims. Her lesbian tendencies thus disrupt family values.

◆ ◆ ◆

Paul Morrissey's *Andy Warhol's Frankenstein* (a.k.a. *Flesh for Frankenstein*, 1973) begins by showing two children who enter father's laboratory and practice dissecting a doll before guillotining it. Ironically removed from the village school because of "contaminating" lower class influences, they are products of an incestuous marriage. Father and mother are brother and sister. While Catherine Frankenstein (Monique van Vooren) rails at the villager's sexual infidelity, the Baron (Udo Kier) is only interested in creating a master-race by using the bodies of the lower classes. Morrisey explicitly evokes class associations present in the original legend.[26] While the Baron engages in necrophiliac activities, the Baroness sexually exploits Nicholas's (Joe D'Allesandro) body in her boudoir. Both she and the Baron procreate for the family name. They have little interest in each other and only wish to rear their children correctly. Both desire to separate sexuality and its discontents from normal family functions. The Baron aims to create male (Srdjan Zelenovic) and female monsters who will procreate, fulfilling the "unfinished business of man on earth, a creation that will replace the worn-out trash that populates and repopulates the earth." The Baron wishes to fulfill the family's major social function—total control over conformist beings. The film ends with the Frankenstein children deciding to continue their father's experiments and (class domination) on the helpless Nicholas.

◆ ◆ ◆

The Universal series attempted to externalize tensions emerging from the family. But they were not entirely successful because the traumas depicted in each film have definable family origins. However, at the time the series began to decline, the Val Lewton group began making a remarkable series of classic films that further emphasize the threatening nature of the family and sympathize even more with beings who are designated as monsters. These monsters become less external and more human. They have undeniable links with family structures that condemn them as abnormal, thereby leading viewers to question supernatural distancing codes within the horror genre while attempting to disavow their relationship to everyday life.

Lewton or "The Ambiguities"

RKO produced a number of low-budget psychological horror films that soon gained classic status.[1] The vast majority of these films deal with the family. It is an important component within *The Cat People* (1942), *I Walked with a Zombie, The Ghost Ship* (both 1943), and *Curse of the Cat People* and *The Seventh Victim* (both 1944).

World War II had drastically destroyed the isolationist innocence of America. This event significantly affected the national culture. Certain genres now explored more complex notions of personality, especially film noir interrogations of the dark side of American society. RKO was an influential studio that produced film noirs ranging from *Citizen Kane* to *Out of the Past*.[2] Val Lewton's unhappy childhood influenced him as did contemporary historical and cinematic events. The Lewton films are macabre versions of the film noir genre, which were replete with psychologically complex motivations that play important roles. Both *The Cat People* and *Curse of the Cat People* feature tormented characters affected by tensions within the family.[3]

In *The Cat People*, Irena (Simone Simon) wishes to be a normal American woman, "I want to be Mrs. Reed now . . . I want to be everything the name means to me but I can't. I need time . . . to get over the evil within me." As an isolated single woman, she blames herself for the feelings society causes. Despite supernatural overtones, *The Cat People* reveals ideologic factors governing female schizophrenia.

In *Curse of the Cat People* (1944), Oliver Reed (Kent Smith) wishes to suppress his daughter's imaginative powers by making her conform to his ideas of normal childhood. He is an unsympathetic bourgeois male who is blind to the imaginative worlds paralleling those described by Hawthorne in "The Snow Image" and "The Artist of the Beautiful." His relationship to

Amy echoes Milton R. Stern's description of Mrs. Glendenning's household in *Pierre*: "There is merriment and comfort only as long as appearances are not disturbed and Pierre himself later realizes that his mother dotes on him only because he is a perfect appearance, a mirror for her own pride and her own values."[4]

In *The Leopard Man* (1943), an uncaring mother forces her young daughter outside late at night to purchase flour. She ignores her daughter's genuine fears over a possible attack by an escaped leopard. On her return the daughter finds the door bolted. Her mother has locked the door so her terrified daughter cannot return empty-handed. When mother realizes the real danger, she cannot move the rusted bolt. Helpless, conscious of her culpability, she watches her daughter's blood seep through the door. A visually macabre prologue and epilogue frames this sequence. Both show the family's younger brother making a leopard's shadow image on the wall. His final shadow play occurs directly above his sister's coffin. The image evokes unspeakable family tensions suggestive of his subconscious desire for his sister's violent death. It anticipates another younger sibling's desires in *The Funhouse* (1981).

Another repressive mother indirectly causes her daughter's death later in the film. Despite differing class backgrounds, both mothers ignore their daughters' true feelings. Forced to meet her lover outside her home, Consuelo Contreras dies in a locked cemetery. Following Lewton's cinematic practice, we never see the perpetrator. The action is left to our imagination. Clo-Clo (Margo), the film's most attractive character, meets her death seeking an elusive $100 bill needed to support her family.

◆   ◆   ◆

Irena's condition in *The Cat People* results from some past dysfunctional family situation that outweighs supernatural explanations. Like George Romero's *Martin*, she is from the Old Country. We never learn about her former life, but it was not good. Wishing a normal relationship with a "regular guy," Oliver Reed, Irena ultimately realizes its impossibility. Irena may be what she says she is: a savage cat woman transforming her body to attack human adversaries. However, another explanation is possible. Irena's condition originates from the very American normality she wishes to embrace in an escape from Old World loneliness. She mistakenly believes incorporation into "normal" institutions will cure her. Appealing to Oliver for understanding, hoping that her new American status will help her, Irena is betrayed on all levels. She feels herself alienated from the conformist arena of marriage and family. Irena becomes a conveniently designated monster, a cat woman society may either destroy or incarcerate within a mental institution. Anticipating Mary and Gregory's plans for Jacqueline in *The Seventh Victim*, Oliver and Alice conspire to incarcerate an unhappy female they refuse to understand. Irena faces the fate of many independent nineteenth-century females whose desire for independence provoked patriarchal discipline and punishment. As in *Frankenstein* the real monsters are human.

Irena is an innocent being. Her mental decline is really a reaction against those conspiring against her—Oliver, Alice (Jane Randolph), and Dr. Judd (Tom Conway). Whether Irena actually turns into a cat woman or psychopathologically believes that she does, one point is clear. Like the dangerous panther in a cage, she refuses social training. Irena will never fulfill Oliver's dream of obedient wife and mother. She reacts against the marital order. Her "uncontrollable" nature threatens the status quo. As a single woman, brought up by her mother after her father's mysterious death, she threatens the American family.

Opening credits and mise-en-scene evoke Irena's feelings of psychic entrapment. A panther screen appears prominently in the background. It later appears in her apartment. A Freudian-influenced caption about ancient sin, clinging to the valleys and low places like depression within world consciousness, concludes the credits. The quotations are from an apocryphal book, *The Anatomy of Atavism* by Dr. Judd, an unscrupulous psychiatrist who uses his skills to dominate sexually female patients and to incarcerate them if they prove obstructive. Opening images reveal the clash of opposing forces competing for Irena's soul: supposedly atavistic tendencies and institutional medical discourse.

In the film's opening scene, Irena obsessively sketches before a panther's cage. Oliver gazes at her, waiting to engage her attention. When Irma narrowly misses throwing a discarded sketch into the litter basket, Oliver quickly retrieves it. He points to a nearby sign—"Be it not said, and said unto your shame / That all was beauty here until you came."[5] Oliver represents civilized neatness and order. Like Paul Holland of *I Walked With a Zombie* and Captain Stone of *The Ghost Ship*, he desires a "clean," regulated world. However, Oliver discovers dark forces beneath his blandly repressed world of normality.[6] Even everyday objects have sinister overtones, for example, a zoo litter basket resembles a tree trunk, nature's scratching post for cats and panthers.

As Oliver speaks to Irma, sharing the frame, a panther prowls restlessly in its cage behind them. When they leave, the camera pans left to reveal one of her discarded drawings. A close-up shows the image of a large cat impaled by a sword. The following scene between Oliver and Irena in her apartment develops the drawing's threatening associations. Prominently framed in her window is a model of a knight impaling a cat. The camera tracks out, revealing Irena framed by the window, left of screen, her figure directly opposite the model. Oliver sits in darkness at her left.

Their positions parallel the male/female oppositions in Irena's drawing. As the sword/phallus impales/penetrates a feline animal, Irena faces danger from two patriarchal allies: a mythologic knight dominating the animal world and his twentieth-century representative. Conditioned to think of herself as "evil" and avoiding normality, Irena symbiotically associates herself with Old World influences of animals and darkness. Struggling against forces that victorious powers of patriarchal light designate as "unhealthy," she mistakenly seeks salvation within the dominant order.

Irena tells Oliver of ancestral legends about King John who drove devil-worshipping Marmalukes out of Serbia. She believes in the "official story." The devil-worshipping Marmaluke cat people supposedly enslaved her people before patriarchal forces liberated Serbia. Irena later tells Dr. Judd that Cat People were exclusively women who were "driven by their own evil to kill their husbands." Torn between intuitive feelings of feminine solidarity and a tempting social normality, Irena becomes a "split subject." Lacking a sustaining female community, she masochistically inhabits a world of darkness, a psychological pit that threatens any single, independent woman who resides within patriarchy.

Oliver attempts to remove her into a clean American world of normality. They marry. But Irena refuses to consummate the union. Psychologically scarred by the hidden effects of her early life, she fears for Oliver's safety. Believing in the official legend concerning her "evil" nature, she sincerely thinks sexuality endangers her husband. Irena's reticence stems neither from frigidity nor malice but from concern for a spouse who eventually betrays her. Until she realizes Oliver's deceit, Irena genuinely loves him. Although he initially humors her, Oliver eventually loses patience and turns toward another woman, who offers him the bland, untroubled American family life he desires. For Oliver social stability counts. He is blind and powerless to help Irena cope with her family induced trauma. His gift of a bird to ease her mind proves futile. As Wood perceptively notes concerning conclusive mise-en-scene components, "The sequence ends with a long-shot of Irena standing desolate with the bird in her hand. In the foreground is a model of the ship, reminding us of Oliver and his work, balancing the expression of Irena's mysterious suppressed nature with the work of conscious control."[7]

The Cat People contains many scenes that juxtapose both worlds. Irena's panther screen dwarfs Oliver's boat. When she and Oliver visit the Maritime Museum, a statue of the Egyptian cat goddess Bubastis incongruously opposes masculine celebrations of nineteenth-century achievements. Irena's bathtub has cat claws. Tiger lilies adorn a shop window when she later spies on Oliver and Alice during their meeting.

People, as well as objects, represent alternatives to the everyday marital world. Following his optimistic pronouncements to his future bride, "You're Irena. You're here in America. You're in love with me, Oliver Reed, a typical American and you're going to marry me," the wedding celebration sequence undermines this. Irena, Oliver, and his friends dine in the Belgrade restaurant, an environment with Old World associations. The mise-en-scene emphasizes her futile desires for normality. A shot of objects resembling squatting cats introduces the sequence. During the celebration Irena encounters her "double," a sinister, single cat woman who resembles her in physique and voice. She greets Irena knowingly as "My sister," smiles at her as if recognizing the obvious failure of her flight into normality, and leaves mysteriously.[8] Lesbian overtones strongly suggest the real nature of Irena's original community. In a later scene showing Oliver and Alice dining together, single women dominate the restaurant. In the background are two females together and one solitary woman. Like Irena, but unlike Alice, they dress in black and have similar hairstyles. Without male escorts they indirectly represent patriarchal fears of the independent female.

Irena's yearning for family life provides no real salvation. Oliver never fulfills any romantic dreams of a knight in shining armor, only a patriarchal nightmare of a powerful knight impaling a cat. He proves unable and unwilling to help Irena and is deviously complicit in a dangerous romantic ideology that results in her mental disintegration. Following the canary's death, Irena unhappily collapses before Oliver; she articulates a false and irrational vision of monogamy: "I envy every woman in the street. They must lead normal happy lives. They're happy and their husbands are happy." Neither Oliver nor Alice attempt to present a more balanced picture. They believe in the myth. Irena becomes more unhappy and isolated. Oliver's later confession to Alice is crassly immature. He says, "I've never been unhappy before. Things have always been swell with me. I had a happy time at school. . . . I've just never been unhappy."

Social rather than supernatural factors govern Irena's deteriorating mental condition. Everyday "normal" people are responsible for her eventual nervous breakdown. Ironically Hollywood's archetypal "sweet American sidekick" Alice, waiting for her man until her rival's convenient removal, proves to be Irena's most dangerous foe.[9]

Alice is no one-dimensional heroine. Despite friendly overtures she really hates Irena and indirectly schemes her downfall. Although she knows

Dr. Judd's promiscuous reputation, she suggests him to Oliver as a possible "healer" for Irena. This All-American Girl plans strategic moves. When Oliver confesses his marital unhappiness, she stages a tearful breakdown which mirrors Oliver's immature thoughts concerning marriage. "I know what love is. It's just the two of us living our lives together happily and proudly. No torture and doubt." When Oliver mentions his marital estrangement from Irena, Alice replies slyly, "You and I, we'll never be strangers." She eventually achieves her goal. Although Irena attempts a compromise by taking Judd's advice about removing the feline artifacts, it is too late. Oliver confesses his love for Alice. The confession scene ends with a bleak view of Irena, her back to camera, slitting a velvet divan with her fingernails. She now realizes the futility of salvation from a morally devious society.

Failing to be a good, normal wife, Irena becomes an outcast liable to be incarcerated in a mental institution. Oliver, Alice, and Judd plan this for her. By not showing any explicit monster, *The Cat People* casts deliberate ambiguity in the audience's mind. Alice's pursuit, the guilty lovers stalked in Oliver's office, and Judd's death result more from the defensive actions of a wronged woman than from any uncontrollable monster. Judd's unprofessional seductive actions toward Irena in his office cause his death, an understandable action of a vulnerable woman attempting to defend herself.

Irena dies outside society. Returning to the zoo, she releases the panther from its cage. Bleeding to death, Judd's swordstick blade still inside her, she resembles the impaled cat at the end of King John's blade, weakening before patriarchy's eventual victory. The panther springs out and kills her. It then leaps over a wall before a car destroys it—a symbol of Oliver's beloved "clean" American technology. *The Cat People* concludes with the death of both "animals." Oliver and Alice flinch before Irena's body. The camera refuses to show us what they see. Oliver and Alice turn away. Irena remains in the darkness, an "abject" monster created by the dominant patriarchal order.

◆ ◆ ◆

Directed by Robert Wise, *Curse of the Cat People* is an appropriate sequel. Lacking supernatural associations it warns of the family's dangerous nature. A family may create "monsters" out of sensitive individuals without indulging in Baron Frankenstein's elaborate preparations. In contrast to its predecessor, *Curse of the Cat People* emphasizes relevant social factors that are normally concealed beneath supernatural codes in other horror films.

In *Curse of the Cat People*, Irena is no longer dangerous or monstrous. Summoned out of Amy's unconscious mind, she is a fellow playmate who inhabits a world of innocence and spontaneity the adult world cannot comprehend. The film complements the Universal *Frankenstein* series. In *Frankenstein* the creature wished to approach the world of childhood, seeing in it an alternative existence tragically beyond its grasp. In *Curse of the Cat People*, Irena fulfills the Frankenstein creature's goal of a potentially liberating relationship with childhood innocence. The relationship between Amy and Irena represents a dialectical fusion of opposites. Monsters emerge from the unconscious. They may be dangerous. Alternatively they may embody aspects of human experience society denies. The Universal and Lewton films suggest this. *Curse of the Cat People* stresses the family's abnormal nature by contrasting it with alternatives within the fantastic realm. *The Cat People*'s Irena appears as a gentle being from a nonpatriarchal dimension. Barbara Farren (Elizabeth Russell) represents the tormented side of Irena in *The Cat People*— a character that anticipates Hitchcock's Marnie.

The film is far from the conformist vehicle many contemporary child psychologists acclaimed.[10] As in *The Cat People*, the adult world appears blind and hypocritical. The family is a dangerous trap for sensitive individuals. Although Oliver does not use any of Judge Schreber's painful educational devices on his young daughter, Amy, his attitude duplicates the same type of "soul murder" practiced against Irena in the earlier film. Daniel Schreber's disavowed perception of his father's brutal practices cause him to believe he is under psychic attack; Amy's safety valve is her retreat into the fantastic.[11]

Living in a charming Tarrytown suburb, Oliver and Alice now have a seven-year-old daughter. However, this ideal household contains a dark secret. As in *Rebecca* (1941), a dead wife's presence haunts the film. Oliver now understands the psychological conditions behind Irena's death, but he denies both its social origins and his own culpability. In his mind Irena is still a "sick" individual.

Curse of the Cat People begins on a bright summer day. Miss Callahan (Eve March) leads her class through the woods. She stops and describes the area in an imaginative way—"songs and lovely melodies"—before relating the supernatural legend of Sleepy Hollow. During her description a black cat suddenly appears on a tree. One of the boys scares it away by firing an imaginary machine-gun at it.[12] Civilized toleration of make-believe violence is more acceptable than Amy's desire for a fantasy friend. The camera then tracks right along a line of children playing a game. It stops, tilting up to reveal Amy as she unintentionally hinders its progress. Her peer group criticizes her: "She's dreaming again"; "We never have any fun with Amy, she spoils everything." Amy's lack of team spirit, individuality, and imaginative powers are more socially dangerous than a black cat's imaginary destruction. Miss

Callahan attempts to excuse Amy, "Amy's a nice girl . . . only a little bit . . ." The dialogue ends here as if teacher (as well as audience) are hesitant of diagnosing her condition as normal or abnormal. Carrie White inherits Amy's role three decades later. Amy's final ostracism occurs when she strikes a boy who accidentally crushes a butterfly she chose as her companion.

The worried parents visit the school. Miss Callahan wishes the Reeds to recognize the normality of Amy's desire for an imaginary playmate. Oliver objects to this. Refusing to recognize his own imaginative feelings and guilt over Irena's death, he wishes to force his daughter into accepting the bland, unimaginative American way of life yearned for in *The Cat People*. Amy's imaginative qualities evoke repressed guilt feelings in Oliver. To him she is Irena reincarnated. As he reveals to her teacher, Amy "doesn't seem normal," she has "too many fancies and too few friends," "she could just about be Irena's child."

Oliver continues to believe in complete conformity. He echoes Mrs. Glendenning's attitudes—a woman of whom Milton R. Stern comments, "Everything is but layer upon layer of appearances to be manipulated into conformity with her will—a will not of aspiration but of Hautia-like social pride." Like her, Oliver's paternalism "sees everything in its own image, seeing only what it will tolerate, perpetually lost in the self-deceiving projection of finding only what it wants to find."[13] Within the Reed home, Oliver's mixed messages confuse his daughter. When her friends fail to turn up for her birthday party, Oliver finds out that she used a tree as a magic mailbox. Oliver angrily overreacts, blaming her for taking literally a story he told her when she was three years old. He warns her against dreaming. However, when Amy questions her parents for urging for her to make a wish over her birthday cake, they tell her, "This is different. Go ahead, blow." She wishes to conform, an aim Oliver approves of—"you'll make Mummy and Daddy very happy." Their servant Edward (Sir Lancelot) further confuses Amy by referring to a Jamaican magic ring. Amy becomes perplexed about adult standards for separating reality from imagination. Oliver even attempts to bribe her into conformity. He makes her a gift of a model boat, as ineffective as the one he presented Irena with in *The Cat People*. But Amy wishes for a sincere, honest, and genuine imaginary friend apart from her home life.

As she waits outside the house for her friends to arrive during her abortive birthday party, Oliver smugly remarks, "In my day kids arrived at birthday parties before anyone was ready for them." He then takes out a game of tiddledywinks and becomes engrossed in it. Alice watches in amusement. Two scenes illustrate contrasts between a little girl punished for imaginative qualities and a hypocritical adult exhibiting the childlike behavior he constantly condemns in his daughter. As Amy waits outside for her friends who never arrive, Oliver plays in solitary narcissistic pleasure. Later, when the adults play bridge while Amy suffers from a nightmare upstairs, another contrast occurs. Awakening from her dream, Amy believes her friend (invisibly) comes to comfort her. At the same moment, Oliver sits in a trance as if experiencing the events upstairs. He disrupts a game as Amy did in the film's opening scenes. However, prompted by Alice, he returns to social reality.

Amy seeks another world that recognizes her imaginative qualities. Irena represents her repressed desires for a loving maternal figure. Amy imaginatively recreates the former cat woman's positive self. They briefly experience a pleasurable bonding as sisters condemned by rigid family structures, finding solace within each other. Amy and Irena achieve what the Frankenstein creature and young Peter could not in *Son of Frankenstein*.

Despite Oliver's traumatic first marriage, he never discards Irena's photos even though he wishes to prevent Amy learning about his past life. But Amy finds one and discovers Irena's name. Oliver then destroys all photos except one. It shows he and Irena together, smiling, during happier days. Oliver stills feels guilty about the former wife he helped to destroy. Because of her discovery of this photo, Amy finds more evidence of Oliver's duplicity. The photo enables her to resurrect Irena mentally by creating an imaginary playmate. An imaginative sequence shows the camera tracking in to Irena's photo burning in the fire. It then dissolves to a pine branch sketch (one of Irena's own sketches from the earlier film?), mixing into shots that show Amy and Irena playing together. Irena returns from the dark world patriarchy has thrust her, rising like a phoenix from the fire, meeting a sympathetic human being and playing as her counterpart in *Frankenstein* could not. She returns as a positive image, not as a fetishistically coded monster.

Irena's world opposes patriarchal family normality. By placing Irena in another realm, which is open only to childhood innocence, *Curse of the Cat People* depicts her as a person different from the earlier film. Safely outside Oliver and Alice's realm, Irena functions as a friend to their daughter, who faces the same dangerous social conformity she did in *The Cat People*.

During Christmas another contrast appears between childhood's imaginative world and false family values. The Reeds invite local carolers into their home. Their invitation reflects social formality, not spontaneous desire. One singer lavishly praises the Reed home. However, a little child exposes this as another adult example of social hypocrisy in an aside to Amy, "She says it at every house we go to." While the grown-ups gather at the piano to sing, "Shepherds shake off your drowsy sleep," a song that celebrates Oliver's bourgeois admiration of work as opposed to "unhealthy," imaginative realms, Amy stands away. Turning she hears Irena singing outside. Moving closer to her real friend, she listens to a counterpart French version that has values reverse to the one sung inside the home,

A dark Gothic world embodying Amy's vulnerable fears soon appears. Wandering outside her home one day, Amy discovers the Farren mansion. Its Gothic architecture represents the repressed tensions inside the Reed home, darkly counterpointing its clean, bland, normal exterior. The Farren home reveals malignantly psychic hearths of darkness also present within the Reed domain.

Oliver believes that Amy is not really his child. Mrs. Farren (Julia Dean) mentally abuses her neurotic Barbara (Elizabeth Russell), denying her in a similar way. Barbara represents an advanced, adult version of Amy. Both suffer from parental indifference and denial. Oliver embodies the supposedly rational side of child-rearing while Mrs. Farren embodies its dark, irrational features.

Amy's visit to the Farren home occurs at the same time Miss Callahan visits Alice. Her entry into this Gothic domain firmly connects with her own supposedly unthreatening, family home. Alice and Miss Callahan discuss ways of making Amy "normal." The Farren house with its Gothic elements of garden griffins, crouched creatures in the porch, winged figures on the staircase, threatening shadows and dominating hallway curtains, suggests the dark consequences behind such social conditioning. Identical grandfather clocks also appear in both homes. Miss Callahan remarks, "A house connected with people's thoughts and wishes. This is the house I like to see." She notices Irena's favorite painting from *The Cat People*—small boy surrounded by sinister cats. Explaining the incongruity, Alice replies, "It's part of our life, a part of our past"; she then mentions Oliver's reluctance to part with it. She admits guilt inhabits her home, "It's almost as if there's a curse on us. It seems to be directed at Amy. I sometimes think Irena haunts us." These words actually reveal Alice's guilt feelings over Irena. Like Oliver, she wishes to make Amy conform. Alice and Oliver wish no trace of his former wife to remain in their daughter.

The Farren household's Gothic interior expresses the dark consequences behind such social conditioning. Suffering from a traumatic mysterious accident, Mrs. Farren continually abuses her daughter. A stuffed cat on a branch devouring a bird in her inner room symbolically expresses tensions within the Farren family relationship. This object acts as a dark family signifier resembling Norman Bates's stuffed animals (*Psycho*) and the winged avenging furies in *The Birds*. Like Marnie's mother, Mrs. Farren uses Amy to antagonize her own daughter. Before Amy returns to her home, the audience sees Barbara hiding behind a curtain, listening to her mother describe her as "an imposter, a liar, and a cheat." These words parallel Oliver's own attitude toward both his present and his former wife who "told lies to herself and believed it."[14]

The Curse of the Cat People succinctly condemns the family institution within the terms of its own particular discourse. Nonconformists suffer mental disorientation and eventual death.[15] The returned Irena tells Amy, "I come from deep darkness and great peace. I wanted a friend too. I've been lonely." Barbara Farren frequently appears as she descends down a dark basement stairway. Amy ventures into the dark Farren household each time her family situation deteriorates. All these are natural "sisters" within a socially proscribed darkness.

Eventually all three sisters unite in a brief moment of solidarity. Amy returns to the Farren house after traumatic experiences at home. Jealous of a rival who alienates her mother's affections, Barbara seeks Amy's destruction. Mrs. Farren attempts to hide Amy, but she dies of a heart attack. Wind rushes through the house from an open door. It darkly parallels the wind in the Reed garden that heralds Irena's first invisible presence. Barbara appears in a high-angle shot framed against blowing curtains and dark shadows. Observing her mother's body, she exhibits a look of malignant fury. She says, "Even my mother's last moment you've taken from me." Amy calls in terror to Irena, "My friend." As Barbara moves toward her, Amy imagines Irena appearing. Her image superimposes itself on Barbara.[16] Amy then embraces her, calling out "My friend." Her tender emotions turn Barbara's grip into a caress. The three sisters offer each other comfort against a threatening family world.

But the moment is temporary. Oliver arrives to rescue his daughter. He finally decides on compromise. Reconciling with Amy, "From now on you and I are going to be friends. I'm going to believe in you," he acknowledges Irena's presence by stating that he sees her in the garden. Father's deceptive strategy works. Irena disappears from the frame, and normality is restored. Like Peter Frankenstein, his daughter returns to the family. But Barbara remains alone. Traumatically damaged by her family background, it is much too late for her. Her eventual fate undercuts the superficial happy ending suggestive of a deliberately ambiguous conclusion.

◆　◆　◆

Family repression structures *I Walked with a Zombie*; its supernatural motifs veil material factors. In the movie a family destroys independent female sexuality—this process has economic and psychological implications. Refusing to free his wife, Paul Holland (Tom Conway) embodies certain nineteenth-century patriarchal attitudes present within Hollywood cinema.

Nineteenth-century male selfhood involved property, talent, social prestige, ambitions, and wife. Any loss involved grave psychological consequences: the most traumatic fear was sexual dispossession. American literature contained no trace of European influenced comic treatments of cuckoldry. The whole issue was deadly serious. As David Brion Davis notes, "A husband's loss of prestige and power could best be symbolized in the outrage of sexual dishonor. Social disorganization could be represented in its ultimate form in the union of sex and death."[17] Such factors influence *I Walked with a Zombie.*

Although set in the West Indies, *I Walked with a Zombie* is still an American family horror film. Combining *Jane Eyre* and *The Heart of Darkness*, the film could be equally located in a Gothic Southern plantation as are *The Foxes of Harrow* (1947) and *Mandingo* (1976), with symbiotic associations between masters and slaves.[18] A shadow world exists; darkness and light intermingle. Betsy (Frances Dee) first sees Paul Holland framed in darkness against a bright sea. Paul soon destroys her romantic feelings, speaking of glittering putrescence beneath illusionary beauty. Day scenes appear pallid and anemic, quickly receding before encroaching darkness. The singer (Sir Lancelot) serenades Betsy with his satirical calypso about Holland family tensions during day and night. T-Misery's blackened slave icon dominates the Holland courtyard and serves as a transition point in certain scenes. Lewton's own description of the figurehead (known to the whites as Saint Sebastian and to the natives as T-Misery) subtly defines its nature: "The wooden breast of the statue is pierced with six long iron arrows. The face is weathered and black. Only a few bits of white paint still cling to the halo above his head."

The figure anticipates the film's conclusion: victory of voodoo over Christianity, darkness over light, putrescence over life, and a Black culture's psychic revenge over White oppressors. *I Walked with a Zombie* is an important 1940s family horror film that emphasizes the institution's internal decay.

As the zombie of the film's title, Jessica Holland (Christine Gordon) is a beautiful walking corpse. Her contradictory nature evokes nineteenth-century conceptions of sexual connections between beauty, death, and putrescence. Davis notes that American "literary descriptions devoted more care and realism to sudden death than to the sexual relation."[19] These associations echoed contemporary estimates of female economic and social value. A woman was not just a piece of property—she was indelibly connected with her husband's status. As a patriarchal status symbol, she could not express sexual freedom outside rigidly defined behavioral codes. Transgressive activities evoked a different symbolic coding for any fallen woman by changing the image into walking death.[20] No matter how externally beautiful a sexually active woman appeared, she embodied decay and death.[21] Sexual sin meant death. Davis cites 1836 New York newspaper reports about the discovery of prostitute Helen Jewett's body. They contained morbid associations between death and illicit sexuality.[22]

Such associations motivate Paul Holland. Betsy gazes in fascination at the glittering ocean; Paul's back is to the screen. As a sailor's song fills the soundtrack, he abruptly interrupts her contemplation. He says, "It's not beautiful. Everything seems beautiful because you don't understand." Destroying her illusions Paul tells her that the flying fish leap not in joy but terror when they attempt to escape predators. The water really "takes its gleam from millions of tiny dead bodies. It's the glitter of putrescence. There's no beauty here—only death and decay."

Paul's Rochester figure imposes a masculine, brutal discourse upon Betsy. He regards his interpretation as *the* correct one. Betsy's first-person narration presents a submissive attitude. Although noting "cruelty and harshness" in his speech, she also finds "clean and honest" qualities. "Clean" and "honest" usually embody sinister qualities for Lewton. They represent an "official version" his films contradict. Betsy's introductory voice-over mediates this "official" version, undermining the credibility of a screen heroine the audience might readily identify with. *I Walked with a Zombie* is a visually textured complex film that demands attention from the viewer. Although Betsy's opening words at the film's beginning, "I walked with a zombie" might represent Lewton's jibe at a studio title, its tone also reveals a superficial and naive heroine.

The island's name derives from a Saint Sebastian figurehead from the first slaver ship that brought White oppressors. It has indelible associations with the Holland "first family" holding economic and institutional power. As Betsy travels to the Holland estate, an aged Black coachman tells her of the "old man" in the family courtyard. Betsy deliberately ignores the coachman's history of slavery and changes the subject. She says, "But they came to a beautiful place, didn't they?" Understanding her nature the old man smiles knowingly, "If you say so, Miss. If you say." Viewing the figurehead Betsy sees only a few remnants of white remaining on the almost totally dark body. As an "ambiguous figure fusing the film's oppositions,"[23] it symbolizes many pertinent themes—the return of the repressed darkness that seeks to overpower White normality, Black disenfranchisement, Paul's attempts to subdue Jessica, and Mrs. Rand's takeover by voodoo forces.

By day the Holland estate exhibits a comfortable façade of normality and conceals divisive fragmentary tensions. Paul and Wes Rand (James Ellison) are sons of the same mother by different fathers. Marrying men symbolizing integral components of colonial domination (Holland was a plantation owner and Rand, a missionary), Mrs. Rand (Edith Barrett) personally embodies ideologic forces structuring the family—state and religion. She maintains family unity with every weapon at her disposal, even a disruptive sexually rebellious daughter-in-law such as Jessica. Mrs. Rand and Mrs. Brenner of *The Birds* have similar aims but use different methods in enforcing family obedience.

She has suitably colonized her daughter-in-law into silence and obedience. Once a beautiful woman who threatened family unity by her independent existence and adulterous liaison with Wes, Jessica is now a "beautiful zombie"; her condition was supposedly caused by a violent fever. Although Paul appears as a wronged and embittered husband, he is really a dominating patriarch who verbally demeans his wife. Wes later mimics Paul, suggesting another side to his debonair brother. "'You think that's beautiful, don't you Jessica? You think you're beautiful Jessica.' One day he'll start on you just as he did on her. What he could do to that word 'beautiful.' He uses words as other men use their fists."

I Walked with a Zombie reveals the family as a real heart of darkness.[24] Every character acts according to socially proscribed roles, masking their real feelings. This also includes Betsy whom Paul later describes as "clean" and "honest." But "clean" and "honest" Betsy is as duplicitous as *The Cat People's* Alice. Both seek to remove an inconvenient rival. Consciously wishing to perform a selfless sacrifice by reuniting Paul and Jessica, she uses a dangerous insulin shock treatment to revive the family "sleeping beauty."[25] Standing outside Jessica's bedroom, both Paul and Alice appear disappointed at the treatment's failure. Wes suddenly emerges out of the shadows, accusing them of plotting Jessica's death, challenging his brother with the same crime leveled at him, "I'm not in love with another woman." Every character in the film harbors murderous desires that are stimulated by dark family structures. Although Wes plays a desolate romantic lover role, he is also an alcoholic and adulterer. He stirs up trouble against Paul from motives of malice and jealousy. Paul later blames himself for Jessica's condition. He tells Betsy that he does not really know whether he was really responsible. All characters are trapped within social conformity, psychologically crippled in one way or another. In *I Walked with a Zombie*, family life is a hearth of darkness destroying everyone.

Day and night symbolically express revealing psychological tensions. The day scenes articulate bland, everyday, social normality. Night more ominously expresses the return of the repressed in supernatural metaphors. Voodoo Hounfort drums significantly punctuate evening conversations within the Holland estate. When Betsy escorts Jessica to the Hounfort in an attempt at another "cure," the barriers she passes parallel those within her normal world.[26] She first encounters a horse's skull decorated with garlands. Horses are the island's only transport. Wes frequently rides a horse. The second barrier is an Aeolian harp reminiscent of Jessica's beautiful gilt parlor harp. A human skull signifies the family's "death in life" condition. Black zombie Carrefour guards the Hounfort as T-Misery dominates the Holland courtyard. On reaching the voodoo god's dark hut, Betsy is dragged inside. She faces Mrs. Rand. Both stand in a low-angle shot at opposite ends of the frame, identifying them as dark family representatives. One mentally subdues a sexually promiscuous daughter-in-law; the other attempts to destroy physically the same "threat" with dangerous insulin treatments. Both women use medicine but eventually turn to voodoo.

The calypso sequence embodies family contradictions. It begins at daylight after Wes detains Betsy at a café. A native balladeer (Sir Lancelot) begins singing "The British Grenadiers." His song has obvious anti—imperialist associations. The Hollands brought the first slaves with them on a ship with T-Misery as figurehead. The singer begins a satirical critique against the ruling family, using pointed lines, "There was a family who lived on the isle of Saint Sebastian a long long time . . . the Holland man he took a wife . . . a wife as pretty as a big white flower. He kept his wife in a tower. She saw the brother and stole his heart and that's how the badness and the trouble start. The wife and the brother they want to go. But the Holland man he tell them no."

Before he can continue—"the evil came and burned her mind in the fever flame"—he learns of the couple's presence. Making a barbed apology ("creeping into his heart like a little fox"), he informs Wes that he would never have sung had he known he "was with a lady." The infuriated Wes dismisses him, but the singer returns at night, resuming his calypso after Wes falls into a drunken stupor. He advances toward Betsy. Referring to Jessica ("Her eyes are empty and she cannot talk"), he includes the island's new arrival in his continuing refrain—"and a nurse has come to make her walk. The brothers are lonely and the nurse is young. Shame and sorrow for the family." Mrs. Rand then emerges from the darkness suppressing both the singer and the song's implications.

The calypso singer is no stereotypical threat.[27] He functions as a cinematic chorus by stimulating questions and alternative readings for the audience to consider. Unlike Carrefour the singer inhabits day and night, uniting distinct worlds of reality and fantasy by revealing their dialectical association.

Sound motifs also complement several visual details. During Betsy's first dinner with Paul and Wes, we hear the Hounfort drums after the latter speaks of (the then unseen) Mrs. Rand—"mother of us both and much too good for both of us." Drums break out after Wes concludes his sentence, "When Paul's father died, she married Dr. Rand, the missionary and after the death of my father she ran the mission." An empty chair at the corner of the dining room signifies mother's unseen dominating presence. These sound motifs denote Mrs. Rand's involvement in colonialism, family, religion, and voodoo. During another dinner sequence, drums sound when Wes begins a violent argument with Paul over Jessica, "You were so reserved and gentle with Jessica that night!" Even their clothing is significant. In both dinner sequences Paul wears a dark suit while Wes wears a light one.[28] Paul later confesses guilt feelings to Betsy. "Before Jessica was taken ill, there was a scene, an ugly scene. I told her she couldn't go, that I'd keep her here by force if necessary." Drums break out at his words, "keep her here by force." Drum beats punctuate Paul's words to Betsy after her return from the Hounfort. "You think I want Jessica back. Clean decent-thinking Betsy, I wish it were true (drums begin) for your sake." The drums suggest other motives behind this supposedly "good" brother's suave, reassuring manner.

I Walked with a Zombie never provides explicit answers, but it reveals a repressive family unit that is responsible for personal and psychological damage. Mrs. Rand's desire to maintain a fragile institution acts as catalyst. She finally claims responsibility when the Hollands face legal investigation over Wes's accusations.

> She is dead. Living and dead. I did it. I entered into their ceremonies—pretended to be possessed by their gods. . . . I kept seeing Jessica's face—smiling because she was beautiful enough to take my family into her hands and tear it apart. The drums—the chanting—the lights—everything blurred together. And then I heard a voice, speaking in a sudden silence. My voice. I was speaking to the Houngan. I was possessed. I said that the woman in Fort Holland was evil and that he must make her into a zombie.

She calls upon supernatural powers to discipline Jessica into bodily submission as Mrs. Brenner unconsciously evokes the birds against Melanie Daniels in *The Birds*. In both cases paranoia over the family and accompanying aggressive tendencies are common factors within these different treatments of family horror.

Wes and Jessica later die at sea. He kills her to prevent the Hounfort claiming her body. Searchers hunt for the bodies in the final sequence. Illuminated by moonlight and phosphorescent sea, Jessica's floating body recalls the beauty/putrescence/decay motifs in Paul's earlier speech to Jessica. The sexual threat is now a corpse. But the institution is not entirely untarnished. As Wes and Jessica's bodies enter the Holland estate, a religious voice-over delivers the official verdict.

> O Lord God, deliver them from the pain of eternal death. The woman was a wicked woman. Dead in her life. Dead in the selfishness of her spirit. . . . Her steps led them down into evil. And the man followed her. Pity them who are living.

A significant cut destabilizes the validity of this discourse. It also disrupts Paul and Betsy's happily-ever-after embrace. Most Hollywood films conclude with a closing shot of the lovers embracing. But T-Misery's image interrupts the camera's last track-in movement to Paul and Betsy. It suggests family guilt will remain. Like Oliver and Alice, Paul and Betsy will never entirely escape their personal complicity within an oppressive family hearth of darkness.

◆ ◆ ◆

The major characters in *The Seventh Victim* and *The Ghost Ship*—Mary Gibson (Kim Hunter) and Tom Merriam (Russell Wade)—are orphans in a hostile world. Both seek authoritative parental figures. Brusquely expelled from her seemingly secure private school, Mary Gibson enters the outside world in search of her only living relative, a sister who has financially supported her for several years. Embarking on his first voyage, young orphan Tom Merriam seeks a father figure. He believes Captain Stone (Richard Dix) is his ideal mentor. However, Mary and Tom find their role models seriously flawed. Jacqueline Gibson (Jean Brooks) moves from one social trap to another; Captain Stone exhibits paranoid authoritarian tendencies on the isolated ship he ruthlessly dominates. Although Mary and Tom eventually survive, there is no certainty they will escape similar family traps.

Supported by her sister, Mary lives a sheltered existence in Highcliff Academy until she learns of Jacqueline's disappearance and the subsequent nonpayment of her fees. Offered the possibility of a demeaning assistantship by the imperious Miss Lowood, she decides to leave and find her sister. On her way out, the submissive Miss Gilchrist warns her to never return. Highcliff Academy is a repressive institution headed by Miss Lowood, who treats her staff like a dominating mother. Highcliff Academy anticipates Mrs. Redi's La Sagesse cosmetic company. Both managers oppress their female employees. Formerly friendly with Jacqueline, Frances Fallon (Isabel Jewell) parallels the submissive Miss Gilchrist. The devil-worshipping Palladist cult macabrely parallels Highcliff and La Sagesse. They are all rigidly structured patriarchal organizations dominated by stern parental figures. Attempting to escape institutional commitment (including marriage), Jacqueline threatens them all. *The Seventh Victim* is another Lewton allegory of the single woman's fate within patriarchal society. Like Irena, Jessica, Julia Farren, and Nell Bowen of *Bedlam* (1945), Jacqueline is another family victim.

Although Mary is the "good sister," her pursuit of Jacqueline eventually causes her sister's death. Her actions parallel those of Alice and Betsy. Mary desires marriage and family, but this can only happen after the death of a transgressive "other." During the penultimate sequence of *The Seventh Victim*, Mary and Gregory Ward confess their love for each other, a love they believe impossible while Jacqueline lives. Gregory speaks of committing Jacqueline to an asylum, echoing Oliver's plans for Irena in *The Cat People*. Mary dutifully listens. The next and final sequence in the film depicts Jacqueline's suicide. Jacqueline fulfills their unconscious desires by carrying out what the Palladists failed to do. As J. P. Telotte notes, "The greatest threats that emerge from the Lewton films, after all, typically prove to be the most logical or rational of people."[29]

Jacqueline's husband Gregory Ward duplicates Oliver Reed. Both men lack sympathy for female dilemmas. Gregory believes Jacqueline inhabits "a world of her own fancy. She didn't always tell the truth. In fact . . . she didn't know what the truth was." Oliver similarly condemns Irena and Amy in *Curse of the Cat People*. Dr. Lewis Judd (Tom Conway) of *The Cat People* repeats his devious manipulation of vulnerable females in *The Seventh Victim*. Judd speaks of Jacqueline as "always a sensationalist, trying to seize on to something, anything to bring her happiness." Unlike *The Cat People*, he succeeds in conducting an affair with his patient under the guise of medical care. But Jacqueline's condition is suggestive of dissatisfaction with social norms, not any narcissistic search for sensation. Finding no outlet for her real desires, she commits suicide. Jacqueline is a tragic victim, the only character who never deludes herself about the bleak nature of social existence. Her final encounter with Mimi (Elizabeth Russell) recalls Irena's meeting with her soul sister in *The Cat People*. Society has no use for transgressive single females. It uses every means at its disposal to victimize Jacqueline, blame her for her condition, and then cause her annihilation.

Jacqueline never deceives herself by wearing appropriate social masks like the male figures. Irving August (Lou Lubin) never achieves his desired wish to be a hard-boiled, victorious detective. He dies an ignominious death at the hands of a frightened woman. Dr. Judd never practices his skills. He explains this as solipsistic disinterest. "I don't practice anymore. I find it easier

to write about mental illness and leave the care to others." Despite supercilious superiority, Judd is a frightened man. He runs in fear, expecting the Palladist's immediate arrival in Jacqueline's apartment. Judd is a failure like poet
Jason Hoag. He fails to cure Jason's girlfriend as well as Jacqueline. A cut scene
reveals that Judd accidentally tips the Palladists off concerning Jacqueline's
whereabouts later in the film.[30] Once a talented poet, Jason is another flawed
male. He fancies himself a contemporary Dante searching for an elusive Beatrice. Jason hopes his "muse" will inspire him to further achievement. Another
cut scene reveals that despite finding one in Mary, his new work is still flawed.
Gregory dons the mask of a bourgeois rationalist husband. He refuses to discern the real forces disturbing Jacqueline and becomes an accessory to her
eventual suicide. As he tells Mary, he helped rent the room with the hanging noose above the Dante restaurant. "That room made her happy in some
strange way I couldn't understand." *The Seventh Victim* presents masculinity
as weak and dangerous.

Like Betsy in *I Walked with a Zombie*, Mary blinds herself to the realities of a nihilistic and hostile society. Seeking her sister and envisaging herself like the heroine of a nineteenth-century novel, she follows her quest as a
family duty. Like Betsy, she pursues unselfish actions, ironically causing her
sister's destruction. Jason challenges her, "Do you really want to find your sister?" Enquiring about Jacqueline's whereabouts, Mary revealingly remarks, "I
almost feel as if I've never known my sister." Answering a knock on her apartment door, she finds Jacqueline outside, darkly counterposing to her supposedly positive image.[31] Another crucial line, edited from the release print, has
Mary wishing her sister dead so the search can end.[32] Never really knowing
Jacqueline or sympathizing with her psychological dilemma, she eventually
becomes *The Cat People*'s Alice to Gregory's Oliver Reed.

By depicting the Palladists as "an unexceptional-looking collection of
people,"[33] *The Seventh Victim* emphasizes their relationship to the world of
everyday normality. Operating according to a rigidly defined set of rules,
unsympathetic to breaches of their covenant, the Palladists echo rigid families. They refuse to sympathize with Jacqueline's plight. They follow the same
patterns of conformity and obedience active within Highcliff Academy and
La Sagesse. Like other characters, they play roles to conceal empty lives.
Although the film's title refers to Jacqueline, all the characters are victims in
one way or another.

By entering their society, finding it wanting, and leaving to attempt an
independent existence, Jacqueline threatens everyone. Her very presence
opposes restrictive social codes. The Palladists embody the repressed desires
of the film's normal characters. Wishing Jacqueline dead (as Gregory and

Mary do), they aggressively act against their victim as a result of paranoid feelings rooted within family institutional structures.

Although set at sea, *The Ghost Ship* repeats *The Seventh Victim*'s "orphan" motif. Like Mary Gibson, Tom Merriam sets off on a voyage of discovery into the adult world. The environment he enters contains similar features of entrapment. While Mary confronts her "shadow" self in Jacqueline Gibson and conveniently disavows it at the climax, Tom Merriam's encounter with his fatherly alter ego, Captain Stone, results in a far greater realization of kinship. Despite a studio imposed happy ending, the visual structure of *The Ghost Ship* contains far darker overtones as it hints at Tom Merriam becoming another Captain Stone.

Like Mary Gibson, Tom is an initiate to adulthood's dark world. Although Mary is newly orphaned since her sister's disappearance at the start of *The Seventh Victim*, Tom is a real orphan eager to prove himself in the outside world. But this world contains irresolvable dark and ambiguous features. The film's opening shot reveals the camera tracking back from a row of knives in a shop window. Young Tom encounters a blind musician singing "Blow the Man Down," aurally signifying his potential fate under a father's knife. Defective in vision as the Finn is in speech, the blind man understands the true nature of a dark world Tom enters. The film suggests the deceptive nature of appearances. Both the beggar and Finn appear dangerous threats in contrast to the initially benevolent Captain Stone. Formerly friendly Sparks and the crew prove ineffective at the moment of Tom's greatest danger.

Like Irena, Amy, and Lewton's other vulnerable figures, Tom seeks friend and family. He believes Captain Stone will provide both. Ascending the ship's ladder he enters Stone's cabin. Glancing briefly at Ellen's photograph, Tom sees Stone descending the ladder leading to the bridge. Both face each other at opposite ends of the frame. Identically positioned like father and son with the former's conspicuous motto WHO DOES NOT HEED THE RUDDER SHALL MEET THE ROCK between them, Stone sees his new third mate as an echo of his younger self. "An orphan, serious, hard-working, anxious to get somewhere," whom he has hired without seeing. Stone's desire for a "clean ship, an obedient ship," unhealthily evokes those similar wishes of Oliver Reed and Paul Holland. His persona hides a latent paranoia. Set on a maritime landscape, *The Ghost Ship* is by no means irrelevant to the urban situation. Like Melville's *Moby Dick* and Jack London's *The Sea-Wolf*, the seascape metaphorically expresses land issues. Echoing Captain Ahab and Wolf Larsen, Captain Stone logically enacts patriarchal structures of brutality begun in the family.

Initially young Tom Merriam sees in Captain Stone a benevolent father-figure, the first older man who treats him as a "friend." As the voyage continues, Tom gains insights into his seemingly benevolent father. During the only tracking shot in both *The Ghost Ship* and most of Lewton's works, Stone escorts Tom along the deck speaking of the "great joy" he has in authority. Like Paul Holland, Stone revels in control and dominance. Two lines parallel the opening dialogue between Paul and Betsy in *I Walked with a Zombie*. When Tom naively speaks about the Altair being a "beautiful" ship for a first berth, Stone replies "She's a beautiful ship—to command." As Sparks later tells Tom, "The Captain wants a clean ship," to rule over his seamen subjects in his "hobby of authority."

The mute Finn Tom encounters before boarding the Altair echoes Carrefour's role in *I Walked with a Zombie*. Positioned at the boundary between two worlds as an "obedient seaman," intuitively sympathetic toward Tom's plight, he also represents his alternative alter ego. In two shots he occupies an opposite position in the frame paralleling Tom. If Stone represents a version of what Tom could be in the film's opening scenes, the Finn represents his oppositional counterpart. Tom is treated as a dumb being during his forced confinement on the Altair. His attempted pleas to the crew draw no response. Tom is as "mute" in their eyes as the Finn. When the bosun musters the crew in an early scene, the first mate remarks, "Keep your eye on that man. I don't want any trouble on board," once he learns of the Finn's condition. As a marginal figure within the crew, he is the only character to sympathize with Tom, and he eventually acts to save him.

Despite each member of the crew possessing individual human characteristics, Stone regards them as little better than the mutton in the ship's hold or the sheep in San Sebastian's courtyards. Believing in the captain's right to control the lives of his crew, he acts as a godlike figure. He either cares for their everyday needs or kills them by divine right. In his Jehovahlike posture, Stone's authoritarian position benefits by his crew's complicity. Unlike Louie (Lawrence Tierney), who dies in the chain locker, the remainder either obediently follow orders or turn a blind eye like Sparks.

Stone's only salvation is his fiancee, Ellen Roberts (Edith Barrett). Seeing in Tom another version of the Captain, "Lonely, austere, bitter . . . without friends or family, condemning yourself to the heights . . . heights you call authority," she loses the battle to change him. Stone's paranoid authoritarianism wins. Informing him of her divorce on board the Altair, she receives no joyous response. Stone wears his captain's uniform instead of the civilian suit he wore in San Sebastian. Now "the captain," rather than "a captain" on land, he tells her of fears involving insanity and his insecurity against those who question his authority. Rejecting female companionship, preferring his isolated patriarchal rule, Stone chooses not to "heed the rudder." When Tom accidentally arrives on board the Altair after failing to indict the captain for murder, he finds himself an intended sacrificial Isaac to Stone's paranoid Abraham. Escaping Sparks's fate by the Finn's timely intervention, Tom commands the ship back to port.

At first sight the climax appears positive. Tom descends the ladder. The movement counters his ascent in the opening but parallels Stone's during their initial meeting. The first person he sees is the blind beggar of the opening scene. Still singing "Blow the Man Down," he offers an ironic message: "Being a sailor, you'll need luck." The camera pans left as Tom eventually meets Ellen's younger sister. With the concluding soundtrack score, the studio obviously intends a "happy" ending. But the woman is in shadow and Tom moves into the darkness. Tom really escapes Stone's fate, temporarily. The beggar still sees him as a "sailor" who needs luck. The shadowy presence of Ellen's sister suggests that she, too, may be as ineffective as her elder sibling in redeeming Tom. Both Tom and the girl walk into a dark background whose shadows suggest more than "an affirmative ending, indicating an initiation accomplished and an individuation hard won."[34]

The Lewton films subtly question family norms within the guise of the fantastic. Lacking supernatural monsters, depicting tensions within a deliberately ambiguous shadow world of tormented emotions, they present a vast array of victimizers and victims all trapped within the family. In the next decade the family appears as the direct origin of monstrous productions, an acknowledgment leading to the achievement of *Psycho*. It will no longer be possible to suggest supernatural elements as the cause of events that have their material causes within the psychic constraints of the family—at least for a few decades.

4

To *Psycho* and Beyond:
The Hitchcock Connection

Alfred Hitchcock's significance is well acknowledged in contemporary cinema studies.[1] Not only was he a great director but he also disclosed key motifs within the realm of family horror. Although, like Freud, limitations of personality and cultural background affect radical realization of motifs within his material, Hitchcock's cinema reveals characters whose dilemmas originate from the family's rigid institutional structures. Many features usually concealed by the horror genre's spectacular mechanisms occur in their most maturest realization within his work, but these features are by no means peculiar to the director. They also occur in other films made within the same era such as *The Bad Seed* (1956), *Homicidal* (1962), and *Lady in a Cage* (1964). Within this era material factors behind horror become predominant. Working in America as an outsider, the director intuitively discerned key motifs that operated within his adopted country's cultural tradition, particularly those involving the family's socially repressive role.

As Robin Wood convincingly demonstrates, Hitchcock's films reveal tormented personalities that struggle against patriarchy's Oedipal trajectory.[2] Whether neurotic or murderously psychotic, his characters are tragic victims of a family institution that imposes rigid patterns of masculine and feminine behavior upon its subjects. Although Raymond Bellour depicts Hitchcock as the grim documenter of a monolithic Oedipal trajectory,[3] many films contradict this. Hitchcock's characters often struggle against Freud's "necessary" developmental pattern, either by opposing patriarchal power (*Spellbound, Notorious, North by Northwest*) or negatively regressing into psychotic behavior. His films frequently depict dangerous family institutions that frustrate the free expression of alternative tendencies within individual personas (*Rope, Psycho*).[4] Far from being misogynistic texts that encourage violence against women, Hitchcock's cinema actually reveals an arbitrarily violent patriarchal culture. His castrating mothers and violent castrated sons enact the Oedipal trajectory's socially sanctioned psychic violence. Anticipating later grotesque representations, Hitchcock's films unveil the real concealed causes behind the spectacular bloodbaths in *Friday the 13th, Halloween,* and *Nightmare on Elm Street.*

Combining key traits of religious guilt, psychosis, and apocalyptic catastrophe, Hitchcock's cinema illustrates Charles Derry's tripartite division of 1960s horror cinema—the Horror of Personality, the Horror of Armageddon, and the Horror of the Demonic.[5] *The Birds* (1962) combines all three motifs. Whether we understand Tippi Hedren's characterization of Melanie Daniels as a Norman Bates–like lost soul or frightened girl-child seeking a mother, her presence causes the winged assault on Bodega Bay. The hysterical mother in the diner regards her as a Salem witch. But Melanie is also a victim. As Raymond Bellour demonstrates, the first attack follows Melanie's dominance under Mitch's male gaze.[6] But the developing cataclysm rushes toward uncontrollable apocalyptic dimensions. *The Birds* does not conclude with the Hollywood "happy ending" of Mitch spanking "sassy" Melanie. Instead forces unleashed from within the patriarchal id now threaten civilization. The birds are a twentieth-century embodiment of the ancient Greek familial avengers— The Furies. Attacking the children's party and answering the unconscious anger of Mrs. Brenner (Jessica Tandy) against Melanie's presence (an association suggested in the editing sequence), they represent a violent evocation of repressed paranoia, which enacts literal and symbolic castration.[7] The birds pluck out the eyes of Dan Fawcett and Annie Hayworth. Attacking Melanie in the attic, they finally discipline her into a catatonic, ideal daughter for Mrs. Brenner.[8] Like Jessica in *I Walked with a Zombie*, she is no longer a sexual threat to the family. However, unlike *Zombie, The Birds* presents a foreboding conclusion that anticipates works of the 1980s. Like Jason and Michael, they become increasingly out of control, turning against the forces that initially evoked them.

Marnie's Mrs. Edgar (Louise Latham) is another of Hitchcock's repressively monstrous mothers. Although she does not conjure winged monsters from the id against her daughter, she is responsible for her condition. She represses a traumatic childhood incident and her daughter's sexuality.[9] Like Mrs. Thompson in *A Nightmare on Elm Street* (1984), she conceals essential information that is necessary for her child's survival. In Hitchcock's cinema family, repression produces victims and victimizers, jailers and prisoners.

Scottie Ferguson and Norman Bates murderously embody the darker side of Freud's scenario. Reactivating a birth trauma in *Vertigo's* opening scene, Scottie (James Stewart) regressively seeks the lost pre-Oedipal "breast," symbolically represented by Madeleine/Judy (Kim Novak). Living in an unrealistic world of romantic love, his narcissistic, voyeuristic gaze turns sadistic once his illusions are shattered.[10] Norman Bates's gaze turns from voyeurism to sadism once the female image destabilizes his precarious sense of masculinity. Hitchcock's work concisely depicts the murderous consequences of repressive family institutions.

Whether responsible for a murderous offspring (*Strangers on a Train, Psycho, Frenzy*), hindering their son's safety (*North by Northwest*), resentful at potential or actual daughters-in-law (*Notorious, The Birds*), or responsible for their daughter's or younger brother's psychopathological tendencies (*Marnie, Shadow of a Doubt*), Hitchcock's cinematic mothers are dangerous beings. They are functionaries of an oppressive order—but this is only one aspect. Despite their authoritarian role within the family hearth, mothers are as much victims of patriarchal institutions as those they oppress. Within the nineteenth century (and much of the twentieth), the dominant ideology allowed the female domestic power as long as she confined her reign to the hearth. Family life became a battleground between the sexes as the wife/mother oppressively dominated husband and offspring in thwarted satisfaction for her lack of outside opportunities. Strindberg's dark family dramas depict such situations. Ibsen's *Hedda Gabler* is equally monster and victim within a patriarchal social structure that allows no positive outlets for her energy. Confined to the home, lacking external outlets for creativity and independence, the mother became a complicit patriarchal agent who molds her children within the same restrictive patterns that imprison her. Encountering recalcitrant children that recall her own repressed energies, she exerts swift reprisal on any offspring reminding her of any lost independence. Mother became a social ally of an Oedipal trajectory responsible for her own oppression.

As Michel Schneider points out, Freud's supposedly universal pattern of gender roles is really socially determined. Parents successively mold offspring within acceptable patterns.[11] The mother represents the male-child's first object-choice from whom he must separate himself according to socially acceptable masculine roles. Conversely the female child develops her attachment to the mother and eventually succumbs to the maternal role herself. In Freud's essay titled "On Narcissism," both parents act in instilling idealized roles within their offspring.

Reacting against conservative Freudian ideas concerning gender roles, feminist "object-relations" psychoanalyst theorists such as Nancy Chodorow and Carol Gilligan argue for a more equal child-rearing relationship between males and females, antithetical to patriarchal modes of gender reproduction.[12] In *The Reproduction of Mothering*, Nancy Chodorow analyzes psychoanalytic mechanisms designed continually to manufacture socially approved gender roles. Disavowing her "masculine" qualities the female uses these aggressive tendencies to rear and control her future children. Similarly in seeking separation from the mother, the male-child overreacts to his mother's feelings and wishes by often projecting fears and desires onto her.

Combating the fantasy of a perfect, all-powerful, devouring mother, Chodorow argues that such a deterministic view ignores social conditions that cause psychopathological behavior which results from male fears toward the female. By refusing to acknowledge their bisexuality, males devalue and dominate the feminine realm. In any society that exhibits close bonding between mother and child, Chodorow notes occurring features of male narcissism, pride, and phobia against mature women.[13] Focusing upon masculinity's problematic nature, the psychoanalytic feminist school contains findings relevant to American culture and Hitchcock.[14]

Patriarchal family structures make everyone monsters and victims. Working within an entertainment system, producing works with key associations to screen memories and dream works, Hitchcock's family dramas fictionally elaborate dominant social patterns. Whether depicting the powerful influence of an unseen, powerful, deceased wife (*Rebecca*), male marital insecurity (Johnnie Aygarth in *Suspicion*), or fear of the feminine (*Spellbound*, *Notorious*), Hitchcock's cinema presents a thwarted world populated by family victims. Except for rare instances of revolt against the father's law (*Notorious*, *North by Northwest*), Hitchcock presents a bleak wasteland where psychotic characters paradoxically evoke the very violence controlling them. *Shadow of a Doubt* and *Psycho* reveal sexual, economic, and institutional mechanisms behind actions performed by later heirs of Uncle Charlie and Norman Bates such as Jason, Michael, and Freddy.

Like *Psycho*, *Shadow of a Doubt* is important for understanding the evolution of the family horror film.[15] In the second sequence Young Charlie (Theresa Wright) lies prone on her bed. Thinking of an uncle whom she believes will save her family from bourgeois sterility, she conjures him up like a monster from the id. Although *Shadow of a Doubt* is not within the horror film genre confines, it has a close relationship, revealing the essential interdependence of all Hollywood genres.[16]

The first scene introduces us to Uncle Charlie (Joseph Cotten) who escapes police pursuit in a quasi-supernatural manner. The next scene shows Young Charlie waiting in Santa Rosa. These two sequences foreshadow *The*

Exorcist: the Philadelphia urban wasteland anticipates Iraq's blighted desert landscape as Santa Rosa parallels Georgetown. Uncle Charlie's appearance in Santa Rosa answers his niece's prayer; she is frustrated with her family situation. Regan's later demonic possession in *The Exorcist* is no arbitrary occurrence—it also results from family tensions.

The family is an important motif in *Shadow of a Doubt* and *Psycho*, sexually, psychoanalytically, and economically—the last factor is crucially significant to America's capitalist society and cultural tradition. For Benjamin Franklin the American Dream was a sober, industrious, and frugal capitalist economy through which Americans can "soon become masters, establish themselves in business, marry, raise families and become responsible citizens."[17] The family manufactures individuals for dominant economic requirements, but its Oedipal trajectory does not always function as a well-oiled industrial machine. Uncle Charlie and Normal Bates are two notable exceptions.

The respective conclusions of *Shadow of a Doubt* and *Psycho* attempt to depict Uncle Charlie and Norman as individual aberrations. However, the bleak, emotional tone of these endings alert us to their bankrupt nature. They parallel ideologically imposed "happy ever after" conclusions of classic horror movies.

Shadow of a Doubt's final scene shows Young Charlie and Graham (McDonald Carey) standing outside a church in broad daylight. Isolated from the community by their knowledge of Uncle Charlie's real character, they certainly do not appear to be a happy, normal heterosexual couple. Their dialogue attempts to restore audience confidence in a secure world. Graham holds his sweetheart's hand as she stands on the church steps. He looks at her but she does not return his gaze. She utters, "He didn't trust people. He hated the whole world." All-American, youthful-looking Graham responds, "The world's all right. It just goes a little crazy sometimes, just like your Uncle Charlie." From inside the church the minister speaks the funeral service— "The beauty of their souls, the sweetness of their characters live on with us for ever." Although the dialogue satisfies the Hays Code, Hitchcock clearly means us to see the real meaning. Hero, heroine, and community deny the real implications of preceding events. Like Shinbone in *The Man Who Shot Liberty Valance*, Santa Rosa prefers to "print the legend" and repress the monstrous facts dormant within its particular hearth of darkness.

During the last five minutes of *Psycho*, arrogant psychiatrist Dr. Richman (Simon Oakland) attempts to reassure audience uncertainty over Norman's abnormality. Although he describes Mrs. Bates as a "clinging, demanding woman," he places the burden of guilt upon Norman. Dangerously disturbed "ever since his father died," bad Norman actually created his psychotic mother! The dialogue presents a conservative 1950s rationale for Norman's behavior. If only he had a father to teach him masculinity, none of this would ever have happened! The explanation is as glib and unconvincing as Graham's in the earlier film. *Psycho* already shows us more than Dr. Richman tells us. Law and medical authorities believe they can rationally tie up loose ends within logical discursive frameworks.

The next scene destroys such reassurance. Hitchcock's camera follows a policeman bringing Norman a blanket. Norman's supposedly self-created mother's voice speaks. The image changes to show Norman in his cell as the camera tracks into a close-up.

> It's sad when a mother has to speak the words that condemn her own son. I can't allow them to think I would commit murder. Put him away now as I should have years ago. He was always bad and in the end he intended to tell them that I killed those girls and that man.

Mother is incapable of swatting a fly. She lets it remain on her son. But who is speaking? Is it Norman's recreation of mother or mother's recreation of Norman? There are no dividing lines. Only psychotic victims of a family situation. As the camera ceases framing Norman's smiling face, our sense of security vanishes. We no longer hear Richman's explanation. Instead we see a split second superimposition of mother's grinning skull on Norman's smiling face, its death-in-life imagery leading to the final shot of Marion's car dragged from the swamp's excremental depths by a chain clearly reminiscent of an umbilical cord. This chain reaches in the direction of the audience, breaking the barriers between cinema screen and everyday life.

Supposedly normal life-affirming bonds of family mother love oppose capitalist ideology's cherished beliefs. Family ties are death-orientated, not life affirming. They are as pathologically strong as the chains dragging Marion's car from the swamp. Beneath the Oedipal trajectory's patriarchal goals of genital sexuality lie repressed oral and anal forces awaiting excessive return in violence and psychosis. Despite the family's repressive role in capitalist society, social and psychic mechanisms may malfunction.

Psycho's final scene is not reassuring. The car does not entirely rise from the depths of the swamp. It may, like us, descend once again into darkness. Beneath any living skin lies the skull, the dead visage of the past, which constantly associates death with life. Norman's facial grimace during his attack on Lila in the fruit cellar intercuts with mother's grinning, socketless skull. He is a split personality, who psychotically enacts the logically violent consequences of patriarchal control.

The swamp in *Shadow of a Doubt* is Santa Rosa's film noir world of the Till-2 club where Young Charlie's alter-ego Louise works as a waitress. Like Bedford Falls in the shadow world of *It's a Wonderful Life*, the landscape represents the dark underside of everything normality represses. Linked to Philadelphia's urban wasteland in the film's opening shots, it expresses the ruthless nature of economic factors in the American Dream. Admiring Young Charlie's ring, Louise expresses her willingness to die for such a gift. She admits both her spiritual kinship with Uncle Charlie's victims as well as the fact that her economic situation will eventually result in possible isolation and death. As an economic loser in the American Dream, her final end may parallel the tramps in the opening scene. Louise lacks Young Charlie's affluent family situation which allows her to remain at home after graduation.

Shadow of a Doubt's introductory scenes visually express a duality common to the horror genre and Hitchcock. Raymond Durgnat significantly notes relevant contrasts between poverty and middle-class daydreams of bourgeois affluence within the opening scenes.[18] The introductory six shots of Philadelphia inversely echo the six shots leading to Young Charlie's room.[19] In terms of movement, direction, and editing, they form a leftward pattern, opposing the latter's rightward direction. Uncle Charlie's first shot is also left to right. It parallels Young Charlie's in the Santa Rosa segment. He caresses his cigar in a leftward direction (when his landlady enters the room) anticipating the position of his niece's hips as she lies on her bed. Before either character speaks a visual bond unites them.

The camera pans left to the money scattered on Uncle Charlie's bedside table, before tilting downward to reveal more on the floor. Then the scene changes to reveal the door through which the maternally stout, middle-aged landlady enters. She informs him of the "friends" who wish to see him. Then she notices money scattered around like litter. For Hitchcock's murderous characters, money is never as important as it is for normal, bourgeois acquisitive characters like Marion Crane. Marion steals money in *Psycho* for her new family life with Sam. The camera presents a point of view shot that shows its magnetic effect on her, tilting down and tracking in to it on the bed. After Marion's death, Hitchcock ironically parallels this "look." A tracking shot begins from her dead eyeball to a wrapped-up newspaper containing the money on her bedside table. In both cases a clear connection between sexuality, death, and money exists.

Hitchcock presents direct associations between family and capitalist relationships. Uncle Charlie's victims were former entertainers who sold their bodies by marrying into money. In *Psycho* money dominates Sam's and Marion's physical relationship. She refuses any further sexual encounters, preferring a platonic, family-related dinner at home before her father and mother's photograph. In both films economic factors within personal relationships cause insecurity and unhappiness. Uncle Charlie and Norman Bates represent monstrous embodiments of civilization's dark repressed forces. They are free from the everyday, economic constraints that control law-abiding citizens within the family. Money means nothing to them. Uncle Charlie leaves it lying around like litter; Norman Bates puts it into Marion's car before sinking it in the swamp. Even if he knew of its existence in the wrapped-up newspaper, he would have thrown it away in any case.

After Uncle Charlie escapes police pursuit, the next sequence shows Young Charlie. Prone on her bed, in a reverse direction to that of her Uncle, she muses in boredom. Her father Joe (Henry Travers) stands in the doorway, his position paralleling Uncle Charlie's landlady. She has "just been thinking for hours" about her family life. "I simply give up. A family should be a wonderful thing. And this family's gone to pieces. We just go along and nothing ever happens . . . we're in a terrible rut." Joe's reference to his recent salary raise echoes the landlady's concern for money. Young Charlie retorts, "How can you talk about money when I'm talking about souls? All we do is eat and sleep." Her family lacks any sense of communication and conversation, existing in a daily round of dinners, dishes, and bed.[20] She speaks of her mother, "Yes, poor mother, who works like a dog. I don't know how she stands it. She's a wonderful women. She's not just a mother."

The Norton family exist in a state of living death. Reacting to their bored existence, Young Charlie evokes her uncle like a demonic being. He represents the return of repressed forces within his family, especially murder and incest. The initial sequences contrasting uncle and niece suggest an incestuous link. As a single wandering male, Uncle Charlie dynamically counterpoints Joe's civilized conformist husband/father figure whom wife and daughter domestically dominate. Uncle Charlie takes over his position at the head of the table. If Uncle Charlie represents Joe's opposite, Herbie (Hume Cronyn) mirrors his repressed counterpart. Single, mother-dominated, sexually repressed, he and Joe seek refuge in plotting each other's elimination in fantasy games. Herbie recognizes their real position within society. As he says to Joe, "For all you know you might as well be dead," aptly anticipating the "death-in-life" family metaphor within *Psycho*.

The Norton family exists in a state of boredom. It seeks fantasy outlets for repressed tendencies. Bespectacled daughter Anne immerses herself in romantic fiction, "characterized by a sustained autistic withdrawal from reality into movies . . . and predominantly books."[21] She parallels Uncle Charlie's youthful devouring of fiction before his bicycle "accident." Anne also loves horror stories, expressing maternal resentment in nursery rhymes, "I broke my mother's back three times." As the youngest in the family, Roger endures the same type of maternal dominance as his uncle once did. When Emmy (Patricia Collinge) receives news of her brother's impending visit, she cries, "It's my brother, the younger brother, the baby," despite the fact that the baby is now a mature male. As she speaks of family tendencies to always spoil its youngest member, a high-angle shot reveals an extremely peeved Roger. When Uncle Charlie's train arrives at the station, its shadow envelops young Roger. Uncle Charlie murderously embodies the entire Norton family's repressed tensions.

Shadow of a Doubt illuminates many crucial motifs within contemporary family horror films. Young Charlie sees her uncle as a romantic figure who will unite her family. However, as in *Vertigo*, deceptive romantic illusions contain dark undertones. Her words to Joe—"Guess we'll just have to wait for a miracle. I don't believe in good intentions"—have ironic consequences. Her Uncle telepathically receives her thoughts. He sends her a telegram—"A kiss for little Charlie from her Uncle Charlie"—before she thinks of doing the same. Young Charlie's thoughts contain supernatural overtones that echo later motifs within the horror genre. She states to Emmy, "I know a wonderful man who can save us," to which her mother responds, "What do you mean, save us?" Reading his telegram at the drug store, she excitedly exclaims, "He heard me! He heard me!" However, her redeemer is a dark Satanic figure returning to the Edenic family world of Santa Rosa. Like Ethan Edwards in *The Searchers*, the wandering male returns home to stir deep tensions within the family hearth.

The meeting of uncle and niece resembles two lovers reuniting. After a series of individual midshots following Uncle Charlie's descent from the train, both stand at opposite ends of the frame. They rush forward and embrace. The reunion between Emmy and Charlie forms an interesting parallel. Emmy occupies her daughter's earlier position left of frame, while her brother occupies the right. Filmed in similar romantic imagery, Charlie reinscribes his sister within her former, predomestic status. He says, "Standing there you don't look like Emma Norton. You look like Emma Spencer Oakley, the prettiest girl on the block." The underlying dark sexual pathology concludes when Uncle Charlie gives his niece an engagement ring worn by his last victim. By symbolically marrying her, he violates the family's incest taboo. As she states to her uncle later in the kitchen scene, "I know you . . . I have a feeling that inside you there's something nobody knows. I'll find it out. We're like twins. I have to know." The ring also links her with Charles's victims. She hums the Merry Widow Waltz, "the tune which symbolizes the sublimated romantic dream of which all the characters are, variously, victims."[22] As she makes coffee a mixed-in image of the dancers within her uncle's fantasy overwhelms her.

Hitchcock depicts the family as a suffocating entity that produces psychopathic killers. Uncle Charlie anticipates the later Hollywood fascination with serial killers. His suave demeanor and gentlemanly bearing foreshadow Thomas Harris's Hannibal Lecter (*The Silence of the Lambs*). Despite complying with Hollywood censorship codes, the film contains enough clues to explain the reasons for Uncle Charlie's psychopathology. Although not as explicit as *Manhunter* (1986), the film suggests parental abuse as the cause for its character's actions. Something occurred in Charles's early life that has conditioned his adult behavior. Although *Shadow of a Doubt* hints at a past "bicycle accident," other explanations are possible. With its connotations of a fall, it reminds us of the descent within *Vertigo* and inextricable associations with the birth trauma whereby the male child's closeness to the maternal breast results in the schizophrenic change from "good object" to "bad object."[23] The film suggests that Emmy's sibling smothering—when "Everybody was sweet and pretty. The whole world. Not like the world today"—had dark overtones, foreshadowing incestuous themes in films such as *I Dismember Mama* (1972) and *The Killing Kind* (1973). In the second film Terry (John Savage) actually whistles the Merry Widow Waltz prior to murdering a mother surrogate (Ruth Roman); the first film reveals mentally disturbed murderer Albert (Zooey Hall) with Edenic fantasies similar to those of Uncle Charlie. Taking little Annie (Geri Reisci) to the Bridal Room of a Victorian hotel, enamored of her pre-Oedipal associations, he muses, "There was a time when men were gentlemen and ladies were pure."

The Merry Widow Waltz imagery has significant associations. As Paul Gordon notes, the sequence belongs to the early years of Charles and Emma's parents, possibly the same period as the photograph Charles gives to Emma—1888. The year also witnessed exploits of the patron saint of serial killers—Jack the Ripper. Charles's mother is a contemporary of his "Merry Widow" victims. Charles's "obsession with the victims he seduces and then kills represents "a continued mother-fixation from his early childhood."[24]

Charles gives Emmy the photo when he is in bed. Surrounded by sister and niece, he is in an infantalized position reminiscent of his earlier family life. With two females "mothering" him, the scene contains further incestuous associations. Like Norman Bates, Charles "demonstrates a typical fear of powerful women which runs throughout Hitchcock's films."[25] As Robin Wood notes, "The mothering sexual/possessive devotion of a doting sister may be felt to provide a clue to the sexual motivation behind the merry widow murders."[26]

Charles also voices paranoid male resentment against a matriarchal society. He engages in a virulent dinner table polemic against his contemporary "generation of vipers"—"You'll see them in the best hotels by their thousands, eating the money, drinking the money, losing it at bridge, aged fat greedy animals" who "live on what their husbands earned." Nostalgically yearning for a mythical family Eden, suffering from denial mechanisms, he wishes to reenter a family hearth whose incestuous web destroyed him. Charles is a family created Lucifer, compulsively doomed to repeat the past, avenging himself on surrogate maternal representatives. Trapped within a damned cyclical grip of "eternal return," he reveals to his niece a world she never suspected. "You live in a dream world, Charlie, and I have brought you nightmares." The nightmare never ends. Although her uncle falls to his death after attempting to murder her—an action that fulfills his niece's desire—"I don't want you to touch my mother. If you don't go, I'll kill you myself. You see, that's the way I feel about you," there is no satisfactory resolution. She actually achieves what her uncle never achieved. She murders a blood relative who is not a surrogate victim. She must live with the knowledge of what this entails. *Shadow of a Doubt's* bleak conclusion shows the lovers distant and apart. Sharing a fatal knowledge with Graham, Charlie understands the dark underside of family life.

Psycho's family hell reveals associations of capitalism and sexuality similar to *Shadow of a Doubt.* Beginning with a pattern of descent whereby "we are to be taken forwards and downwards into the darkness of ourselves,"[27] the bird's-eye camera view reveals a shabby hotel room that signifies the desolate nature of Sam's and Marion's affair. Economic and social circumstances blight their personal lives.[28] They both suffer from a dead family past. Burdened by alimony payments to his ex-wife and his deceased father's debts, Sam expresses reluctance for more domestic obligations. Desiring respectability Marion refuses further premarital adventures. She plans a future dinner "in my house with my mother's picture on the wall and my sister helping me to broil a big steak for the three of us." Despite Sam's ironic response to Marion's family desires—"And after the steak, do we send Sister to the movies? Turn Mama's picture to the wall?"—he acquiesces. The move from sexual illegitimacy to family legitimacy has drastic consequences.

From Marion's dialogue mother appears to be the dominating partner in her parents' relationship. She seeks approval for her new relationship with Sam from "mother's picture on the wall." Like Mrs. Bates, Marion's mother exercises repressive power beyond the grave. In Marion's office Caroline speaks of her own mother's oppressive influence. Mother's doctor gave her tranquilizers on her wedding night and continues to interfere with her marriage, making it as barren as the desert landscape picture above Marion's desk. Flaunting his economic power, drunken capitalist Cassidy speaks to Marion about the home he intends to buy for his daughter. As Robin Wood states, "Cassidy's relationship with his 'baby' takes us a step into the abnormal because it is highly suspect: she will probably be better off without the $60,000 house, which is itself a symbol of her father's power over her."[29] Seeing money both as power and key to her desired union with Sam, she decides to steal.

As Marion prepares to leave, the mise-en-scene reveals her family entrapment. To the left of the bathroom and its visible shower curtain, is a photograph of mother and father. Near her closet is a baby's photograph indicative of parental desires to keep offspring in a dependent position as long as possible. Gazing at the money, Marion believes it will guarantee a new respectable life. But unlike the mythical bird of her city, Marion will not rise rejuvenated from a funeral pyre. Her burning desire for economic entry into family life ends in a stagnant swamp.

Fleeing a barren urban landscape (appropriately photographed in the bleakest black and white photographic tones), Marion travels through an equally bleak desert environment before finally arriving at a Californian used-car lot. This location also symbolizes the American dream's impoverished nature. Rushing through a deal, she enters a restroom to use some of the stolen money for the purchase. The restroom's excremental associations anticipate anally aggressive destructive forces within the shower sequence. Marion ironically counts out a waste product fetishized within an economy of capitalist exchange, which is based upon violence and repression. Her actions evoke destructive psychic demons. By stealing she violates the Father's Law of property based on female submissiveness. Mentally recreating Cassidy's outraged cries of economic male castration, "Well I ain't about to kiss off $40,000! I'll get it back, and if any of its missing I'll replace it with her fine soft flesh!" her earlier expression reveals perverse pleasure, anticipating mother's grinning skull. Marion's economic and sexual desires for marital respectability evoke death, not life. Cassidy's off-screen curse evokes a patriarchal punishment as vicious as the winged Furies of *The Birds*. Ironically the chosen avenger is another victim of the same family trap that affects Marion.

Psycho contains no disavowing supernatural veils, enabling it to reveal the relevant material conditions that generate horror. It sees economic oppression, mental pathology, and excessive violence within civilization's nurturing unit—the family. Like *Shadow of a Doubt*, *Psycho*'s characters duplicate each other in one way or another. The family rules the lives of every major character. Respectable dreams of idyllic family life dominate Marion. She manipulates Sam into accepting a more traditional relationship. Mother dominates Norman. Norman exercises the ultimate patriarchal control over Marion by wielding the phallic knife. Sam's dead father dominates him economically, as does his ex-wife. Lila (Vera Miles) assertively reproduces her sister's hold on Sam, urging him to investigate the Bates Motel. They register there as man and wife, ironically paralleling Sam's and Marion's earlier deceptions. Arboghast bullies Norman, believing his detective powers and assertive masculinity will solve the case. The Crane sisters resemble each other, as do Sam and Norman. Both men later occupy opposite ends of the frame in the motel office. Earlier Marion and Norman faced each other in similar positions. Sam's reflection in the mirror echoes Marion's on her arrival. Like Arboghast, Lila believes she will gain control and knowledge. She finally confronts Mrs. Bates. But the clue to the enigma is death, not life. The sanctified hearth is death-orientated. Wielding the phallic knife, symbolizing in extremis, the logical manifestation of family repression and violence, Mrs. Bates is both jailer and prisoner. Existing beyond the grave, she murderously exercises the same disciplinary functions she did in life. Her murderer is also her victim. *Psycho* bleakly reveals the family as a Death Instinct Agency, dominating both living and the dead, forcing every victim compulsively to repeat the past.

Psycho's victims destructively reenact an eternal *fort-da* existence within a societal institution that causes frustration, deceit, violence, and murder. Marion aggressively steals Cassidy's money before dying under Mrs. Bates's knife. Her name parallels Norman's. Both Marion and Norman vainly attempt to escape their own "private traps" caused by the dead weight of family ties. They both exist symbiotically. Marion's California license plate—NFB 418— has ominous associations. The first and third letters parallel "Norman Bates." "F" may denote her Edenic, never-reached goal of Fairvale, where Sam lives. The number "418" echoes the date on the motel register of Norman's last guest, that is, 4/18, which numerically adds up to "13." Marion and Norman face each other in exact profile three times during the film: when she first signs in, in her motel room when Norman invites her to dinner, and when Norman brings a tray of sandwiches outside her room. *Psycho* weaves together a chain of coincidences, setting in motion events of almost supernatural correspondence. As the subject of neurosis, Marion becomes the object of psychosis. As Marion pauses before writing her address on the hotel register, Norman turns around to get the room key. Marion writes down a false Los Angeles address taken from the folded *Los Angeles Times*. As Marion does this Norman pauses before the key for room number three, glances surreptitiously over his shoulder, and takes down the number one key, as if telepathically cognizant of Marion's "lie." Matched close-ups suggest Marion's actions evoke a demonic avenger after she has wandered off the main highway. As Norman says, "Nobody ever stops here anymore unless they've done that," a statement resonating with purgatorial overtones.

Psycho needs no supernatural monster. Its mirror imagery adequately suggests Sartre's axiom of hell existing in other people, especially those affected by family ties. Everyone remains within a family net of private traps. Exploring Mrs. Bates's bedroom, Lila momentarily reacts to the shock of her own reflection in the mirror behind her. Before leaving Phoenix, Marion gazes at her image in the mirror before glancing again at the stolen money. In the car lot restroom, she counts out $700 before a mirror. As she goes to the Bates Motel desk, she and Norman briefly appear in the same mirror. Her image remains there while Norman goes to the other end of the desk. Marion's reflection appears again in her motel room mirror when Norman invites her to dinner. Significantly, before leaving Norman suggests she remove her wet shoes. Ironically this echoes her parting words to Sam when she advised him to put on his shoes before leaving the Phoenix hotel room. Returning with the tray, Norman's reflection appears on Marion's window. As Arboghast begins interrogating Norman, his reflection occurs on the same motel desk mirror as Sam's does when he also questions Norman. *Psycho* is a visually rich film in terms of strategic dualisms, implicating everyone within a socially created hell. It reveals a generic development no longer dependent on monsters or the supernatural nor on any fetishistic disavowal mechanisms. Despite later misappropriations, *Psycho* is a great achievement of family horror.

Like Santa Rosa's Till-2 Club, the Bates Motel expresses the true nature of a social reality based on power, economics, and violence. It bleakly articulates elements existing in the world outside. Mrs. Bates's control over Norman represents the logical conclusions of the Phoenix dominance exercised by Cassidy and Caroline's mother over their respective offspring. Even if parental figures are no longer alive, they leave a legacy of economic and ideological entrapment as the barren lives of Sam and Marion show.

Fairvale, California, is by no means remote from the Bates Motel. The Fairvale sequence begins with a shot of Sam writing to Marion, immediately following Norman's successful submergence of Marion's car. A tracking shot follows, moving away from Sam to reveal his rudimentary store. Pitchforks and knives appear prominently, the latter having obvious associations with the shower sequence. A middle-aged lady enquires about insecticides, "And I say, insect or man, death should always be painless," in ironic contrast with the death previously witnessed. Later Mother/Norman will not wish to swat even a fly! Lap dissolves link Fairvale and the Bates Motel: one ends with Norman disposing of Arboghast's car in the swamp to connect with Sam's store; another concludes with Lila's face at the sheriff's house after she learns of Mrs. Bates's death to Norman putting the phone down prior to moving mother's body to the fruit cellar. The final close-up of mother's grinning skull leads to the County Court House where Fairvale's citizens gather outside. Visually and thematically inextricable connections exist between the pathologic Bates family relationship and a supposedly uncontaminated outside world.

Even a seemingly redundant scene involving the Chambers House has relevant associations. The Chambers live in a typical (Hollywood) small-town American home. Decorated with a landscape painting on the staircase wall, biblical mottos in the living room, nineteenth-century miniatures, and lace covers on chair and mantelshelf, it counterpoints the repressive interior of Mrs. Bates's bedroom. Mrs. Chambers's (Lurene Tuttle) delight in thinking Norman recently married—"Norman took a wife?"—as well as her match-making Sunday dinner invitation to Sam and Lila outside church reflect unquestioning acceptance of social proprieties. Both she and Sheriff Chambers (John McIntire) exhibit the same type of sexually repressive attitudes psychotically motivating Norman and mother. Sheriff Chambers pauses significantly in telling Lila about Mrs. Bates's sexual liaison: "This guy she was—in love with" (the last words uttered disapprovingly). His wife also expresses small town values: "Norman found them dead together—in bed" (the last two words expressed in a shocked tone). Ignored by most critics, the Chambers sequence is important. We learn Mrs. Bates was certainly no pillar of Victorian values. Although repressing Norman's sexuality and stunting his emotional growth, she also engaged in an adulterous affair whose consequences had devastating psychological effects on Norman. As well as wishing to preserve his destructively symbiotic bond with mother after death, part of Norman's personality obviously reacted against hypocritical behavior on the part of a dominating parental figure. Torn between desires for mature sexual experience and a repressive mother's adherence to law and religion, Norman became the psychotic instrument of patriarchal repression. *Psycho* never spells the message out, either visually or thematically. But its consequences are clear.

Exploring the Bates home, Lila wanders within its repressively Gothic interior. Discovering Norman's bedroom she discerns an environment whose contents of cuddly rabbit and Beethoven record reveal two sides of its occupant.[30] His arrested development and potential for creative experience destructively merge in maintaining family values.

Hitchcock's works present explicit themes within several Hollywood films, that is, the root causes of traits appearing within other genres revealing their relationship to family horror. Whether the frustrated youngsters of Nicholas Ray's *Rebel Without a Cause* (1955) or Mark Lamphere and the "mother's boy" killer of Fritz Lang's *Secret Beyond the Door* (1948) and *While the City Sleeps* (1955), these characters react against the family in different, albeit similar, ways. Hitchcock's cinema still remains unchallenged in unveiling key elements within family horror, but other lesser works contain revealing features. If they are not as accomplished as Hitchcock's, they illuminate a cultural context the director recognized and responded to.

◆ ◆ ◆

Mervyn LeRoy's *The Bad Seed* (1956) is a popular adaptation of a successful Broadway play. Although outside the generic codes of horror, the movie has many similarities to family horror. Influenced by conservative psychiatric tenets of heredity's dominance over environment, *The Bad Seed* attempts to explain the murderous activities of eight-year-old Rhoda Penmark (Patty McCormack) as the result of genetic factors. Before the film begins, young Rhoda has already committed cold-blooded murder, and she kills two additional people—classmate Claude Daigle (who won a coveted penmanship medal) and handyman Leroy (Henry Jones). Her mother, Christine (Nancy Kelly), learns she is the surviving daughter of a criminal mother, who is responsible for a genetic "bad seed" that jumps a generation. Realizing her daughter lacks any moral sense, she attempts a murder-suicide. She gives Rhoda a lethal overdose of sleeping pills and shoots herself. However, the shot alerts the police who arrive in time to save mother and child. An additional ending, shot to satisfy contemporary censorship requirements, shows young Rhoda going out into a storm to search for the incriminating penmanship medal. Lightning strikes her metal detector and divinely incinerates the young miscreant.

In terms of the film's discourse, Rhoda is entirely evil, lacking any redeeming features. *The Bad Seed* champions reactionary, hereditary psychiatric theories against the socially environmental findings of William James, B. F. Skinner, and J. B. Watson. Filmed in Hollywood pedantic style, *The Bad Seed* didactically articulates its ideologic message. However, even this rigid film has antihegemonic features.

As Kathy Merlock Jackson shows, contemporary influences, such as the rise of juvenile delinquency, resulted in *The Bad Seed*'s popularity.[31] At the time of its release, the police dealt with over one million cases, most involving normal families from middle-class neighborhoods. Although television representations concentrated on bland family depictions in *Father Knows Best, Leave It to Beaver, The Life of Riley,* and *Ozzie and Harriet,* serious contemporary social problems existed within the American Dream. However, the Cold War–McCarthyite era avoided liberal, environmentally based theories that were critical of social institutions. Instead Congress and the FBI blamed selected scapegoats for the problem. *The Bad Seed* is a contemporary status quo film, scapegoating young Rhoda as an "evil" child.

In the film Rhoda Penmark is no product of a problematic family institution but a naturally evil child, the ideologic descendant of *The Scarlet Letter's* Pearl and the possessed adolescent girls of the Salem witch trials. She anticipates "evil children" in *The Exorcist, The Omen, It's Alive,* and *The Children* (1981). Lit in high-key lighting to signify her "pure" qualities, hair scrupulously coiffured, polite to her elders, constantly curtseying, eternally wearing appropriate "feminine" frocks, she also represents the ideal childhood model of Eisenhower's America. As a neighbor remarks, "Isn't she perfection!" Within the film's ideological construction, Rhoda is evil because of her genetic background. Neither society nor family are to blame for Rhoda's condition. Learning of her contaminated hereditary origins, Christine blames herself by accepting responsibility for an event that is beyond her control. "It isn't what she's done. It's what I've done." Lacking her husband's patriarchal presence, she fails as a parent and thus becomes J. Edgar Hoover's culprit for juvenile delinquency. *The Bad Seed's* reliance on conservative genetic theories morbidly parallels Nazi eugenic theories. Rhoda is an exclusively bad child. Like Puritan accounts of possessed children, guilt becomes conveniently externalized. Eisenhower's America simply *could not* have produced such a monster!

Did Rhoda automatically turn herself into the 1950s model of idealized childhood behavior? *The Bad Seed* suggests an alternative interpretation. Rhoda's monstrosity represents the logical conclusion of contemporary patterns of family child rearing. Existing as a unit in the service of the state, the family attempts to produce conformist products to enter the world of capitalist production. As a perfect, obedient child, wearing appropriate costumes, Rhoda answers adult desires for childhood conformity. As a precocious individual, never interacting with any of her peer group, assertive, and competitive to the extent of murdering a rival for a desired penmanship medal, Rhoda darkly embodies the American family dream. The perfect child is actually a killer. She carefully learns social roles realizing their importance as conformist masks. As her teacher, Miss Reid remarks, "There's a mature quality in her that is disturbing in a child." Rhoda becomes a monster to fulfill institutional ideals of competition, obedience, and role-playing.

She uncannily resembles a Nazi child uncomfortably demonstrating capitalist society's repressed affinities with fascism. Contemporary child manuals instructed parents they could raise superchildren. Existing in a society threatened by nuclear war, with an absent father (William Hopper) who occupies an important military position in Washington, young Rhoda callously exterminates any threat to herself, whether from a young child or an older woman. She is definitely a "bad seed." But the origins of her monstrosity are social, not genetic. Rhoda merely enacts on a local scale the logical consequences of her father's Cold War—Pentagon activities. In an era now aware of secret military and scientific radiation testing on uninformed subjects, it is more than coincidental that the film never discloses what Rhoda's father actually does.

The film's epilogue resembles a Freudian slip completely contradicting its premises. Opening with the message, "You have just seen a motion picture whose theme dares to be startlingly different," it introduces each individual cast member bowing to the audience. Nancy Kelly follows Patty McCormack, who previously curtseyed in young Rhoda's most winning manner. The camera pans to the left, following Kelly's introduction as she looks off-screen, "And as for you young lady!" She rushes to spank young Patty in the most patriarchally approved manner. This scene is revealing. It counters everything previously seen that is suggestive of the importance of human responsibility and parental control, not genetic determinism. *The Bad Seed* wishes its audience to "have its cake and eat it," weakly asserting a family power previously denied.

◆   ◆   ◆

Although produced as a gimmicky response to *Psycho, Homicidal* (1961) is not entirely devoid of interest. Lacking *Psycho's* complexities in favor of teasing the audience with gender mystification, *Homicidal* has several family horror themes. Denied access to her true gender, Emily (Jean Arless) expresses her real femininity in pathologic violence by avenging the oppressive nature of her masculine construction as "Warren" on those responsible. Concealing the nature of her birth from a ruthless patriarchal father who desires a son, Emily's mother and nurse Helga conspire to falsify the birth certificate and rear Emily as Warren (also played by Jean Arless). From the very moment of birth, social forces collaborate to purge Emily/Warren of any trace of femininity. At one point Warren tells his half-sister Miriam (Patricia Breslin) of Helga being "part of a system" that kept him away from the nursery, to toughen him up and keep girls out of his life, paying his friend Carl "to start fights with me when I was a kid." Warren shows her Helga's whip that was used to toughen him and make him strong, adding that she followed his "father's orders." He reminds Miriam of her own victimization. "Can you forget what he did to your mother? He divorced her so he could remarry and have a son."

Despite *Homicidal's* pedantic direction and unconvincing performances, the film remains an interesting footnote in the social construction of horror, linking the family's violent nature with capitalism. For Miriam's father, "Making money was the only thing he knew how to do." She, ironically, remarks to Warren (who regards his future inheritance as a "cheap price to be his son"), "I'm glad to know you're not like him." Hating the appropriately named Miriam as a reflection of her concealed femininity, Warren uses her name in his Emily masquerade the night he murders Judge Abrams. Several scenes frame the two "women" as twin *personas*, the one expressing resentment against the other for her freedom to live a true sexual identity. Both Warren and Emily are conflicting masquerades: one a woman imitating a man, the other a socially defined "male" wearing female clothes. Both are monstrous creations within patriarchy.

Homicidal explains its monster as expressing "a rage of an infant whose doll is taken away with the strength and imagination of an adult." Lacking mature development the person kills when there is no outlet for rage. Divorced from following her real inclinations, Warren/Emily suffers physical and mental child abuse at the hands of parents and nurse. Her particular "Shape of Rage" expresses itself in jealously toward Miriam, wielding the knife as a distorted manifestation of her repressed sexuality. Emily is Warren's "monstrous feminine," a nightmare phallic woman emerging from violent patriarchal roots. Unfortunately, *Homicidal* lacks adequate coherent construction to make it a really significant critique of the family. It ends with the fragile, feminine doll Warren steals from Miriam in the opening scenes, blown off the window ledge by the rushing wind and falling upon the whip used to brutalize and educate throughout formative years. This image is more poignant than the entire film.

◆　◆　◆

Directed by Burt Topper for Allied Artists, *The Strangler* (1963) is a low-budget work that recognizes the social roots of family horror. Beginning with a caption which thanks police department and psychiatric cooperation for "reconstructing the character in accordance with their realistic reference," *The Strangler*'s Leo Kroll (Victor Buono) is an overweight, mother-dominated Norman Bates, who strangles nurses as surrogate victims for his oppressive mother. Opening with a close-up of Leo's eye, tracking to an iris-frame close-up of a nurse undressing, the ensuing events reveal Leo's sadistic-voyeuristic pleasure in his murderous gaze. Later undressing his fetish-object doll, the camera reveals his orgasmic expression as he drops the doll on the floor.

Obviously indebted to *Psycho*, *The Strangler* presents Leo Kroll as a continuing victim of mental abuse by his bed-ridden mother who instills guilt feelings within him. The dialogue makes clear that Leo has known little else except psychic assault from childhood. "What would any girl want you for? You're not good looking. You're fat. You know very well that some people think you're funny . . . even as a little boy nobody liked you. You have no money. And women want money." Leo also remarks that he pays the hospital bills for his mother's private room. Although freeing himself from mother's physical presence by causing her heart attack, Leo finds her psychic hold still continues. Like his later successor in *Don't Go into the House* (1979), mother haunts him from beyond the grave, her voice mingling with a girl's rejection in extradiegetic dialogue prior to Leo's destruction.

♦   ♦   ♦

Relatively ignored since its initial release, Walter Grauman's *Lady in a Cage* (1964) represents one of the bleakest family indictments following *Psycho*. With credits resembling Saul Bass's Hitchcock work, it begins with a voyeuristic "bird's-eye view" into the Hillyard home. Lacking monsters or reassuring psychiatrists, *Lady in a Cage* presents family, urban society, religion, and capitalist decay as interconnecting threads within an oppressive existence. Filmed in high-key lit black-and-white photography, eschewing both film noir stylistics or classical horror's expressionistic visual devices, *Lady in a Cage* presents the most uncompromising attack on the family in any sixties film. With its excessive hysterical style, it has many parallels to Hollywood family melodrama. The film is an excessive attack on a Mrs. Bates figure imaginatively conceived by a repressed son. Shot on a modest budget, its dominating use of bar motifs *frames* not only its ensuing family drama but also credit sequences and the Paramount studio logo. *Lady in a Cage* owes much of its success to the collaborative factors of director Walter Grauman, producer/scenarist Luther Davis, and Olivia de Havilland, James Caan, and William Swan.

Opening with credit sequences depicting traffic chaos and urban wasteland, it reveals the bleak detritus behind middle-class suburban existence. A child prods the sleeping figure of a tramp while a dog lies dead in the street, obviously run over by the frantic speeding traffic. As a teenage couple sexually embrace in their car during sweltering July heat, their radio blasts out a religious broadcast. Radio Tabernacle calls for an "anti-Satan missile." "While we have been conquering polio and space, what have we done about the devil?" Echoing the horror genre's connections between sexuality and repression, this introduces *Lady in a Cage's* predominant concerns.

Images of decay and despair open a film that never attempts any reassuring conclusion. As the camera voyeuristically inserts us through air conditioner vents, we see Malcolm Hillyard (William Swan) in his mother's bedroom putting a letter near her phone. After addressing "Darling" on the letter, he meets Mrs. Hillyard (Olivia de Havilland) outside. Due to a household accident, she depends on a walking cane and an automatic lift to travel between different floors of her house. Their relationship resembles more of a husband/wife rather than mother/son. Coquettishly smiling while Malcolm tensely strains at maintaining a placid appearance, Mrs. Hillyard asks whether he has left her "one of those little love notes you used to write before." Mother and son face each other in rituals of polite repression that conceals their incestuous bond. Agreeing to his request to read the letter after his departure for the 4 July weekend, the following shots illustrate entrapment. The camera frames Mrs. Hillyard through the lift bars. As Malcolm reenters his mother's bedroom to retrieve the breakfast tray, the camera zooms in to revealing lines on his letter, "I'll kill myself." The next shot shows him framed through the lift bars from Mrs. Hillyard's point of view. *Lady in a Cage*'s opening scenes acutely illustrate a claustrophobic relationship between mother and son. Malcolm desperately attempts to impose a smiling face upon smoldering desperation. These introductory scenes reveal intense repression which demands hysterical release in paranoia and violence.

As Malcolm reaches for a cigarette in the living room, its music box case reveals his actions to his mother. She firmly and sweetly suggests he cut down on his smoking. Reacting obediently to mother's commands, Malcolm returns the cigarette to its box and joins her in the kitchen. Noting her contradictory health fads with a concealing veneer of good-natured humor, Malcom departs for his weekend with friends Paul and "Peggy." During his weekend break, he will act as cook to Paul's butler with "Peggy" as the guest of honor. William Swan's performance visually clarifies the nature of his weekend liaison without needing overexplanatory dialogue. He is clearly a family victim attempting to escape from a repressive parental figure. Mother not only follows changing health fads that she imposes on her son, but she also, parasitically, depends for her affluent existence upon a brutal world outside whose violent nature she conveniently ignores. Speaking of her stock market investments, she suggests that increasing Cold War tensions may work advantageously for her. Recognizing this selfish thought, she blithely represses it with the comment, "It's a terrible way to make money, don't you think?"

As the opening credits reveal, Mrs. Hillyard's bland, bourgeois existence depends upon repressing capitalism's ugly nature which exists outside her clean home. Noisy, polluting urban traffic, disruptive exploding firecrackers, decomposing dog, or drunken wino represent civilization's excremental elements conveniently expelled from middle-class consciousness. The credits freeze-frame these scenes with bars paralleling the confining lift-cage, forcing her to recognize the reality of her existence.

Paul's departure succinctly suggests a connection of ensuing events with his own repressed feelings. Walking to his car he puts on dark glasses. The act symbolizes the dark nature of succeeding events. Immediately the camera pans right to a handyman who places a ladder against a line supplying power to Mrs. Hillyard's home. This causes the first temporary power short. Paul's car then bumps against the ladder, causing the second short that leads to the permanent power collapse. As Paul beeps his horn in farewell, Mrs. Hillyard responds inside her kitchen, "Have a good time, love." The ensuing invasion represents the monstrous incarnation of Paul's repressed antagonisms against his suffocating mother. Her response has ironic associations she does not realize. She will certainly not have a good time. Returning to her lift, she becomes trapped halfway up the stairs when the power finally ceases.

Initially believing her whole neighborhood is affected and that help will soon arrive, an exterior point-of-view shot (rising up like a lift representing her imaginary sense of control) reveals the outside world. This exterior domain is as oblivious to her feelings as the interior of her home shot in foreboding single static shots. She then switches on her hand radio seeking her earlier bourgeois solace in sweet classical muzak. The station she tunes in tells of the recent discovery of a nude female's decapitated body. She immediately switches off, her last controlling action before outside forces invade her home.

Although she believes in benevolent neighborhood response to her plight, people really do not care. Independence Day vacationers, oblivious to the sound of her alarm bell, travel by in their cars. An air-conditioning repairman chooses not to investigate and drives away in his truck. The only figure who appears is religious fundamentalist wino George L. Brady Jr. (Jeff Corey).

As a detritus emblem of a capitalist existence Mrs. Hillyard has never acknowledged, Brady is the first repressed force invading her sanctity. With "Repent" tattooed on his hand, he also embodies the dark side of those sanitized positive thinking secular poems Mrs. Hillyard once penned. While Brady approaches the house, Mrs. Hillyard begins a developing descent into insecurity and madness. Gazing at the automatically powered escalator light, she ponders civilized dependency upon electricity. "Without light, this could really be a tomb." But realizing depleting batteries, she decides to switch out the light and save them. As she does this, Brady approaches the outside door. Sweating in her now un-air conditioned tomb, she begins her first retrogressive descent, opening her dress to masturbate her breast. The following fantasy is not pleasurable, eventually evoking demonic son Randall Simpson O'Connor (James Caan).

As the phone rings for the first time, Brady breaks into the house. Until the climax the audience does not know that Malcolm phones his mother to see if she agrees to his request for independence. As Brady explores the house, the phone rings a second time. Its ringing poignantly denotes a son's desperate suicidal plea to his mother. Her limited reliance on capitalist status symbols of suburbia and stock market prove futile before Brady's assault on her home. Brady is a pathetic example of a repressed, weak, vulnerable son who needs a "nursemaid" to control his deranged tendencies, a dark embodiment of Malcolm Hillyard.

After picking up two of Mrs. Hillyard's delicately carved miniature figurines and throwing them against the wall, crying "Graven Images" and "Repent!" "Repent!" Brady runs off with several bottles from the Hillyard wine cellar and an expensive toaster. Mrs. Hillyard's trust in the graven artifacts of capitalism disintegrates as they are the first objects under assault.

Brady pawns the toaster at Mr. Paul's junkyard shop. Full of civilization's cast-off, superfluous products, it counterpoints the neat Hillyard home. Middle-aged Mr. Paul bears the same name as Malcolm's Independence Day guest. Hoping to close his business early so he can take his wife and mother away for the weekend, Mr. Paul pays George for the toaster and curbs the adolescent horseplaying of three recently arrived delinquents—Randall (James Caan), Elaine (Jennifer Billingsley), and Essy (Rafael Campos). As Elaine uncovers their loot, Mr. Paul hands her a joint he finds in the contents. They exchange gazes, her lascivious black-eyed (from one of Randall's abusive actions) glance seeing Paul's one-eyed lensed spectacles. Mr. Paul's "castrated" appearance echoes Malcolm's in the film's beginning. These matching close-up gazes counterpoint earlier midshot/reverse shot positions showing Malcolm and his mother. Both reveal sexuality as a power weapon whereby dominating females attempt to control weak males.

This junkyard sequence also sets in motion the ensuing violence. Suspicious of George, Randall and his companions follow him to the Hillyard home. The delinquent trio parallels the group of two males and one female with whom Malcolm supposedly spends the weekend. Counterpoised to the neat, cleanliness of the Hillyard household, the junkyard represents the repressed world of violent, anal-excremental forces beneath a tidy civilization. The sequence concludes with George leaving the junkyard and passing three, predominantly displayed, toilet bowls hanging above him.

George enlists overweight hooker Sade to help loot the Hillyard residence. As she astutely recognizes, he needs maternal assistance. "And you need someone to keep you away from the wine long enough? Nursemaid, uh!" Making him toast in a toaster far different from the more expensive model he has hocked, Sade represents a proletarian version of Mrs. Hillyard. While Mrs. Hillyard remains deliberately oblivious of the capitalist forces supporting her privileged existence, Sade depends on them for her very survival. Functioning at night, overweight in contrast to Mrs. Hillyard's affluent, diet-conscious slimness, she lives in a humble, one-room apartment. She also acts as dominating mother to her middle-aged dependent child, George Luckman Brady, Jr., (Luckman being his maternal name—"That's my mother, German"). She later finds a gold baby cup dedicated to "Baby Malcolm Cornelius Hillyard, 7lbs, 3ozs" in their next raiding expedition. Cornelius is obviously Mrs. Hillyard's maiden name. Both women exercise maternal power over their respective offspring. Sade's later cradling of the helpless George in her arms does not save him from Randall's murderous assault. Also, when Mrs. Hillyard's phone rings for the third and final time, Sade pulls out the cord. She unknowingly contributes to Malcolm's suicide by symbolically cutting a suffocating umbilical cord between mother and son.

The three delinquents invade the home; they force Sade to carry their loot and assault George. While his accomplices loot the house, Randall faces his victim for the first time. He is a violent resurrection of the repressed version of own son who has now committed suicide. His appearance foreshadows Mrs. Hillyard's descent into insanity following her long confinement in the cage. Before George's and Sade's second invasion, she attempts to compose mentally one of the bland, insipid, *Reader's Digest* affirmative poems she used to pen.

> Oh, I have worshipped thee false god, for thou art false, electricity. . . . Killowat is his name. And we did burn incense to his power. But lo, one day, our god killowat left us. Can we go back to the gods of our childhood—reindeers, Santa Claus?

Her atavistic religious fantasies echo George's; they are both victims of civilized religious ideology. *Lady in a Cage* develops further dualistic motifs. While George echoes Malcolm's passivity, Randall is a monstrous proletarian son who attacks her privileged existence. Unfortunately, despite promising economic and class associations, the film remains restricted within hysterical rage, viewing Randall as an unredeemable monster. Despite having parallels to Malcolm as an incestuously abused child, he remains a negative figure throughout the film and resembles later images of Michael Myers, Jason Voorhees, and Freddy Krueger as a conveniently externalized monster. Unlike the Frankenstein monster and Norman Bates, he has no redeeming features with which to elicit audience identification and sympathy.

Affirming herself as "a human being, a thinking, feeling creature," Mrs. Hillyard learns of Randall's self-described "animal" nature and his long years of incarceration in state institutions. Oblivious to her own institutionalization within bourgeois home and family, she rages at him. "I see. You are one of those many bits of offal produced by the welfare state. You're what so much of my tax dollars goes for the care and feeding of." Thanking this gracious lady, Randall delivers an aromatic burp at her. This "culinary aftermath" ironically counterpoints Malcolm's pretend 4 July weekend gourmet assignation.

Believing that her world has ended due to a nuclear explosion, she switches on her radio to hear, ironically, a program dedicated to "The Man of Tomorrow." As she collapses in hysterical laughter, the camera pans right from the watching figures of Randall, Elaine, Essy, and Sade to the hot sun outside the window. Returning to the sun by match dissolve, the camera shows the world outside, isolated, and oblivious to Mrs. Hillyard's dilemma. She muses on her current plight, interpreting it within the darkest tones of Melville and Poe.

> We made us cities and towns and thought we had beat the jungle back, not knowing that we had built the jungle in. I suppose every hospital room's a jungle, every neat little room where somebody's having his body opened or lies dying. Every marriage bed, love bed, lust bed.

Immediately a music box begins its tune, the same music box containing the cigarettes she earlier forbade Malcolm to touch. Reviving at the sound, she stands up to see Randall looking at her and blowing a kiss, a dark parody of the civilized, denied incestuous bonds linking her and Malcolm. George revives, his head still covered, believing he is blind. "Blind! Why hast thou blinded me? . . . He's blinded me. Am I so much more guilty than the others?" His vulnerability also denotes Malcolm's earlier blindness to his mother's dangerous hold over him as well as his ensuing guilt feelings. Although lacking the mature realization of *Psycho*'s dualistic patterns, *Lady in a Cage* has its own double motifs depicting a dark pathological family.

Discussing their plans with his associates in a bathroom (containing a tub that Elaine believes could hold more than one person—a recognition having obvious overtones), Randall decides to kill everyone. Musing over the state's capital punishment penalty, Elaine orgasmically entertains the thought of the "hot seat" in Mrs. Hillyard's tub—a revealing sex-death association that clearly parallels the "death-in-life" existence Malcolm endured from suffocating, sexually repressed mother-love. Noting Essy's shadow outside the bathroom, Randall teases him into joining Elaine in the tub before feminizing him with Mrs. Hillyard's lipstick. Their violent power play with Essy suggests dark, unspoken, activities within the Hillyard family relationship. On Sunday Randall decides to murder George, Sade, and Mrs. Hillyard. When George asks why, Randall states the mere fact of his existence suffices. Mrs. Hillyard then understands, "That's what we've all done. We're here."

On a typical Sunday morning, introduced by "normal" scenes of church bells ringing, a man mowing his lawn, and paper delivery, Randall and his group dress up in Hillyard family clothes grotesquely parodying the normal family. He delivers his Judgment Day verdict on George. Despite the pathetic wino's pleas, Randall stabs the helpless tramp beneath a Mayan head with its obvious sacrificial associations. Repressed tensions within a morbid family situation symbolically erupt into uncontrollable violence.

After church bells toll, Randall turns toward Mrs. Hillyard. She attempts to save her life by offering ten thousand dollars from the bank. Despite Essy's desire to give some of the money to needy relatives and Elaine's wish for bourgeois respectability "to have kids," Randall has no urge to reproduce monsters. "Kids! Yours and mine! I wouldn't trust them with a dull kitchen knife. They'd cut us up the moment we'd close our eyes!" Mrs. Hillyard vainly attempts stabbing Randall in the back with metal prongs. After this failure, he discovers a symbiotic family tie with Mrs. Hillyard.

Searching for her bankbook, Essy returns with Malcom's letter. Noting the opening address, "Darling Mother," he draws certain conclusions—"This whole letter. He sounds real—what you say—gay." Randall notes the relationship's incestuous overtones. "I bet you had him at it since he was twelve, kept him sucking." He then learns of Malcolm's frustrated attempts at independence and suicide threat over the family inheritance. "I'll be thirty next Wednesday. I won't have many more chances in life. Each time I try to leave you, you decorate a room or dress up the house, or charm me."

Randall recognizes parallels to his own situation. "You still got him at it. How did you charm him, baby? . . . I had a holier-than-thou old crow of a grandmother. She tried to keep me at it, too. I would have killed her, if she hadn't died. She was trying to kill me, like you were trying to kill Malcolm." His family history anticipates later themes in Thomas Harris's novels, *Red Dragon* and *The Silence of the Lambs* whereby family victims become future serial killers. Condemning her for stunting Malcolm's development, Randall reads damning lines from the letter. "Release me from your generosity. Release me from your beauty. Release me from your love." Hearing the concluding lines, "I'll kill myself," she faints. Randall sees her as another embodiment of his deceased grandmother. "Old crow, old crow baby."

While Mr. Paul's invading army distracts Randall and his group, Mrs. Hillyard manages to fall on to the floor from her lift prison. Attempting in vain to call for help on the phone, she also realizes her culpability, "My son has killed himself . . . I may have killed my son." She crawls outside, blinding Randall with the bent prongs within her breast as he attempts to drag her inside. She thus "castrates" another son. Randall now becomes a family victim like Malcolm and George, destroyed by the violence inherent within the morbid structure of a patriarchal family. Although Elaine and Essy initially obey him by dragging "that old crow" inside, they mock his position. "I ain't blinded. . . . What do you think I am? An old wino?" Relishing the Oedipal plight of their former tormentor, they creep outside seen only by Mrs. Hillyard's blurred gaze. Her deceased son's off-screen voice—"Release me from your love. Release me from your generosity"—echoes through her brain, opposing her incestuous entrapment. She finally realizes her guilt. She says, "It's all true. I'm a monster, a monster."

Crawling outside she pushes Randall away from her into rushing traffic. This stops the vehicles for the first and only time in the film. Spying Elaine and Essy attempting their escape, she cries, "Murderers, monsters." Her cries also implicate the watching motorists and audience. Elaine's and Essy's attempted escape in a car knocks against the power line, inversely paralleling Malcolm's earlier action and restoring electricity. Mrs. Hillyard is propped, catatonically, against her house, her brow moistened by drops from a now functioning air conditioner. The final shot shows hectic traffic resuming. Life attempts to return to its normal pace. But this is clearly impossible. As Mrs. Hillyard realizes we are all monsters, that is, victimizers and victims caught within an oppressive family structure that produces both monsters and victims in a relationship in which either may change places.

The attack on the family is direct and uncompromised in these films. It needs no distracting mechanisms to divert viewers. *Lady in a Cage* represents the most nihilistic embodiment of this assault by revealing the family institution as both morally bankrupt and dangerous. However, Hitchock's more artistic vision and those by lesser talents was so direct that only two alternatives became possible. Succeeding films could either carry the assault to its logical conclusions and call for a new society without authoritative families—an impossible task for Hollywood, or ignoring the evidence, future films could assign family trauma to a supernatural agency by again using traditional Puritan, cultural, scapegoat mechanisms. Some later films took this latter path but not without some revealing contradictions appearing within the individual texts.

5

Return of the Native: The Satanic Assaults

Despite the emphasis of the 1950s upon material aspects of family horror, many succeeding films were reluctant to continue this process. A Satanic cycle of films such as *Rosemary's Baby* (1968), *The Exorcist* (1973), and *The Omen* (1976) variously attempted to disavow relevant social factors by ascribing traumatic family circumstances to the aggressive return of an old native lying dormant since the Puritan witch trials. Satan, not problem families, was really responsible. Using this disavowing interpretation, several films allowed audiences to have their cake and consume it. They witnessed families in disintegration, but they were ideologically reassured that the cause was supernatural, not social. At least this is what was attempted.[1] Belonging to an era witnessing the Kennedy assassination, Vietnam, and the emergence of anti—status quo minority movements, these films are contemporary examples of Hollywood's use of a disavowing paranoia that mobilizes whenever society suffers turmoil.[2]

Released in 1968, the traumatic year of the Tet Offensive, massive antiwar demonstrations, police brutalities during Chicago's National Democratic Convention, and the assassinations of Robert Kennedy and Martin Luther King, *Rosemary's Baby* struck a resonant chord within the American public. Although director Roman Polanski's skill contributed to its success, he was deeply indebted to forces within the American cultural tradition, the original novel, the Paramount studio system, and the involvement of Robert Evans and William Castle. Evans produced several films reflecting the changing mood of contemporary America. Castle directed several neglected works within horror cinema.[3] *Rosemary's Baby* is not an isolated auteurist product.[4]

A reverse image of the American Dream occurs. The young American couple, Guy (John Cassavetes) and Rosemary (Mia Farrow) become Joseph and Mary in a new Satanic order inversely paralleling the Christian Messiah's birth. The film perversely criticizes the American family and its religious associations. During Rosemary's dream, the Kennedys participate in the ceremony leading to her supernatural impregnation. Guy turns into the devil and rapes his wife. These events occur at the very time the Pope visits New York City. Satan's coven operates within the Big Apple, no longer in a dark forest outside the City on a Hill. Both Satanic mythology and American Gothic evoke Rosemary's fears concerning the Bramford coven's cannibalistic desires for her unborn baby. The New Age is dawning. Like Wilbur Whately in Lovecraft's "The Dunwich Horror," young Adrian will one day summon his father to exercise a last judgment different from Christian expectations.

Condemning the film "not only for several scenes of nudity" as well as "the perverted use ... of fundamental Christian beliefs" and "mockery of religious persons and practices,"[5] the Catholic Office failed to consider the film's indebtedness to its own religious dualism. The upturned cross on Adrian's black crib at the film's climax is merely one example. Pertinent mirror imagery frequently emphasizes Christian impotence. Deciding to cease waiting for Hutch (Maurice Evans), Rosemary looks into a window showing a model of the Nativity scene to see her haggard reflection dwarfing the scene. In her last attempt to oppose the coven, she wears a blue dressing gown over a white nightgown, resembling traditional icons of the Virgin Mary. The Castavet foreign guests are Satanic Wise Men bearing gifts.

Rosemary's Baby's satanists represent no positive alternative. Like the vampire community in Larry Cohen's *A Return to Salem's Lot* (1987), they are another dark institutional order. Aged cosmopolitan couple Roman (Sidney Blackmer) and Minnie Castavet (Ruth Gordon) incarnate the Old World's threat against the New. The coven's recommended doctor, Dr. Sapirstein, belongs to a race whom Christianity has persecuted. During Rosemary's dream, a Black helmsman on the yacht abruptly orders her down during a storm. "You'd better go down below, Miss," his superficial courteous tones express hatred against a representative of a persecuting race.

The Kennedys also appear in Rosemary's dream. John F. Kennedy wears a navy uniform on the yacht. He turns his back and Roman Castavet takes his place. Hutch arrives at the dock but is barred from the yacht. As Rosemary queries his exclusion, Kennedy replies, "Catholics only. I wish we weren't bound by these prejudices but unfortunately we are." Going below Rosemary sees the vague figures of Roman, Minnie, and Guy among the coven. Jackie Kennedy offers condolences, "I'm so sorry to hear you aren't feeling well."[6] The

Kennedys belong to the same religious group as Rosemary. Catholicism is as exclusive as satanism with its particular rites. The dream sequence implicitly suggests the real reasons behind JFK's surprising 1960 electoral victory. One of the Bramford's former notorious inhabitants was a Keith Kennedy.

The film's opening scenes show a familiar New York landscape. As credits roll a mother's lullaby occurs on the soundtrack. The camera slowly pans left across the city, moving in an anticlockwise direction, suggesting Satanic desire to reverse two thousand years of Christian dominance. After passing Central Park, it reveals another part of the city where Gothic architecture strongly contrasts with New York's skyscraper image. The camera stops over the Bramford building. Almost imperceptibly it tilts down, finally resting at an unusually steep angle above the brown Victorian apartment block. The Bramford represents the repressed Gothic house that stands within a clean, modern America, familiar from Hawthorne, Poe, and Lovecraft, as well as *King's Row*, *Curse of the Cat People*, *Meet Me in St. Louis*, and *Psycho*. An abrupt cut leads to a medium long shot of Rosemary and Guy entering the courtyard with the agent to inspect an apartment. The film ends with a reverse camera movement following a medium long shot of Rosemary kneeling before Adrian's cradle, humming the lullaby heard earlier on the soundtrack. In the final shot the camera does not continue to reverse its earlier motion panning back to the modern world. It remains fixed on the Bramford.

This visual predestination is deliberate. Rosemary discovers she is the selected vessel to bear the Satanic messiah chosen, in the coven's words, "from all the women of the earth." Opening lullaby and overhead panning shot plunge the spectator into the film. Abrupt cuts to and from the ground in the second and penultimate shots of the film lead audiences to share Rosemary's sense of entrapment. Mother love finally claims her.

Rosemary and Guy are fresh, likeable young Americans, representing a welcome world of normality after the overhead shots. Rosemary is a lapsed Catholic. Protestant-reared Guy is a struggling young actor, hoping for the all-important break that will enable him to "get ahead." He has already appeared in TV plays and commercials as well as legitimate stage productions such as *Luther*. Both want to start a family—a desire that has unforeseen consequences.

As they inspect the apartment whose previous eighty-nine-year-old tenant (Mrs. Gardenia) died in a coma, the camera follows them dollying in and out, contributing to a mood of surveillance by unseen forces. The interior's brown and yellow colors express decay and age. A piano plays in another part of the building, its sinister scales evoking *Repulsion*. Despite a note left by Mrs. Gardenia ("I can no longer associate myself"), an ominous looking herbarium, and a dominating chest of drawers before a seemingly innocuous linen closet, the young couple decide to rent the apartment and begin plans for family life. The next scene shows them having dinner with Rosemary's mentor Hutch. He tells them of the Bramford's reputation and its previous occupants—the cannibalistic Trench sisters, Satanic magician Adrian Marcato, and Keith Kennedy. The camera pertinently cuts to food and wine while they discuss cannibalism, associating normal with abnormal. The Bramford's last scandal involved the discovery of a dead infant's body wrapped in a newspaper. Hutch regards the Bramford as an evil building, his terms evoking other dark abodes in Poe's "The Fall of the House of Usher" and Lovecraft's "The Shunned House." Returning to their dark, unfurnished apartment, they hear Minnie and Roman's voices next door, picnic on the rug, and make love while Guy jokes about the Trench sisters. Succeeding scenes show Rosemary redecorating the apartment in brighter colors of gold and white while Guy watches his performance on a TV commercial. A fast instrumental rendition of the main soundtrack theme accompanies her activities. The young appear determined to move in, laugh at old ideas, and join in the normal American way of life by starting a family.

Entrapment begins when Rosemary meets Terry in the basement's dark laundry room. The Castavets had adopted her some two months before Rosemary's arrival, saving her from a street life of drug addiction. Although believing they initially wanted her for "some kind of ulterior motive, maybe some kind of sex thing," Terry is grateful toward them, showing Rosemary an oddly smelling locket they gave her. The following shot shows the Bramford forces stirring within the Woodhouse bedroom at night. Following the coven's chant next door, the camera tilts up from Rosemary's head, panning right to the yellow wallpaper (paralleling the action it takes after Terry's death). A sinister moving shadow appears on the wallpaper.

Terry's suicide immediately follows. After leaving a suicide note, she jumps from one of the upper floors. She lies in a pool of blood, her locket distinctly visible round her neck. After giving condolences to the eccentric Castavets, the Woodhouses return home. The next scene shows reality and fantasy merging. Guy sleeps while Rosemary remains awake as the camera repeats its previous movements of the last bedroom scene. As Minnie's voice echoes from next door, "Sometimes I wonder how come you're the leader of anything!" delightfully revealing the Satanic family participating in the same type of domestic squabbles as its normal counterpart, Terry's dead body superimposes on the wallpaper. A nun appears in Rosemary's dream, speaking with Minnie's voice. A brief flashback from her Catholic schooldays shows the nun scolding Rosemary for revealing the cheating that was behind her school team winning at sports. Terry's death evokes guilt feelings, resulting in the merger of separate worlds and leading toward Rosemary taking the place of a chosen bride from old Italian immigrant stock. Satanism in *Rosemary's Baby* is the repressed side of Western Christian deceit.

The next day Rosemary views Minnie's distorted face through her peephole. She invites them to dinner, wishing company to forget Terry's death. Despite Guy's depression at losing an important role, they both attend. The Castavet apartment with its deceptively warm browns, reds, and yellows, as well as Roman's red sweater, garishly contrasts with the Woodhouse home's youthful colors. During dinner Guy and Roman make disparaging references to the Pope's forthcoming New York visit. Roman expects a newspaper strike's abrupt cessation the day before because "no Pope ever visits a city where the newspapers are on strike." Guy remarks on Catholicism's "show biz" aspect thereby encouraging Roman's digs at its ritual, robes, and jewelry. Despite Rosemary's lapsed Catholicism, she still venerates its head. "Well, he is the Pope. I guess I've been conditioned to have respect for him and I still do, even if I don't think he's holy any more." Roman then strategically mentions Guy's role in *Luther*, John Osborne's play about Protestantism's oppositional father. When Rosemary and Minnie do the dishes, Rosemary tells Minnie about her "fertile family," her isolation from them due to Guy's Protestant background, and their nonchurch wedding. As Rosemary glances into the other room, she sees an ominous mass of dark cigarette smoke above Roman's chair. Guy looks furtively toward Roman as the two women join them. Returning to their apartment, Rosemary comments over missing pictures from the Castavet apartment. Guy enthusiastically tells her about Roman's knowledge of an older thespian generation. The Old World Order has already ensnared the younger generation.

Minnie and her middle-aged friend Laura-Louise (Patsy Kelly) officially adopt Rosemary as Terry's successor, giving her the tannis-root locket. Although Rosemary dislikes its smell, Guy pressures her to wear it. From this point on Guy's entrapment becomes clear. He wins a long sought-after role owing to the sudden blindness of rival actor, Donald Baumgart. Preoccupied with his new role, neglecting Rosemary, he displays guilty feelings, having sold both his soul and his wife to emulate the theatrical success of Roman's idols, Henry Irving and Forbes-Robertson.

After visiting Hutch for advice, she returns to find a changed Guy. Apologizing about his selfish preoccupation, he suggests starting a family. His lines—"I even figured out the right time to start"—have ominous connotations. Since the Pope visits New York on Monday, 4 October, the date of conception means that Rosemary's baby is planned for the early hours of 25 June, the opposite calendar date to 25 December.

As Rosemary and Guy dine before a specially lit fire during "baby night," the doorbell announces Minnie's arrival. However, as Rosemary fervently prays, she does not enter. Guy brings Minnie's specially prepared chocolate mousse for dessert. He feigns ignorance of its chalky undertaste. Rather than eating it all, she deposits the remainder elsewhere while Guy's back is turned. When she feels dizzy, Guy takes her to bed. A nightmare begins. Her bed floats on an ocean with Freudian and surrealistic overtones. She travels on a yacht captained by a resuscitated JFK. An abrupt cut shows Guy stripping her on the apartment bed. She returns to the dream where she is either nude or clad in a bikini. Hutch vainly attempts to join her. Like the Pope, he is an impotent father figure unable to help her in time of need. Guy pulls off her ring to prepare for nuptials with the Prince of Darkness. Feeling herself elevated Rosemary sees Michelangelo's Sistine Chapel Fresco above her, showing Adam's creation, inversely echoing her role bearing the doppelganger to the New Testament's second Adam. She hears Guy's voice, "Easy. You've got her too high," as they carry her through the linen closet that separates her apartment from the Castavets'. Rosemary notices a burning church on her right and a picture of Adrian Marcato. A group of obscenely naked worshippers look at her. Guy is among them. As a robed Roman paints designs on her body, Guy whispers to Minnie, "She's awake. She sees." Minnie reassures him, "She don't see. As long as she ate the mousse she can't see nor hear. She's like dead." Guy approaches Rosemary. Slowly transformed into the devil, his scaly hands claw her body as smoke arises during intercourse. The Pope appears. He holds out his ring to her. It resembles the tannis-root locket.

Entering a dream world where boundaries blur, Rosemary undergoes immersion into the dark forces behind Western civilization. Society and satanism wish to use her body to produce offspring. She has no identity of her own; she exists only to bear the expected male child. *Rosemary's Baby* thus deals with female entrapment by conservative forces. The aged coven articulates the old order's eternal function of dominating the younger generation to continue family tradition. Everything mirrors its opposite. The nun from Rosemary's schooldays speaks with Minnie's voice. Guy turns into the devil. Roman captivates the young actor with tales about his theatrical predecessors. Hutch is as distant and removed as the Pope on the night of Rosemary's violation. Rosemary's final glimpse of the Holy Father's ring shows Catholicism's relationship to its darker counterpart. Catholicism and satanism are opposite sides of the same family coin. Both wish their subjects to be fruitful and multiply.

Rosemary awakens the next morning to find scratches on her back. Guy confesses that he impregnated her as she slept. "It was fun in a necrophilic sort of way." However, with its dark overtones of marital rape, Rosemary's family bliss has a sour taste. From this point the old order begins domination. The Castavets advise her to leave Dr. Hill (Charles Grodin) and attend the more prestigious, older Dr. Sapirstein (Ralph Bellamy). He prescribes a daily health drink (made by Minnie) and avoidance of all modern remedies. The day after meeting Roman, Hutch becomes seriously ill while the Woodhouses become further isolated, neglecting their younger friends, associating more with the elderly Castavet group. During a New Year's Eve party, Roman makes a curious toast—"To 1966. The Year One"—a reference understood by all except Rosemary.

Developing severe pains she cannibalistically attempts to devour raw meat, only ceasing when the toaster reflects her haggard face. Although her younger friends counsel returning to Dr. Hill, the sudden cessation of pain results in continuing with Dr. Sapirstein's remedies and Minnie's drinks. However, after receiving some witchcraft books left to her by Hutch in his will, she begins to put clues together over such unusual incidents as Baumgart's sudden blindness, Guy's rushing home during Hutch's visit, his concealment of a possible witch's mark on his body, and the coven's possible cannibalistic intentions toward her baby. A visit to Dr. Sapirstein's reception room reveals a *Time* magazine cover, "Is God dead?" prominently displayed, and learning of his affinity for tannis root, she rushes back to her former physician Dr. Hill. Skeptical of her charges against a prestigious colleague (and obviously not wishing to jeopardize his own career by opposing a senior member of his profession), Dr. Hill informs Guy and Sapirstein. Temporarily escaping her enemies at the Bramford, Rosemary manages to flee to her apartment only to discover the coven already there. Collapsing in labor, she gives birth during an infernoesque ninety-four-degree heatwave.

On awakening she learns of her baby's death. But suspicious of the continual use of a pump to relieve her breasts of milk and hearing a baby's cries from the Castavets', Rosemary eventually discovers a secret entrance behind the linen cupboard that connects her apartment with the Castavets'. Creeping along the corridor, she sees the burning church painting glimpsed during her "dream." The coven congregates in the living room. It includes the Castavets (who had supposedly departed from Kennedy Airport for a European tour) and Guy. A black-draped cradle with an inverted cross stands ominously in a corner. Rosemary looks inside, seeing (unseen to the audience) the same golden-yellow eyes of her nightmare Satanic penetrator. Roman answers her anguished, "What have you done to his eyes?" with "He has his father's eyes." Rosemary drops her knife after discovering she has borne the Satanic messiah.

During this inverse Nativity, foreigners bear gifts, a Japanese takes photographs, and Rosemary sits shocked in the corner. Rejecting Guy's advances and Roman's initial attempts to persuade her to wean her child (instead of Minnie and Laura-Louise), Rosemary maternally intercedes when she notices Laura-Louise rocking the cradle too fast. Overruling Laura-Louise's objections, Roman allows Rosemary to fulfill her maternal functions. He answers Rosemary's final hesitant, "You're trying to get me to be his mother," with "Aren't you his mother?"

Rosemary becomes trapped in a dark parody of her designated ideologic role within Western civilization. Traditional behavioral patterns overwhelm her. She gently rocks the cradle. The baby stops crying. As the opening soundtrack lullaby begins again, the coven look on approvingly as Rosemary fulfills her proper family role. For *Rosemary's Baby*, satanism is no potential alternative but a conservative agency. The film regresses from the previous decade's treatment of social horror. Although seeking to destroy two thousand years of Christian hegemony, the Marcato group aims at replacing one oppressive structure with another. Worshipping Satan as Christians submissively bow to their Lord and Savior, the aged satanist structure is as patriarchal as its opposing order and is bound within strictly defined gender roles. Finally outnumbered by the coven, Rosemary submits to her allotted role of mother love. *Rosemary's Baby* emphasizes female predestination. As Minnie says, "He chose you out of all the world, Rosemary. Out of all the women in the whole world, He chose you. . . . He arranged everything that had to *be* arranged, 'cause He wanted you to be the mother of His only living Son."

Although framed within traditional discourses, *Rosemary's Baby* is still an innovative work. The monster—now within the normal American family—has the potential to destroy Western civilization.

◆ ◆ ◆

The Exorcist and *The Omen* complement *Rosemary's Baby*. Both Regan and Damien are twentieth-century descendants of the American cultural tradition's Satanically possessed child. In *The Scarlet Letter*, Pearl originates from an adulterous liaison between Hester and Dimmesdale. Born out of acceptable family wedlock, her nonconformity in dress and behavior lends credence to community suspicions that she is actually Satan's daughter. Hawthorne did not invent this association. It belonged to a Puritan culture with which he was intimately familiar. As Cotton Mather's *Haec ipso miserrima vidi* illustrates,

Puritanism regarded childish pranks and hyperactivity as signs of demonic possession.[7]

The Exorcist was the first modern horror film to begin excessively using distracting special effects generic devices. Most reviewers missed its radical family critique and regarded the film as a "macho-masochistic religious porn film."[8] But the Satanic possession motif veils the real cause: eruption of repressed energies against the family institution. Three factors influence the Satanic theme: Puritanism's historical legacy, contemporary psychological treatments of the family, and changing perceptions on childhood imagery in cinema.

As Richard Slotkin demonstrates, the Puritan tradition has always exercised a dominant hold on the American consciousness, particularly with its "scapegoat" mechanism. Cotton Mather never understood the Goodwin children's constant expression of desires to injure and murder their elders in response to strict family upbringing. Mather's reports of childish "gymnastics" anticipate Regan's bodily reactions in *The Exorcist*. Old solutions became current again. In an era of recession, oil embargoes, the debilitating effects of Vietnam, and crisis of confidence in presidential leadership, cinema provides an ideological answer by invoking a traditional enemy—Satan.

Despite antipsychiatry's current marginal status, this 1960s movement focused attention toward social and familial contexts. Although schizophrenia may not be an oppositional reaction to family oppression, R. D. Laing, Aaron Esterston, and David Cooper suggest the role of the family in generating insanity. Noting social factors that influence Freud's Schreber case, Morton Schatzman reveals child abuse veiled within supernatural discourse.[9] Certain films attempt raising these antihegemonic factors to counter supernatural mystification within the content.

The Exorcist appeared at a time of fundamental changes within the family. Despite its enshrinement within American ideology, the unit bore little relationship to ideologic representations. Increasing divorce rates, one-parent families, developing minority relationships, and economic necessities resulting in two breadwinners questioned the role of 1950s TV model families like the Cleavers and the Rileys. No longer could parents dominate their children. Offspring rejected the idea that "Father Knows Best." The development of children's liberation and growing adult insecurity resulted in the child's new incarnation as either Tatum O'Neal's foulmouthed, streetwise tough or as Satanic progeny. Although Tatum belonged to a Hollywood tradition of tough-nosed kids such as Jackie Coogan, Jackie Cooper, and The Dead End Kids, little Jodie Foster presented a more sexual incarnation in *Taxi Driver* (1974) and *The Little Girl Who Lives Down the Lane* (1976).[10]

The Exorcist's Regan attempts to answer these troubling depictions. Satanic forces are really responsible for the antifamily children in *Lolita* (1962) and *Wild in the Streets* (1968).

Beneath *The Exorcist's* supernatural veil are family tensions. The MacNeil and Karras families are in an advanced state of disintegration. There is little need for any Satanic assault. Regan (Linda Blair) misses her absent father. She resents Chris's (Ellen Burstyn) involvement with director Burke Dennings (Jack McGowran). Dennings's foul-mouthed, sexually explicit nature influences her. When her neck later turns 360 degrees, she speaks in Denning's voice, victoriously possessing her mother's lover. Father Karras (Jason Miller) exists in an uneasy relationship with his aged mother. His father died several years before. Already suffering from religious doubts, he feels guilt over abandoning her in slum premises she stubbornly refuses to leave. His career choice of priesthood (rather than affluent professional life) torments him. As a celibate male he has repressed feelings of guilt, resentment, and rage. The demons tormenting Regan and Karras represent distorted parental figures. While Regan's possessor is male, Karras's tormenter is female. Father returns to possess Regan; mother speaks from inside Regan's body, temporarily revealing herself during the exorcism.

Demonic forces also blur normal gender identity. A male sounding demon (speaking in Mercedes McCambridge's voice) possesses Regan, turning her body monstrous and granting her excessive phallic strength.[11] During his nightmare Karras briefly sees a grotesque female demon as his mother ascends, then descends, the subway stairs. His vocation generates dark feelings of homosexual repression. Both he and Father Merrin (Max von Sydow) encounter a being who opposes not only their religion but ordained gender roles. The possessed Regan is an "abject" male and female mixed entity embodying alternative, oppositional elements repressed by the family. But the demonic is definitely no positive, revolutionary element capable of expressing liberatory feelings as it remains defined within the conservative terrains of the Gothic. *The Exorcist* is another example of a Hollywood unable (and unwilling) to follow suggestive implications to their logical conclusions, presenting the alternative in non-abject imagery. Like the 1980s horror cycle, *The Exorcist* presents alternatives as alien and "other." From the 1970s onward, the genre fails to develop the social insights of the *Psycho* era. Society and the family no longer produce monsters and psychopaths—only "other" external forces. However, despite this failure, horror films usually contain contradictions. This is certainly so with *The Exorcist*.

Darkness fills the screen. Eerie music accompanies the opening as credits roll to an Arabic chant. The image fades to a blue, filtered sun gradually changing to sunset. Reminiscent of "The Dawn of Man" prologue to Kubrick's *2001: A Space Odyssey* (1966), *The Exorcist*'s beginning contains strong deterministic influences. A feeling exists of Old World contamination awakening. The Arabic East's enigmatic nature opposes Western Catholicism. Simmering infernoesque heat arises from the desert. It leads to a long shot of an excavation site as an Arab leads his flock past. Individual shots show picks penetrating the ground. Mechanical shovels oozing out dirt anticipate Regan's excremental activities.[12]

Some workmen discover a buried object. They send a boy to summon Father Merrin. The camera follows his path tracking and panning ominously leftward, finally panning left to right before the shot ends in an abrupt cut. The next image shows Father Merrin, his back to the camera, in a long shot framed between the boy's legs. Merrin is the first major character introduced in this way, a technique used for every significant player (with the exception of Karras and Dennings). The camera movement signifies an unseen force seeking to move toward human pawns for some cosmic chess game. Later the camera frames Chris from behind in a high-angle shot; her back is away from us as she reads a script in bed. The camera later pans left as she enters Regan's room to close the open window. Regan's back faces her mother. Merrin's later reintroduction occurs when he walks up a small slope in Maryland's Woodstock Seminary, his back to the camera. As Friedkin points out, "We come up behind them, almost like an unseen force." Demonic energies focus on Merrin using the MacNeil family to trap their victim. They also aim to ensnare Karras whose family circumstances parallel the MacNeils.

As Merrin approaches the object, the camera tracks left to right, tilting down and tracking in before another abrupt cut. A Christian St. Joseph medal enigmatically appears within an ancient archaeological level. Although subtitles translate Merrin's Arabic comment as "This is strange," he actually says "What's *this* doing here?"[13] As an addition to the film version, the medal functions very much like a talismanic barrier preventing the emergence of evil forces until its removal from the archaeological site. It also links supernatural and family realms. Karras's mother wears a similar medal; Father Dyer receives it from the MacNeil family in the epilogue.

Merrin then examines the mound where the medal appeared. He extracts a piece of rock from the hardened clay. As he clears it, his expression turns to dismay as he recognizes the implications behind this Christian medal as a guardian device. He finds a green stone amulet containing the head of Pazazu, a minor Assyrian demon that personifies the southwest wind and whose domain involved sickness and death. The soundtrack emits a sinister buzz.

The Pazazu amulet awaits release after thousands of years. *The Exorcist* attempts returning to classical horror motifs of evil as an external manifestation that awaits unwary Americans. Europeans excavate a foreign land, unwittingly unleashing a buried object which will attack the family. *The Exorcist* prologue depicts a Hollywood "Orientalism" ascribing blame to a convenient external source—the Arabic world. However, this revisionist version of the Puritan Captivity Myth does not entirely succeed. Within the film are internal factors revealing family tensions as the real reason behind supposed demonic assault. The amulet's color resembles the clay from one of Regan's sculptures Lt. Kinderman (Lee J. Cobb) discovers below the steps after Dennings's death. There are grounds for ascribing his death to a daughter who is jealous of her mother's love rather than to a convenient "bogeyman." The amulet also appears in Karras's nightmare after his mother's death.

Succeeding shots contrast Father Merrin with the East's alien nature. Three close-ups emphasize his aging, mummified face as he sits in a café taking tablets to alleviate his heart condition. His position in a crowded bazaar, surrounded by a foreign culture's noisy clatter, strongly suggests Eastern culpability for his ailment. As Pazazu's demonic domain of sickness and death, Iraq is antithetical to Western Catholic health. Stern-visaged Arabs gaze at Merrin while he takes his tablets. An Arab leads away a blind beggar. The next image shows an infernoesque blacksmith's fire, the camera zooming in to the blacksmith's one good eye. It resembles later shots of Regan's eye moving in their sockets. A hammer strikes an anvil, a sound also occurring during the exorcism. The Iraq prologue functions as an overdetermined set of associations that seeks to project family horror on a disease-ridden Eastern culture.

Even time undergoes threat. A clock suddenly stops in the curator's office while Merrin examines the amulet. He departs, saying, "There is something I must do." Passing a prostrate group of Arabs praying on prayer mats, he walks through a dark marketplace down a narrow street. An Arab watches him from the roof. As Merrin staggers from his heart condition, a carriage suddenly rushes past him nearly knocking him down. Inside the carriage, a sinister, aged, obese Arab woman leers evilly at him. Approaching the excavation area after identifying himself to two trigger-happy Arab guards, Merrin finally encounters his foe. As rushing wind dominates the soundtrack, Pazazu's head appears against the sun. The buzzing sound heard earlier at the amulet's discovery reoccurs. A sinister Arab guard watches Merrin. As two dogs fight their growls anticipate Regan's possessed sounds. The camera tracks into Pazazu's head. The prologue's final image visually presents Western civilization's dualistic imagery of binary oppositions. Pazazu's statue stands left of frame, its serpent penis signifying "evil" connotations behind Regan's future demonic possession. Solitary Father Merrin stands facing Pazazu right of screen. In the long shot framing these combatants, the prologue's red sunset mixes into the middle space. A combat between two forces will begin.

The prologue attempts to present the struggle in Western Christian terms between the two opposing forces of good and evil. Pazazu represents Satan. But Pazazu was a marginal figure in Assyrian religion. Pazazu was no Satan but a minor deity existing within a divine pantheon of deities whose complex motivations and actions resembled their human counterparts. Assyrian deities were arbitrarily good and evil unlike their Christian successors. *The Exorcist*'s manifest text attempts a logocentric metaphysical order, but latent elements are contradictory.

The "affirmative" epilogue contains no assured final victory. Chris has not altered her atheistic beliefs. She represses past events. Faintly bruised Regan has no memory of demonic violation, except for one brief action. Staring at Father Dyer's collar, she suddenly reaches up and kisses him. Then, embarrassed at this unexplainable action, she runs to the limousine. Before leaving Chris hands Karrass's medallion to Dyer. Resembling the prologue's St. Joseph medal, it brings the action full circle. Dyer then pauses at the top of the steps where Karrass fell to his death. The camera cuts to the boarded windows of Regan's room. Dyer pensively looks at the steps then walks away. The epilogue has no sense of reassurance. The Jesuits have won one battle but not the entire war. The circumstances causing Regan's possession remain.

The Exorcist indicates that Regan's family life is not ideal. The twelve-year-old girl lives with her actress mother in a glossy Georgetown house during the filming of a student revolt movie, *Crash Course*. We never learn the reason for her parents' divorce, though tensions arising from Chris's status as a successful star and his obscure career are possible causes. Regan lacks her father at puberty's crucial onset. Despite a superficially happy relationship between mother and daughter, all is not well. Chris's histrionic manner dominates the set as she violently argues with director Burke Dennings. Both indulge in obscene language. They may also do so at home. Although secretary Sharon (Kitty Winn) cares for Regan during Chris's location work, the family situation is uneasy. The temporary domicile's dark interior and "haunted house" creakings suggest unresolved tensions.

Chris works on a film that deals with a contemporary movement disrupting American society. Standing up for students who want to learn against their demonstrating counterparts, she faces opponents wearing shrouds and death masks. Returning home she passes St. Mike's church, briefly seeing Karras attempting to console another priest over loss of faith. Children in

Halloween costume pass her. Then the camera abruptly cuts to reveal two middle-aged white nuns, their robes flowing in the wind. Like the Iraq prologue, this sequence hints at ominous forces within the surrounding environment that are ready to attack American normality.

The MacNeil family relationship contains repressed tensions. Regan's name originates from King Lear's destructive, ungrateful daughter. Although mother and daughter engage in friendly activities, visual clues suggest negative tensions. After Chris has caught Regan in a chase through the house, they both sink to the floor giggling. As they do so the camera tracks in, placing both in shadow, perhaps "tellingly revealing the lies they live with."[14] The basement scene provides further evidence. Regan sails a sculptured clay "worry bird," its feather plume and comically painted nose aimed directly at Chris. Clawed feet and lowered wings resemble Pazazu. Its long pointed nose parallels the deity's serpent penis.[15] Trapped within the socialized realm of girlhood whose familial construction disavows any trace of "masculine" aggressiveness, Regan projects repressed feelings elsewhere. Unlike *The Bad Seed*'s Rhoda Penmark, she will not play the sweet, obedient, little girl role.

Regan's model is the first manifestation of her repressed feelings. The worry bird's phallic nose resembles the penis tacked on to the Virgin Mary's desecrated image in the church. Regan's attack is not only an anally excremental assault against Western civilization's supreme symbol of motherhood but also a subversive return of socially repressed "phallic" qualities traditionally denied to women. During her demonic possession, Regan embodies aggressive qualities in her assaults upon the forces of law, medicine, religion, and motherhood—patriarchal institutions that depend on the family to maintain female subordination.

Regan obviously misses her natural father and is jealous of Chris's relationship with Dennings, the first person she murders. During the basement sequence, she mentions her fantasy playmate, "Captain Howdy," who excludes Chris from participation on the Ouija board.[16] Although the film never mentions the name of Regan's father while the novel does (Howard), the very fact of the fantasy playmate's gender, his resentment of Chris, and his refusal to answer Regan's question concerning Chris's attractiveness, strongly suggest Captain Howdy is Regan's imaginary incarnation of her missing father.

Regan reacts against family lies. At bedtime Chris discovers Regan's possession of a movie magazine containing scandalous gossip. It contains a photo of them both on the cover. Mother and daughter engage in a teasing dialogue extremely suggestive of the lies and double-talk within their family relationship. Chris refuses to discuss the magazine's contents, concentrating instead on the cover photo. Regan's knowledge of the magazine's report concerning her mother's involvement with Dennings becomes clearer in the next few lines after she suggests inviting him to her birthday party. Chris is surprised.

> REGAN. Well, welllll you like him. . . .
> CHRIS. Yeah, I like him. Don't you like him? *Regan looks away without responding.*
> CHRIS. Hey, what's goin' on, what is this, huh?
> REGAN. *(A bit sullenly.)* You're going to marry him, aren't you? *This leads to Chris's vigorous disavowal.*
> REGAN. You don't like him like Daddy?
> CHRIS. *(Serious now.)* Regan, I love your daddy. I'll always love your daddy, honey. OK? Burke just comes around here a lot 'cause, well, he's lonely, ain't got nothing to do.
> REGAN. Well, I heard—differently.
> CHRIS. Oh you did. What did you hear, huh?
> REGAN. (Carefully noncommittal.) I don't know.[17]

The seeds of Regan's possession lie within the family. A further scene emphasizes this. During Regan's birthday, Chris attempts to phone her ex-husband. Regan overhears her, looking down from the top stairs. Her despondent look reveals her recognition of Chris's earlier lie concerning loving her father.

> CHRIS. He doesn't even call his daughter on her birthday, for crissakes.
> SHARON. Well, maybe the circuit is busy.
> CHRIS. Oh circuits my ass! He doesn't give a shit![18]

Learning the lie behind her parent's relationship, Regan deteriorates. The next night Chris finds Regan frightened in a shaking bed. In the morning people discover the Virgin's desecration in the church. Regan later disrupts Chris's party, prophesying an astronaut guest's death in space and pissing on the carpet. When Chris discovers Regan's shaking bed, she takes her to a doctor. Regan spits in his face, swears at him, and announces her possession in a masculinized demonic tone, "Keep away! The sow is mine!" After Dennings's death, Regan bloodily masturbates with a crucifix and assaults her mother. Reverting to an anally aggressive mode, she reacts against conformist forces of religion and family, finally attacking her mother for lying to her. The final horrific revelation sees her speaking in Dennings's voice. Enacting a violently grotesque parody of her mother's sexual relationship, Regan has finally possessed her lover. Rejecting her real father who "doesn't give a shit," she submits to an alternative symbolic patriarchal realm by becoming a demonic "Bad Seed."

The Karras family is also deeply troubled. Existing at the opposite end of the social scale, Father Karras faces the priestly dilemma of loss of faith. After watching Chris on location, he descends to a subway station, its dark interior illustrating his religious and parental sense of alienation. A train's approaching light suddenly breaches the darkness. Karras ignores a derelict wino's pleas for help, shutting his eyes against his presence and painfully retreating into solipsistic torment. Reacting against life's sordid nature, he disengages himself as he later withdraws from pathetic, clutching, elderly patients in the impoverished hospital that houses his senile mother. Karras earlier appears in long shot, walking despondently along a New York slum street. As he passes, ragged, grimy urchins wreck a car. Entering a dark and squalid room, he finds his aged mother in poor health. Karras feels extreme guilt over his mother's condition as well as repressed resentment over her contribution to his malaise. As his uncle later remarks, if Karras had not chosen the priesthood, he could have become an affluent psychiatrist who was able to support his mother. His guilt increases when she later blames him for her incarceration within the neuropsychiatric ward, an accusation repeated in the later exorcism. Agreeing to return her home, Karras undergoes extreme spiritual anguish when he learns of her body's discovery three days after her death. Karras's family circumstances provide fertile soil for the return of the repressed.

Falling into a drunken sleep after his mother's death, he sees the Iraq medallion descending in a dream. His mother ascends the subway stairs while Damien attempts to reach her. He vainly calls her, but she continues to descend. During this dream subliminal flashes occur, showing a white-faced female demon. This figure later appears during the exorcism when the demon obscenely refers to Mrs. Karras performing fellatio in hell. Associations with Karras's repressed homosexual feelings are present. The female demon's face also briefly superimposes itself on Regan's as she utters, "You killed your mother, you left her alone to die." Damien Karras feels guilty for his mother's tragic death which was bereft of the Last Rites. Linked with repressed homosexual tendencies endemic to his vocation, the demon's female persona counterpoints Regan's male Captain Howdy. Regan and Karras internally struggle against familial gender roles—a struggle that receives no other articulation in *The Exorcist* except via demonic codes.

During the exorcism demonic taunts link Karras's repressed feelings over his mother to the earlier subway scene. The demon mimics the wino's plea as it taunts Karras about his mother. It attacks both Regan and Karras over their socially acceptable gender roles. Possessing Regan, reversing her developing genital sexuality into a monstrously masculine anal-aggressive-ness, the demon taunts Karras over his repressed homosexuality. As he says to Karras, Regan is not his only target.

> REGAN/DEMON. What an excellent day for an exorcism.
> KARRAS. You'd like that?
> REGAN/DEMON. Intensely.   .
> KARRAS. But wouldn't that drive you out of Regan?
> REGAN/DEMON. It would bring us together.
> KARRAS. You and Regan?
> REGAN/DEMON. You and us.[19]

Karras is the real goal of the demon, not Father Merrin. During the exorcism's second stage, Merrin sends Karras away when the demon uses his mother's body and voice. Returning Karras finds Merrin dead from a heart attack. He assaults the giggling Regan, daring the demon to possess him. Karras's assault is really ambiguous. It may signify his return of faith. Or he may attack several personal demons—his mother who makes him feel guilty, the female demon of his nightmare expressing repressed feminine tendencies, and a possessed little girl whose genderless body opposes social normality. He provokes the demon to enter him and receives the Last Rites as he lies dying outside the MacNeil residence.

The families in *The Exorcist* live in a deteriorating America that no lon-ger offers any coherent solutions to individual family dilemmas. Despite the prologue's desperate attempt to externalize evil, dissonant forces are defi-nitely within the family. *The Exorcist* visually associates both families long before Chris and Damien meet. After the camera tracks in to the ominous wall shadows during the MacNeils' supposedly good-natured horseplay, an abrupt cut to the dark subway station follows showing Karras rejecting the wino. After he leaves his mother, the next sequence reveals Captain Howdy's Ouija board in the MacNeil basement. Both scenes emphasize mothers and absent fathers. Regan's questions over mother's relationship with Dennings and her feelings toward her father follow Karras's announcement of his loss of faith in a crowded bar. Regan's screaming in the hospital interrupts Kar-ras's nightmare. Events in the normal everyday scientific world have dark counterpoints. Scenes showing arteriogram needle insertions into Regan's cartoid artery signify crucifix penetrations. Her bodily responses, writhing on a bed with electrodes attached to her head, parallel demonically possessed levitations. Significant dualities occur between institutionally acceptable dis-courses of patriarchal control and demonic counterparts. Both seek physical control of the female body. *The Exorcist's* world reveals the family as the real threat, not the imaginary Iraq of the prologue.

♦   ♦   ♦

As a big budget Twentieth Century Fox studio response to *The Exorcist's* (Warner Brothers) success, *The Omen* lacks its flawed counterpart's productive ambiguities. Although lending itself to readings illustrating tensions between childhood's wholesome appearance and resentment against parental figures, these ideas never really develop. Damien is clearly Satan's child. An aura of predestination predominates leaving little room for suggestive parallels between familial and demonic realms. Brought into the home by prospective presidential candidate Robert Thorn (Gregory Peck), Damien eventually arrives in the White House over his adopted parents' graves. If, as Kathy Merlock Jackson suggests, the real point of contemporary child-as-monster films was not so much "the evil of children, often the victims of demonic possession themselves, but rather the ineffectiveness of the family, church, and state—America's most highly valued institutions—to guard themselves against deception and destruction,"[20] this links these powerful children with the institutions they react against. The family is ineffective as a controlling device. Patriarchy is in crisis. But the films supply no deeper reason for the revolt, only demonic possession. However, even *The Omen* suggests insecure adult paranoia over uncontrollable offspring rather than demonic possession. But its overwhelming pessimistic aura of supernatural predeterminism often overshadows a significant family trauma.

The visual style suggests an underlying nihilism. Although day balances night, light contains no positive assurance because it is weak and anemic. When the Thorns arrive at their British home, Robert smugly comments, "Nothing is too good for the wife of a future President of the United States." He closes the shutters, placing the dining room in darkness. While young Damien remains outside with his nurse Holly (Holly Palance), Robert and Katherine (Lee Remick) conceive their second child whom they eventually lose.

Repentant satanist Father Brennan (Patrick Troughton) warns Robert in his comfortable ambassadorial office about Damien. Baboons attack Katherine and Damien during their drive through a safari park. Bright daylight never fills the screen. Night constantly seeks control. Thorn and Jennings (David Warner) descend from Jezreel's daytime excavated exterior to a darkened room. There an archaeologist-exorcist (Leo McKern) presents Robert with ceremonial knives necessary for Damien's physical and spiritual extinction. The film's final scene emphasizes this uneasy visual alternation.

Witnessing the Thorns's burial, Damien turns and smiles to the audience. Daylight recedes into darkness. The credit sequence is ominous. Opening in darkness to Jerry Goldsmith's Satanic chorus, Damien's figure slowly appears on the right. Credits roll on the left. However, unlike John Carpenter's Jack O'Lantern of *Halloween* (1978), Damien is never completely illuminated. He remains shadowy and indistinct, thereby demonstrating light's ineffectiveness before the demonic messiah.

The film's action begins at night. Thorn's car rushes to a hospital in Rome where his wife is due to give birth. Several shots show him entering. They conclude in an overhead long shot as he sits framed by the banisters. Powers of darkness begin a circle of entrapment. Informed by Father Spiletto (Martin Benson) of their baby's death, Robert agrees to his plan of substituting another child. Fearful of Katherine's death if she discovers the truth, he acts out of feelings of love and concern. By deceiving his wife, he unleashes a chain of events that eventually cause their destruction.

Like *Rosemary's Baby* and *The Exorcist*, family lies generate Satanic assault. While Guy betrays Rosemary for selfish reasons of material gain and Chris deceives Regan over negative feelings toward her husband, ironically Robert lies out of genuine compassionate feelings. However, it is still a deception, causing repressed consequences to emerge in Satanic guise. Agreeing to Father Spiletto's suggestion, the image of both men dissolves to reveal a nun holding a baby. The baby's face merges with Robert's on the screen. The image changes revealing the actual (as well as the symbolic) basis for this merger. A plate glass window reflects Robert's face as he looks. The real world contains its dark opposite. As future ambassador to England and prospective presidential candidate, Robert's political ambitions parallel Damien's role as "Chosen One." Damien reflects a darker version of an American office that has the power to destroy the world as well as to save it for democracy.

The next scene shows Father Spiletto's reflection suggestive of conspiracy by all present. Robert wishes to deceive his wife for positive reasons. Spiletto has deadlier motives. In either case a family deception occurs. The scene changes, showing both men framed on the opposite side of the glass to the nun and child. Spiletto remarks, "Your wife need never know. It would be a blessing for her and for the child. . . . On this very night God has given you a son." As Robert's face merges with his new son, their very juxtaposition suggests ominous consequences arising from Robert's well-meaning lie. The sequence ends with the Thorns leaving the hospital; their car passes a leering gargoyle.

Behind Robert's supposedly positive desires lie classic Freudian narcissistic motifs regarding the child as less of a being in its own right but more of an object for parental desire. As Freud points out in his classic essay "On Narcissism," familial circumstances often result in parental self-deceptions and a dangerous disregard of childhood's actual nature. By selecting Damien as a particular male-child object-choice, Robert's narcissistic attitude exhibits parental blindness. Although *The Omen* explicitly depicts Damien as Satan's offspring, Robert's attitude echoes Freud's flawed parents who "are under a compulsion to ascribe every perfection to the child—which sober observation would find no occasion to do so—and to conceal and forget all his shortcomings. (Incidentally, the denial of sexuality in children is connected with this.)"[21] Even with Satanic overtones, the film illustrates acutely the dangers of family self-deception and its catastrophic consequences. As a monk later tells Thorn, "For everything holy, there is something unholy—this is the essence of temptation." Wishing his son to be "perfect" like all parents, Robert discovers a different reality expressed in supernatural terms.

This duality expresses itself in Father Spiletto's scarred visage. Robert discovers him in a sanctuary containing refugee monks and nuns who are repentant of Satanic involvement. Half of Spiletto's face is horribly burned. Hell's abnormality coexists with Christian normality. Even worldly cynical photographer Jennings is not exempt from this duality. One of his first ironic comments during Damien's garden birthday party is "I don't know whether we've got the heir to the four million here or Jesus Christ himself." Like David Hemmings's photographer in *Blow Up* (1966), he finds a different world contrasting with naive trust in objective photographic reality. Snapping Father Brennan, Holly, and himself, he finds the developed images containing a line (invisible to objective reality) that pierces the bodies, prophesying their deaths. Holly commits suicide in front of the garden party, hanging herself as a masochistic sexual sacrifice to the Antichrist, "Damien, look at me. I'm over here. Damien. I love you. It's all for you." Swinging on a rope her body smashes through a window. Father Brennan dies outside a closed church that cannot offer him sanctuary. A lightning rod kills him. The editing suggests Damien's involvement, intercut shots showing him chanting and playing suggestively with billiard balls while Katherine suffers from a headache. Jennings accidentally photographs himself in a mirror inside Father Brennan's room. Accompanying Thorn to Jezreel he dies macabrely, a glass sheet falling from a truck decapitates him.

The camera views Jennings's death from an overhead high-angle shot filmed in slow motion visually suggesting both omniscient predestination and the victim's perception of approaching death. It is a frequent visual device. Damien knocks over Katherine's chair as he rides past in his tricycle, causing her to fall over the balcony. Grasping the banisters for temporary relief, a slow-motion overhead shot presents her perception of a fishbowl dropping below and smashing into fragments. The vision anticipates her later demise when she falls through a hospital window on to a waiting ambulance. Her fingers gradually slipping, she looks at Damien observing her before she finally falls—a fall that results in the miscarriage of her newly conceived child. As Thorn and Jennings explore a deserted Etruscan cemetery to obtain evidence of Damien's real parentage, the camera observes them from above, panning right as they move, anticipating the sudden canine attack. In the film's penultimate scene, the camera presents Robert's perception of the police bullet moving toward him. Shot in slow motion, the gunshot's flame fills the screen in close-up as the bullet slowly proceeds to kill the only person who could save the world from its eventual hellish expiration.

As Jennings finds out, Damien may inherit four million but he is definitely not Jesus Christ! His mark 666 reverses the Holy Trinity. *The Omen* attacks all of Western civilization's cherished institutions—family, religion, and politics—transforming them into microcosmic facets of death and armageddon. The manifest explanation emphasizes demonic agency, but other textual features suggest paranoid parental feelings toward children. Observing Damien before she falls below, Katherine suspects her supposed firstborn. Previously Damien assaulted her when she attempted to take him to church, ignoring the advice of Holly's replacement Mrs. Baylock (Billie Whitelaw). The incident's physical effects and the mental aftermath of a safari park baboon-attack make her request an abortion to avoid bearing any other children. Suspicious of her son, she naturally believes him to be the Antichrist.

Although warned by Father Brennan that Damien is "the son of the devil who will kill his earthly parents," Thorn ignores psychiatric advice concerning an abortion. "She thinks the child is alien or evil. Another child would be disastrous." Despite his determination to fight destiny and ignore his wife's pleas—"It was foretold that her pregnancy would be terminated. I'm going to fight and see that it's not"—his efforts are in vain. While he drives home, young Damien rides around in his tricycle watched by Mrs. Baylock. As a single, unattached female, Mrs. Baylock also threatens family values. Watching Damien ride in a circle, she smiles as if encouraging a savior who will avenge all her burned and tortured sisters. After Katherine falls from the balcony, she pleads with Thorn in hospital, "Don't let him kill me"; she fears her five-year-old son's supposed power. Father and mother harbor paranoid feelings toward their offspring. Without Satanic explanation *The Omen* could have profitably developed this theme of parental insecurity over child rearing. However, it moves toward old Puritanistic scapegoating tendencies.

Convinced of civilization's impotence, Robert travels to an archaeological excavation site in Old Testament Jezreel where he receives two ceremonial knives from an exorcist who instructs him to kill his child on hallowed ground. Retrieving his child from Mrs. Baylock's frenzied protection, he carries him to a church. Ironically Robert attempts to become a patriarchal Abraham by sacrificing a Satanic Isaac within a Christian church. Pausing before his son's pleas, "Daddy, please! Please don't!" (which may be cries of a child who does not understand his true identity), Robert's cry, "God help me," leads not to God preventing his act, as in the Old Testament, but a police bullet leading to his death. The film's final image reveals Damien between the president and first lady who are attending Thorn's funeral. He looks at the camera. The Antichrist not only finds a new family but is in the heart of Western civilization's most powerful center—the White House. The image fades into darkness.

Although less accomplished, *Damien—Omen II* (1978) contains several notable features concerning its messiah's family progress. Adopted by his uncle Richard Thorn (William Holden), Damien attends a military school with stepbrother Mark, Richard's son from his first marriage. Although loved by Richard and his second wife Ann (Lee Grant), wealthy Aunt Marion (Sylvia Sidney) suspects his negative influence on her beloved nephew Mark. Although both boys laugh at her, Damien (Jonathan Scott-Taylor) becomes a convenient scapegoat for Aunt Marion to attempt financial control over the family like Cassidy in *Psycho*. Threatening to leave her millions to charity instead of the Thorn Corporation and emphasizing Anne's subordinate position as second (childless) wife—"Neither boy is yours"—Aunt Marion represents the first of many adults in the film whose actions force Damien into his predestined role as Satanic messiah. Because Damien is as yet unaware of his destiny, the film's postprologue presents him as victim of family tensions and adult desires. He is forced into a particular role he initially reacts against. Damien's fate results as much from adult insecurity as Satanic desire.

Until Sgt. Neff (Lance Henriksen) suggests Damien read *Revelations*, the youthful Antichrist is unaware of his identity. Unknown to him a mysterious raven disposes of any possible threats to his destiny while military (Sgt. Neff) and corporate forces such as Paul (Robert Foxworth) carefully groom him for his destiny. Both Sgt. Neff and Paul are single men, the former carefully drawing parallels with Damien—"I see you're an orphan. That's something we have in common." They also negatively embody a twentieth-century military-corporate establishment seeking control over world affairs. Paul sees the Thorn Corporation's economic success in exploiting famine rather than electronics, using low-cost food to blackmail the Third World in retaliation for the 1970s oil crisis. Despite the film's insistence on Damien as the Antichrist, if he did not exist establishment forces would invent him as a convenient alibi. Both male authority figures see Damien as an object to realize their own ambitions. Their actions parallel the traditional family act of molding children into conformist products.

Damien's anguish at discovering his identity is genuine. Reading *Revelations*, while the Military Academy practices a graduation march, he rushes outside in horror, uttering a cry of desolation, "Why?" "Why me?" Sgt. Neff and Paul are the real forces in Damien's destiny. Having no alternative, Damien follows his chosen role. Offering genuine feelings of love and friendship to Mark, he finds his last hope for salvation rejected by a paranoid stepbrother. Like the Frankenstein creature, Damien sincerely desires a friend. But Mark sees him as a monstrous threat. Angrily killing Mark by mental telepathy, Damien finally screams in emotional agony when he realizes his deed. His last chance of changing his destiny fails.

The film also suggests family complicity with Satanic forces. Without family antagonism and adult manipulation, Damien would not be an Antichrist. Like his Christian counterpart, religious and family forces mold his destiny. Ann eventually reveals herself as the "whore of Babylon," killing Richard with ceremonial daggers to save Damien's life—"I'll always belong to him, always." However, her call to Damien results in her destruction, fulfilling biblical prophecy. Suggestions of some dark liaison between them exist. Earlier the Thorn family watched a Hollywood, clean, wholesome family movie that concludes with a happy ending. They then joke about the film's illusory nature. While Mark is upstairs running the projector, Damien rests intimately on his adopted mother's breast. The climax suggests darker associations between a maternally disguised "whore of Babylon" and future Antichrist. By destroying her Damien murderously reacts against a suffocatingly incestuous relationship, designed to manipulate his individual personality. Walking to his car in military uniform, the film pessimistically shows a new Messiah produced by satanism, capitalism, and the family.

Graham Baker's *The Final Conflict* (1981) sees thirty-two-year-old Damien (Sam Neill) occupying his uncle's and father's positions as head of the Thorn Corporation and ambassador to the Court of St. James. Fulfilling his Satanic and capitalist destiny, Damien first appears criticizing a rough-cut Thorn advertising short that concludes with biblical imagery he detests as "trite, rhetorical, cliched, and inane." Satanism no longer represents a threat to the Puritan "City on the Hill." It achieves its aims within the contemporary political and corporate order. Damien's criticisms indirectly apply to the inability of the *Omen* films to realize subversive aspects within the demonic discourse.

Satanism becomes another metaphoric description of "big business." Alternatives are also flawed. As represented by Father De Carlo (Rosanno Brazzi) and his monastic order, Christianity resembles a Mafia hit-squad. Both forces act ruthlessly. By aiding the Western powers in blaming a Marxist liberation front for Israel's destruction of the Aswan Dam and unethically obtaining both the British ambassador post and UN Youth Council presidency, Damien collaborates with a corrupt American president (Mason Adams) in fulfilling his goals. Despite Sam Neill's rebellious Luciferian demeanor, Damien is only another bureaucratic embodiment of corporate capitalism.

However, *The Final Conflict* does contain some significant motifs. Damien's desire to obtain the Youth Council post links up with the satanist cycle's attack on patriarchal structures. Conversing with TV journalist Kate Reynolds (Lisa Harrow) on a talk show, he desires to give youth a greater say in world affairs. Rather than complying with the old order's desires to brainwash the younger generation, Damien wishes to help them gain a voice in their own future. However, *The Final Conflict* presents this movement in a negative light by linking it with an Antichrist twentieth-century version of the "Massacre of the Innocents." Ordering his "Disciples of the Watch" to kill all newborn babies to ensure the reborn Christ's death, his strategy involves assault on the family. Among his followers are young children, Wolf Cubs, a nurse, and a vicar, who willingly carry out his orders. Damien's adult disciples (representing rebellious members of institutional orders such as religion and law) and their younger counterparts (the Wolf Cub sector of the Boy Scouts eager to do their "good deed for the day") respond to his Satanic order. In his prayer to Satan, Damien rejects Christianity's false illusions, preferring the realities of human existence. His father is the "Lord of Silence, supreme Lord of Desolation whom mankind reviles but aches to embrace." Praying to save the "world from Christ and his grubby mundane creed," Damien existentially appeals to the "grandeur of melancholy, the divinity of loneliness, the purity of evil, and the paradise of pain." He later tells Kate that although most people confuse evil with their own lusts, "Pure evil is as pure as innocence." Damien is a twentieth-century Byronic hero, heir to Uncle Charlie of *Shadow of a Doubt*. Reacting against Christ's doctrine of Original Sin, "draining man's desire in a deluge of sanctimonious morality," Damien champions the recognition of contemporary life. "What perverted imagination has fed man the lie that hell lies in the bowels of the earth. . . . There is only one hell, the leaden monotony of human existence. There is only one heaven, the ecstasy of my father's kingdom."

As a thirty-two-year-old ambassador, paralleling John F. Kennedy and Alexander the Great (whom he admires for his command of an army at the age of sixteen), Damien is still single. He explains to Kate that apart from skepticism, his busy life affords him no time for marriage. *The Final Conflict* contains several visual suggestions of Damien's sexual preferences, a condition the film finds "appropriate" to a Satanic messiah. Hostile to women, family, and the Second Coming, Damien keeps a blasphemous crucified Christ model in his upper room, its posture reversed from its usual appearance. After praying to his father, Damien ascends and leans on it, embracing the wooden arm in a homosexual gesture, attracted and repelled by his divine opposite. Failing to satisfy Kate in the normal missionary position, he gives up any attempt at heterosexual union and sodomizes her after uttering a dualistic creed, "Breath is pain. Death is pain. Beauty is pain." *The Final Conflict* can only ascribe Damien's sexuality as demonic and evil, not oppositionally radical.

Damien and Kate's son, Peter, begin a genuine friendship, based on feelings the film unconvincingly codes as monstrous. Although Peter's father died soon after his birth, Damien never really knew his father. Like Sgt. Neff in *Damien— Omen II*, both are orphans. He sees in Peter the lost friendship he had with Mark Thorn, and he tells Kate, "It's not every day you get a chance to be a boy again." Eventually, Peter falls under Damien's control, seeing in him the father he never had, and he becomes increasingly alienated from his mother. Father De Carlo warns Kate of the consequences, "Your son is with Damien Thorn in body and soul. Your son has become an apostle of the Anti-Christ," recognizing the religious implications of this unholy bond "between men."

Although using him to find Christ's location, Damien exhibits great fondness for Peter, gazing in fascination at his bloodied cheeks, as he smears him with the blood of a monastic assassin during a fox hunt. By the time Kate interrupts Damien's attempted initiation of her son, the real implications become apparent—"I love you beyond all others. Beyond life itself." Peter warns him of a possible trap. Arriving at the Abbey containing the risen Christ, Peter gives up his life for his master, shielding his body from De Carlo's knife, unlike his New Testament counterpart. Once Kate realizes the ultimate estrangement between mother and son, she stabs Damien from behind.

The Final Conflict moves to its ultimate conclusion, one of the weakest and most unsatisfying within horror cinema. Staggering to face his great adversary, Damien looks up at an abbey window. A large Christ figure emerges from darkness into light to dwarf his Satanic opponent. Dying, Damien utters, "Nazarene. You have won . . . nothing." From the film's perspective, Damien emerges the winner. Although he fails in preventing "a second ordeal of Jesus Christ," *The Final Conflict*'s conclusion contains no affirmative victory. Despite the appearance of a quasi-biblical text proclaiming messianic victory and anemic dawn scenes, the outcome has little sense of elation. It parallels

Damien's vampiric description of Christ's return—"I feel his presence like a virus, a parasite feeding on my energy, draining me of power." The film presents a dissipated climax. Despite a quotation from Rev. 21.4 proclaiming new life and resurrection, this does not include Peter. The penultimate scene shows Peter's dead body carried by a shadowy figure (the messiah?) and delivered to Kate. Peter remains still. He does not rise. Despite *The Final Conflict*'s attempt to ideologically conclude the 1970s cycle of Satanic movies in a year seeing the resurgence of fundamentalist Christianity, it cannot entirely extinguish a radically potential fatal attraction.

◆   ◆   ◆

Although *Exorcist II—The Heretic* (1977) was, and is, a critical and commercial failure, it appropriately belongs in any conclusion on Satanic films. Deliberately intended as an alternative philosophic answer to the original film, John Boorman attempted a significant breach with many restrictive codes preventing dialectical movement toward new goals the horror genre should, and must, attempt. Whereas *The Exorcist* maintains familiar binary oppositions between darkness and light, good and evil, God and Satan, content merely to reproduce old formulas with sophisticated special effects, *Exorcist II* attempts a far more ambitious breakthrough. However, its innovatory techniques resulted in serious misunderstanding. It did not give audiences what they wanted. Boorman tried to blend opposites, engaging viewers within a sophisticated visual interplay, avoiding traditional Gothic codes, and attempting to move towards new generic horizons.[22]

Although the family institution receives little direct attention, it nevertheless functions as a key motif in the film. Ostensibly remembering little about her demonic possession, Regan (Linda Blair) undergoes analytic sessions with Dr. Gene Tuskin (Louise Fletcher), a divorcée with two young children. Both women are free from traditional family ties. Regan's mother is away on location. Responding to Dr. Tuskin's question about dreams, Regan replies, "You know why I come here. To make my mother feel better. She feels guilty. Her divorce, her career, away all the time." Despite expectations concerning another replay of family demonic elements in *The Exorcist*, *Exorcist II* clearly disappoints traditionally minded audiences. The film generates meanings on a higher plane, involving each major character's break with institutional definitions of meaning toward radical personal development. *Exorcist II* is a heretical horror film. It seeks to reconcile oppositions on every level by moving toward higher meanings, suggesting the horror genre's eventual future redundancy in a changed world bereft both of traditional families and horror films. *Exorcist II* attempts a dialectical interplay between reductive concepts of good and evil toward a higher metaphysical unity. The film attempts to unify separate domains of masculine/feminine; science/religion; satanism/Christianity; east/west; different levels of space and time, attempting transcendence toward revolutionary sophisticated meanings that lead toward the abolition of restrictive gender and family definitions. Downplaying *The Exorcist*'s reliance on traditional codes and fetishistic special effects, *Exorcist II* suggests the demonic realm itself contains oppositional forces suggestive of future progressive social developments. It dialectically recognizes it as a contradictory entity containing both positive and negative features, necessitating a mental leap toward a new form of unity, thus diminishing the latter force. *Exorcist II* does not engage in a Puritan Holy War between good and evil. It implies both terms are now anachronistic. Only by merging into the dark realm, allowing oneself to be "brushed by the wings of Pazuzu," advancing beyond institutional constraints, and restrictive institutions can real progress occur. This entails not only abolishing church and family but also restrictive ideologic barriers separating men and women, youth and age, science and religion.

As a church emissary investigating the circumstances of Father Merrin's death, Jesuit priest Father Philip Lamont (Richard Burton) initially sees Regan's and Dr. Tuskin's experiments as a means to an end. He hopes to restore Father Merrin's reputation, release his works from papal censorship, and prove he was not "a Satanist at the end." The Roman Catholic hierarchy not only wishes to preserve the contemporary status quo as Lamont recognizes—"Satan has become an embarrassment to our progressive views"—but to protect the world of religion from any contaminating forces. They desire to maintain traditional barriers. From the opening scenes of Dr. Tuskin's laboratory, the audience realizes that *Exorcist II* furnishes no grounds for this. Far from being the impersonal laboratory where Regan underwent electrocephalic torture in the original film, Dr. Tuskin's laboratory resembles a glass hive whose mirrors reflect the potential for unity between everyone. Rather than expressing traditional generic dualistic motifs, Dr. Tuskin's laboratory suggests fusion of opposites. When Lamont arrives at Dr. Tuskin's office, Boorman shoots his reflection through the glass door as he looks at an autistic child. This parallels an earlier shot of Regan. As Regan stands briefly outside, Lamont's reflection appears to her left. As the door slides open moving to the right with Lamont's reflection, we see Regan looking at Lamont, who is now off-screen. The door slides to the left, restoring the former images as Dr. Tuskin introduces them. The mirror imagery suggests an eventual symbiosis between them.

Speaking of Regan's former possession, Father Lamont and Dr. Tuskin debate different interpretations. While Father Lamont insists on evil as "a spiritual being, alive and kicking, perverted and perverting weaving itself insidiously into the fabric of life," Dr. Tuskin regards it as a mental illness, "like the casualties of a diseased society." The film suggests neither interpretation is exclusive. Structured according to a cleverly arranged dualistic order, *Exorcist II* seeks to reconcile opposites, a strategy revealed in mise-en-scene and narrative. This begins in the first mental synthesizer experiment. All participants experience Father Merrin's death in the original exorcism. Before this scene Regan and Sharon watch one of Uri Geller's spoon-bending performances on television. Behind them a fragmented glass wall suggests humanity's limited understanding. Potentials exist but like the glass wall, they are fragmented and uncoordinated.

During the experiment Regan and Dr. Tuskin wear head receivers to experience Merrin's death. As Regan's mind remembers, images of Merrin and the possessed Regan appear on opposite ends of the screen. As demonic Regan points at Merrin, he collapses from a heart attack. The demon's hands clutch at Dr. Tuskin's heart. Regan rushes to her side massaging Tuskin's left breast as her demonic ghostly self grasps Tuskin's heart. Lamont puts on Regan's headset, gazing in fascination. At this point Regan begins to assert control, urging Dr. Tuskin to relax, pleading with Lamont to bring her back. Several dissolves reveal significant links between characters and levels of time. The demon's face merges with Regan's while Merrin's mixes with Tuskin's. It suggests a dialectical unity between different levels of good and evil, science and religion, victim and victimizers across time and space. Eventually, Lamont accedes to Regan's pleas, his command, "In God's name," leading the demonic Regan's ghostly hand to retreat from Dr. Tuskin's breast.

As one of *Exorcist II*'s most technically sophisticated scenes, the sequence diffuses barriers suggestive a necessary transcendence all characters must undergo to advance beyond social constraints. Traditional restrictive categories of family, religion, and science become redundant. Chris MacNeil is absent from the film. Dr. Tuskin is a divorcée bringing her children up on her own. Father Lamont is honest enough to confess his sexual desires before Dr. Tuskin. Wishing to redeem Father Merrin from heresy, he will become a heretic himself leaving the church to battle the negative forces affecting mankind. However, he must first fight himself. Regan must finally confront her destructive demonic counterpart in Georgetown's haunted house. Lamont's wishes to synthesize with Regan are not entirely pure. He desires her sexually as his temporary fall into Regan's seductive demonic self reveals. Like Regan, he must advance beyond patriarchal thought, avoiding religious dualities of good and evil. The synthesizing machine symbolizes *Exorcist II*'s theme of merger, advancing beyond traditional concepts of good and evil and institutionally constrained church, science, and family. Despite Linda Blair's unsatisfactory acting skills, she is *Exorcist II*'s messianic figure which embodies the horror genre's hidden utopian desires. Eventually evolving into a superhuman presence, defeating the final demonic attack, she represents feminist potentials for a new society. Seeing her in Teilhard de Chardin's progressive terms as signifying rational unity of science and religion, Lamont finally understands. He speaks of de Chardin's and Merrin's belief "that we'd come together in a kind of world mind which we'd all shape." But he recognizes humanity still has a long way to go. "If it happens before we are ready we might find ourselves pointing in a wrong direction—towards Satan."

Following Merrin's earlier path to Ethiopia in search of the young boy (Kokomo) he once exorcised, Lamont cannot rely on his masculine powers. As he walks through a disease-ridden village, Regan recognizes his need for her guidance. Struggling against Satanic contact, Regan appeals to him, "Call me by my dream name." Lamont eventually does, having already experienced the dark order's supposedly contaminating nature by flying on Pazuzu's wings. "Pazuzu, prince of the evil spirits of the air. Take me to Kokomo." Like Regan in the earlier film, he has to undergo contamination to advance. Experiencing Kokomo's (James Earl Jones) supposedly demonic presence in a heat exhaustion nightmare, Merrin realizes religious faith hinders further progress. Awakening from his traumatic illusion, Lamont finally meets the real Kokomo. No longer a Pazuzu witch doctor, he is a civilized doctor engaged in scientific experiments to end his country's frequent locust plagues. To Lamont's question, "Were you possessed by Pazazu as a boy?" Kokomo noncommittally answers, "That's what my mother used to tell me." Like Kokomo, Lamont and the audience need to reject old ideas of family and religion.

Showing Lamont his laboratory's hive of locusts, Kokomo unites science and religion to develop a higher order. Noting locust tendencies to act destructively whenever they merge too closely—"The key factor is the brushing of the wings"—Kokomo places his hopes in a new being, "the good locust" whose "children will be our agents in the swarm breaking the chain reaction" and restore harmony. The image dissolves to Regan rising from her bed.

When Lamont next appears before Regan, he no longer wears his clerical collar. He rejects Catholic patriarchal constraints for a new heretical frontier. Merrin previously thought, *Does great goodness draw evil upon itself?* Perhaps the question may be better rephrased: Do positive potentialities within the human personality attract negative institutional constraining forces such as the family, church, law, and science, interacting externally and internally (particularly in causing guilt or Original Sin)? At this juncture Regan and Lamont face further barriers. Meeting Regan in the Museum of Natural History, Lamont still speaks to her in institutional language about Kokomo. "He told me that Good and Evil are struggling within you. We must fight it."

Reexperiencing Merrin's Gethsemane through the synthesizer one last time, Lamont hears the demon's final taunt to the dying priest, "You're dying Merrin and your hopes die with you." But Merrin speaks beyond death. He recruits Lamont, telling of his life mission to protect future saviors such as Kokomo and Regan from Pazuzu. Here *Exorcist II* moves into revolutionary directions. Merrin's exorcisms are no longer understood as restoring the patriarchal status quo as in *The Exorcist*. They transcend all social, religious, and family boundaries necessitating a new social order.

At the original scene of Regan's possession, everyone engages in one final battle with evil forces. Repressed tensions emerge. Sexually attracted to Regan, Satanically contaminated by "the wings of Pazuzu," and violating his church's warnings against spiritualism, Lamont confronts his personal demons. Falling into the embraces of a sexually demonic Regan, Lamont attacks her pure counterpart. However, paralleling the climactic moment in *Curse of the Cat People* when Barbara nearly murders Amy, Merrin finds salvation. Speaking in her voice and Kokomo's, Regan evokes Lamont's memory of the revolutionary and heretical knowledge he gained in his quest. This enables him to fight his demonic seducer. As the battle rages, Pazuzu's locust hordes arrive, destroying the house and attacking Regan. She defeats them by using the same motions young Kokomo did during an earlier locust attack in Africa. Diverse worlds of time, space, science, and religion merge in opposing negative forces that affect humanity.

Two versions exist of *Exorcist II*'s climax. The European version ends with Lamont's death fighting the demonic Regan and tearing out her heart. Holding the dead Sharon in her arms, Dr. Tuskin looks at Regan who is now conscious of her special powers. The American version concludes with Lamont alive. Unlike Father Karras he recognizes affinity with his female side. Rejecting Catholic patriarchal authority, he accepts a feminist salvation offered by Regan, defeating the sexually possessive urges toward her the demon promoted. By doing this he advances beyond the violent masculinity that characterizes Father Karras's final assault upon the demonic Regan in the earlier film. Denying his religion's patriarchal authority and freely relinquishing power to a young woman, he obtains both a personal and revolutionary salvation. Walking up to the dying Sharon, who confesses, "I chose evil," Lamont understands her dilemma, choosing to sympathize not condemn, comforting her before death. "No Sharon. Your hunger for belief was your truth. Deo absolve nominis patri." Dr. Tuskin entrusts Regan into his care and sees them both walk away. The final image shows her face lit up by a police car. Her transcendental expression reveals higher awareness of a new world order, uniting all opposites, moving toward positive human development. By emphasizing the female and putting the male in a secondary position, both versions of the film are complimentary. *Exorcist II* envisages a future beyond patriarchy and family.

Exorcist II—The Heretic suggests a utopian goal—abolition of all institutional constraints oppressing human development. The film is one of the most revolutionary achievements within the genre, suggesting potentials still unrealized. *Exorcist II* looks toward a time when the genre will eventually wither away. It is a neglected pioneering work whose critical and commercial failure results from deliberate assault on the horror film's traditional boundaries. But horror's fetishistic codes are still strong and dominant. Unlike the Frankenstein and Lewton films, alternative possibilities are no longer brief but instead are capable of realization. However, *Exorcist II* remains a solitary exception. Its radical potentials remain still unrealized. Traditional codes of denial and disavowal still remained powerful.

6

Far from Vietnam: The Family at War

The Vietnam War influenced many 1970s horror films explicitly and implicitly in style and content. With the exception of *The Green Berets* (1968) until nearly a decade later, major Hollywood studios avoided explicit representations of the conflict. However, echoes of the Vietnam War function as subtextual elements in different genres such as westerns, biker movies, and science fiction. They frequently operate as a significant "political unconscious."[1] The horror genre was not exempt, certainly not family horror. Diverse examples such as *Night of the Living Dead* (1968), *Last House on the Left* (1971), *The Night Walk* (1972), *The Crazies* (1973), *The Hills Have Eyes* (1977), and *Dawn of the Dead* (1979) significantly associate family institutions with the Vietnam War.

Family, fatherland, or motherland are rhetorical devices emotionally manipulated in any wartime situation. During the Vietnam War, President Johnson used Puritan Captivity Narrative motifs, contrasting South Vietnam's agrarian "City on the Hill" with marauding, demonic, Indianlike Viet Cong. Richard Slotkin reveals connections between Western frontier imagery and contemporary descriptions of war situations.[2] The former influences 1970s horror films such as *The Texas Chain Saw Massacre* and *Race with the Devil* (1975). Puritan Captivity Narrative imagery occurs in one interesting 1984 prerevolutionary horror film—Avery Crouse's *Eyes of Fire*. It displays pertinent cultural traditions linking demonic forces with family repression.[3] A common motif in all these films is a state of siege where the family unit struggles against outside forces. These forces represent distorted embodiments of repressed tensions. Understanding these influences reveals the reasons why so many Vietnam films and literature present the conflict as a peculiarly American dilemma. Cultural perspectives, mediated via family and popular culture, play a crucial role, forming most of the Vietnam generation's perceptions of the conflict. Oliver Stone's *Born on the Fourth of July* (1989) presents Mrs. Kovic (Caroline Kava) as a malign influence that molds her Ron (Tom Cruise) to fight communism. She represents an equivalent of the horror genre's monstrous-feminine whom Ron must expel from the text to undergo his personal odyssey toward remasculinization.[4] Several contemporary horror films use Vietnam's traumatic effect on American society making relevant metaphoric connections, explicitly (*The Night Walk*) and implicitly (the vast majority of representations). Homeland protection means defense of the family from violation. The enemy is a demonized "other." However, during the 1960s and 1970s, ample evidence appeared documenting American atrocities against the Vietnamese people. Ideologic codes were thrown into crisis. The average American farm boy soldier was no longer Audie Murphy but a cold-blooded killer. Certain contemporary horror films suggest violence as the inevitable outcome of socially conditioned repression. The family plays a crucial role here. What if the monster now came from the American family as in *The Night Walk*? Or *Forbidden Planet*'s creature from the id now became *The Night Walk*'s Andy, Romero's zombies, and Craven's shadow families? Tobe Hooper's *The Texas Chain Saw Massacre 2* (1985) introduces another member of the Sawyer family—Vietnam veteran Chop Top. In *Apocalypse Now* (1979), Vietnam alone does not make Kurtz and Willard killers. A cold, technological bureaucratic society, using administrative jargon such as "terminate with extreme prejudice," produces killers, especially family produced masculine monsters.

During the 1979 Toronto Film Festival, Wes Craven associated America's various wars with family repression.

> The family is the best microcosm to work with. If you go much beyond that you're getting away from a lot of our roots of our own primeval feelings. . . . It's very much where most of our strong emotions or gut feelings come from . . . from those very early experiences and how those are worked out. I grew up in a white working class family that was very religious. There was an enormous amount of secrecy in the general commerce of our getting along with each other. Certain things were not mentioned. A lot of things were not spoken of or talked about. If there was an argument, it was immediately denied. If there was a feeling it was repressed. As I got older, I began to see that as a nation we were doing the same things. Most of us grew up thinking the Indian was the bad guy who mysteriously disappeared. We never thought that we might have exterminated all indigenous nations in the United States to get their land. Most of us

did not look very carefully at what we were doing. We didn't look at how we got Puerto Rico and most of Texas and what happened in the Bay of Pigs. We are just finding out now what really happened. So it was a nation that was very much kept secret.

In *The Hills Have Eyes*, nobody even tells anybody what they saw. Everybody's trying to protect everyone else, so nobody tells the truth, (which) costs us in time and unpreparedness because you're not psychically facing what really is happening. So within the family I feel there are all these things. It's not that there are violent people out there waiting to break into our own affluent circle. No. We are those people. It's like in the 'sixties. We are not the enemy. They're us. We have done the most violent things. . . . There's a famous phrase in the United States: "Why are we dragging these things out? Why do we have to talk about Vietnam again? It's over." It's not over with—it's going to come in through another door.[5]

One significant play noted this denial. Produced by Joseph Papp for the New York Shakespeare Festival Public Theatre in 1971, David Rabe's *Sticks and Bones* delivered a devastating assault on the relationship between American family values and the Vietnam War. Written as an ironic assault upon manufactured ideologic values generated through a favorite long-running TV sitcom, *The Adventures of Ozzie and Harriet*, Rabe turns the format on its head by delivering a scathing attack on an institution created and nourished by a consumer capitalism constantly disavowing dependence upon American military imperialism. Beginning in a TV room, the play depicts a crisis situation when the Nelson family confront their blinded veteran son David and the ugly realities he brings into their lives. Nurtured by junk culture, Ozzie, Harriet, and Ricky live in a cocooned world oblivious to the Vietnam War. As Pamela Cooper points out, "Ozzie's family is a microcosm of the American capitalist culture which has bred the media, the journalists, ultimately the war itself."[6] They have to confront one living example of Vietnam's human wreckage, that is, their son David, whose blindness elevates him into a world of different realities that disrupt the family's imaginary existence. As Rabe indicates in his "Author's Note": "In any society there is an image of how the perfectly happy family should appear. It is this image that the people in this play wish to preserve above all else."[7] David's assault upon this image exposes family racism and leads Ozzie to finally murder David's Vietnamese lover Zung. Behind the conventional family façade lies repressed hostilities that eventually erupt into violence.

Sticks and Bones moves toward this logical conclusion. The first act presents the family's difficulties in understanding and describing what is happening, and the second act shows them destroying each other. To restore family unity, Ozzie murders Zung, literally expelling Vietnam from the American narrative. David commits suicide under family pressure, thus removing his threatening presence from its complacent historic ignorance. As Cooper eloquently states, David "embodies the threat of exposure to reality, and is the living expression of his parents' own repressed guilt, hatred, and hostility. As the invader who becomes a victim, David has both a symbolic and naturalistic function in the play. Through him, Rabe extends the metaphor of battle to the home front: his power struggle with his father is war in the domestic arena."[8]

Sticks and Bones is crucial in understanding Vietnam family horror films. As in Rabe's work, the war returns home either in the figure of a wounded son or other metaphoric guises such as zombies. These latter figures allegorize aggressive cannibalistic desires returning to the homefront with a vengeance.

◆ ◆ ◆

Paul Schrader's *Rolling Thunder* (1977) screenplay and Coppola's *Apocalypse Now* also illustrate violent patriarchal psychopathology. Vietnam is clearly an excuse. Conditioning has already occurred. Despite condoning Major Rane (William Devane), Schrader's collaborative screenplay reveals the deep psychosis within violent masculinity. Returning home to San Antonio in 1973 after five years as a North Vietnam POW, Rane describes the experience as making him and his colleague Sgt. Vohden (Tommy Lee Jones) "better Americans." Once he is home, he faces a wife who wishes a divorce and an alienated son. A gang attacks his home and tortures him to reveal the location of money San Antonio donated to him during captivity. As if recognizing the selfishness behind his refusal, they shoot him and his family, commenting, "Big macho man." The gang function as Rane's repressed unconscious by also eliminating his troublesome family. He exhibits "manly" silence under extreme pain when the gang thrusts his hand into a garbage disposal slicing it to shreds. Refusing to deposit the money in a bank, Rane's patriarchal stubbornness results in his family's destruction. Like Nathan Slaughter, he openly welcomes violent outside forces. Awakening in hospital, a metal claw replacing his right hand, Rane's only thought is to find "the men who killed my son." With pliant groupie Linda (Linda Haynes), a master sergeant's daughter who both teaches him to shoot with his left hand and sexually disproves his fears of impotence, Rane sets out in pursuit. "Rescuing" Vohden from uncomfortable domestic surroundings, he dons his uniform and avenges male pride. *Rolling Thunder* presents a bleak message: violence is the only catharsis for Vietnam veterans frustrated by years of long captivity and unfulfilling family life.

◆ ◆ ◆

Stylistically *Apocalypse Now* combines not just visual motifs from horror and Vietnam War movies but other films such as conspiracy thrillers, Westerns, films noir, detective thrillers, Godardian avant-gardes, and literary adaptations, which leads Kim Newman to describe the entire work as a "Genre holocaust."[9] Although *Apocalypse Now*'s intertextual structure resembles postmodernist pastiche construction, its dominant visual motifs are film noir and horror, a union foreshadowed in Val Lewton films. Following Kurtz's passage up the river, Willard becomes fascinated with his quarry's personality, a fascination akin to that between hunter and monster in classic horror films. Kurtz's final appearance two thirds into the film, surrounded by darkness, visually evokes the monster's appearance within horror. But the monstrous quarry turns pursuer into a fellow monster, emphasizing an intrinsic connection between supposed opposites. *Apocalypse Now* has several associations with breaking traditional barriers of contemporary horror. It represents Willard and Kurtz as monsters from the military-political establishment's id. The CIA and military institutions wish to deny its own creations. They order Willard to "terminate with extreme prejudice." Both men were once typical, conformist Americans. Heroes are now adrift within a chaotic, historical situation. Newman sees *Apocalypse Now* as the product of an era where the "horrors and neuroses of the age have had to percolate through the entire stratum of cinema."[10]

When Willard and Kurtz unite physically and mentally, *Apocalypse Now* anticipates male Gothic Vietnam movies of the 1980s such as *Platoon* (1986) and *Off Limits* (1988), which also contain a similar blending of identities. Uniting film noir and Gothic horror, these films show American values as the real source of problems affecting Vietnam. For Oliver Stone, Sgt. Barnes is a psychopathic Captain Ahab. Stone reduces Vietnam's crucial historical and political implications to an Oedipal battle between two fathers for the son's soul. In *Apocalypse Now*, Kurtz's (Marlon Brando) only concern in his last hours is for Willard (Martin Sheen) to reveal the truth to his son. Willard reads Kurtz's letters to his son during the boat journey up the river. Like Major Rane, women are less significant for these fathers. Willard has no son. Returning home after his first tour of duty, he only "spoke once" to agree to a divorce. "Groomed for the top slot in the corporation," Kurtz reneges from family and military values by becoming a violent monster. Although rejected by the High Command, he really pursues the logical policies of American imperialism, policies homefront beneficiaries disavow. Vietnam has not made monsters but provided a cataclysmic environment for male violence that is repressed within military and family institutions.

◆　◆　◆

George Romero's *Night of the Living Dead* (1968) appeared in a year of political and social turmoil. Although it does not have the direct allegorical associations of *The Night Walk* or *The Crazies* (1973), Vietnam is a "political unconscious" that structures the text. *Night of the Living Dead* shares two components within *Sticks and Bones*: the family's warring, cannibalistic nature and media denial of unpleasant realities. Although *Night* does not operate as a direct Vietnam allegory, the conflict hovers on the margins of the text, unconsciously influencing it like a Lacanian "structured absence." *Night* is essentially an apocalyptic horror film. Its sadism, violence, and perversion represent the breakdown of surplus repressive mechanisms that maintain bourgeois notions of sexuality and logically culminate in characters devouring each other physically and metaphorically.[11]

This does not rule out other meanings. As Sumiko Higashi notes, the metaphor could "include Western consumption and imperialist exploitation of Third World peoples," including the Vietnamese.[12] On this analogy the zombies represent a politically unconscious version of the "return of the repressed," bearing unpalatable truths by their very presence and attacking normal values as David does in *Sticks and Bones*. *Night* is the cinematic extension of Rabe's play.[13]

Night opens on a deserted country road. A car gradually approaches the camera. Successive shots show it moving into an old cemetery, its sign splattered with mud, illustrating affluent America's neglect and erasure of the dead. As the car slowly drives past tombstones, a long shot places the Stars and Stripes in the foreground. Romero's credit appears superimposed over the flag. A young brother (Russell Streiner) and sister (Judith O'Dea) emerge from the car. Dialogue emphasizes the visit as a family obligation, one resented by Johnny but dutifully accepted by Barbara. They bring a manufactured cross wreath to place before the grave of a barely remembered father. Johnny caustically expresses his feelings concerning mother's role in this journey. He says, "We have to move mother out here or move the grave to Pittsburgh. We still remember. I don't even remember what the man looks like so we drive three hundred miles into the country and she stays home!"

Arriving there on Sunday, the first day of daylight saving time, the couple stand before the grave. Barbara kneels down to pray while Johnny stands by impatiently contemptuous of the whole ritual. He also suspects local officials of removing the wreath after their annual visit, repainting it, and selling it to them again. Johnny cynically understands capitalist profit motivations behind reusable consumption. Spiritual values are non-profitable. He impatiently urges Barbara on, "Come on Barbara. Church was this morning. No real sense in going to Church." Thunder booms followed by a lightning flash. As a man wanders in the distance, Johnny decides to reenact a childhood incident, thereby frightening his sister. Recalling grandfather's earlier admonition, "Boy, you'll be darned to hell," he begins teasing her, "They're coming to get you, Barbara." His actions foreshadow his final appearance in the film as a devouring ghoul dragging his sister outside. Johnny's behavior also reveals repressed hostility and orally aggressive incestuous desires. However, his recycled repetition of childhood fantasies results in his death and Barbara's flight to a deserted farmhouse.

Even the seemingly deserted house contains a hidden example of unrestrained consumption. Exploring the interior Barbara discovers a half-eaten face upstairs. About to rush outside, she encounters Ben (Duane Jones). He immediately begins to take charge of the situation. Although Romero places no emphasis on Ben's racial origins, it recalls a Vietnam situation of nonwhite ethnic groups bearing an overly proportionate share of combat during the conflict. However, as the film develops, the issue becomes less one of heroic Black versus cowardly Whites but more irrational aspects of destructive masculinity, a theme Romero develops in the remake as well as in other films.

Eventually, they discover others in the house who represent two family types—a traditional nuclear family (Harry, Helen, and injured daughter) and Tom and Judy, the horror genre's surviving young couple who usually walk away into the traditional sunset. *Night*, however, presents everyone as flawed, destructive, and irrational, constantly at war with each other, trapped within family gender constraints that head toward annihilation. Although no Vietnamese appear in *Night*, the zombies metaphorically express the war returning to America. Paralleling Puritan Captivity Narrative demonic Indians, they embody American repressions returning to confront a paranoid nation that is unable to project them elsewhere.

Like Johnny and Barbara, *Night's* second family unit is also divided. Together only because of daughter Karen who is sick from a zombie bite, they exist in a state of mutual tension and loathing. *Night* contains succinct parallels between Johnny and Barbara and Harry and Helen. Both males dominate females within the family. Frustrated, trapped males resort to frightening or bullying women to compensate for masculine insecurity. When Johnny returns as a cannibalistic zombie, taking orally aggressive incestuous desires to their logical conclusions, young Karen revives to enact grotesquely family tensions by partially eating father and stabbing mother. The family breeds cannibalism and violence. Both women also passively submit to their deaths, enacting conservative Freudian tenets concerning women's place within patriarchal society, a scenario Romero changes in the later version.[14]

Although Ben is a single male, he becomes involved in a masculine one-upmanship contest that destroys any potential for united action. Ironically, neither Father (Black or White) really knows what is Best. The conflict occurs in the home, a battleground between two males competing for space and territory. They refuse to unite against a common enemy. The battle occurs inside and outside; the ghouls embody repressed family tensions.

Romero constantly destabilizes his characters within particular sections of the frame, illustrating family tensions and media lies. When Johnny and Barbara go through the graveyard, the camera tilts down from an overhead shot of the sky to frame them awkwardly at the right. This occurs while Johnny complains about the visit. As Barbara runs from the pursuing ghoul who has "come to get her," rapidly edited, left-and-right tilted camera angles stress frenzied pursuit. Although supposedly safe in the house, a quick jump-cut association of shots shows a number of animal heads on the wall, hinting at *Night's* reversal of the boundaries that involve the once separate realms of human and animal. After Ben orders Barbara to search for wood, the camera pans diagonally right from a mountain lion's head to a music box. As Barbara touches it, the instrument begins to play. The next shot shows her fragile face fragmented through the box's opening panels. Finally sitting alone in the house listening to radio reports of cannibalism, a series of intercut shots alternate between zoom-ins to her face and a radio dial, leading to an abrupt close-up of a hand emerging from the cellar door.

Although television news shots appear formally composed in contrast with *Night's* mainly visual paranoid style, one Washington, D.C., shot uses a handheld camera to reveal government instability behind the news media's reassuring composure.[15] The news report contains contradictory statements, which ironically results in Tom's and Judy's deaths when they learn of a supposedly safe rescue station and attempt to pump gas into the truck.

Caught within their own private worlds, *Night's* families refuse to unite against a common enemy embodying repressed paranoia. Described in the radio broadcast as "ordinary people in a state of trance" who are engaging in an unprecedented epidemic of murder, the zombies appear to be ordinary people, young and old silent majority representatives in various stages of decomposition. They logically represent the implications of America's culture of consumption, a culture highly dependent on Third World and Vietnam exploitation. While living families verbally tear themselves apart, the living dead dismember their victim's flesh before redneck hunters arrive. This last group engage in a "search and destroy" mission, using attack dogs as in Vietnam, shooting anyone (whether living or dead) indiscriminately.[16] Filmed from a helicopter at the start of *Night*'s final sequence, the group appears indistinguishable from its quarry and is often accompanied by the same type of bland media commentary that accompanied GIs during Vietnamese "search and destroy" missions. Like Harry Cooper they shoot first rather than ask questions.

Night breaks the last generic taboo when the hunters shoot Ben, the final survivor, eventually dragging his body out to burn on a funeral pyre. Shot in grainy black and white documentary footage, the image echoes Vietnam reportage, as does the last live shot of a flame emerging from the funeral pyre with unmistakable napalm associations.

The family lies at the heart of *Night of the Living Dead*. Romero's zombies are the logical successors to Hitchcock's winged aggressors in *The Birds*, arising like Furies responding to psychological tensions. Six years later the assault is more vicious and abhorrent. Family ties contain seeds of disaster. Judy's desire to join Tom in the truck leads to their deaths. Barbara and Helen eventually submit to living dead monsters who are enacting aggressive desires. Ben and Harry engage in an antagonistic patriarchal contest over control of the home. Their monstrous doubles patiently wait outside, hoping to continue human power struggles to their most logical conclusions. While America fights and lies to itself in a besieged house, its military machine ruthlessly attacks a Third World nation that stubbornly refuses to be a convenient demonic "other." Operating within a different generic code, *Night* understands what contemporary American and later Hollywood productions always attempt to avoid: the enemy is really us. As a family horror movie emerging from a particular historical era, *Night of the Living Dead* is one of American cinema's most important cultural achievements.

◆　◆　◆

Wes Craven's *The Last House on the Left* continues this assault.[17] Violent outside forces attack a seemingly pure family. Reworking Ingmar Bergman's *The Virgin Spring* (1958), *Last House* emphasizes that its dark family group actually represent violent forces within the average family. Unlike Kathryn Bigelow's *After Dark* (1985), which illustrates Reagan era conservative tendencies by separating "good" and "bad" families, *Last House* explicitly equates the two. Emerging from a different historical era when America did not depict Vietnam as a "noble crusade," *Last House* reflected a country facing involvement in a war involving military atrocities against innocent people. For Wes Craven, both Stillos and Collingwoods are "us."

Last House begins by depicting opposites, gradually blurring barriers, until the audience's emotional involvement with violent actions leads not to catharsis but self-disgust and self-awareness. Although the film appears violently pornographic on the surface, it is far different from later slasher films. Although works of the 1980s emotionally manipulate their audiences into willing complicity and sadistic voyeurism, *Last House* condemns any audience member who complies with excessive violent displays. It is an extremely complex film that unveils an ugly sadistic lust most horror films pander to. Violence corrupts perpetrators and voyeuristic viewers. By presenting the horror of violence, *Last House* confronts every viewer with the direct implications of the genre's spectacular experience. Like Hitchcock's work, *Last House* presents a bleak picture that stimulates viewers to recognize associations with the world outside.

Although contemporary youth culture preferred distinguishing themselves from their less-fortunate working-class counterparts in Vietnam, they inextricably shared in the decade's violence. Certain youth culture movements vociferously condemning the Vietnam War cathartically reveled in a violent America that engendered not only the Manson Family but the aggressive stage acts of The Doors, Janis Joplin, Jimi Hendrix, Alice Cooper, and The Who—a rock fashion that had its final dark culmination in The Rolling Stones Altamont performance. Michael Herr's *Dispatches* notes significant parallels between Vietnam and the West Coast cultural matrix of rock and cinema. The peace movement was by no means peaceful in its demonstrations, its CND locket worn by violent activists as well as Scorpio in *Dirty Harry* (1971). John Collingwood presents such a locket to his daughter Mari in *Last House*'s opening scenes, remarking on the incongruity between her membership of the "love generation" and her interest in "Bloodlust," a rock group that dismembers live chickens as part of their stage act. The Collingwood family live in the American Dream's self-deceptive image; it contains disturbing contradictions they choose to ignore.

The Stillo family represents the Collingwood's dark side. Like Tom Doniphon and Liberty Valance in Ford's *The Man Who Shot Liberty Valance*, they mirror each other in a repressive social structure. *Last House* explicitly reveals the violence within such repression. While one family represses its dark desires, living a 1970s version of *Father Knows Best*, the other exists in an oppressive world, nakedly exhibiting the Collingwood family's dominant power-structures. Like *Night of the Living Dead*, Vietnam lurks as an absent factor that structures *Last House*'s violent excessiveness. The Collingwoods and the Stillos represent the difference between America's delusive view of itself and the brutal violence unleashed outside in a far country, a violence returning home to confront its beneficiaries. John and Estelle Collingwood initially believe in their respectable distance from violence and excessive sexuality. But, as the climax reveals, the two worlds are not so far apart. One brief scene shows a sheriff's deputy reading a *Classics Illustrated* edition of *Caesar's Conquests*. Although shot for laughs, the scene's humorous intent cannot entirely deny associations with America's overseas imperialist venture.

Last House opens with Mari Collingwood's (Sandra Cassel) idyllic countryside home. As she showers a Norman Rockwellesque mailman delivers her birthday cards. During these opening scenes, a ballad commences. Its prominent lines tell of a road that "leads to nowhere. And the castle stays the same. And the father tells the mother 'wait for the rain.'" Unlike *The Virgin Spring*, where the road did lead somewhere, *Last House* presents a contemporary nihilistic vision of an era when institutional roads lead nowhere. The song punctuates key segments throughout the film.

Subsequent scenes reveal repressed sexuality within the Collingwood household. They contradict the initial peaceful imagery. Noting his daughter's breasts, John (Gaylord St. James) complains that she is not wearing a bra. Mari rebuts her mother Estelle's (Cynthia Carr) moral support of father, referring to her torpedo bras of the 1950s that tied breasts up "like little lunatics in a straitjacket." John sees similar contradictions between Mari's membership of the peace generation and her affinity for Bloodlust. The Collingwood family represses the violence and sexuality excessively seen in the Stillos.

As cinematic descendants of Fenimore Cooper's Bush clan, the Stillo family is a grotesque caricature of American family life. Krogh Stillo (David Hess) has served time for the triple slaying of a priest and two nuns. His partner Weasel's (Fred Lincoln) crimes include child molesting, Peeping Tomism, and assault with a deadly weapon. Krogh keeps his son Junior (Marc Sheffler) firmly under parental control with heroin injections. Predatory, witch-like Sadie (Jeramie Rain) is the group's mother-figure. This dark family has Western counterparts such as the Clantons in Ford's *My Darling Clementine*, the Cleggs in *Wagonmaster*, and the Hammonds in Peckinpah's *Ride the High Country*. Like the Tobins in *Man of the West* and Hooper's slaughterhouse family, they are extremely dangerous. Although Marx dismissed the European "idiocy of country life," American cultural representations present a much darker picture of economic and geographical losers.

Last House parallels both families. The Stillos secretly yearn for respectability, wanting new names and identities to escape their present outlaw status to become a normal family like the Collingwoods. After murdering Mari and her friend Phyllis, they change into respectable middle-class attire. Sadie acts as a mother figure toward Junior and regrets his inability to get on with his father. Krogh conceived him at the age of fifteen. "It sort of broke him very short having responsibility." While John Collingwood accepted his social duties, Krogh's early assumption of parental care pushed him toward a life of crime and murder. Stillo father-son tensions echo Collingwood father-daughter alienation. When John fails to make Mari conform, Krogh uses more dangerous means to ensure parental obedience. Junior is merely an object who has to obey. His name articulates his demeaning status; he has no identity in his own right. In one of *Last House*'s most poignant scenes, Mari attempts to reach him, finding out that beneath the pain lies a gentle being whom she renames Willow. His life reveals continual physical and mental abuse within the family.

Seeing Mari and Phyllis slumming in a dangerous area, the Stillos kidnap them. As they indulge in sexual appetites, juxtaposed shots show the Collingwood birthday preparations. John's tasting of the cream on Mari's birthday cake ironically echoes Weasel's earlier comment to Sadie, "You've got the cream of American manhood." John kisses Estelle, "It's truly respectable. I want to attack you." His behavior is reminiscent of the married couples in *Psycho* who choose a night in a sleazy hotel to engage in cheap thrills which are taboo within repressive marital relationships.

Last House reveals the brutal effects of such taboos. Civilization rests upon repressing alternative channels of desire that often erupt in sexually violent forms. To its credit *Last House* depicts the violence brutally but not pornographically. The Stillos begin a morning drive. As their car travels through the beautiful countryside of the film's opening shots, the landscape cinematically changes. As the camera tracks right, a rapid succession of shots reveals the river swirling like a raging torrent. Violence begins to pollute the formerly peaceful countryside. As alter egos to the Collingwoods, the Stillos enact the dark consequences of repressed family violence. John Collingwood's repressed desires emerge in monstrous form. The Stillos viciously abuse and murder the two girls, taking family control to its most logical conclusions. The deaths are filmed in a documentary style resembling concentration camp and Vietnam war footage, a style also used in the closing images of both versions of *Night of the Living Dead*. Mari resembles a helpless camp victim who walks to her death in the lake after Junior vainly attempts to save her.

Craven films the murders graphically and brutally; he allows viewers neither sensory pleasure nor distancing special effects. He depicts the total ugliness and brutality of violence without using the distancing spectacular mechanisms present in most horror films. But other features emerge. Despite their self-indulgent slaughter, the Stillos stand alone, silent, disgusted, realizing what they have done. They never appear as distanced brutal monsters. In spite of (and because of) their atrocities, they are still identifiable human beings. Because they have the capacity to feel disgust for their acts, they are capable of redemption.

But like so many brief possibilities within the genre, the opportunity never arises. As a generic product, emerging from a particular cultural tradition, involving the inevitability of violence and self-destructive Last Stands, *Last House* moves to its final cataclysm. Accidentally discovering the Stillos' involvement, the Collingwoods plan a brutal revenge. Victimizers become victims. The Stillos arrive at the Collingwood home never suspecting Jacobean revenge feelings lurking within their seemingly kind hosts. Weasel awakes from a dream in which he imagines the Collingwoods knocking out his teeth with a chisel. His nightmare becomes reality. Estelle entices him outside. After she ties him up, she bites off his penis; she then slashes Sadie to death. Krogh forces Junior to commit suicide after he attempts to defend John Collingwood, but Krogh's physical prowess proves useless before John Collingwood's chainsaw.

The final scene reveals a grim aftermath. As a sheriff arrives, the Collingwoods embrace, silently self-aware of the enormity of their actions. They resemble the Stillos, now realizing the violent tendencies that were once hidden beneath a normal family exterior. The image freezes. There is no external enemy functioning as a convenient scapegoat like a Frankenstein monster or demonic child. The real enemy is the family whose repressive mechanisms result in atrocities. For *The Last House on the Left*, the road leads to nowhere.

◆　◆　◆

Bob Clark's *The Night Walk* is one of the earliest films that dealt with the family producing a monster during the Vietnam conflict. Like one of Leslie A. Fiedler's heroes in *Love and Death in the American Novel*, Andy Brooks (Richard Backus) flees to the Vietnam wilderness to escape his suffocating mother's influence. Whatever his home situation, he still serves God, country, and family. Unlike Huckleberry Finn his "lighting out" for new territory has disastrous consequences. Although he is killed in action, he hears his mother's voice willing him back to life. He returns as a disintegrating vampire to "bring the war home" to a society that has used him to further its aggressive aims. Donning the uniform that denotes him as patriotic savior and future embodiment of the status quo, he drinks his hometown's blood, whether from a friendly truck driver, family doctor, or girlfriend, ironically replacing the blood shed on his tour of duty. Confronting draft board head Dr. Allman (Henderson Forsythe), who obviously ignored Andy's traumatic family circumstances to send him out in furtherance of American imperialism, Andy tells him that having died for America he, in turn, must undergo the same process, albeit by a vampire that embodies the real nature of American involvement. As a blood-sucking zombie, Andy undertakes those very actions political cartoonists frequently condemned the White House for. But Andy's condition originates from the family—a monstrous product of society has returned demanding recognition from the very institution that sent him to Vietnam and expected him to take his place as a future husband and father.

Andy's condition metaphorically represents the logical outcome of patriarchal conditioning. Unfeeling, operating like a dehumanized automaton, having no identity beyond military and family roles, Andy is the ultimate embodiment of patriarchy's dutiful son. But he turns against the institution that produced him by vampirizing girlfriend and future wife Joanne (Jane Daly)—reacting against a figure whose ideologically approved role will further entrap him. Like *Alice, Sweet Alice* (a.k.a. *Communion* [1976]), *The Night Walk* incisively reveals the family tensions that trap everyone within restrictive roles. Christine (Lynn Carlin) and Charles (John Marley) Brooks have ceased to have any real affection for one another, enduring their miserable existence by whatever substitutionary forms exist. Complicit in her own self-oppression, Christine dotes on Andy, devoting all her energies toward making him her ideal male. Like Harriet in *Sticks and Bones*, she denies the dangerous reality of a situation that affects her own family. Ignoring his lonely daughter Cathy (Anya Ormsby), excluded from Christine and Andy, Charles finds companionship with the family dog or withdraws into alcoholic oblivion. Finding no other alternatives, Cathy accepts her subordinate role within the family. Filmed a year before American withdrawal at a time when foreign policy toward Vietnam reached total disintegration, *The Night Walk* astutely depicts a weak family situation where the return of a decomposing son hastens internal collapse. Shocked at his son's final appearance, Charles commits suicide while Christine drives Andy to a graveyard. Insanely singing the lullaby that accompanied Andy's return to life in the opening sequences, she covers the grave containing his rapidly decomposing corpse. Family and American foreign policy collapse before a being that represents its logically monstrous consequences.[18]

♦ ♦ ♦

George Romero's *The Crazies* continues the Vietnam associations begun in *Night of the Living Dead*, developing connections between family and politics that culminate in *Dawn of the Dead* and *Day of the Dead*. Biological warfare material accidentally infects the water supply in Pittsburgh's Evans City district causing sections of the population to go insane. This insanity releases socially repressed tensions that erupt both violently and sexually. The precredit sequence replays elements from *Night of the Living Dead*. Like Barbara and Johnny, a young brother and sister enact family tensions.[19] A father interrupts the children's game where the brother teases his sister by pretending to be a monster. Having murdered his wife, he sets the house on fire. Later in the film, a harmless-looking grandmother stabs a soldier in the eye with her knitting needle, avenging herself on a social structure that has condemned her to a useless senior-citizen status. Another family enacts repressed incestuous desires when a father and daughter indulge in forbidden sexual activity.

Although the stated cause for the virus is an incompetent cover-up by the military of biological warfare contamination (obviously destined for Vietnam at that time), the actual craziness really represents family repressed desires as the precredit sequence reveals. Family and military are both authoritarian institutions. The Army quarantine of the indigenous population parallels Vietnamese relocation. *The Crazies* reveals a society steadily disintegrating. Neither military nor scientific establishments are in control. *The Crazies* reveals disintegration of all levels of civilized society—family, law, science, medical, military, and government. All are interdependent structures and collapse like a fragile house of cards. Romero sees wider implications arising from family horror—an insight that makes his work extremely insightful.

The central characters are a trio that anticipates Romero's development of the triangular motif in *Dawn* and *Day*. David (W. G. McMillan) and Clank (Harold Wayne Jones) are veterans. While Clank was regular Army, David managed to join the Green Berets. However, like Peter in *Dawn*, David exhibits a sensibility that is at odds with his military background, which is critical of social masculinity. He tells his pregnant girlfriend Judy (Lane Carroll) he regrets his former machismo values, recognizing them as social constructions. David knows the mental damage to his personality, noting associations between success in becoming "Evans City's only Green Beret" and his days as a high school football hero. He rejects macho values of school and military machines. Anticipating Romero's other oppositional male characters, David is the film's most sympathetic character. Although he is living with Judy, they have no immediate plans to marry, and begin family life. Gentle and sensitive despite his military background, David's nature explains why he never suffers from the virus. Clank steadily becomes violent, anticipating the characterization of *Dawn's* Roger. Judy also exhibits signs of instability. Both die at the hands of official and unofficial forces of a violent America. The military shoot Clank while a gang of prowling teenagers (paralleling *Night's* redneck posse) kill Judy on their own "search and destroy" mission.

Many scenes have undeniable Vietnam associations which make explicit *Night's* implicit images.[20] The disintegrating chaos of *The Crazies* has political connotations. A protesting priest immolates himself with a Zippo lighter. Some troops burn corpses with flame throwers. Shot through the head, Clank's death parallels Eddie Adams's 1968 photo of the death of a Viet Cong suspect. A helicopter chases David and his group through the woods. He shoots it down as easily as the Viet Cong were able to defeat their technologically advanced foe by using the simplest weapon. Beginning with a family situation breakdown, *The Crazies* extends this to the world outside, revealing intrinsic connections between family values and military/political structures.

◆ ◆ ◆

The Hills Have Eyes uses a similar family binary oppositional structure as *The Last House on The Left.* Like *The Texas Chain Saw Massacre* and *Race with the Devil*, *The Hills Have Eyes* fuses several Hollywood genres—horror, the western, and the road movie.[21] Classic Puritan Captivity Narrative conflict appears between the Carters and the cannibal family. Thanks to technology the formerly static homestead is now on wheels, but it is still liable to Indian assault whenever it stops for the night. Although the cannibal family lacks the demonic associations of their counterparts in *Race with the Devil*, there are several significant parallels. Both are losers in the affluent American Dream. Craven's dark family is the most extreme example. Furthermore, the marauding family's cannibalistic activities echo Puritan fears of ritualistic Witches' Sabbath activities. Finally, *The Hills Have Eyes* contains political features not too distant from contemporary audiences. The cannibal family subsist on an American Air Force nuclear test site, constantly used by low-flying fighter planes. Despite living in this dangerous environment, subject to constant death and annihilation, they survive by using captured technological items from their enemies such as binoculars and walkie-talkies. The family's tribal structure and stubborn existence within a nuclear testing site recall a people General Curtis LeMay threatened to bomb "into the Stone Age." It also echoes Viet Cong tenacity in using guerilla tactics against a technologically superior enemy. As with *Sticks and Bones, Night of the Living Dead, The Last House on the Left,* and *The Night Walk,* an affluent American family face their dark opposites. Craven's surviving family members understand the nature of concealed and repressed brutal energies—knowledge that enables them to live a privileged existence. In the final battle they draw on American practical know-how and hidden reserves of violence to defeat their enemies. At the conclusion Doug realizes the dark realities hidden beneath the American Dream—a nightmarish violent reaction against any enemies whether they are internal economic losers or demonic Vietnamese who threaten the national interest.

The film's opening scene shows Grandfather Freddy attempting to flee the area, telling his granddaughter Ruby that her family has gone too far in their marauding activities. He wishes to leave before the Air Force, state troopers, and National Guard investigate. Up to this point he has been a willing accomplice. However, because the last robbery involved a successful attack on an Air Force PX, Freddy realizes that government investigations may reveal his complicity. Freddy's activities resemble those of corrupt South Vietnamese officials. Attempting to barter whisky and radios for essential food to combat starvation, Ruby hopes to leave with him. Like Junior in *The Last House on the Left,* she wishes to begin a new life and break away from violent family control. Freddy caustically dashes her hopes, emphasizing her lack of civilized refinement; he condemns her to the savage existence from which she wishes to escape; "Do you think you could pass for regular folks? . . . You stink like a hog." Living in a formerly prosperous area, now deserted, he left his mutant son to die after splitting his head with a tire iron in 1939, believing him responsible for burning down his home and killing his infant daughter. Resenting his son for causing the death of his wife in childbirth, he sought any convenient excuse to expel him from the home. Jupiter, however, survived, kidnapped a whore, and reared his own family: Mars, Pluto, Mercury, and Ruby. Rejected by father and, affluent society, they live a precarious existence in the desert, avoiding starvation by kidnapping and eating affluent vacationers. Although Jupiter's activities are inexcusable, he and his family are demonic Furies that haunt the American Dream which unjustifiably excludes them. Rather than recognize his past guilt, Freddy regards Jupiter in Puritan cultural terms as a "devil kid" who grew into a "devil man," ignoring the relevant social conditions that influence his rejected family's activities.

When the Carter family arrives, Freddy hides Ruby and warns them to stay on the main road. Traveling from Columbus, Ohio, the Carter family is an affluent beneficiary of the American Dream. Dominated by overbearing, ex-law officer Big Bob Carter, retired after twenty-five years on the force, the predominantly female family unit meekly submits to him.

Apart from attempting to balance Bob's blunt patriarchal sensibilities with anemic religious feelings and polite gentility, Ethel Carter blithely ignores unpleasant realities and bows to his wishes. Bob sees his family as subordinate; he names its younger members, Bobby and Brenda, with the initial letter of his own name, a practice also applied to household pet Alsatians, Beast and Beauty. The children are little better than animals. All are patriarchal property. Elder daughter Lynn's husband is New Yorker Doug, whom Bob often views suspiciously, measuring him according to masculine definitions. Fulminating against American outsiders, whether they are Blacks from Cleveland or wilderness hillbillies, Bob takes his family to view a "real silver mine" which Ethel's Aunt Mildred left them for their silver anniversary. Bob decides to proceed despite Freddy informing him of the mine's depletion for over forty years (a time period roughly synchronizing with Freddy's abandonment of Jupiter in the wilderness and also ironically recalling the biblical Israelite exile in *Exodus*). Freddy tells Bob about the Air Force's use of the site as a gunnery range, adding ominously, "Now, nobody's back there but animals." Later scenes show Jupiter's family moving quickly, like silent Indians, against the desolate background.

After the Carter family departs, Jupiter blows up Freddy's truck to prevent his escape. Awaiting the expected assault, he utters ominously, "There'll be hell to pay now." The silver mine formed the basis for the area's previous economic prosperity. Both the Carters and Freddy's rejected family have pertinent economic associations as winners and losers in the American Dream. Jupiter's family represents repressed vengeance against a social Darwinist structure that leaves victims to fend for themselves. Jupiter's family later destroys Bob, the patriarchal beneficiary of an economic system that condemns them to starvation and historic erasure. They also avenge those other losers in the American Dream—Blacks and hillbillies—victims whom Bob oppressed in his former law enforcement days.

Despite Freddy's warning Bob decides to find the silver mine. Oblivious to both dangerous low-flying jets and signs marking the presence of a nuclear test site, he urges his family to travel into a hostile wilderness. While the family trailer ventures further into "Indian Country," Jupiter's family keeps them under surveillance using captured binoculars and walkie-talkies. Like their Viet Cong counterparts, they use enemy equipment, eventually attacking when their opponent's technologically advanced vehicle runs into trouble. Jupiter's code name is "Papa Duke," its Vietnam associations anticipate Colonel Kilgore's "Big Duke" of *Apocalypse Now*. Pluto later uses a walkie-talkie to trick Bobby into giving valuable information concerning firepower, recalling Viet Cong access to American communication networks during the post—Tet era. Jupiter's family uses military equipment casually thrown away in the test site. Returning from his expedition, Doug arrives with several items such as wire, noting the amount of material the Army threw away that was financed by his tax dollars. He comments on there being "enough stuff to open an army surplus store." Then (and now) a high percentage of American tax revenue went toward the military budget, destabilizing President Johnson's New Deal aspirations toward the Great Society in the Vietnam era. Much U.S. equipment fell into enemy hands after the ignominious retreat from Saigon in 1975. Contemporary viewers of *The Hills Have Eyes* would be familiar with television footage showing helicopters thrown overboard from aircraft carriers two years before the film's release. A contrast appears between wasteful military expenditure and the revenue that could have transformed America into the democratic aspirations of a welfare society, a program that could have helped Jupiter's family.

Ironically, a low-flying U.S. fighter plane destabilizes Bob's trailer and car. The plane's appearance occurs three times in the narrative and is associated with the silver mine. It first flies over Freddy's gas station when he denies the silver mine's existence. The other two occasions follow Bob's vehement desire to find the mine's location; he believes that Freddy has looted his property. Speeding dangerously on the rudimentary dirt road after the jet's third appearance, wind rushing through the car blows the map (listing the site as a nuclear testing ground) into Bob's face. Brushing it away, he swerves to avoid a jackrabbit and crashes.

Bob and Doug decide to seek help separately, leaving the women and Bobby at the "homestead." Bobby jokingly mimics male authoritarian control over Brenda, a power he does not possess. Ethel fears gigantic poisonous rattlesnakes. Her only wilderness experience is derived from ABC TV's Sunday afternoon *Wild Kingdom of Omaha*. While she seeks "The Lord's help," Lynn discovers a large black tarantula inside their trailer. Both incidents foreshadow later invasions. The tarantula's appearance anticipates Pluto and Mars, who infiltrate the family trailer like marauding Viet Cong.

Adhering to Ethel's request for family prayer, the Carters stand silently outside the trailer. Although Ethel wishes "The Lord to watch over us," succeeding point-of-view long shots ironically reveal demonic forces watching the vulnerable family. After Bob and Doug depart, the remaining group (including Ethel) laugh about an earlier incident in Miami when Beast tore a helpless poodle to pieces. Despite repression, violent tendencies lurk beneath the seemingly placid exterior of an all-American "white bread" family.

Before the ensuing debacle, the Carter family repressively denies any sense of danger. After killing the tarantula, Lynn disavows an unpleasant reality to

Brenda by replying "Nothing" to her sister's query, "What is it?" Viewing the foreboding landscape, Ethel blandly comments, "It's a kind of pretty place, plenty of fresh air." Hearing heavy breathing on the intercom, Ethel dismisses the sound as animal noise. Her daughter Lynn, streetwise from living in New York, is more alert. "If animals out there are smart enough to run a radio, we're up shit-creek." Mother expresses horror for the wrong reasons. "You never used language like that till you moved to New York." Returning after discovering Beauty's gutted carcass, Bobby also represses unpleasant knowledge; he refuses to tell his sister about his find. He finally tells Doug many hours later, after Pluto locks him out of the family trailer. Bobby's inability to speak indirectly results in the deaths of Lynn and Ethel and in baby Catherine's kidnapping. All these denials strengthen the shadow family. Like Freddy Krueger, they live and grow on their victim's fear.

Finding Freddy, Bob learns his family history before Jupiter kills him with a tire iron that is similar to the one Freddy used against him in 1939. Jupiter stalks Bob, who suffers from a heart condition, and eventually overpowers him. Like his murdered father, he impales Bob on a tree and sets it alight, Satanically inverting The Light of the World's crucifixion. Jupiter symbolically reenacts the event Freddy blamed him for—burning the family home and incinerating his little sister.

While Doug, Bobby, and Mildred run off to save Bob, Pluto and Mars attack the women inside the trailer. The two bothers battle over Brenda. Mars exercises the elder brother's authority as he forces Pluto outside her bedroom—"Not till you get to be a man." As Mars rapes Brenda, the frustrated Pluto, raging like an angry child, destroys items in the kitchen. This familial antagonism is a darker version of the bantering rivalry between Bobby and Brenda. Pluto's actions echo Brenda's resentment of Bobby's authority when his father gives him his handgun before leaving to find Freddy's gas station.

As Doug tends his dying father-in-law, Mildred falls into hysteria. She cries, "That's not my Bob." Mortally wounded during the trailer raid, she eventually dies. Bobby and Brenda begin mourning her but soon realize they are facing extreme danger. Unknown to them Jupiter and his family eat Bob's cooked flesh. Between mouthfuls Jupiter ritually speaks of annihilating his family and memory—"I'll eat the heart of your stinking memory." He regards Bob as a hated symbol of a system that has condemned his own family to a scavenger existence. Living outside an affluent civilization, Jupiter's family resorts to cannibalism to avoid starvation. Like an American Indian, he regards Bob as a territorial invader. He speaks angrily as he consumes his flesh, "Don't you come out here and stick your life in my face."

The remaining Carters discover untapped sources of energy that enables them to copy enemy tactics and survive. Beast kills Mercury, retrieving his walkie-talkie so Doug can now overhear enemy movements. Doug and Bobby communicate by walkie-talkie over long distances as they plan to "search and destroy." Bobby and Brenda cease mourning to exercise pragmatic American ingenuity. They use Mildred's body as bait to trap Jupiter, their actions mirroring their antagonist's deceptive cunning in using their father's body as bait. Setting an explosive device in their trailer, they hope to destroy him. But Jupiter survives and attacks them. Bobby and Brenda collaborate, their earlier cowardice and hysteria forgotten, in a violent family assault against their antagonist that is reminiscent of the Collingwood revenge against the Stillos in *Last House on the Left*. Confronted with life-threatening danger, the Carter family exercises the very same qualities that have enabled Jupiter's clan to survive for many years.

The last third of *The Hills Have Eyes* reveals little difference between both families. While Brenda axes Jupiter in the back, Ruby uses a poisonous rattlesnake to bite Mars in the neck before he stabs Doug to death. Ruby changes her allegiance from Jupiter to the Carters, stepping into Lynn's shoes as the mother who protects the baby. She saves Doug as Brenda saves Bobby from Jupiter. Beast savages Pluto to death, repeating his deadly Miami attack on another dog. Freed by Ruby, Doug picks up Mars's knife and frenziedly stabs him to death—a duplication of Brenda's vehement axe assault on Jupiter. Civilized family values are nonexistent; both families are identical. Ruby can easily transfer from one to another.

The film ends with a low-angle freeze frame red filter shot of Doug. Looking at Mars's body, he appears fully aware of the repressed violent nature that links him to Jupiter's family. Monsters are definitely within the American family.

◆ ◆ ◆

George Romero's *Dawn of the Dead* represents one of the peaks of 1970s horror cinema. It is a logical sequel to *The Crazies* in its critique of destructive masculine values. In *The Crazies* the collapse of society and the military damned the future relationship between David and Judy. Although Clank still shares destructive macho values, David understands their inherent redundancy. Clank anticipates *Dawn*'s Roger (Scott Reininger) and *Day of the Dead*'s Captain Rhodes (Joe Pilato); David's cinematic descendants are *Dawn*'s Peter (Ken Foree) and *Day*'s John (Terry Alexander). In later works Romero

increasingly moves toward attempting to define a new society without patriarchal family structures. His future groups reject Western sexist and racist
formations and move toward a future postcapitalist world where hierarchical
barriers no longer exist. Romero's female characters gain equality with their
male counterparts, sometimes even exercising "male" prerogatives of leadership. Both *Dawn* and *Day* strongly suggest patriarchal structures contaminate
white males. A new order is essential, uniting individuals of different ethnic, gender, and class backgrounds. The future is with women and minority
groups that are outside dominant social norms. Both Afro-American, Peter
and the Jamaican helicopter pilot, John, are new, sensitive male figures breaking ideologic barriers to coexist with women and other men in new social
groupings. *Dawn*'s climax, showing the pregnant Fran (Gaylyn Ross) piloting
a helicopter with Peter, presents "the potential for a new kind of family" in
a world where the traditional family "is no longer an operative part of our
lives."[22] The family motif lies at the heart of *Dawn of the Dead*.

As Robert C. Cumbow notes, the film contains several suggestive Vietnam metaphors with its helicopters, commando weaponry, and an eventually victorious multitudinous zombie army. As with *Night* Romero develops
important links to both capitalist consumption and media breakdown.

> The image of the living dead at a shopping mall turns the film into a black
> comic picture of an America hypnotized in an orgy of acquisition and conspic-
> uous consumption. By using the zombie ghouls as an image both of "them" and
> "us," *Dawn of The Dead* turns the question of America's economic and military
> world leadership back on itself.[23]

Although inextricably linked to Vietnam's effect on American culture,
Dawn also anticipates the united worlds of mass consumerism and dehu-
manization of the Reagan era. The movie opens in a Philadelphia TV studio
in total chaos.[24] Unlike *Night*'s TV where reports from a studio attempt some
semblance of control, *Dawn*'s media world is in complete disintegration. In
Night Romero made a cameo appearance interviewing a Washington politi-
cian. He now appears briefly, impotent before studio monitor controls, vainly
attempting to instill some sense of order in the surrounding confusion.

Dawn's opening scene is a close-up of Fran sleeping against a studio
wall. Disturbed voices echo offscreen. People argue continually. Romero critiques television's bland superficiality; its supposed objectivity and control
contrast strongly with its tendency to collapse in any major crisis. Revealing this overwhelming vision of chaos, Romero castigates media dishonesty
and emotional instability. Fran learns that half the televised rescue stations

are inoperative. Her studio manager prevents her remonitoring correct information due to his concern for ratings. "Without those stations on the screen every minute people won't watch us. They'll tune out!" Technicians leave or interrupt a studio transmission. Her lover, traffic news helicopter pilot Steve Andrews (David Emge), arrives with an escape plane. Fran hesitates because of her position of public responsibility within the broadcasting institution. A cameraman says, "Go ahead. We'll be off the air by midnight anyway. Emergency networks are taking over. Our responsibility is finished, I'm afraid."

Previous scenes depict the station's entire lack of "responsibility." While Fran attempts to save lives, intercut scenes show a talk show host performing a verbal inquisition on a guest scientist who is trying to explain reasons behind the zombie outbreak. An overly emotional studio audience harangues him. The situation's relationship to informed news shows such as *The McLaughlin Group* (a show based on who shouts the loudest) and the debased forum of a talk show situation is unmistakable. Audience aggressiveness foreshadows later irrational forces of zombies and bikers. As Fran succeeds in temporarily erasing the false rescue stations from the screen, the scientist condemns the studio hysteria. "And it's precisely because of incitement by irresponsible public figures like yourself that this situation is being dealt with irresponsibly by the public at large." Emotional instability leads to a totalitarian martial law proclamation which states that "citizens may no longer occupy private residences no matter how safely protected or well stocked. Citizens will be moved into central areas of the city." Parallels with South Vietnam's disastrous relocation policies occur.

Later scenes show which section of the population is affected. A SWAT team moves in to expel Puerto Ricans, Hispanics, and Blacks from an apartment complex. It is a politically motivated act of class and racial harassment. SWAT member Wooley (anticipating Rickles in *Day*) voices economic resentment, "I'll blow their asses off . . . their little low life Puerto Rican and nigger asses right off. How the hell come we shift those low-lifes in those big ass fancy hotels anyway? Shit man! This better than I got." His ecstatic killing spree anticipates both Roger's later macho glee in his zombie excursions as well as the bikers' assault on the mall. Appalled at Wooley's actions, Peter shoots him to end his indiscriminate slaughter. Wooley is little different from the zombies.

After "wasting" zombies in the basement, Roger suggests Peter join him in an escape plan. By this time Peter becomes totally disgusted with his institutional affiliation and the acts it authorizes in the name of law and order. Like Fran, his responsibility is over. Although recognizing the zombies as a dangerous force, as the only Black in the team he sympathizes with the minority community he is ordered to slaughter. Peter also notes the perversion of family ties. He sees a wife rushing to embrace her zombie husband who promptly begins devouring her. A young SWAT team member commits suicide after witnessing these scenes. Visibly upset by killing his "brothers" in the basement, Peter develops a death wish, deliberately taking his time to reload as a black zombie slowly crawls toward him. Roger saves him. Peter understands why the besieged community left their dead in the basement instead of incinerating them: "'Cause they still believe there's respect in dying." He is moved by the words of a one-legged Puerto Rican priest returning from giving the zombies their last rites. "You are stronger than us . . . but soon I think . . . they be stronger than you. When the dead walk, senors . . . we must stop killing . . . or we lose the war." The priest does not just identify himself (and implicjtly Peter) with the zombies/"us." He also articulates the need for a new philosophy to replace ideologic capitalist, racist violence.

Encountering some Philadelphia cops looting and fleeing the city, Peter and Roger team up with Fran and Steve. Escaping in Steve's helicopter, all four begin a journey where personal adjustment toward changed circumstances determines survival and personal growth. Old habits such as monogamy, family life, and capitalist consumerism are now redundant. But as *Dawn* reveals, they linger on. As they fly over the countryside, Romero reprises *Night's* concluding redneck hunt. Satirizing American macho immaturity, a sardonic mock country and western song ("I'm a man") accompanies images of military and redneck anachronistic masculinity.

The group discusses their new status. Steve still believes himself inside the law as they consider landing on a military airfield.

PETER.   Oh yeah! You got the papers for this limousine?
STEVE.   (Angrily.) I got JAS ID. So does Fran.
PETER.   Right! And we're out here doing traffic reports? Wake up, sucker. We're thieves and bad guys is what we are. And we gotta find our own way.

Dawn documents the attempts, failures, and possible success in finding this new way. Arriving at the mall, the group finds zombies wandering aimlessly about. Steve explains their presence as due to "some kind of instinct. Memory . . . of what they used to do. This was an important place in their lives."

As an affluent symbol of capitalist consumption, the mall's materialist environment challenges the group. Initially drawn toward the complex for basic supplies, this last bastion of the old society eventually contaminates them, resulting in the return of old values such as property and family. Discovering food in the civil defense storage system—"Looks like a free lunch"—Roger and Peter find the nerve center and press controls with "the keys of the kingdom" in their possession. Consumerist mechanisms begin. Escalators move. Fountains jet. Muzak accompanies the stumbling zombies. Delighted by a free shopping spree Peter and Roger ignore personal safety. Joined by Steve, who desires entry into this elite masculine group, the trio neglects Fran. They return to save her from a zombie at the last moment. Unaware of opening a dangerous Pandora's Box—"Let's get a TV and radio." "How are we going to get back?" "Who the hell cares?"—they overrule Fran's objections. Steve persuades her to stay by using manipulative arguments concerning necessary material security for future family life.

> Those things are out there, everywhere, and the authorities would give us just as hard a time, maybe worse. We're in great shape here, Frannie. We got everything we need right here. I'm not just being stubborn. I really think this is better. Hell, you're the one who's been wanting to set up shop.

The mall's zombie inhabitants are an old society dominated by consumer capitalism—middle-aged, students, yuppies, Blacks, nuns, and Hare Krishna devotees. Peter understands their connections to the living. Intermittent media broadcasts describe zombies as functioning on "a subconscious, instinctual level"; their remaining skills are being "remembered behavior from normal life." *Dawn of the Dead* shows that capitalism programs reactions, making them appear instinctual. The film never suggests struggle will be easy. When the group expels the zombies from their capitalist Eden, Peter watches them eagerly awaiting their return.

> STEVE. They're after us. They know we're in here.
> PETER. They're after the place. They don't know why. They just remember, remember they wanna be in here.

Short of fuel and entranced by their easy access to the mall, the quartet faces the dangers of mindless consumerism which inversely echoes their zombie counterparts. Humans and zombies are equal victims of conspicuous consumption dominating personal behavior. As the infrequent TV commentary asserts, the zombies have "little or no reasoning power." Neither does the bickering TV studio audience nor the quartet. They partake in a hunt that eliminates every zombie intruder in their domain. Initially, Fran joins the men, strapping on guns (echoing Steve's desires to be just one of the boys) with Peter and Roger. However, after the hunt she walks away disgusted, realizing the infectious danger of violent behavior. The men plunder the mall's wealth, setting up an acquisitive and materialistic society that gradually contaminates them.

Roger's gradual transformation into a zombie is not accidental. Reveling in macho excess and bravado, his blustering prowess resembles Clank of *The Crazies* and Wooley. Endangering the group's strategy to block the mall doors, he becomes increasingly childish and crazy until a zombie bites his leg. Like Wooley's hatred of minorities who live in apartment complexes beyond his economic means, Roger resents the zombies threatening his consumerist Eden. His joy at "whipping 'em" has possessive undertones as his exuberant "We got it all" shows.

The earlier hunt for basic supplies turns into frequent plundering forays for inessential items. They raid the armory, take useless money, coats, hats, tools, supermarket food, and photo-slide viewers, wheeling Roger around on a trolley like the family "baby." Romero equates their armory raid with zombie behavior. African tribal music with undertones of cannibalism comments on their desires.

Dawn equates capitalist acquisitiveness with deteriorating relationships. Enjoying access to consumer plenty, all appear bored. Fran skates alone on the ice rink or tediously tries out cosmetics and wigs before a mirror. Both she and Steve revert to the marital structures they attempted to escape from in their flight from Philadelphia. After Roger's death Peter prepares a romantic dinner for them. Discreetly exiting, he leaves the space free for Steve's proposal. Looking at his ring, she rejects its acquisitive romantic overtones. "We can't, not now. It wouldn't be real." Reacting to Steve's photographing her as she collects clothes in the mall, she snaps, "Great! When you finish the roll drop it off at the drug store!" A slow zoom-out from both of them in bed emphasizes the sterile Antonioni-like nature of their relationship as Fran stares listlessly into space. Ultimately a domestic argument erupts over Steve's desire to keep the vacant TV channel on. As the original screenplay notes, "Peter watches the two sheepishly. It is a domestic scene. The group has become a family, with all the disadvantages of comfortable living, including the inability to communicate with each other." Fran realizes this. She says, "What have we done to ourselves?" The sequence leads to a brief rapprochement as Steve shows her how to pilot the helicopter, acceding to her earlier request. Both appear happy, operating the craft in an equal, nonpatriarchal relationship. The reunion is fragile. As an alienated Peter attempts to ease his frustration by playing squash on the roof, one of his balls drops down among waiting zombies outside. A reckoning awaits.

Dawn's final third ironically parallels the quartet's earlier invasion of the mall. This time they have to defend their territory against a marauding army of bikers. While Peter realizes the necessity of avoiding a hopeless confrontation against overwhelming numbers, Steve possessively engages in open combat to defend his consumer kingdom. Ignoring Peter's advice, "Just stay out of sight. They're after the place. They don't care about us," Steve avariciously responds, "It's ours. We took it. It's ours." Like Roger, he is already on the road to becoming a real zombie. As a biker tells them on the intercom, "Hey, you in the Mall. You got fouled up real bad. We don't like people who don't share." As a professional army living off the land, the bikers parallel *Night's* redneck posse, rapacious zombies, and the macho military values Peter rejects. The biker leader (Tom Savini) echoes Wooley's earlier racism by taunting Peter as a "chocolate man." The gang plunders the mall in a violent parody of the zombies instinctual desires and the original quartet's raiding expeditions. One biker attempts to steal a TV set before another shouts, "Hey man, what are you going to watch on that thing." The bikers holler like marauding Indians, sharing implicit associations with marauding Viet Cong. One sounds a U.S. cavalry bugle like Col. Kilgore's bugler in *Apocalypse Now*

The zombies regain control of their kingdom by consuming any retreating bikers. Steve turns into a zombie that instinctually leads the hordes to the secret hiding place. Sickened by killing, Peter decides to commit suicide like the young SWAT team member in the earlier assault on the apartment block. Fran starts the helicopter. Everything appears lost as zombie forces advance.

Dawn's original screenplay concluded with Peter's and Fran's suicides. The final film ends differently with pregnant woman and surviving Black flying off, with limited fuel, into an uncertain future. This ending is the logical culmination of tendencies inherent in Romero's earlier work and *Dawn* itself. By depicting a tentative beginning represented by two oppressed groups in Western capitalist society, *Dawn of the Dead* represents not just one of Romero's greatest achievements as director but an important development suggestive of future directions for a genre that is currently trapped in a nihilistic blind alley.

Before Peter escapes he relinquishes his rifle to a zombie groping for it. This same zombie earlier grabbed Roger's rifle as Peter urged him to let it go. Now Peter voluntarily releases his weapon as he realizes that old masculine military values no longer apply. His action contrasts with Steve's zombie persona. He emerges from the lift still carrying his useless pistol.

As the helicopter ascends, dawn breaks. The zombies regain their consumer kingdom. Flying off with limited food and fuel supply, Fran is essentially alone and pregnant. There is no hint or possibility of any Hollywood romantic relationship with Peter. The future is tentative and uncertain. But Fran and Peter realize that the old order is dead as is the traditional family.

Sacrificial Victims

Family horror films of the seventies reveal intense contradictions. They illustrate R. D. Laing's theories on family schizophrenia and often deny supernatural causes for more material explanations. Read according to Michel Foucault's definitions of discourse and power-knowledge formations, horror film monsters are defined according to a particular set of institutional guidelines as "abject" due to their antagonistic protest against family restraint.[1]

Spectacular devices of violent excess attempt to disavow underlying material causes.[2] However, many family horror films depict social factors governing the return of the repressed. Parental figures become trapped within dangerous institutional and economic circumstances. Existing in a child-orientated society, feeling obliged to present offspring with every material advantage, most parents lack the necessary financial resources to fulfill this American Dream. Definitive manuals supposedly guarantee harmonious child rearing and the avoidance of mistakes. Disobedient children then become threats. Imprisoned within a system that is oblivious to real needs, a dangerous situation may result which reproduces a cyclical chain of victims and victimizers. Some fictional representations see the child terrorizing loving parents. This appears in *The Bad Seed* and one early *Twilight Zone* episode, remade with the necessary Reaganite entertainment "happy ending" in segment three of *Twilight Zone—The Movie* (1983).[3]

Seventies' horror films display contradictions between personal feelings and social conditioning. The monster reacts against family constraints. But this opposition often hints tentatively toward alternative paths. In Larry Cohen's *It Lives Again* (1978), two mutant babies suggest a new human evolution. Significantly named Adam and Eve, they react against a violent, pollution-ridden human society. They respond to those who do not fear them, but any danger provokes murderous reaction. Cohen reveals relevant authoritarian structures that threaten his creatures. However, potential utopian worlds remain blocked within an ideology that constrains most fictional representations by coding alternatives as violent and monstrous. Sometimes gaps appear within this framework.

Grave of the Vampire (1971), *Sisters* (1971), *The Possession of Joel Delaney* (1972), *Jack's Wife* (a.k.a. *Season of the Witch* [1974]), *Martin* (1976), *Alice, Sweet Alice* (a.k.a. *Communion* [1976]) and *Housewife* (a.k.a. *Dial Rat for Terror, Beverly Hills Nightmare, Bone* [1972]), *It's Alive* (1974), *God Told Me To* (a.k.a *Demon* [1976]), and *It Lives Again* (1978) articulate both the decade's great achievements as well as the genre's inability to advance beyond traditional constraints to achieve the epistemological breakthrough that *Exorcist II—The Heretic* suggests. *Willard* (1971), *Ben* (1972), and *The Amityville Horror* (1979) are lesser works that contain significant insights. *Grave, Sisters, Possession, Jack's Wife, Martin,* and *Alice, Sweet Alice* present characters struggling in different ways against family oppression. In *Grave of the Vampire* and *Alice, Sweet Alice,* James and Alice face overwhelming odds. Each film concludes with both becoming monsters. Joan Mitchell of *Jack's Wife* and Martin reach different degrees of awareness. While Joan lives, patriarchal violence prevents Martin's consciousness from blossoming out into personal salvation. All these neglected films emerge from a low-budget cinema that is often free from major studio self-censorship restraints and better able to articulate radical ideas than major studio productions.

◆   ◆   ◆

John Hayes's *Grave of the Vampire* anticipates many of the decade's themes.[4] At this stage the threat emerges externally from European vampire Caleb Croft (Michael Pataki). Like Norman Bates, he demonically appears to answer repressed desires. On a dark night in 1940, a college couple drive to their convenient mating spot—a graveyard! Young Paul produces a ring, puts it on Lesley's finger, and proposes to her. "It was my grandmother's ring. The only thing I own is my car." The dead hand of the past and allied economic problems weigh heavily upon them. Lesley suggests moving into her parents' boarded house to save money. Like Sam and Marion in *Psycho,* Paul and Lesley face oppression from institutional forces—money and family. Awakening in answer to their repressed feelings, decomposing vampire Caleb Croft leaves his coffin, attacking the couple as they make love. He drags Paul out of the car, breaks his back on a tombstone, and rapes Lesley in an open grave, brutally enacting "death-in-life" implications behind their conformist desires.

Croft retreats to a basement and murders a housewife who is compulsively listening to a radio crime program's violent broadcasts.

Recovering in the hospital Lesley meets Olga, an independent-minded widow who lost her husband to medically overprescribed drugs. She represents an alternative feminist path for Lesley, warning her against the profession's institutional use of drugs. "The pills help you to forget you're alive." Both women reject medical authority. However, believing she bears Paul's baby, Lesley refuses an abortion despite warnings of the possibility of nurturing a monster. "What is inside you cannot be a human being. It's a parasite. It will kill you." She decides to bear the child, a grey-skinned vampire child who refuses milk, preferring blood from its mother's breast. Like Rosemary Woodhouse, Lesley's maternal feelings overwhelm her, and she accedes to her baby's demands. The two women set up house together, their potential lesbian relationship frustrated by Lesley's acquiescence in the traditional maternal role. *Grave* understands the powerful nature of patriarchal conditioning destroying alternative channels of female expression. The ideology of motherhood operates similarly in *Rosemary's Baby* and Rodman Flender's *The Unborn* (1990), destructively oppressing an actual lesbian relationship in the latter film. Reared by the two women, the boy remains in the shadows, constantly watching other children play normally in the sun. The scene dissolves to show him fully grown several years later. Now a mature adult (William Smith), he lives alone after the two women die. Viewing Lesley's prematurely aged body in her coffin, he vows revenge on the father who has literally caused his mother's youth and blood to drain away.

He eventually tracks Croft down, discovering his new identity as a university professor who naturally prefers night classes. Although he is enjoying a brief love affair, suggestive of possible redemption and release from his affliction, the final outcome is pessimistic. Before staking Croft in the traditional manner, he receives the paternal curse, "Be damned." Gradually turning into a fully fledged vampire, he stumbles toward his girlfriend, warning her to get away before it is too late. The vicious circle of patriarchal ideology continues, damning all who fall into its trap.

◆ ◆ ◆

Coscripted by Louisa Rose, Brian De Palma's *Sisters* is a brilliant reworking of Hitchcock's *Psycho* and *Rear Window*. It uses the genre's potential to express cinematic reaction against patriarchal oppression. But *Sisters* is a paradoxical work. Justifiably hailed as one of the most significant achievements of 1970s cinema, it is also the work of a director who is notorious for his exploitation of sensitive themes within American society—feminism, Vietnam, and social urban malaise.[5] Although Robin Wood claims that his works reflect the dilemma of "a fundamentally feminine man who, because he is a man within a patriarchal culture, can view his femininity only in terms of castration," this cannot justify every De Palma film.[6] As any viewing of *Dressed to Kill* reveals, De Palma's camera represents the closest approximation to Laura Mulvey's influential thesis, *Visual Pleasure and Narrative Cinema* which reveals women as voyeuristic objects of the sadistic male gaze. Although De Palma's work contains overtones of male insecurity and hysteria, these never function in a satisfactory manner to contradict powerful negative images of violence against women. *Sisters's* emergence as one of the most radical works of the 1970s results more from accidental borrowings of progressive elements within Hitchcock and Louisa Rose's collaboration in the screenplay.

As a protest against patriarchal oppression of female sexuality, *Sisters* indirectly reworks the horror film's premise of woman as monster. *The Cat People's* Irena now appears within two schizophrenic entities: identical twins Dominique/Danielle (Margot Kidder) and journalist Grace Collier (Jennifer Salt). Patriarchal structures oppress them. While the sisters attempt to escape Emile Breton's (William Finley) marital/medical institutional dominance, Grace tries asserting independence against mother's demands that she give up her "little job" and get married. Viewing a brutal murder from her apartment, Grace fails to persuade mother and the law (official law enforcement officers and overbearing private detective Charles Durning) of the validity of her independent vision. While Emile Breton collaborates in denying the reality of Danielle's actions, the law ignores Grace's claims to knowledge of a murderous event.[7]

Sisters's visual structure of split-screen techniques, linking Grace and Danielle/Dominique, develops the horror genre's dualistic component into a radical critique of patriarchal oppression. The film shows monstrous alter-ego Dominique lurking beneath sweet, compliant Danielle; Dominique is violently opposed to any masculine oppression, whether it is the surgeon's knife or bourgeois romance.

Like Marion Crane in *Psycho*, Grace Collier falls into a patriarchal heart of darkness. Pursuing her investigations she views a videotape documentary about Siamese twins Danielle and Dominique. Joined together by the hip, their association evokes an earlier scene when Grace and Danielle appear together with hips touching before a wardrobe containing two sets of clothes. Usurping traditional male prerogatives, Grace becomes Dominique in a later nightmare sequence. Viewing the tape Grace hears the commentary, Danielle "only appears healthy because of her sister." Occupying Dominique's position in the nightmare, Grace sees her mother suddenly appearing to photograph her when the word "freak" occurs repeatedly on the soundtrack. Denying mother's constant pressures to marry, Grace's nightmare sees her body wheeled off for an operation that castrates her mentally and physically. As the climax reveals, her independent voice becomes nonexistent.

Emile hypnotizes her to forget. Prior to her capture, Grace follows the kidnapped Danielle into a mental hospital. Like Samuel Fuller's Johnny in *Shock Corridor* (1962), she discovers an institution that represents the repressed underside of American society. She encounters inmates obsessed with cleanliness and tidiness who are compulsively fulfilling the proscribed roles of bourgeois society. After undergoing hypnosis Grace forgets everything, paralleling Danielle in the climax. Now fully submissive she is mother's ideal daughter like Melanie in *The Birds*. She last appears in a little girl's room, an environment identical to Norman's room in *Psycho* and *Psycho IV*.

Dominique reacts violently against patriarchal oppression. Objecting to Emile's designs on her sister, she conveniently dies during an operation. But Dominique lives on and returns from the depths of Danielle's psyche to revenge herself on males, whether they are innocent (Philip) or guilty (Emile). She finally castrates her castrator, who crawls to embrace Dominique/Danielle in a dark, romantic *Liebestod*. Male oppressor and female oppressed briefly unite in a poignant dying moment. Ironically Dominique castrates Emile with his own surgeon's knife. Lacking the phallus he is now no dangerous authoritarian threat to her. *Sisters* ends pessimistically with a passive, brainwashed Grace. But the final shot reveals Charles Durning's arrogant detective figure, his ladder leaning against a telegraph pole, impotently focusing his gaze through binoculars at now-redundant evidence. Male control becomes a joke.

Despite *Sisters*'s achievement, De Palma's later films exhibit incoherence and confusion. Although his *Vertigo*-influenced *Obsession* (1975) unveils destructive male voyeurism and incestuous desires within the family (with mother and daughter as capitalist property items), it contains few advances beyond Hitchcock. The stylistic excesses of *The Fury* (1977) overwhelm family motifs. Scattered insights within *Blow Out* (1981) and *Body Double* (1984) become overwhelmed by sadistic indulging in scopophiliac mechanisms. *Raising Cain* (1992) reveals contemporary horror themes of child abuse, but De Palma's trivial postmodernist practices and rhetorical showmanship engulf them in empty spectacle.

◆　◆　◆

Neglected, but far more significant than De Palma's *post—Sisters* opus, is Warris Hussein's *The Possession of Joel Delaney*. Despite several faults, such as stressing the obvious and representing the Puerto Rican community as a group of superstitious voodoo devotees, it handles family motifs far more successfully than its publicized successor *The Exorcist*. *The Possession of Joel Delaney* achieves an effective balance between supernatural motifs and material causes by never allowing the former to overwhelm the latter. The reasons for Joel's possession are succinctly ambiguous, leaving the viewer to draw conclusions. Did dead psychotic Puerto Rican criminal Tonio Perez possess Joel's body to avenge himself on an oppressive White community?[8] Or is Joel's dark side using possession as a convenient excuse to react against his incestuous sister and act out guilty feelings concerning his membership of an affluent racial class? Whatever the conclusion the family generates horrific events in a film containing the racial, economic, and class characteristics of *I Walked with a Zombie*.

The film's title is apt. Two forces strive for possession of Joel's soul, Tonio Perez and Joel's possessively incestuous sister, Nora (Shirley Maclaine). Both threaten his individual personality by forcing him into particular roles such as possessed killer or idealized family member. His possession has economic undertones. Joel represents the repressed return of an economically exploited underclass. Joel (Perry King) monstrously reacts against Nora's possessive desires to smother his wishes for individual expression and personal space.

The precredits sequence shows a middle-aged woman's face in close-up. She stands in a somberly colored claustrophobic background in a tightly packed elevator. Voodoo music briefly occurs on the soundtrack, one of the many indications of subversive forces awaiting expression. The camera pans left, stopping at Nora Benson. She looks apprehensive. The lift's oppressively crowded interior parallels the film's suffocating brother-sister relationship in a society based upon Black and Puerto-Rican exploitation. In the following party sequence, intercut shots juxtapose affluent White guests with primitive voodoo masks placed in the demeaning position of trendy artifacts. A Black man stands alone. His face exhibits ethnic alienation.

Nora's face lights up as she sees a young man rushing toward the lift. They appear to be lovers. However, during the party we learn they are brother and sister. Nora looks at him. Her face expresses revealing desires that far exceed the sibling relationship. Joel has recently returned from Tangiers. Throughout the party he is either with Nora or under her surveillance in various parts of the room. Several guests comment on their unusual relationship. A woman remarks that they are both like "young lovers." Another succinctly comments on Nora's vivaciousness, "Some women bloom after a divorce." Her male companion suggestively says, "I never thought she'd go backwards. I hate to see an attractive woman go backwards." Erica Lorenz's husband, Justin (Michael Horden), leaves Nora and joins his wife. Both laugh together in a conspiratorial manner. Nora's discarded lover remarks on her recent coolness toward him. Sherry and her male entourage enter. Successive shots cut between Joel and Sherry's conversation and Nora's dominating gaze. Oblivious to her ex-lover's conversation, she jealously watches both. The party sequence ends with a long-shot of Joel and Sherry speaking together—for the first time he ignores Nora's look. A final close-up reveals Nora's annoyance. These opening shots display Nora's incestuous desires.

The following sequence associates Nora's incestuous possessiveness with economic roots. It follows the Puerto Rican maid, Veronica, on her daily work routine. Beginning with a shot of Veronica leaving a bus, the camera turns 360 degrees to show her passing through heavy traffic to begin work. As Veronica enters Nora's house, the scene changes to show Nora lounging in bed and speaking on the telephone. Caustically referring to a career woman who "doesn't have to work," Nora's remark ironically contrasts with Veronica's domestic activities. Nora speaks on the phone to Veronica giving her the day's orders. The following long-take visually illustrates Veronica's daily routine. Possessively dominated by Nora's gaze, she enters her room with a breakfast tray. Nora chides her when she is about to place it on a bureau. She tells her to position it by her bedside. The command coincides with Nora's reflection in the bureau mirror as she gazes at Veronica. As Veronica positions the breakfast tray, the camera follows her, framing Nora, who is now actually within the image. It continues to survey Veronica as she goes to the other side of the room to open the curtains. Although the image no longer contains Nora's actual physical presence, her reflection gazes on Veronica from another mirror to supervise her every move. The camera then dollies left, framing Nora as she leaves her bed to give Veronica additional instructions for dinner as she unquestionably assumes Joel's presence. By using subtle, nonrhetorical camera movements, Hussein excellently reveals the oppressive nature of White power.

Another scene depicts Nora's possessive character and reveals her desires to keep Joel in a state of childish dependence. It begins with a close-shot of Joel's hair being brushed. The camera zooms out, revealing Nora acting in this maternal manner. Joel gets up, moving to her dressing table. He picks up a silver-plated brush and recognizes it as his mother's. The ensuing dialogue reveals marked differences between brother and sister. Nora remarks, "I kept my mother's things." Joel curtly replies, "I didn't." A small, circular dressing table mirror significantly frames Nora's face at the very moment Joel picks up the brush, visually echoing Nora's earlier mirror surveillance of Veronica. Mother's photo also appears near the mirror, hinting at a *Psycho* situation affecting these affluent people.

The next scene shows Joel suggestively reclining on his sister's bed. He ironically compares her to women he met in Tangiers. "I met a woman like you in Tangiers . . . women like you who go all the way to Tangiers to get laid. Then when they come back they haven't changed at all." The film suggestively leaves open the exact nature of Joel's relationships in Tangiers and its possible repetition-compulsive undertones.

Although Joel appears affable toward his sister, he really harbors deep feelings of hatred and resentment. As psychiatrist Erica (Lovelady Powell) later tells Nora, traumatic family circumstances, which involved their mother's nervous breakdowns and eventual suicide, adversely affected Joel. Feeling abandoned by his father, Joel developed hostile feelings toward his maternally inclined sister. Seeking freedom from a negative family situation whose patriarchal constraints resulted in his mother's death, he reacts against anyone who embodies restrictive incestuous possessiveness. Releasing Joel from mental hospital incarceration, Nora takes personal responsibility for her sick brother, ironically remarking, "And you'll stay with me. It'll be like old times."

Joel's resentful feelings toward Nora and the family emerge in the ice-skating sequence. Accompanying her children, David and Carrie, on a day's outing, his expression turns savage when Nora appears on the scene. He whirls Carrie round in an increasingly dangerous game before they both slip on the ice. Learning of Nora's dinner plans, which include his acquiescent presence, he becomes critical because she did not ask him. Significantly his first possession occurs on the very night he decides to be absent. He attacks Mr. Perez, who killed Tonio to stop his psychotic murders. Seeing her crazed brother led away, Nora notices Mrs. Perez, a woman with whom she later finds she has much in common.

Joel wishes to live apart from White society; he prefers to inhabit the East Village Puerto Rican ghetto. He reveals desires for a greater sense of community involvement in his session with Erica. Joel equates Erica with Nora, regarding both as dominating women who attempt to destroy his individuality by making him conform to particular social patterns. He clearly resents any family defined role. During his birthday party, everyone attempts to categorize him as the "world's greatest" brother, lover, or uncle. Falling into a trance to find Sherry's lost earring, his subsequent actions are extremely suggestive. He ties the retrieved object to a balloon and sends it floating away. Like Uncle Charlie and Norman Bates, he has no use for expensive artifacts.

He scares Sherry by holding her hair dangerously near the lighted candles. She is his future sacrificial victim. Joel resents her as a designated wife and sexually free woman during his Tangiers period. He hates her, seeing Sherry as another Nora. Both women were sexually active during his absence. Joel and Sherry's sexual reunion is violent and frenzied, climaxing in her painful cry, "You hurt me. What have I done to you?"

Sherry becomes Nora's convenient surrogate, someone upon whom Joel displaces his resentment against Nora's possessive, incestuous desires. This appears when Nora discovers Sherry's decapitated body. The sequence opens with a long-shot revealing Sherry's trunk, her head hanging above it. A tilted angle-shot of Nora's face follows. Two close-shots of the body appear intercut with Nora's reaction. The sequence concludes with a subliminal fusion of Sherry's face onto Nora's, identifying the two women and suggesting Nora's recognition of the fact. A zoom-in to Sherry's head concludes the sequence.

Joel and Tonio have similar backgrounds. Visiting Joel's Puerto Rican ghetto apartment, Sherry comments on its parallels to Joel's dark side. Joel regards Tonio as his surrogate dark alter ego. He tells Erica that "he stands for everything Nora hates." Erica later informs Nora about the relationship. Tonio's father abandoned him at an early age, leaving him to his grandmother's care. Mrs. Perez also tells Nora that Tonio became seriously disturbed ("evil") following his grandmother's death and attempted to kill her. A dark family scenario lies beneath these violent actions, a scenario suggested in the film's opening scenes. Tonio's murders parallel Joel's. They represent surrogate revenge against his mother. Tonio even gave Joel his own apartment. On her visit there Nora sees two significant items: a Trotsky poster and a drawing of a hand with a cut palm that resembles one she saw at the Perez household. Both represent political and spiritual reactions against capitalism. As in *I Walked with a Zombie*, voodoo represents Black opposition against White family orientated civilization.

Two scenes visually represent two conflicting worlds. Briefly glimpsing Mrs. Perez during her first ghetto visit, Nora sees the hand painting on the left of her room and a large cross to the right. When Joel visits Erica's apartment for his psychiatric appointment, individual shots show voodoo masks and foreign artifacts that visually oppose the soundtrack's demure Western classical music. Sound and images collide in anticipation of the conflict evident in the film's climax when a possessed Joel forces the Bensons to dance to classical music in rhythmically inappropriate ghetto jive movements. When Joel goes to Erica's window, further signs of his possession appear. He stretches out his palm, placing it on the glass. Two brief inserts follow, that reveal the hand drawing in Tonio's apartment and its painted original representation inside Mrs. Perez's room.

Nora selfishly refuses to recognize New York's economic squalor; she prefers her life of privileged affluence. While visiting Joel at the mental hospital, she criticizes his preference for living in the East Village. Attempting to find Joel in the city hospital, she pushes aside a poor woman and attempts to use her class superiority on the Negro receptionist. Becoming more concerned about Joel, she ventures deeper into the ghetto and discovers the oppressed sectors of society she usually ignores in her secure affluent existence. Before visiting spiritualist leader Don Carlos, she pauses outside his shop. A voodoo mask appears to the left of the window, a Christ statue to the right. Nora's reflection appears between both objects. Deciding to enter the shop, she moves to the left and into the voodoo world. On leaving she encounters ghetto squalor; she is the only White in the area. Nora becomes increasingly oppressed by this environment and finally halts a taxi in a panic. During her frenzied escape, a Black Muslim female grins at her from across the street.

Both worlds intersect at the beach house Nora takes her children to for safety: the revenge of the economically deprived community and Joel's violent, unrepressed reactions toward Nora's incestuous feelings. As she discovers Erica's decapitated head in the kitchen, the camera pans right to reveal a possessed Joel dressed like Tonto Perez. He begins a process of class vengeance—humiliating David for his inability to gut a fish like any poor boy, forcing him to strip to experience the cold, running his knife under Carrie's throat, making her eat dog food, and forcing the family to dance ethnically to classical music. Eventually, the police arrive and shoot Joel. The children run to their father. Unconcerned over their safety, Nora runs to her dying brother.

After Joel dies Nora looks up. Her eyes reveal a demonic look. Clearly possessed she looks in fascination at Joel's knife. The police look on. An ambiguity results. Does Tonto possess her? Or has Nora finally succumbed to her own dark desires by incorporating Joel's soul within her own body in a manner similar to how Freddy Krueger stores his young victims? Nora looks at a cop, raising the blade as the film ends in freeze-frame; she is isolated from her children who stand with their father. She wields the phallus patriarchal society denies her. She becomes the film's monster and reveals the real nature of Joel's possession—incestuous desires within the family.

Earlier scenes anticipate the film's conclusion. Visiting Joel's room Nora found a flick-knife. Accidentally opening it, she gazed at the blade in fascination, putting it quickly away when Sherry arrived. After the skating rink sequence, she put on her dark glasses, smiling, in close-up, at Joel off-camera.

Her appearance parallels Joel's when the audience first sees him completely possessed. A close-up reveals his twitching face before he smiles and puts on dark glasses while on his way to kill Erica. Like Sherry, Erica represents another surrogate for his sister. The family collapses under the weight of its own psychosis.

Neglected both during and after release, *The Possession of Joel Delaney* is one of the decade's most important family horror movies. It explicitly links the institution to allied factors of class, racial, and economic oppression without resorting to special effects or Satanic mystification.

◆ ◆ ◆

George Romero's *Jack's Wife* significantly explores the oppressive Catholicism and patriarchy affecting its heroine. Married to a prosperous but overbearing attorney, affluent suburban housewife Joan Mitchell has every type of material possession. All she lacks is independence. *Jack's Wife* opens with a dream sequence that presents her everyday dilemma in fantastic form. In the dream Joan submissively walks behind her husband, following him everywhere. Subjective shots reveal tree branches hitting her face as her husband moves on, oblivious to his wife's discomfort. Finally, he places a dog collar around her neck and incarcerates her in the dog pound. A later daydream presents her bored demeanor as she listens to the mindless chatter of her female coffee circle. Alienated within her tidily furnished living room, she sees her prematurely aged face as it is reflected on a mirror. Joan seeks to define her existence apart from husband, home, and medical discourse. Attending a psychoanalytic session, her psychiatrist dismisses her feelings by describing her as "the least qualified person to understand dreams." Joan, however, intuitively realizes her sterile bourgeois existence and her constraining Catholic background.

Although not a horror film in the traditional sense, *Jack's Wife* has many associations with family horror. As a borderline generic offering, the film shows how Joan attempts to remedy her situation in a society that lacks alternative paths. Attending a party Joan meets a woman who claims to be a witch. Attracted by the movement's nonpatriarchal elements, she begins to experiment with hexes and rituals. However, Joan's search never leads to any real liberation. Her interest in covens becomes another escapist path similar to her coffee mornings. She lacks specific direction, a problem that affects many countercultural movements of the 1960s. Although she communicates with an appropriately named familiar spirit named "Virago," Joan's witchcraft interests are as aimless as her coffee mornings. Breaking Catholic taboos by taking a lover, Joan's extramarital activities become as unfulfilling as her marital relationship. Her lover, Gregg, is as unpleasant and condescending as her own husband; he constantly dismisses her desires for independence. Believing herself to be Satan's tool, she drifts into an affair and accepts no responsibility for exchanging one form of domination for another. Her fantasy involvements are merely escapist.

After accidentally shooting her husband one evening, Joan finally becomes a single woman. But her personal inadequacies and social constraints ensure she will never achieve any real independence. During Joan's final initiation into the coven, the group binds her with a cord. This action parallels her husband's placement of a dog collar around her neck during the earlier dream sequence. Like the covens in *The Seventh Victim* and *Rosemary's Baby*, it really represents another form of patriarchal domination. The concluding sequence shows her at a party. Despite her new status as a single woman, Joan is still referred to as "Jack's Wife." Her bereavement changes nothing. Despite awareness of marital entrapment, she lacks the necessary initiative to change.

◆ ◆ ◆

Martin's condition is more extreme. Like Joan Mitchell, Martin (John Amplas) retreats into fantasy. He is trapped in a dangerous situation from which he will never escape; he is a victim of family conditioning and misrecognition. Although he is nineteen years old, his family already defines him as a monster, an eighty-four-year-old vampire, making him an undeniable example of R. D. Laing's family schizophrenic victims. Although Joan (*Jack's Wife*) lives a sterile existence that moves toward a stage where she cannot distinguish fantasy from reality, Martin turns in the opposite direction. Already defined as a monster, he acts out a family determined role model and attacks young females. Martin fantasizes his exploits, envisaging them as old Universal horror movies. At the film's opening, he arrives in Pittsburgh's declining Braddock district to stay with his elderly cousin Cuda (Lincoln Maazel). Cuda sees Martin not as an emotionally abused adolescent but as a dangerous vampire. He ignores the reality of his decaying environment and chooses instead to retreat into superstitious reaction. Martin's accent reveals he has not just arrived from Europe. He is clearly American. Although the audience never gains insight into his former family life, his condition clearly results from emotional abuse. However, like *The Cat People*, *Martin* remains ambiguous about what social factors made its titular figure into a monster. Cuda represents traditional horror film audiences that choose to retreat into fantasy rather than recognize social realities behind supernatural manifestations. Speaking of Braddock, "This is a town for old persons," Cuda denies a deadening environment that causes apathy, boredom, and retreat into casual sex. His granddaughter Christine (Christine Forrest) spends most of her time in bed bickering with her boyfriend Arthur (Tom Savini). Meeting Martin as he arrives in Braddock, Cuda takes him past a scrap yard that symbolizes the community's sterile existence.

Martin is another of Romero's imaginative explorations into horror. The film reveals material factors often concealed within the genre. Victimized by negative family situations that constantly deny real needs and aspirations, the major characters in *Martin* all suffer from a stagnating social system that affects personal behavior. Martin and Cuda retreat into their own fantasy worlds; Christine uses sex as a convenient narcotic. The world of *Jack's Wife* is not too far away from this particular "vampire movie." However, Martin does attempt to break away. He tries to change Cuda's false beliefs and family misrecognitions by attempting to make his uncle see him as a sensitive and vulnerable person. Showing him a knife at the dinner table—"See it has two blades, a real one and a trick one. Things only seem to be magic. There is no real magic"—he finds it is all in vain. Cuda prefers to live in his own fantasy world, defining Martin as a monster even while his society crumbles around him. This particular scene is insightful. It also condemns the traditional desire of horror film audiences for false, spectacular, magical special effects rather than attempting to recognize the dangerous nature of the real world that surrounds them.

The actual danger lies in Braddock's industrial decline and its dehumanizing effects. Hostile and aggressive housewives patronize Cuda's store. Punks annoy women in the shopping malls. Neighbors obsessively pursue artifacts such as motorcycles. Winos and criminals haunt deserted warehouses. A radio announcer titillates his listeners by reporting a strangler's activities. He exploits Martin's need for sympathy and denies his call for help by featuring him as the local vampire. Braddock's very environment trivializes humanity's real needs, a process aptly signified by an ice cream van's use of Mozart's *Marriage of Figaro* and Beethoven's *Ninth Symphony* as calling signals.

Although Cuda does react against certain social definitions, for example, by rebutting a patron's insinuations that concern Martin living under the same roof as Christine—"It looks the way you want it to look, Mrs. Brennan. Martin knows how to behave"—he is not above manipulating Christine. Reacting to her desire to leave with Arthur, Cuda attempts to destroy her relationship by telling him of the "shame in the family"—Martin's supposed condition—"Perhaps it is best for her never to get married." Christine eventually departs, using Arthur as an exit visa from a claustrophobic family environment; she promises to keep in touch with Martin, a promise Martin knows she will soon forget.

Although Martin initially performs his predestined family role of vampire by attacking young women and sucking their blood, he does enter into a sexual relationship with Mrs. Santini. The characterization of Mrs. Santini resembles both Joan Mitchell and Christine; she uses Martin for sexual release from her everyday mundane existence. Martin gradually loses his desires to suck blood. Attacking another housewife who also uses sex to escape everyday reality, he feels no basic need to drink her blood and possibly allows her to live. His next Universal fantasy recreation of the event shows the woman still alive. Gradually, Martin begins to slowly awake from the monster-label his family has applied to him—an action that reveals a possibility of change.

Martin progressively reveals that family and society create monsters. Unlike Joan Mitchell, Martin gradually moves further toward reality. But, like the *Frankenstein* films, violent patriarchal action prevents further development. Believing Martin to be responsible for Mrs. Santini's death, Cuda stakes him through the heart. In actuality Mrs. Santini had committed suicide rather than confront her everyday sterile existence. As Cuda sprinkles garlic over Martin's garden grave, the ice cream van's *Ninth Symphony* jingle plays. There can be no real "Ode to Joy" over this monster's death.

During his dreams Martin fantasizes a female beckoning and calling his name, giving him the type of recognition he never achieves in everyday life. She is his feminine alter ego, representing a new form of alternative existence beyond family. As a monster existing in Braddock's bleak environment, Martin has limited choices—a family-defined vampire, a proficient killer, or sexual psychopath—he is living in a world that nurtures the psychosis from which he intuitively seeks release. His premature death is all the more tragic. Martin gradually recognizes that repressive family ideologic factors define him as a monster, but before he can advance, he becomes the sacrificial victim of a vicious patriarchal system.

◆ ◆ ◆

Although the "Terrible House" often functions metaphorically as a Gothic motif in many horror films, it also has a specific economic basis. Home ownership, with its financial commitments and social obligations, is a fundamental component of capitalist society. The home anchors individuals within the system. Overburdening owners with high mortgage payments and property renovation, the home acts as an entrapment, ensuring that its victims comply with capitalism's maintenance. Salaries, wages, interest rates, desires for economic success, and continuing employment are all interrelated. Even Mrs. Bates hoped to benefit from a motel until the state constructed a highway elsewhere. Tensions associated with home ownership occur in certain horror films.

Willard (1971) presents its economically and family oppressed twenty-seven-year-old hero (Bruce Davison) who pathologically desires to maintain a family property he would be better off selling. Psychically dominated and pushed by his aging mother (Elsa Lanchester) and her senior citizen friends to bootlick his way up the corporate ladder, Willard turns to Ben and his rats as allies against a repugnant adult world. Living in a deteriorating Gothic home where he is forced to act as a repairman by a mother who constantly fills him with guilt for his very existence—"Twenty seven years ago tonight you were born in pain and suffering. They didn't think I could live"—Willard eventually takes revenge against his dominating boss (Ernest Borgnine). However, despite his alliance with a dark animal world, Willard's dominance by home ownership results in him becoming just another oppressor. After killing his boss with a little help from his friends, he soon begins to exhibit traits of the masculine self-confidence of a corporate world that originally oppressed him. Willard becomes another home-owning patriarch who disavows connections with the socially outcast rat world. Ironically Willard's attempts to court Joan (Sondra Locke) as his future wife lead to Ben's revenge against his former master for drowning the rats. Like Ygor in *The Ghost of Frankenstein*, a former victim turns into just another oppressor and pays the price

The disappointing sequel *Ben* (1972) reveals the adult world as entirely bankrupt. Law enforcement figures exhibit no redeeming features as they attempt to exterminate the rat population. The film suggests a new type of relationship between young Donny (Lee Harcourt Montgomery) and Ben. Like the *Frankenstein* films, the world of childhood contains no prejudice against beings that society deems monstrous. Although Donny's family life is less oppressive than Willard's, the film presents his widowed mother struggling for economic survival both in her own business ventures (threatened by the rats' presence) and by Donny's hospital bills. The capitalist world outside affects family relationships. However, though Ben and Donny survive at the end, their relationship will never effectively oppose the dominant order.

◆　◆　◆

Despite lapsing into incoherence toward the end, Stuart Rosenberg's *The Amityville Horror* (1979) contains significant associations between family life, home ownership, and supposedly supernatural horror. Although several explanations appear for horrific events, the strongest is the economic factor. As George (James Brolin) and Kathy (Margot Kidder) Lutz tour the

Amityville home (whose exterior resembles a human skull), intercut shots reveal the family killings of a year before. Home purchase, ownership, family tensions, and murder intermingle. The film contains several suggestions that George's deteriorating condition has economic rather than supernatural causes. His aberrant behavior represents reaction to the pressures of home ownership. Business is "falling apart," the IRS continue to harass him, and he has overcommitted himself. "You marry a dame with three kids. You buy a big house with mortgages up to your ass. You change your religion and you forget about business." Kathy pressures him into buying a home. Following a domestic squabble she pleads, "Be nice. This is a big event in my family. We've always been a bunch of renters. This is the first time anyone's bought a house." Telling George of the house's supernatural associations, Caroline (Helen Shaver) states, "Energy cannot be created or destroyed. It can only change forms." Caroline's explanation links family home ownership with supernatural motifs. Despite incoherences, *The Amityville Horror* is one of the few films that link the economic responsibilities of home ownership to family horror.

Like *Martin*, *Alice, Sweet Alice* (a.k.a. *Communion*) is set in a declining industrial ghetto. Set in 1961 New Jersey, *Alice, Sweet Alice* is more than a cinematic homage to earlier films such as *Psycho*, *What Ever Happened to Baby Jane?*, and *Don't Look Now*. It bleakly indicts oppressive forces of family and religion as responsible for producing monsters. *Alice* is definitely an innovative radical family horror film.

Set in an Italian Roman Catholic area, *Alice*'s credits show a female communicant holding a cross. She lifts it up, revealing its lower end as a blade. With its satirical Bunuelesque overtones and parody of Nicky Cruz's conversion narrative, *The Cross and the Switchblade*, this image aptly signifies Catholicism's repression of female sexuality and its unrepressed eruption into violence. A virginal Bride of Christ is also a psychotic murderer.

Alice presents a coherent structure of duality and mirror imagery from its very opening. Young Father Tom presents eight-year-old Karen Spages with a gold cross in honor of her first communion. This arouses the jealousy of her twelve-year-old "problem" sister Alice who dons a monster mask to frighten her. Before Alice reveals her real face to rectory housekeeper Mrs. Tredoni, she progressively strips away two rubber masks: monster and old woman.

Adolescent psychotic fantasies echo Catholic ritual. Karen's strangling accompanies the communion service. As young female communicants line up, successive shots show an old woman in a communion veil and elderly nuns in an attempt to reveal the past's institutional hold on the future and the continuation of the tradition to stunt female growth. Whether as future wives or single women, these young communicants have no alternatives—family and religion block any potential for real development.

As the ceremony proceeds, violent instinctual forces appear. A figure wearing Alice's yellow raincoat murders Karen and burns her body. This secular cremation pollutes the communion service. *Alice* depicts Catholicism and Satanic violence as alternative manifestations of a malignant social order. Before Alice receives the Host, she moves her tongue like the demonic Regan in *The Exorcist*. A cry, alerting the congregation to the smoke from her sister's burning body, prevents her from swallowing the Host.

Sole ignores the distracting supernatural overtones by concentrating on the Catholic community's social and family relationships. Divorced from her husband Dom, Alice's mother Catherine nurtures a warm personal relationship with Father Tom. However, already alienated from her religion by breaking one of its taboos, she can neither admit nor consummate her desires for the young priest. Both repressed lovers can only communicate within acceptable guidelines of parishioner and priest. "Bad sister" Alice is illegitimate. Mother and daughter are outcasts within a restrictive society. Despite her sexual desires, living in a community hostile to remarriage, Catherine faces a frustrating future of loneliness, single parenthood, and eventual aging, resulting in her finally becoming like Mrs. Tredoni. She also faces family conflict. Her sister Annie hates her and Alice as well as Catherine's ex-husband Dom. Like Catherine, Dom breaks two Catholic taboos by divorcing and remarrying. Alice's hatred of her legitimately conceived sister Karen parallels feelings between aunt and mother. Releasing repressed emotions in sibling hatred and stuffing her already overweight family with food (like Beatrice Arthur's mother in *Lovers and Other Strangers* who uses the same tactic to sublimate her husband's sexual appetites), Annie is another social victim of a restrictive family situation. This condition affects every character in the film who are all family sacrificial victims. Already damning Alice for her illegitimate status, Annie regards her as the monster responsible for both Karen's death and the subsequent knifings in the community.

Alice eventually reveals Mrs. Tredoni to be the real monster and victim. Representing Catherine's possible future, she is the logical result of repressive forces within religion and family. Like Catherine, she sublimates her feelings for young Father Tom, conceals sexual desire, and wishes to be constantly in his presence in her role as housekeeper. Having lost her own daughter during her very first communion day, Mrs. Tredoni psychotically reenacts the trauma through a distorted version of Christian ritual. Convinced that children bear the burden of their parental sin, she sacrifices Karen as a ritual offering for Catherine's earlier illegitimate procreation, punishes Dom for breaching Catholic norms, and finally murders her son-lover figure, Father Tom, preserving him from sexual pollution by Catherine. Like Karen, Catherine is illegitimate. For Mrs. Tredoni she is a "whore." Like Dominique/Danielle, Mrs. Tredoni can safely embrace Father Tom after stabbing him, nullifying his sexual threat by castration.

Unconsciously aware of the psychological damage institutional values cause, Mrs. Tredoni acknowledges her affinity with the monstrous, wearing Alice's creature mask and yellow raincoat in her murderous activities. Although *Alice* ends with community realization of Alice's innocence she, too, becomes polluted by the social system. Witnessing Father Tom's murder, Alice walks away in a state of shock. The final camera movement tracks back from her. She walks forward holding Mrs. Tredoni's bloody knife—another family sacrificial victim who will continue to repeat a past trauma. *Alice, Sweet Alice* is an unjustly neglected work. Although promoted on video packets because of Brooke Shields's brief appearance as Karen, it significantly highlights the real material factors behind family horror—a bankrupt social system resulting in misery and oppression.

◆ ◆ ◆

Larry Cohen's work reveals similar achievements. He is one of the most remarkable figures working in low-budget commercial American cinema. His talent transcends many genres; his films often echo each other. Generic horror work such as *It's Alive, God Told Me To,* and *It Lives Again* articulate motifs in other films such as *Housewife, Black Caesar,* and *Hell Up in Harlem.*

Although not explicitly a horror movie, *Housewife* contains many themes integral to Cohen's work within that genre. Fusing satirical black comedy with caustic critique of capitalist lifestyles, *Housewife* contains Cohen's first assault on the nuclear family. He explicitly reveals the modern consumerist family as dependent upon a fragile lifestyle of hypocrisy and repression. *Housewife* represents a son's destructive revenge fantasy against parents who abandon him. Serving a prison sentence for dope smuggling, Kenneth Lennick lies on a dirty prison floor as if imagining the entire film. After frequent fragmented subliminal images accompanying parental denial of his real existence throughout several scenes, he finally appears toward the end. Rather than respond to his appeal for help, Bill (Andrew Duggan) and Bernadette Lennick (Joyce Van Patten) create a fantasy about an absence they now fully believe to be true. They tell everyone he is serving in Vietnam. Ensuing events of humiliation, chaos, and murder follow the intrusion of aggressive Black handyman Bone (Yaphet Kotto) into their lives. Appearing in answer to their traumatic discovery of a rat in their supposedly clean Beverly Hills swimming pool, he represents a racially class-motivated return of the repressed against the Lennicks. At the climax he suddenly disappears as mysteriously as he appeared. Bernadette (Joyce Van Patten) then rehearses alibis to disavow her responsibility for Bill's murder before the camera. She uses denials similar to those used in fabricating the story of Kenneth's absence. "I don't know whose idea it was. It wouldn't have been mine. I would remember it. Wouldn't I? Wouldn't I." She speaks these words in darkness after Kenneth destroys the lightbulb that stimulates his prison cell fantasy. The cinematic frame and Bill Lennnick's (Andrew Duggan) television image advertising a car plunge into complete blackness. The film represents Kenneth's revenge against two disavowing and selfish parents. In his first film, Cohen depicts Kenneth as a modern avatar of the Universal Frankenstein monster who is denied by his parent. Bone is also a fantasy projection of affluent class fears. As the film develops, this once threatening figure proves less monstrous than the upper-class couple who initially conjure him into existence. Although more of a satire than horror film, *Housewife* has key associations with Cohen's later work.

Cohen's two Fred Williamson films, *Black Caesar* (1972) and *Hell Up in Harlem* (1973), develop his ideas. Using the classic rise and fall structure of traditional gangster movies, Cohen emphasizes that the fall lies not in individual hubris but infection by capitalist lifestyles. As the godfather of Harlem, Tommy Gibbs (Fred Williamson) destroys not only himself but also his friends and family. His entire actions really strengthen a system he opposes. Capitalism contaminates everyone. Despite misleading advertising associations with the 1970s "blaxploitation" genre, Cohen stresses minority group membership as providing no real antidote to the system. Both *Black Caesar* and *Hell Up in Harlem* emphasize families as dysfunctional and self-destructive. Tommy emotionally destroys his mother in *Black Caesar* and indirectly causes his father's death in the sequel. The climax contains a deliberate irony. After rescuing his son and lynching his opponent in a classic racist Southern manner, he tells his offspring, "I'll love you like I loved my father." Both father and young son light off for the territory toward some undefinable future.

Cohen's mutant babies of the *It's Alive* films are logical successors of Bone and Tommy Gibbs. They are social productions of a corrupt system. *It's Alive* is one of the decade's most important family horror films, developing themes within Gordon Douglas's *Them!* (1954). Both films climax in the storm drains of Los Angeles, a key psychoanalytic metaphor for an excremental waste repressed by an obsessively clean materialist society. But there are several differences.

As a Cold War production, *Them!* presents its monsters as external representations of the Communist threat to American society. The first victims are an American family; the sole survivor is a traumatized young girl. Representing the official forces of law enforcement (cop James Whitmore and FBI agent James Arness) and science (Edmund Gwenn and Joan Weldon), the humans eventually invade the queen ant's nest and incinerate her eggs. Although *Them!* often contains parallels between human and ant society, they are both separate. The climactic sequence involves restoration of the typical American family when the humans return the Lodge children to their mother after wiping out the ant colony in the storm drains.

Two decades later, *It's Alive* presents its monster as the logical product of the typically affluent American family.[9] Like the Lennicks of *Housewife*, the Davies family exists in a disintegrating social order whose implications they ignore. Although *It's Alive* gives no manifest reason for the mutant's appearance, pertinent elements associate family repression with social collapse. Circumstances change. *It's Alive* no longer presents a fatherly figure such as Dr. Medford of *Them!* who makes reassuring scientific diagnoses. Nervous fathers waiting outside the delivery room reveal contemporary insecurities and lack of confidence in technological development. One expectant father looks for a spoon to stir his coffee. Another loans his pencil, commenting wryly, "After a whole year you get used to the taste of lead in your coffee." The ensuing conversation involves urban pollution. "There is an overabundance of lead in everything we eat. We're always poisoning ourselves." Los Angeles smog produces the comment, "It doesn't make any difference whether we breathe it or eat it!" An exterminator husband-to-be mentions insecticides creating a new breed of bigger and stronger roaches. Another nervous father kicks the malfunctioning coffee machine. Frank (John P. Ryan) finally quits the room in disgust after hearing about the snail problem in Beverly Hills— "They can wipe out a lawn in just a few minutes." This sequence draws implicit connections between institutional cleanliness and its negative consequences. It anticipates Frank's discovery of his baby's slaughterhouse activities in the antiseptic delivery room. The repressed returns with a vengeance. *Them!* earlier contrasted a radio bulletin reporting the elimination of dangerous diseases and an unstable political situation.[10]

The credits of *It's Alive* open on an unfocused subjective shot of individual torches flashing back and forth. They almost finally merge into a blinding light formation evoking *Housewife*'s postcredits opening image. This sequence anticipates the film's continual use of flashlights. Taken to his elder son's school, the hostile Los Angeles Police Department cops flash their beams in Frank's face. In the storm drain Frank's mutant baby shields its face from

Frank's light. This opening credit sequence places the audience in a similar dominated position by identifying us with both "creator" and "monster."

Red police neon lights form another recurrent visual motif, that is, emphasizing the real threat to individuals—institutional law enforcement turning on those they supposedly protect. Flashing red lights appear when Frank emerges from the hospital following his son's escape, outside his elder son's school, and when the police escort Lenore (Sharon Farrell) from her house in the concluding segment.

Both lights represent hostile signifiers of institutional forces ready to attack anyone deviating from socially defined normality, a normality with which Frank once identified. Hired by the drug industry to conceal any possible blame for the mutant's birth, Dr. Norton (Shamus Locke) suggests using Frank as bait to trap his own son. Institutional forces of law and medicine draw no distinction between Frank and his son. Both are equally monsters.

After the last credit, the camera pans left over the exterior roof of the Davies home, dissolving to a midshot of the house, leading to the bedroom. Lenore begins to feel her labor pains. Caressing Lenore as he prepares for the hospital, Frank dresses and goes to Chris's room. He is asleep, his pet Siamese cat on the bed. The brown wallpaper letters spell out the family's harmonious ideal "L.O.V.E." Frank wakes Chris up by nuzzling the cat's head against his face, an act Tom Milne describes as a "perfectly credible yet somehow outlandish note . . . a first foreboding indication that he has an obscure reluctance to come into contact with, to really accept his own flesh."[11] Like Cohen's other tormented hero in *God Told Me To*, he appears reticent about accepting the role of father. Frank reassures Chris concerning fears that stem from a TV program. "Is Mom going to die?" Opening scenes contain faint traces of uneasiness about to erupt virulently. The final interior shot shows Frank and Lenore framed in the nursery doorway. As the camera tracks out, it reveals the expected child's crib. From the blue walls we see that Frank desires a son. Lenore and Chris do not share his patriarchal expectations. Chris says, "I don't care what it is as long as you're O.K." Lenore replies, significantly hinting at her preference, "We'll give you a call when we find out whether you've got a baby sister or a baby brother." Instead she produces a monstrous product that reacts against social and institutional constraint.

Hollywood's normal family now produces a monster. The Davies home expresses family tensions. Returning home after the delivery, Frank again stands in the nursery doorway. He walks up to the crib, picks up a grinning cuddly toy, and places it on the mantelpiece. Cohen uses several ominous looking toys throughout *It's Alive* to express adult insecurity concerning childhood's real nature. Taken by the police to Chris's kindergarten schoolroom,

Frank is left alone except for his mutant baby's unseen presence. After the baby pulls a toy truck's string, a brief shot of its head leads to a shot revealing a row of grotesquely "Huggable" plastic toys used to teach the alphabet. The final image reveals a close-up of one with open mouth and fanglike teeth that resembles the mutant baby. Whether in home or kindergarten, the adult world can never feel secure with childhood.

In a later scene Frank believes Chris has returned home. A shot of the crib reveals something moving beneath the blankets. The next shot shows Frank ascending the stairs. We then see his shadow on the wall, its squat form resembling his mutant son, visually affirming affinity between creator and monster.

With its significant Universal Studio–associated title, *It's Alive* develops the premises of the Frankenstein saga to their most logical conclusions by affirming solidarity between creator and monster against the real enemy—institutional forces of law, medicine, and family. Like Frankenstein, Frank initially denies kinship with his son, choosing instead to regard it as an external monster. He psychotically joins in its hunt like Melville's Captain Ahab. Although earlier expressing his anguish on viewing the delivery room—"They stole my baby"—Frank gradually submits to ideologic patterns of thought, thus regarding his son as a monster. The audience also discovers Frank's insecurities concerning fatherhood. Comforting Lenore in the pre-med room, he expresses his desires to have a child, desires he did not share at her first conception. Significantly, eleven years separate Lenore's two deliveries, suggesting a long period of parental hesitation over having children.

LENORE. I'm glad we decided to have the baby.
FRANK. We both want it.
LENORE. It's not going to tie you down? You're not going to feel trapped like last time?

At first, he vehemently believes in the baby's abduction and responds angrily to Dr. Norton's medical interrogations.

NORTON. It kills like an animal and when we find it we have to kill it like an animal.
FRANK. It's not an animal! You can't classify it as an animal! It's human, doctor *(vehemently)*.

He vacillates before Dr. Norton and Lt. Perkins (James Dixon), "You have to do what is necessary. . . . What is there to understand?" Frank gradually submits to social pressure. However, contradictions appear even before the delivery. The Davises once considered an abortion. "Doesn't everybody enquire about it nowadays. It's just a question of convenience and we decided to go ahead." Sacked from his advertising firm by an image conscious boss associated with the hospital ("I have good connections over there. I'm vice-chairman of the fund-raising committee"), Frank changes under social pressure. When the supercilious Clayton (Guy Stockwell) speaks of a colleague keeping a mentally retarded child locked up in his home, Frank (obviously sensing his diplomatically phrased dismissal) retorts, "We're not talking about a retarded child. We're talking about a monstrosity of some kind."

He confesses his insecurities to sympathetically inclined Lt. Perkins who shares a similar family predicament. Telling a colleague about his wife's fears concerning his safety, he understands the family's problematic nature—"We lost our last baby." Learning of Mrs. Perkins's eight-month pregnancy, his colleague answers, "You're lucky you don't have grown-up kids nowadays. People without children don't know how lucky they are." Earlier expressing negative feelings concerning police work—"Hunting and killing babies doesn't seem to be my speciality"—Perkins senses Frank's dilemma and what motivates his aggressive feelings.

> FRANK. Why does everybody look at me as if it's my own flesh and blood. It's no relation to me . . . I've got an eleven year old no different from anyone else.
> LT. PERKINS. Nobody's looking at you *(sympathetically)*.
> FRANK. Maybe I didn't do the right thing. I just wanted to show I felt the same way as everyone else.

Frank changes from Frankenstein the creator to Frankenstein the hunter of the original James Whale version. But he feels deeply insecure. When Dr. Perry (Andrew Duggan) arrives with Dr. Norton to gain university medical rights to the mutant's corpse, Frank denies his parenthood, "It's not my child." He also notes, "When I was a kid I always thought the monster was Frankenstein. You know Karloff walking along in those big shoes grunting. When I went to high school, I read the book. . . . Somehow the ideas got all mixed up." Perry dismisses the parallel. "One must not allow oneself to be obsessed by escapist fiction." Yet undeniable traits within escapist fiction echo Frank's own dilemma. He is the 1970s Frankenstein. He expresses the reality behind the original story and various cinematic representations all involving families who produce monsters. Despite their different natures, a deep bond exists between father and monstrous son, one Lenore significantly recognizes. "Why are you so anxious to be the one to do it? . . . You're his father! . . . You have to be the one to do it!" She understands his violent attitude is a denial mechanism against feelings of paternity and responsibility. Frank sets off in pursuit as Lenore tells Chris why the baby initially reacted violently. "The doctors were trying to suffocate your little brother. He just wants to live."

Institutional forces are the real enemy. An earlier scene reveals an unnamed executive (Robert Emhardt) bribing Dr. Norton with a board position in his Research and Development Department if he ensures the baby's complete physical destruction. As head of a medication company, he marketed untested drugs without government approval. Wishing to avoid another thalidomide scandal, he enlists Norton's aid to cover up. Facing corrupt institutional forces, the baby's violence is understandable and preferable to its opponent's covert activities. Lenore also asserts that the baby loves its father, a love that also exists within Frank.

Frank compulsively reenacts his culture's regeneration through a violence pattern that follows frontier antecedents toward a bloody denouement that will supposedly make civilization secure. The greatness of *It's Alive* lies in its following this pattern and then rejecting its ideologic consequences.

Frank's pursuit of his mutant son in the storm drains also evokes archetypal patterns within the American cultural tradition. The motif recalls Charles Brockden Brown's early psychological fantasy, *Edgar Huntly*. Throughout the novel Edgar pursues the dark figure Clithero, who prefers nightmare and solitude to Edgar's genial daytime arena of society and gentility. Edgar gradually becomes aware of his kinship with the being he pursues, a kinship leading toward eventual identification with his quarry and the realization that Clithero represents his own dark self. As Richard Slotkin points out, "His (i.e., Edgar's) search in the physical wilderness is likewise a mask for his inquisition into his own mind and soul. His search for the guilty Clithero is an unconscious search for his own guilty self.[12] Frank arrives at similar realizations.

It's Alive moves into its final revelation, one of the most touching moments within contemporary American cinema. Frank looks at his son who suffers from a wound he earlier inflicted. As the mutant shields its eyes from the light of Frank's torch, he lays down his gun and walks up to it. Unlike Ahab of *Moby Dick*, he recognizes his true relationship to his son. He also realizes the self-destructive ritual violence society demands of him. Unlike any of the Universal Frankensteins and the vast majority of their cinematic successors, Frank acknowledges his creation. With tears in his eyes, he attempts to explain—"I was afraid like you. . . . No, you mustn't cry because if you cry they'll hear you and they'll come." He puts his coat around the mutant, taking it in his arms as Lenore did earlier in an attempt to conceal its presence from Frank at home, and he flees from the approaching police car in the storm drain. The hunter no longer attempts to destroy a social threat; he understands society is the real menace.

Unfortunately, like *Curse of the Cat People*, this brief utopian moment collapses before the intrusion of violent state forces. The police surround Frank outside the storm drain. Pleading in vain for his baby's life—"It can't hurt anyone. Let him live please"—he faces police abuse and Norton's murderous cries, "Kill it! Kill it now!" Frank then throws the baby at Norton. Both perish in a hail of bullets; the L.A.P.D. in no hurry to discriminate.

Reunited with Lenore, Frank regains her love. As Lt. Perkins is about to drive them home, he receives an intercom message. "Another one's been born in Seattle." The final image shows the car driving off into the night. It is an uncertain future in a civilization where families now breed monsters.

God Told Me To (1976) continues Cohen's radical explorations. Using satirical religious imagery and science fiction motifs, the film develops its particular vision of the new world of "gods and monsters" that the horror genre implicitly suggests but never adequately realizes. This new world not only presupposes the necessary destruction of all crippling institutional formations, such as the family, but also leads toward abolition of traditional gender distinctions. Operating within traditional generic categories while seeking to extend them beyond ideologic recuperation, *God Told Me To* finally emerges as an ambitiously flawed work aptly described by Robin Wood as a "sketch for the great movie Cohen may make one day."[13]

Investigating a random series of killings whose proponents claim divine sanction before their deaths, Peter Nicholas (Tony Lo Bianco) finds himself trapped in a situation that has personal and professional dimensions. As a dedicated Catholic, personally tormented by social definitions of normality, he lives in an individual hell. Separated from his wife Martha (Sandy Dennis) and living an unfulfilling existence with his young mistress (Deborah Raffin), Nicholas finally discovers that the whole institutional edifice upon which he has based his life is nothing but a lie. As a law enforcement officer straining against his religious procreative ordinations, he discovers he is the unsuccessful result of an alien insemination experiment. Although his superhuman powers remain recessively dominated by his human qualities, including civilization's necessary repressive mechanisms, his alien brother exhibits the other extreme. Believing himself a divine incarnation, the alien (Richard Lynch) parallels the same divided self as his tormented brother. Invested with positive light associations, he orders a series of random killings, trying to find his own personal identity within a hostile world and echoing his brother's wish-fulfillment killings of his unborn children.

By linking human and monster in an indissoluble chain, *God Told Me To* further emphasizes one cardinal tenet within the horror genre: the socially sanctioned *old* world of gods and monsters is never safe for the latter. They can only react against its constraints by either unconscious violence (killing unborn children) or exercising random acts of violence. However, though unfocused, these acts strike at the heart of society—capitalism's mean streets, a St. Patrick's Day Parade, and the annihilation of an entire family by its father, a father with whom Peter shares a deep affinity. He violently overreacts against a person who has also carried out his deepest desires.

Peter's relationship with his Martha and "Mary" counterpoint his alien brother's messianic associations. Confronting his sexually ambivalent alter ego in a deserted upstairs apartment after first meeting him in a basement furnace room, he is invited to participate in a procreative act that blurs all acceptable gender boundaries—an act that could result in a new messiah and the literal end of civilization. He rejects this, violently attacking his twin, allowing repressive instincts to rise in horror against this "aberration." The film's final scenes show him led away to mental institutional confinement, answering a reporter's question with a knowingly enigmatic, "God Told Me To." A new world of gods and monsters still awaits realization. Unlike *Exorcist II*, the opposites never merge.

Following *The Private Files of J. Edgar Hoover* (1977), whose repressive family monster controlled American political life for nearly four decades, Cohen directed *It Lives Again*. It is the logical successor to his other work and extends the horror film's generic horizons. Like *Exorcist II—The Heretic*, it contains themes awaiting full realization in a more progressive era. The emphasis is now firmly on protecting the monster from society. *It Lives Again* is not a fully realized work; its positive suggestions are more important than the overall design. But, like many significant 1970s works, it implicitly demonstrates the need for a society that lacks traditional family institutions.

Now part of an underground rescue team, Frank Davies approaches Eugene (Frederic Forrest) and Jody (Kathleen Lloyd), a couple that is expecting their first baby. The Scott relationship is already tense. Jody has given up a promising career in law, subordinating her status to Eugene's. Frank undermines their superficial beliefs in American society as he tells of the medical profession's attempt to suffocate his baby at birth and its "human" quality of forgiving him for wounding it. In *It's Alive* the social order victimized Frank. He now wishes the Scotts to see the difference between their precarious freedom and a murderous state system. Believing in a pre-Reagan era judicial system, Eugene recognizes the government's illegal activities and parallels it to primitive methods of child exposure. Once the Scotts deny social definitions of the "monstrous," they soon encounter state violence. Rescuing Jody from the hospital, Frank's medical team delivers the baby before the police can destroy it. Taken to a secret base, Eugene meets Dr. Perry, who is in charge of protecting the mutant babies, two of whom he significantly names "Adam" and "Eve." Although they are savage, the babies represent the future of the human race, possibly "the beginning of a new race of humanity which is going to eclipse our own, the way the human race is going to survive the pollution of the planet." Perry hopes to eventually train them so they will not threaten the human race. This is a precarious goal. The babies react violently, often brutally murdering those seeking to protect them from society. Despite Perry's optimistic projections, they are still monstrous beings reacting in traditionally violent generic terms.

Facing a vicious social order, they respond in the same manner. As Eugene flinches before the babies, Perry explains the nature of their violent reactions, "Your fear seems to threaten them." Reared within a family social structure having rigid definitions of "normality" and "monstrous," Eugene intuitively reveals his family conditioning. As in *The Birds*, paranoia unleashes aggressive reaction. But *It Lives Again* emphasizes even further that the real threats come from the state not from the monsters. The mutant babies react whenever they feel themselves threatened. But, as with the Universal and Lewton films, brief utopian moments exist when humans and monster empathize outside the rigid boundaries of institutional definitions. *It Lives Again* makes abundantly clear that no positive "new world" will ever occur until negative forces of state, law, and family no longer threaten new developments.

By implicitly suggesting progressive avenues, *It Lives Again* notes obstacles such as traditional family restrictions. The Scotts live in an unequal relationship. Economic constraints force Jody to relinquish her law school graduation to aid Eugene in his career. Jody's mother conveniently blames him as a possible hereditary cause for the mutant birth. Gene is a monster. "It has to be him." Seeking to undermine her daughter's "unsatisfactory" marriage, she collaborates with FBI agent Mallory (John Marley) to eliminate both monsters: Gene and the baby.

Unquestionably accepting social norms and eager to interfere in her daughter's marriage, Jody's mother stimulates a chain of events that have violent consequences. Both she and Mallory are rigid conformists. Mallory's attitude parallels Frank's earlier pathologic pursuit of his monster son. Operating under an assumed name, Mallory later reveals himself as the father of the mutant baby born in Seattle. Conceiving late in life, the mutant's birth dashed his paternal hopes. He returned home to find his wife's body torn apart by the birth, and he immediately shot the baby with his service revolver. Mallory shoots first and asks questions later. But he bears deep-rooted guilt feelings which he represses in his institutional role of hunter. *It Lives Again* contains several indications of his regrets. Continually uneasy in Frank Davies's presence, a father who let his baby live to find it had feelings of love and forgiveness, Mallory eagerly forces law enforcement officials to shoot any mutant baby at sight. After "Adam's" death, he abruptly silences an FBI agent who noted the baby's vain attempt to speak. As in *It's Alive*, the sympathetic Lt. Perkins realizes the presence of alternatives other than violence. But he is trapped within the system. "We'd be better off finding the cause, pollution, drugs, instead of just killing." Perkins notes Mallory's bloody chewed fingernails during their final surveillance of Jody and Gene. Mallory pathologically asserts, "It's got to come back. It's got to kill them. That's its nature!" This exposes concealed guilt over the murder of his own child. John Marley's performance keenly conveys the anxieties and guilt feelings of a father repressing his feelings by violence.

Although Jody refuses to listen to her mother, she is clearly affected. Meeting Eugene again in Perry's secret base, she reacts to his touch, a response he understands as being "because of what we created." Alienation develops when Gene agrees to act as bait to trap his mutant child. But like Frank, Gene also experiences a final crisis of conscience.

When the baby arrives Jody reaches out, realizing its need for love. She persuades Gene to drop his revolver, saving him from becoming another tormented Mallory. Acceding to Jody's appeal, "He just wants to be held," he takes the child in his arms, echoing Frank Davies's progressive movement in the final part of *It's Alive*.

As law enforcement agents isolate the house, Gene and Jody appear as a happy couple nursing their child before a comfortable fire. They are a real family, with feelings of love and tenderness for a being society deems monstrous. But, as with those brief moments in *Frankenstein*, *Bride of Frankenstein*, *Curse of the Cat People*, and *It's Alive*, the social order intrudes by seeking to disrupt any alliance between boundaries it wishes to keep apart. Mallory and the police arrive like the hunters in *Bride of Frankenstein* and the police in *Curse of the Cat People*.

Appealing to Mallory to put down his gun, Gene is unable to prevent the baby from attacking his enemy. Picking up Mallory's revolver, Gene now finds himself in Mallory's earlier position. But he cannot fire. Ironically, Jody directs Gene's aim and urges him to shoot. Appalled by the violence, mother and father act together and kill their child. In the final seconds leading to the act, Gene looks away in anguish as Jody directs his aim before he shoots. Saving Mallory, the couple embraces again, their first real physical contact since their son's birth. The film ends with Gene now in San Francisco. He repeats Frank's earlier role of emissary as he informs another couple about their new arrival.

It Lives Again is one of the genre's most progressive and complicated works. It presents a possible alternative direction. Cohen's films clearly reveal social perversion. Contaminated by capitalist structures, the family is a manipulated unit. It produces everyday monsters. The mutant babies represent a repressed violent reaction against this process. Despite their vicious attacks, they often respond to those who do not fear them. At brief moments a union occurs between humans and monsters that is suggestive of the possibility of a dialectical fusion leading toward positive alternatives, a thesis suggested by *Exorcist II*. But the state intervenes to suppress this possibility. Another remarkable feature of Cohen's work is his suggestion that the family is capable of redemption if it accepts the monstrous and moves toward new forms. *It's Alive III* concludes on this optimistic note. Not all family horror films contain monsters or irresolvable contradictions.

However, this utopianism receives virulent reaction in later decades. While the developing forces leading to the Reagan revolution slowly mobilized to combat the gains of the 1960s, horror films began to take more nihilistic, aggressive directions, seeking to deny and overwhelm suggestions for new radical developments by excessively mobilizing fetishistic devices inherent in the genre itself. This explains the disappointing nature of many later works that indulge in reactionary displays of spectacular violence, denying everything except the most negative meaning. Despite developments of trends in the *Friday the 13th*, *Halloween*, and *Nightmare on Elm Street* films, contradictions could not entirely disappear. Furthermore, the apocalyptic aspect of particular horror films are not entirely devoid of some relevant ideas.

Chain Saw Massacres: The Apocalyptic Dimension

The 1980s saw a drastic change in the form and character of the American horror film. In 1980 a work appeared that heralded the genre's degeneration— *Friday the 13th*. This film initiated another subgeneric movement variously entitled "slasher" or "stalker" film. Although most commentators dismiss these films as worthless trash, they are symptomatic of their particular era and deserve attention. The phenomenon did not emerge unheralded. As part of a corpus described as "Reaganite Entertainment," they belong to a cultural movement that gained momentum in the 1970s, erupting during the next decade. These visually repugnant and thematically debased "slasher" films belong to an apocalyptic dimension influencing contemporary horror. Works such as *The Texas Chain Saw Massacre* (1973), *Race with the Devil* (1975), *Eaten Alive* (1977), *The Brood* (1979), *The Funhouse*, *Scanners* (both 1981), *The Texas Chain Saw Massacre 2* (1986), and *Leatherface* (1988) exemplify a particular apocalyptic vision moving from disclosing family contradictions toward self-indulgent nihilism. To understand this change, a knowledge of this apocalyptic influence is essential.

According to Christopher Sharrett, American culture exhibits a particular apocalyptic strain in the political, religious, and cultural spheres throughout its entire history.[1] As a Puritan "City on the Hill," the young Republic felt a sense of mission as a chosen people extending from the Frontier into world affairs. Full of self-appointed missionary status, American society blinded itself to its negative side with ideologic idealized innocence, a feeling lasting into the mid-twentieth century. With the end of postwar affluence, a mood of despondency and despair infiltrated society and culture. Optimistic components behind the missionary ideal collapsed, revealing a fatality and nihilism also present in biblical apocalyptic literature. With the decline of belief in myths and institutions, a religiously inspired (but secularized) sense of living in the "last days" emerged, a mood modern horror best embodies.

This contemporary apocalyptic mood differs from its religious roots in being nonrevelatory, emphasizing "the unrecuperability of society, with the dissolution and futility of all human effort."[2] Although disagreeing with the definition's application to certain films (particularly Romero's work), the movement does provide a key to the rationale behind slasher films beginning with *Halloween* (1978). For Sharrett, "It is precisely because the modern apocalypse is horrific that the horror film best represents its expression."[3] Because the present lacks belief in any enduring value systems and fails to construct viable alternatives, this prevailing mood of despair also influences cultural artifacts such as the horror genre. Although certain films present, by implication, the need for new alternatives, others wallow in a nihilistic barrage of special effects and vicious assaults usually directed against sexually active females.

Although Jason, Michael, and Freddy lack explicit supernatural attributes, their various resurrections exemplify punitive biblical atavistic actions against youthful transgressors. "The horror film, even as it steadily ignores the supernatural, becomes the best representation of the hold of Old Testament moralism in popular culture, a hold enhanced by dominant ideology."[4] Stability collapses. Family figures in the various *Friday the 13th*, *Halloween*, and *Nightmare on Elm Street* films appear weak and ridiculous. But nothing further results. As Sharrett notes, "The apocalyptic at work momentarily inoculates the spectator with criticisms of a failing dominant order, but then reneges on this criticism by denying that there is any worth in carrying this critical process through to a conclusion."[5] Instead there is only despair and a collective death wish involving cinematic sacrificial victims articulating fears within the audience's psyche.

In contrast to Sharrett, I wish to argue that the full nihilistic apocalyptic vision actually emerges in the eighties. Although he states that films such as *Psycho*, *The Birds*, *Rosemary's Baby*, *The Exorcist*, *The Last House on the Left*, *The Hills Have Eyes*, and *The Texas Chain Saw Massacre* lack any definable rationale for their horrific events, enough evidence exists within the various works to reveal veiled material forces behind such manifestations. Although contemporary theory attacks totalizing concepts such as Marxism and psychoanalysis, the lack of direct causation within the films themselves need not necessarily presume an explanatory rationale. As Pierre Machery and others show, a work is important for what it excludes as well as for what it chooses to display.[6] Jason's neglect, Michael's murderous incestuous desires, and Freddy's child molestations are all socially generated. But the films emphasize excessive violence to the detriment of social meaning by sadistically immersing the audience in a masochistic barrage of special effects. By contrast, events in *The Texas Chain Saw Massacre, Race with the Devil, The Brood,* and *Scanners* have sociofamilial features of earlier horror films. However, an apocalyptic current does attempt to deny material causes.

Sharrett refers to D. H. Lawrence's idea of the apocalyptic as signifying a human tendency to think in religious and ultimate terms about failure within the historic process. It denotes a form of self-destructive escapism appealing to a thwarted collective self arising from a failed consensus.[7] Lawrence's definition suitably fits an era disillusioned by failed 1960s promises and the social breakdowns of Vietnam and Watergate. This era wishes to forget and deny both the historical and any active attempts at social change. A type of crisis cinema emerges that projects collective revenge and irrational tendencies. For Sharrett, "Crisis becomes a means of making sense of, and giving order to the world, but it is also a way of displacing responsibility by regarding extreme situations as predestined, supernatural, irrational and demonic."[8] Within the horror genre an excessive mixture of visual sadistic and masochistic violence emerges to overwhelm the narrative. It represents a pathologic reaction toward the viewer's negative self-image within a historical situation seemingly impervious to progressive change. Family dilemmas remain. Dark families threaten the younger generation. The viewer remains trapped within a repetitive double-bind situation where resolution remains temporary. There are no longer any closed, cathartic, classical endings as various cinematic reincarnations of Jason, Michael, and Freddy show. The family is revealed as dark and destructive, but contemporary cinema shows that there is little, if anything, its victims can do about it.

◆ ◆ ◆

Both versions of *The Texas Chain Saw Massacre* reveal differences between earlier and later stages of the apocalyptic. Where Hooper's first version remains firmly entrenched within the parameters of American history and culture, its sequel contains elements paralleling slasher works of the 1980s, drowning the viewer in spectacular violence and excess. This tends to stifle the film's other meanings involving historic memory and cultural change. The earlier film presents the slaughterhouse family as a dark embodiment of the American dream, losers within American ideology that parallel the working-class satanists of *Race with the Devil.* Hooper's remake and its successor presupposes the family's monstrosity. Its emphasis upon violence and female brutalization engulfs anticapitalist critiques within the narrative. Within contemporary apocalyptic and generic parameters, this confirms Sharrett's findings. "The cynicism of this type of film is geared towards refusing explanation: the apocalypse does not have to do with providing clarity and a revelation of history's purpose. It is concerned with showing civilization at a dead end, but more importantly with expressing the worthlessness of any totalizing system of belief."[9] Although recognizing the latter strategy as an ideologic governed mechanism designed to ward away progressive alternatives, the description does explain the situation facing family horror in the 1980s and 1990s.

Apocalyptic dimensions have historic connections determining particular cinematic treatments of the family that reveal the American horror film as a fundamental component of the national cultural tradition. *The Texas Chain Saw Massacre* is a unique cinematic recapitulation of Richard Slotkin's regeneration through violence thesis. Puritan ancestral fears finally prove themselves more powerful than Enlightenment concepts within the Declaration of Independence. Contrasts emerge between Western civilization's repressive structures and demonized others in a cultural Gothic imaginary.[10]

In this pre-Freudian world, a fundamental link appeared between the Puritan community's repression of dark passionate impulses and Indian culture's supposed blood and myth rituals. The latter group embodied Puritan repressed projections. Puritans maintained rigid physical and spiritual apartheid. They feared succumbing to their neighbor's free sexuality and envisaged cannibalistic impulses. A hunter figure mediated between both environments protecting the community from contamination. But there was always the danger that this savior could become infected. Hawthorne's writings reflected "a Puritan image of the wilderness as the land of terrible unconscious, in which the dark powers of man impress themselves in reality with tragic consequences. The hunter becomes like the beast he hunts; the would-be destroyer of bestial sin himself degenerates into a 'Belial.'"[11] Anticipating horror film devices, the Puritans saw their racial "others" as monsters fit only for extermination.[12]

The hunter myth opposed this Puritan extreme of exorcism and extermination. Its basic premise involved learning from the wilderness, an inconceivable idea during the Mather hegemony.[13] Benjamin Church's narratives stressed practical experiences gained from the hunt rather than Puritan isolationism.[14] As the myth developed, other important tenets appeared: the mysterious aura of identification between hunter and quarry and the symbolic initiation into the other self gained by killing the "beast," an initiation the hunter could use to save his people assuming he survived contamination.[15] The myth influenced particular works within American literature such as Melville's *Moby Dick*, Cooper's Leatherstocking tales, and Faulkner's "The Bear."

A regeneration through violence myth grew. It embodied an irresolvable *anima-id* paradox, often involving a struggle between the hunter and the dark figures of the wilderness for possession of a white female captive who symbolizes Christian moral and social law. The dark enemy represented the hero's deep desires and his soul's most feared adversary—his repressed self. The difference between these two appears in the opposing works of T. B. Thorpe and Nathaniel Hawthorne. For Thorpe the bear represented the embodiment of creative power that the hero gains by merging his identity.[16] Other literary works foreshadowed a resolution of opposites, anticipating the project of *Exorcist II*.[17] But they were generally ineffective, suffering from ideologic constraints that affect alternative movements within Western society. The development of the hunter myth had disastrous consequences for American society. Although the Puritans cleared the wilderness for conversion, Daniel Boone's heirs often did so in the name of capitalist aggrandizement. Rapacious business interests destroyed everything earlier settlers wished to rescue from barbarism. Forests and animals fell victim to profit.[18] So, too, did the original hunters and settlers once they had served their purposes. Don Siegel's partially directed *Death of a Gunfighter* (1969) reveals a ruthless business-minded community's disposal of its former "hunter-savior," Marshall Patch (Richard Widmark). Settled Western homesteads eventually become John Ford's displaced "Okies" of *The Grapes of Wrath* (1940). Even a hunter once "pure in mind" could degenerate into becoming Melville's Indian hater in *The Confidence Man* or Robert Montgomery Bird's Nathan Slaughter in *Nick of the Woods*. The hunter myth could provide an ideologic rationale for wilderness exploitation.[19] So the original regeneration through violence ideal contained flaws.[20]

The Texas Chain Saw Massacre represents Puritanism's worst fears. Its slaughterhouse family is a twentieth-century descendant of Ishmael Bush of *The Prairie*. They represent the demonic Indians of Puritan nightmares by their cannibalistic activities. At the same time the family are losers within the American Dream made redundant by new technology and changing historical forces. Unlike the Indians they neither vanish into reservations nor travel west like the Okies. Instead, they live on the margins of civilization, brutally following the logical consequences of consumer capitalism. Like Romero's zombies, they represent repressed, violent family tendencies.

Sally (Marilyn Burns) and Franklin (Paul Partain) Hardesty are the successful products of "getting ahead," benefitting from a process that has destroyed the Frontier. Like Craven's family in *The Hills Have Eyes*, they venture into a wilderness area that was devastated after fulfilling its use-value. The Hardesty business involved meat, built upon the physical and mental exploitation of the slaughterhouse family. A group of selfish and bickering youngsters venture out and encounter their repressed counterparts in America's most violent state. Like H. G. Wells's Morlocks, the slaughterhouse family emerges and take bloody vengeance on twentieth-century Eloi beneficiaries of their economic exploitation. The radio commentary in the precredits sequence ascribes blame to "outsiders" as a convenient escapist mechanism. Evil lies within American society and the family.

Fenimore Cooper's noble Leatherstocking becomes the mentally sick Leatherface. He is now part of the demonic landscape having succumbed to cannibal tendencies feared by the Puritans. Instead of rescuing the captive white female and returning her to civilization, the hunter pursues her, recognizing her status as a symbol of forces that have made him (and his family) redundant. The killings no longer occur outside a family hearth, but within, serving as a substitute for the place of former employment. There is no longer any noble pursuit as in the deer chase of *The Pioneers*. Similarly there can be no real integration between hunter and quarry after the hunt. Because civilization has made the hunter redundant, this is impossible. Leatherstocking's Kill-Deer becomes Leatherface's chainsaw. Leatherface is no noble, articulate hunter but an obese, inarticulate figure who represents the degeneration through violence of a figure personified by Daniel Boone and Natty Bumppo. Fully identified with his former prey, Leatherface can only make animal sounds. The hunter has turned from clearing the wilderness for civilization. He will take revenge on those who have made him obsolete, especially youthful representatives of the American family. As Hooper shows, the slaughterhouse family represents the return of many repressed qualities—social, cultural, ideological, and historical.

Although the major part of the film suggests a cause for the violent events according to a Marxist-Freudian "return of the repressed" hypothesis, the prologue does contain apocalyptic connotations.[21] A written commentary fills the screen affirming the film's factual basis. The screen goes dark. We hear the sound of a shovel shifting earth. A series of flashbulb shots briefly illuminate the darkness revealing objects that are initially difficult to recognize. We gradually see they are shots of decaying hands, teeth, and a skull. The skull finally appears against the light as the camera slowly tracks away from it. An entire skeleton embraces another, grotesquely parodying domestic embrace. A radio commentary accompanies the camera movement telling of a series of Texas graveyard desecrations. As the camera stops in a static shot, it concludes by blaming "elements outside the State" for the acts.

The radio commentary does deny causality. But, as the film progresses, we learn Hitchhiker is responsible for the desecration. He carries a camera. During the following sequence where we meet the five youngsters, another radio commentary describes events Hitchhiker could not have been responsible for. These include violent incidents in American society, the collapse of a building in the town, the discovery (in another state) of a body lacking genitals, international terrorism, oil spills, and wholesale arson. One report tells of the discovery of an eighteen-month-old child found chained in an attic by its parents, an interesting foreshadowing of forthcoming family violence. As the first major apocalyptic horror movie whose excessive violence foreshadows later works, *The Texas Chain Saw Massacre* stands at a midway position. It does not entirely deny causality, but it also juxtaposes random elements that attempt to avoid material explanations for the events, a technique featuring in so-called "postmodernist" horror films.[22]

The prologue attempts disassociation from causality. A succession of ominous booming sounds and clashing cymbals opposes radio commentary logocentricity. After mentioning "elements outside the state," credits roll. Then the film opens with a shot of the sun, shrouded in mist, a visual motif occurring throughout the film that attempts an aura of cosmic significance. The image links up with several astrological elements. At three key points Pam reads from a book telling of "malevolent planets in retrograde" and Saturn's bad influence. The first occurs in opening scenes, and the second follows their journey past the slaughterhouse prior to Hitchhiker's appearance. The final reading happens after Hitchhiker leaves the van. A low-angle shot identifies the book as *American Astrology: Your Daily Guide.* Pam reads from a section about Capricorn's dominance by Saturn. She uses the text to explain Hitchhiker's disruptive actions, disavowing any attempt to explain rationally events escaping into illusionary explanations. This reveals their unwillingness to face a real danger.

An apocalyptic situation does not completely dominate the film. These young Americans deny ugly social realities and seek recourse to apocalyptic solutions. The analogy parallels the Reagan era's self-destructive immersion in old myths with their denial of material causes. Hooper's film anticipates many key features of Reaganite entertainment and later horror films where violent effects become the raison d'être. At this point of time, the film engages in a dialogic clash between causation and denial, a factor evident in visuals and soundtrack. The predominant sun motif appears when the van arrives at the gas station. It frames Leatherface's respective murders of Pam and Kirk and Jerry's teasing of wheelchair-bound Franklin. "He's coming to get you. I told him where you are." Sunset also appears as Jerry approaches the house—it is accompanied by the clashing cymbals of the opening soundtrack. Although these elements attempt noncausal, extradiegetic signification (similar to the opening scene's dead armadillo), they cannot entirely overwhelm other important motifs.

The film reveals two reasons for the group's journey. They ostensibly travel to investigate grandfather Hardesty's grave after reports of graveyard desecrations. But the real reason for the visit is Sally's desire for a day out. Family circumstances necessitate the presence of her obese brother Franklin. The others regard him as a nuisance. Sally has to look after him as Hitchhiker has to care for Leatherface. Both siblings resent this family duty. Arriving at the family graveyard, Sally accompanies the sheriff to check on the grave. No other young people are present. The majority are either old or middle-aged. Several intercut shots show a drunk. Shot from a high angle, his head grotesquely in the frame's foreground, he acts as chorus telling the "unofficial" version of events. "Nobody listens to an old man . . . but I've seen things . . . things nobody wants to hear about." The next shot shows Franklin's disturbed face. As Sally finds grandfather's grave untouched, the drunk repeats his words concluding, "There's them that laughs and knows better." Played by 1950s blacklisted radio commentator John Henry Faulk, this character's presence again signifies American society's tendency to accept irrational explanations over unpalatable rational causes. Faulk's role asserts a common motif in the horror genre that is recognized by Wes Craven and others: denial of social causation.[23]

One ugly fact links the Hardesty family with their exploited slaughter-house counterparts. As the van nears a slaughterhouse, Franklin identifies the smell, "That's the old slaughterhouse where grandfather used to sell all his cattle. Uncle used to work in one of those places at Fort Worth." As intercut shots show a dead cow's head and live cattle looking aggressively toward the van. Franklin eagerly describes slaughterhouse practices as cattle roar in the background. Pam reads predictions from her astrological manual. He takes out his knife to look at it in fascination. His dark actions evoke a monster from the id—Hitchhiker.

Despite objections—"Well, the son of a bitch will smell like a slaughter-house!"—they pick up Hitchhiker (Edwin Muir) near the Hardesty's former property. Like Henry Frankenstein, Franklin condescendingly dismisses and insults his creation—"I reckon we just picked up Dracula." Learning of Hitch-hiker's family occupation, Franklin then comments, "Yeah, a whole family of Draculas!" There are enough indications during this sequence to show Hooper's familiarity with classical and contemporary horror motifs. Like Frankenstein's monster, Hitchhiker appears in answer to Franklin's gory fantasies.

Like Dracula, he and his family vampirize passing travelers, selling processed bodies for economic survival after the collapse of their original livelihood. "The family who stays together slays together." With his green T-shirt, animal pouch, and long greasy hair, Hitchhiker also subversively embodies the dark aspect of hippie youth culture—Charles Manson and his "family."

As the group drives further into "Indian Country," country and western music plays ominously on the van's radio; the lyrics ironically parody the dark domesticity within the slaughterhouse family.

Hitchhiker's slashing of Franklin's wrist, following his refusal to pay two dollars for a blurred photograph, has dark historical implications. Believing that the photograph captured the soul, many nineteenth-century American Indians avoided the camera. With his long hair and animal pouch, Hitchhiker's hippie/Indian culture persona embodies Puritan fears of Native American Satanic forces. When Franklin refuses to pay, he burns his photograph. Not only does this create a diversion, allowing him to escape, but he also captures Franklin's soul, making him vulnerable to Leatherface's chainsaw. By cutting Franklin's wrist with his own razor after slashing his own hand, Hitchhiker creates a perverse sense of blood brotherhood, thereby bonding Franklin to his own family. Hitchhiker inverts the Puritan Captivity Mythology's regeneration through violence. The sequence ends with him looking through the van windows, kicking and sticking out his tongue at the group. After smearing the exterior with blood, he dances, grotesquely parodying an Indian war dance.

Intending to visit the old Hardesty residence, the group stops at a gas station, Hooper's equivalent to the Bates Motel halfway point before the Terrible House. Hitchhiker's blood smears are noticeable on the van—marking its occupants as future victims. The attendant (Jim Siedow) informs them of the sudden lack of petrol while he supplies them with suspicious looking barbecues. While Pam, Sally, Kirk, and Jerry venture outside, Franklin remains within, watching an imbecilic window-washer clean the van windows. Intercut shots echo Franklin's earlier perspective as he viewed Hitchhiker dancing outside. He gazes in fascination at his knife containing Hitchhiker's blood smears. Eating the barbecue (and unconsciously partaking in the Puritan's taboo cannibalistic Eucharist), Franklin fears meeting Hitchhiker again. Ominously worms are also on sale. The group leaves the gas station after the attendant warns them not to go near the old Hardesty house. He thus lays bait for the unwary travelers.

Arriving at the old house, the youngsters lift Franklin out of the van, then go and leave him as Hitchhiker frequently deserts Leatherface. Attempting to move his wheelchair toward the old house, Franklin spits out his barbecue portion, venting frustration at the others who use him as an excuse to go on a jaunt. Mimicking Sally—"Come on Franklin. It's going to be a fine trip!"— he bursts into tears, sticking his tongue out against her, exactly duplicating Hitchhiker's earlier action (Leatherface later rolls out his tongue after he murders Harry). Hearing what appears to be a rattlesnake, Franklin sees a bag on the floor, then looks up to see a voodoo charm (resembling a skeletal bone from elbow to wrist) above his head.

The associations are revealing. Chewing on recycled human flesh, Franklin again unwittingly participates in a Satanic Eucharist. Ensuing events answer his prayer of vengeance. Kirk, Pam, and Jerry fall prey to Leatherface who suddenly erupts in the slaughterhouse home. Leatherface's home disavows separations between home and workplace within capitalist society. The family hearth is a dark microcosm of the world outside. Furthermore, the youngsters' fates within the terrible house reveals the hidden violence beneath their affluent existence. Unlike the earlier radio commentator, they can no longer conveniently project unwholesome tendencies onto "elements outside the state." They face their dark proletarian family counterparts.

Both Franklin and Leatherface are obese, unwholesome, dependent children within their families. Although Franklin conjures up Leatherface as his Frankenstein monster, this does not save him from his creature's violent energies. Like Henry Frankenstein, he perishes at the hands of his creation, who then sets off in pursuit of Sally. Hunter, not demonic Indian, becomes the pursuer. He chases a selfish female, the cultural descendant of an avatar making his once-heroic role redundant.

In the twentieth century, the hunter's isolation from any form of society is impossible. Lacking Natty Bumppo's final prairie and the isolated wildernesses awaiting Shane and Ethan Edwards at the conclusion of *Shane* and *The Searchers*, the noble hunter now becomes reduced to dependence on capitalism and the family. Recaptured by the gas attendant (who represents the family's father-figure), Sally returns to the house to participate in a grotesque family meal where she is both guest of honor and main course.

The slaughterhouse family macabrely invert normal civilized values. After pausing to switch off the gas station lights—"the cost of electricity is enough to put a man out of business"—the attendant drives home with Sally tied up in a sack. Seeing Hitchhiker on the road, he leaves his pickup truck to admonish a prodigal son beating him with the same stick with which he prodded Sally—"I'll teach you to stay away from that graveyard!" His anger intensifies on seeing the family door, which was damaged by Leatherface's chainsaw in his pursuit of Sally. "I told you never to leave your brother alone." "Look what your brother did to that door!" He punishes Leatherface like a naughty child. Paternal discipline restores family order.

Sally awakes to find herself tied to a chair with severed arms in a grotesque parody of Poe's "King Pest" and Carroll's Mad Hatter's Tea Party. She meets a grandfather entirely different from the one whose grave she visited. The sequence begins with a blurred image focusing into the moon. Jeered at by Hitchhiker, stared at by Leatherface, now wearing a suit and new black wig, she meets Grandpa. Formerly the best killer in the slaughterhouse before age and technology made him redundant, this living corpselike figure, fed by Leatherface, has the honor of her slaughter. Held in the family dining room, surrounded by human skeletons, lampshade, and cannibal feast, Sally finds Grandpa unable to hold the hammer and equal his former prowess. "Nobody could beat Grandpa." Family values are now grotesque and senile.

Sally frees herself and escapes by jumping through a window. It is daylight outside—a shock after the darkness of the preceding scenes. She limps to the highway pursued by Hitchhiker and Leatherface before a tractor-trailer runs over the former. Managing to hobble into the back of a pickup truck, she watches Leatherface as she lapses into hysteria. The penultimate shot reveals the insane, bloodied visage of someone who will never recover. Then we see Leatherface standing, whirling his chainsaw upward, parodying a dance of death. The image abruptly cuts to the blackness that introduced the film. Only Leatherface remains, a perverse embodiment of the family. Although daylight appears darkness remains the real cosmic ruler.

The Texas Chain Saw Massacre is one of the most nihilistic visions of the family, revealing a hearth of darkness that generates violence and destruction. Despite apocalyptic elements Hooper presents his slaughterhouse family as material embodiments of capitalist repression.

◆　◆　◆

Jack Starret's *Race with the Devil* also reveals significant material factors. Although its two couples are not strictly families (having no children), they embody institutional values. They are married, live in a mobile home, and have a family dog. Their consumerist affluence marks them for retaliation by losers in the American Dream. Despite merging different generic elements such as western, road movie, and horror film, *Race with the Devil* is really a horror film with modern parallels to the western. It is a contemporary version of Ford's *Drums along the Mohawk* (1939). An economically underprivileged silent majority replaces Indians as the new version of Puritan demonic forces. Nathaniel Hawthorne's worst dreams occur. Satanists are no longer identifiable Indians but ordinary Americans inhabiting not just the wilderness but rural American trailer parks, roads, small towns, and garages. Middle Americans are now satanists. The mobile trailer replaces Ford's log cabins.

Owned by affluent businessmen, the trailer represents an attempted compromise between opposing tensions in the Western genre—settlement and wandering/home and freedom; the Ideal Male is the virile adventurer and Ideal Female is Wife and Mother.[24]

Credit scenes emphasize wilderness Satanic forces outside America's supposedly safe highways. A dead tree appears against the skyline as the camera tilts up from the road. The camera gradually tracks in as credits roll. Red smoke enters frame right behind the tree. It eventually covers the sky. The tree reddens to a white heat. As the whiteness fills the screen, the image immediately cuts to an oxyacetylene white flame. Dark energies lurk behind constructive technology. A zoom-out shows a mechanic working on a motorbike in a manufacturing firm built up over the years by Frank and Peter. Played by two actors (Peter Fonda, Warren Oates) having associations with westerns and road movies (*Ride the High Country, Major Dundee, The Wild Bunch, The Hired Hand, Two-Lane Blacktop, The Wild Angels, Easy Rider*), both embody capitalist success in the American Dream. Unlike *The Wild Angels* the bike is now safely integrated within consumerism. No longer a threat, it becomes subordinate to the family trailer.

The trailer represents a new form of the pioneer ideal embodied in contemporary annual visits to national parks and summer camps for urban Americans.[25] For Frank and Roger it represents their ideal vacation. Both men had postponed raising children to devote themselves to building up their business during the previous five years. They now take a much-needed vacation. Opening images show a high-angle shot of the trailer leaving San Antonio and passing the Monument to the Defenders of the Alamo, another significant icon in the violent "Last Stand" scenario within American Frontier history. A figure ascending toward heaven appears on the monument. Although we are not close enough to see any inscription, the actual Alamo Memorial reads as follows. "From the Fire That Burned Their Bodies Rose the Eternal Spirit of Sublime Heroic Sacrifice Which Gave Birth to an Empire State." As the film proceeds, this gains ironic overtones. The next shot shows the trailer driving past the San Antonio Bank, its reflection appearing on in its windows. Like *Shadow of a Doubt*'s Bank of America dominating sunny Santa Rosa, capitalism resides within any idyllic environment. These two monuments have key associations. The noble sacrifice of the Alamo defenders actually gave birth to a capitalist Eden for the fortunate few. While Frank and Roger bask in their newly acquired affluence, they forget about the losers outside. Criticizing ordinary trailers as "nothing more than mobile truck houses on wheels," Frank boasts. "We don't need anything from anybody. We are self-contained. Don't need no restaurants, no showers. We've got a $36,000 trailer." However, they accidentally stumble into another sacrificial situation that darkly inverts an earlier Last Stand.

Before Frank turns off the main highway, he remarks to the others, "There it is. Our private road to seclusion." A high-angle shot reveals the trailer pulling into a wilderness area. As the couples leave the trailer, the camera pans left as they walk to the river's edge. Their comments echo Betsy's tunnel vision in the opening scenes of *I Walked with a Zombie*, "This is beautiful, don't you think? Beautiful and peaceful." A high-angle shot zooms out to reveal the dead tree of the credit sequence at frame right facing the parked trailer at the left. A river separates the two objects, its associations darkly inverting Ford's favorite western hymn, "Shall We Gather at the River." The continuing zoom-out dwarfs the trailer amidst surrounding vegetation, reminding us of Puritan isolated communities surrounded by a contaminating wilderness. While Frank and Roger race on their bikes, the two women walk in the woods. Kelly (Loretta Swit) senses the environment's alien nature, a feeling reinforced by family dog Ginger.

Frank and Roger celebrate their first night out on the trail. Frank proposes a toast to the American Dream ideal of happy personal relationships built upon friendship and marriage. "Well I don't want to overload this dinner party with sentiment but I'm going to propose a toast. To the wife I know I'll love forever . . . and the friends I know I don't deserve." The increasingly inebriated duo continue celebrating their affluent achievements. They clink their glasses together, but before they can drink, a fire lights up across the river heralding another sacrifice completely different from the one in 1835 ensuring their affluence. The 1835 Alamo "Sacrifice" was one of the many land-grabbing imperialistic activities (such as "The Louisiana Purchase") which laid the foundations for future American affluence. Witnessing the scene they encounter the nightmare side of American existence pursued by forces that threaten their newly acquired wealth and lives. Frank stubbornly wants to continue to enjoy their vacation. Refusing to return home after Kelly's disturbing swimming pool experience, he asserts, "No way. No way. For five years we've been living in motels and hitting flat tracks. Now we're going skiing." He grasps a ski pole he will later use to defend himself against snakes planted in their trailer.

Race with the Devil is unique in avoiding the genre's usual treatments of satanism. The movement has clear socioeconomic undertones involving conflict between the haves and have-nots in American society. The group is not as affluent as their counterparts in *The Seventh Victim* and *Rosemary's Baby*. When the working-class Henderson couple visits the trailer, Frank condescendingly introduces Mr. Henderson, "This is Mr. Henderson. He's got the

Road King next door." The people who stare at Kelly in the swimming pool are either old or middle-aged. They lack youth's dynamic quality for economic survival in a competitive consumer society. Another economic contrast occurs in the restaurant scene. A country and western singer appears lit up by a red light before a portrait of a nude female with red (Aztec?) headdress. He sings a song highlighting working-class dreams of affluence. "Well I never had much money and when I want I get it. . . . From now on I'm living high even if I have to live on credit." The Hendersons thrive in this rough proletarian environment; they avidly enjoy a violent fight that suddenly erupts. During this time satanists invade the trailer. They hang Ginger and place rattlesnakes in the food cupboard. The very thing the Mather theologians feared happens. Instead of repressing their energies into the work ethic, the community succumbs to satanism, avenging themselves upon Protestant capitalist mores.

As the trailer progresses on its journey, a gradual sense of paranoia develops. Each stopping place is a potential danger spot. On their last stop, they find phones out of order. They are forced to take a detour. Arriving at a seemingly secure haven before dark, the group instead find themselves as sacrificial offerings. A long shot shows their trailer driving up a hill at sunset, its red rim encircling it as it stops, anticipating the trailer's final entrapment by a ring of fire, the same element used by Ford's Indians in *Drums along the Mohawk*. The final shots reveal the satanists not as Indians or monsters but normal mid-Americans seen throughout the film—the Hendersons, the sheriff, and his deputy. Unlike Ford's film an optimistic ending is impossible. Dark repressed forces beneath capitalism and the family emerge to claim final victory, reversing the conclusion of Michael Wigglesworth's 1662 violent poem, "The Day of Doom," where Christianity eschatologically triumphed over forces of darkness. For *Race with the Devil*, the repressed has socioeconomic components.

◆   ◆   ◆

Hooper and Henkel's next collaboration *Eaten Alive* (U.K. *Death Trap*, 1976) is an abysmal mess. It seems to have no redeeming features. Featuring an array of former Hollywood stars now reduced to cameo roles, *Eaten Alive's* beautifully lit studio format contains an incoherent mishmash of themes pastiching sixties horror (particularly *Psycho*) and anticipating the grotesque horror and violence of the eighties. Unlike *The Texas Chain Saw Massacre*, there appears little rationale for ensuing events. Opening with a shot of the moon, reminiscent of sun shots in Hooper's earlier film, *Eaten Alive* is more apocalyptic in its denial of causality than its distinguished predecessor. But it is an interesting symptomatic work.

The main themes of *Eaten Alive* echo *Psycho*. Fleeing from her family into the wasteland of prostitution, a blond female fugitive enters Judd's run-down Starlight Hotel and is brutally slaughtered. Norman Bates is now Neville Brand's portrayal of a middle-aged, drugged derelict who wanders around babbling incoherent monologues that shed no light on his condition. He haphazardly attacks a bourgeois nuclear family of husband (William Finley), wife (Marilyn Burns), and little daughter. The wife forces her neurotically weak husband to attempt shooting Judd's pet alligator after it consumes the family dog. Judd also destroys another father (Mel Ferrer) later in the film. Built upon displaying female bodies, male violence toward women, and chase sequences reminiscent of *The Texas Chain Saw Massacre*, *Eaten Alive* is a self-referential film that denies causation and indulges in pastiche. The family motif is marginal. Carolyn Jones's cameo as Miss Hattie evokes audience knowledge of her role as Morticia in *The Addams Family*. Neville Brand's status as subordinate "most decorated World War Two hero" to Audie Murphy's Number One becomes parodied by the presence of military paraphernalia in Judd's home. The actor's contemporary battle against drug addiction was also known at the time. However, these add little to the film's overall meaning.

But a rationale is present. In "Postmodern Narrative Cinema: Aeneas on a Stroll," Christopher Sharrett outlines pertinent aspects of features affecting contemporary cinema's aesthetic and socially bankrupt condition that are also relevant to *Eaten Alive*.[26] As a film based upon nonoriginal self-referentiality, *Eaten Alive* appears an ideal candidate for the noncausative, apocalyptic, cinematic models that Sharrett sees in *The Texas Chain Saw Massacre* and other works. Acknowledging *Psycho* and its actors' familiarity within other Hollywood productions, *Eaten Alive* is an example of a crisis cinema rich in spectacle but poor in meaning. We have no key to Judd's condition as we do Norman Bates. Once a regular at Miss Hattie's but now expelled for frightening the girls with tales of his "gator," Judd exists within the Starlight Hotel violently ready to exert his repressed energies on any wandering female. We do not know whether this is a regular occurrence. Throughout the film Judd wanders around babbling incoherent monologues. Rather than regard these scenes as Hooper indulging his actor, we should understand them according to Frederic Jameson's account of the individual's schizophrenic condition within late capitalism which involves a "reification of alienation rendering the subject schizophrenic rupturing signifying chains and historical consciousness."[27]

Judd wallows in inaccurate historical and mythic consciousness, denying causation. Believing he gained his African-reared, deathless alligator from explorer (and media exploiter) Frank Buck, Judd avoids real factual explanations. We later learn from another source that the alligator actually tore out his leg. Judd is merely an unmotivated monster. Pursuing his victims he takes on the persona of an eternal Grim Reaper, a mythic figure within a bankrupt society and an impoverished film.

Although *Eaten Alive* contains elements capable of family critique (Harvey Ward's repressive father figure and Sheriff Martin's resemblance to Anthony Eisely's manipulative sheriff in Samuel Fuller's *The Naked Kiss*), these exist within the narrative as floating signifiers devoid of social and historical anchors. However, *Eaten Alive* is not without interest. Introducing Robert Englund in pre-Freddy days, the film stylistically resembles later generic works of signifying excess. It also symptomatically anticipates many elements common to 1980s Hollywood representational strategies which "steer clear of a presentationalism which would suggest a new political awareness of the spectator."[28] Beginning with a dissolve from *The Texas Chain Saw Massacre* moon to Buck's (Robert Englund) belt buckle and immediately getting down to business with the opening lines, "Name's Buck and I'm raring to fuck," *Eaten Alive* begins its spectacular discourse. By additionally charting Buck's frustrated attempts to perform anal sex throughout the narrative, it also contributes what Christopher Sharrett notes as "a nice Bataillean image of sacrificial excess" (personal communication). Here, as in later films, the family motif becomes marginalized and diminished within the narrative.

◆　◆　◆

The family motif also appears in two significant works of David Cronenberg—*The Brood* and *Scanners*. Cronenberg is a director who usually has little interest in family horror. Sharrett sympathetically describes Cronenberg's work as displaying the apocalyptic bankruptcy of myth and ritual in a postindustrial landscape.[29] Many features within Cronenberg's films resemble themes within Rene Girard and postmodernist critics.[30] His work generally reflects anxieties resulting from contemporary social nihilism, and it is doubtful whether Cronenberg offers more than a cinema illustrating helpless pessimism. The films do reveal social disease. But they contain very little evidence for any belief in Sharrett's epiphany involving the "efficacy of rational (bourgeois), individualistic consciousness in a society where technological change is gradually effecting a transformation of humanity."[31] *The Brood* and *Scanners* diagnose a particular family malaise, yet they offer very little hope for progressive cure and viable alternatives.

Despite its characteristic Cronenberg cerebral nature, *The Brood* differs little from classical family horror films. Patriarchy and the family institution are responsible for creating human misery and monsters. Nola Carveth

(Samantha Egger) fulfills Dr. Pretorius's role as a Bride of Frankenstein by producing short-lived monsters embodying her paranoid rage as a family victim. The Brood function as Nola's embodiment of Hitchcock's Birds. Although clearly no "mad scientist," Dr. Hal Raglan falls victim to the obsessional "hubris" characteristic of Universal scientists by his short-sighted compliance with Nola's dangerous creativity. Presenting Nola Carveth as a family victim of mental and physical abuse, *The Brood* reveals social roots within the horror genre's metaphysically constructed monsters. But by moving toward a pessimistic climax, it denies any possibility of ending an eternal circle. It thus anticipates later horror patterns of the eighties. Reared by a self-denying alcoholic mother and a weak father, Nola Carveth initially claims audience sympathy. However, Cronenberg presents her as a twentieth-century version of the classical Gothic "femme fatale," a descendant of Medea and Keats's "Lamia." The director views her according to Rochester's blinkered vision in *Jane Eyre*. No oppositional motifs exist within the text for viewers to deconstruct Cronenberg's "Madwoman in the (cinematic) Attic." Although vulnerable and clearly disturbed, Nola Carveth becomes the psychotherapeutic plaything of patriarchal medical demigod Dr. Raglan (who clearly loses control of his monster). Described by Frank (Art Hindle) as a woman who married him for his sanity, Nola becomes a dangerous force that necessitates destruction. Cronenberg does not condemn the institution that generated her condition. *The Brood* needs a more complex approach. Its monsters, who lack sexual organs and view things "only in black and white," appear as telling revelatory offspring of Cronenberg's antiseptic directorial vision. Although locating pathology within the family, *The Brood*'s perspective is antagonistically antifemale. The director carefully chooses selected targets (Nola, her mother Julianna) rather than engage in depicting the real social causes determining their natures. Frank eventually rescues his daughter, Candice, from her mother's contaminating influence. But in concluding with tell-tale physical warts erupting on Candice's arms, *The Brood*'s apocalyptic nature appears nihilistic, sexist, and unprogressive.

Like *The Brood*, *Scanners* perversely refuses to interrogate implications within its material. Linking apocalyptic, biblical, and classical motifs, the film has deep associations with family horror tenets of gods and monsters. But Cronenberg's vision is nihilistic and pessimistic. Utilizing the genre's duality, *Scanners* presents two rival siblings; Cameron Vale (Stephen Lack) and Darryl Revok (Michael Ironside) are products of a definable past social act. Created by a scientist father, Dr. Ruth (Patrick McGoohan), because of drug experiments on his wife, Cameron and Darryl become rejected like the Frankenstein monster after they serve their respective purposes. Once Darryl becomes a dangerous threat to the fascistic-corporate world order employing Ruth, the scientist resurrects his other creation, retrieving Cameron from the derelict existence where he abandoned him. His action resembles the Universal scientist who attempts to resurrect the creature for his own purposes in many sequels. Emphasizing Colin Clive's original link with the monster and his divine hubris, Cronenberg depicts Ruth as a gray-haired hirsute Jehovah figure constantly dressed in black.

As with *The Brood*, evil as a family creation attracts the interests of the state and psychiatry. *Scanners* condemns institutional forces but collapses into nihilism. Any suggested alternatives are ruthlessly eliminated. Under Kim Obrist's (Jennifer O'Neill) direction, alternative potentials for scanner forces other than those directed by the unacceptable dualities of ConSec and Revok become impossible. They are crushed before they have any chance to develop. Like Larry Cohen's homicidal father in *God Told Me To*, artist Benjamin Pierce (Robert Silverman) recognizes the real causes behind his condition. As a ten-year-old child, he attempted to murder his entire family in 1958. Now channeling his energies into art, he exists in hostile isolation from other scanners and society before his eventual murder.

Traditional concepts of modernist (rather than postmodernist) alienation really influence Cronenberg's films. Despite his cerebral visual style and association with contemporary cultural movements, Cronenberg's cinema really resembles a dead end of twentieth-century modernism. The malaise is diagnosed, but we are offered no cures. Even a postmodernist era does contain some alternative paths despite the shaky foundations of master narratives. Recent postmodernist feminist criticism suggests this. However, Cronenberg's deceptive cinema really reveals a nostalgia for modernist male existential dilemmas, as the final movement of *Scanners* reveals.

Moving toward a final confrontation appearing to offer a positive epiphany, Cameron's and Darryl's battle resembles those concluding battles between the "good" and "bad" monsters from *Frankenstein Meets the Wolf Man* and *Abbott and Costello Meet Frankenstein*. Ignoring any alternative feminist consciousness Kim Obrist offers, *Scanners* moves into a negative binary oppositional conflict of good and evil forces. Although sired by the now-discredited Dr. Ruth, the two brothers engage in a mental battle for supremacy that concludes in a transcendental marriage of Heaven and Hell. Even if we believe in Cameron's victory at the end when Revok's body speaks with Cameron's voice, the final image is ambiguous. Trying to assure Kim, "It's me. I'm Cameron. We've won," the voice expresses no clear assurance of victory. The audience does not know whether this is a trap. The film ends with a close-up of Revok's eyes, resembling that final image of Candice in *The Brood*. The image fades into white, the final color we saw in Revok's eyes after Cameron's eyes popped out. It uncannily anticipates the optical device characterizing Jason's activities in the first three *Friday the 13th* films. There is no guarantee that Cameron wins. Nothing has really changed. Like *Videodrome's* (1982) conclusion, the actual nature of transcendence is vague. Family is clearly the source of Cronenberg's horror in these two films. But his pessimistic apocalyptic vision contains conservative elements blocking any supposed progressive currents in his vision.[32]

◆　◆　◆

Hailing *The Funhouse* as "more distinguished than anything in the genre since *Halloween* and *Friday the 13th*," Andrew Britton acclaims the work's demonstration of how American culture recuperates the Gothic in the interests of conservative entertainment mechanisms.[33] He finds the film's second half disappointing in terms of its "obligatory massacre of teenagers." *The Funhouse*, however, is far more complex and deserves closer attention. Although Hooper demonstrates how the entertainment industry attempts to recuperate Gothic motifs, his treatment is less conservative than either *Friday the 13th* or *Halloween*. The approach is more critical, at least according to the limited possibilities offered within contemporary generic manifestations. Using the figure of the laughing Fun-house clown as a disruptive device, akin to Hitchcock's jester in *Blackmail*, Hooper attempts to open alternative avenues to alert viewers within the context of his film.[34] *The Funhouse* continues his exploration of the American family's repressive nature.

The carnival world Amy (Elizabeth Berridge) enters is a Gothic Bakhtinian counterpart to her confining family situation. Unlike Bakhtin's definition of the carnival atmosphere as representing a liberating arena from social and individual conformity, Hooper's fun fair presents its dark, unrepressed side. He shows its relationship to society and family as a contaminating force of physical and psychic danger. The second sequence, showing Amy's mother and father viewing *The Bride of Frankenstein* on television, reveals the entertainment industry's recuperation of the Gothic. But the carnival environment provides a darker recreation of what really lies repressed within Amy's family situation—violence, exploitation, and sexual repression. Although Dr. Pretorious's announcement "The Bride of Frankenstein" visually associates Amy with Elsa Lanchester and her future status as potential violated bride to the Freak (Wayne Doba), its significance extends far beyond "film buff" parallels. As the original Universal production drew clear parallels between the Gothic narrative and its framing prologue so *The Funhouse* makes similar connections between opening scenes and later narrative.

Despite initial sequences resembling another *Halloween* appropriation, Hooper has a far more significant purpose. The film actually opens with a poster of the Funhouse clown appearing frequently throughout the narrative. An unseen stalker picks up a little boy's mask before going into the bathroom to enact yet another *Psycho* slashing. Before this occurs we note several movie posters on the wall of Universal monsters—Carloff's Frankenstein creature, Lugosi's Dracula, and Lon Chaney Jr.'s The Wolf Man. Initially scared before recognizing little brother Joey (Shawn Carson), Amy vows to get even. She refuses to take Joey to the carnival on Saturday. The sequence ends with Amy's discovery of a Polaroid photo of her in terror (another of Joey's past tricks) with the camera tilting up to the Frankenstein monster poster.

Several associations appear in this sequence. Hooper emphasizes the culture industry's recuperation of the Gothic in *Psycho-Halloween* parodies. But his purpose is not entirely derivative. A tension exists between the family's role as a sexually repressive unit and the entertainment industry's attempt to inoculate dangerous alternative tendencies within the framework of "harmless entertainment." Hooper refers to past (*Psycho*) and present horror films (*Halloween*), drawing viewer attention to such devices. At the same time Joey's activities reveal horror as active within the family. As the younger, weaker sibling, he reacts against his sister very much like the young boy in *The Leopard Man* and Franklin in *The Texas Chain Saw Massacre*. The remainder of the film is Joey's fantastic revenge upon his sister and friends who deny him access not just to the carnival but also to sexual activity. When Joey later overhears Amy dutifully responding to her father's order about not visiting the carnival, he whispers, "Liar." He drops a Frankenstein monster model alerting his parents to his presence. It foreshadows Ritchie's later action in dropping the lighter and revealing the youngsters' presence to the Freak's Barker father (Kevin Conway). Frankenstein monster imagery links both Joey and the Freak. While Joey has Karloff's poster in his room, the Freak wears Karloff's mask during the film's first part.

As Amy's parents watch television, mother prominently drinks whisky. Her actions not only parallel Lea Thompson's similar activities in the opening part of *Back to the Future* (1985) but other characters within the carnival. Before their respective performances William Finley's Count Dracula and Sylvia Miles's Madame Zena quickly indulge in alcoholic sustenance. The carnival's world is one of artificial role-playing that echoes an outside world of socially constructed roles, especially the family. The Barker later apologizes to his son for his alcohol-induced mental abuse. Adult characters resort to alcohol to repress awareness of damaging artificial social roles.

Before she leaves for her date, Amy's father expresses disapproval of Buzz's (Cooper Huckabee) class background. His gas attendant position renders him outside the realm of family acceptability. The carnival has similar social classifications. Discovering that his son has murdered Madame Zena, the Barker rages against the former's violation of social taboos. "You really did it this time. You killed one of the family. I don't care what you do with that dirty business you do with them locals. I don't want you doing anything with our kind."

The Barker turns a blind eye to his son's violent activities in Dallas and Memphis, which echoes Joey's actions toward his sister in the film's opening moments. As he tells Amy and Buzz, "Blood is thicker than water." Ignoring his son's sexual desires, as Joey's parents avoid dealing with violent masquerades in the opening scenes, his parental responsibilities are questionable. He mentally and physically abuses his child, hitting him when he calls him "Father." "Don't you ever call me that! I can't stand the sound of your filthy voice." He also manipulates his offspring into doing one "last bad thing"—in slaughtering the invading youngsters. Father then promises to take him fishing "just like we used to." The Barker has obviously ignored him, echoing the actions of Joey's parents in the opening sequence who regard their son as a nuisance and leave him to his macabre imagining. This carnival father is an alcoholic abusive parent. He later explains his real motives for parenthood to Amy and Buzz. "He's not such a bad little fellow. He does get himself into all sorts of trouble.... I'm sure he's going to be a real comfort to me in my old age." Madame Zena's maternal figure manipulates the Freak, overcharging him for her services and threatening to tell his father. Because the Freak's previous victims were all little girls, his movement toward an older woman (representing his deceased mother) is significant. The carnival reproduces darker aspects of family life.

Although Joey's parents do not treat him like the Freak, they ignore him until he runs away from home. As the youngsters tour exhibits featuring animal, human, and sexual displays, they are constantly reminded that the displays are all "children of God." The Freak's dualistic embodiment of a two-headed animal-human is anticipated by earlier exhibits of a two-headed cow and baby-brother Tad. The Barker later tells Buzz and Amy that he is "just protecting my family." When Amy responds, "Your family! It's not even human!" he replies, "The Lord works in mysterious ways." Normal and carnival families share a common identity. The Freak enacts Joey's repressed desires for vengeance against his sister and her friends who exclude him from their fun. Rescued by his family, unlike the unfortunate Franklin, Joey looks toward the funhouse where Amy and her friends are conscious of their dangerous situation. Amy's earlier threat to him echoes on the soundtrack. He decides to say nothing. Amy sees her father and attempts to call him from behind the air-ventilation fan which blocks off her voice. The family drives off, leaving her to face Joey's family related revenge. His Frankenstein monster will slaughter her friends and nearly kill Amy.

The carnival folk are dark avatars of a repressive family system Amy flees. Displaying his female wares, the sex-show barker voyeuristically gazes at Amy, reminiscent of both Joey's earlier perspective in the shower room sequence and the Freak's later assault. Within the carnival appear family outcasts—representatives of the human detritus capitalism chooses to ignore—a Bag Lady who acts as chorus and a male derelict. Both appear in the film's concluding shot as Amy wanders away from the carnival. Reacting to the final laughter of the funhouse clown, Amy passes both figures. The Bag Lady speaks, "I'm watching you." The derelict touches Amy's torn blouse. Despite the Freak's spectacular death in the funhouse machinery, other dark elements remain at the film's conclusion.

◆   ◆   ◆

Hooper's sequel to the *Texas Chain Saw Massacre* develops the original's apocalyptic associations to greater heights. In this version the slaughterhouse family leaves the rural confines of south Texas for Dallas's economic attractions. They now represent the repressed side of urban (as well as rural) society existing in a dark tunnel beneath a "Texas Battleground Amusement Park." If Hooper's *Funhouse* carnival depicted the entertainment industry's unsuccessful mechanisms in restraining the family's Gothic underside, *The Texas Chain Saw Massacre 2* reveals a similar faulty apparatus attempting to contain family violence beneath mass cultural activities of sport, historic entertainment spectacles, and the junk food industry. Hooper's family is now a legitimate part of American consumer capitalism.

The opening develops family connections with American historical and ritual violence. Following the series standard pattern, *The Texas Chain Saw Massacre 2* begins with a spoken caption. It brings the story to the present day by informing the audience about law enforcement's inability to trace the family. As there were "No Facts" there were "No crimes" so "Officially, The Texas Chain Saw Massacre never happened." This represents an apocalyptic dimension, denying history, moving toward a nihilistic vengeful sacrificial blood ritual whose road (like the record the two drunken youths request from Stretch) "leads to nowhere."

The film's introductory sequence shows two high school youths driving to "the biggest Party in the world"—a Dallas weekend football game. The game is more an excuse for those "blood crazy for a riot." Hooper immediately presents the audience with characters who differ little from the slaughterhouse family. One shoots at a mailbox from the car followed by other bullets aimed at road signs—"Refight the Battle of San Jacinto"—Mesquite, Dallas (significantly the Dallas part of the sign is hit)—"Remember the Battle of the Alamo." They play a road game with a pickup truck prominently displaying the American Flag, a truck we later learn is owned by the slaughterhouse family who are dark versions of normal, business minded, patriotic Americans. The gun-wielding youth wears psychedelic/prismatic sunglasses, concealing his eyes and giving the impression of blindness. Hooper makes an important metaphoric point in this opening scene. As America's notorious violent state, Texas has witnessed several bloodthirsty episodes ranging from the Alamo's Last Stand to the Kennedy assassination. For Hooper the state represents America's spiritual heartland by disavowing the real lessons of history in favor of a memorial park emphasizing nostalgia and entertainment.

The last sign the drunken youths pass and shoot at reads, "See the Texas Battleground Amusement Park," a sideshow belonging to the Sawyer slaughterhouse family. In one of the film's most revealing sequences, Lefty (Dennis Hopper) discovers blood trickling from a mural image of Davy Crockett's mouth within the family owned historical amusement park. It not only equates Crockett with Count Dracula but also hints at the bloody nature of America's violent past. Kicking in the wall, Lefty discovers not Richard Slotkin's "Pyramid of Skulls" but a huge pile of entrails, the hidden detritus of family business enterprise.

Wishing to stop "playing head-banging music and do something real," the film's resourceful heroine Stretch (Caroline Williams) attempts to enlist Franklin's uncle, former Texas Ranger Lefty Enright, into tracking down the chainsaw killers of the drunken youths. Recalling John Wayne's Texas Ranger associations in *The Searchers* and *The Commancheros*, Enright is a latter day Ethan Edwards searching for his lost relative. He is even more psychotic than his Fordian counterpart. Hooper makes valuable points concerning the bankruptcy of a patriarchal structure. There is no Debbie to rescue. Enright is deranged and alcoholic. Initially unresponsive to Stretch's appeal for cooperation, the devoutly religious Enright opposes female involvement in his search. Living in a hotel full of drunken, weekend Dallas football spectators, he dismisses her.

Enright regards Stretch's feminine presence as the real threat to his masculine ideal of lone avenger. Drayton Sawyer (Jim Siedow) also sees Stretch as a distraction to Leatherface's function as an obedient worker within the family business. Discovering Stretch's "influence" on his younger brother, Drayton admonishes him—"S.E.X. Sex! You had to find out about it. Why didn't you ask me? It's a swindle! So don't get mixed up in it." Enright is no hero. He later manipulates Stretch into acting as a decoy to attract the Sawyers into the open despite her possibly brutal death. As a former Texas Ranger, he understands how the system operates. He uses fragmented speech also associated with the Sawyers. "Kill signs been about in North Texas all these years. The Law! They shy away from piecing it together as murder. They call it accidents or disappearances." Enright recognizes the nature of a social order refusing to combine parts into a disturbingly meaningful whole. Dallas awards Drayton Sawyer annual prizes for his chili but prefers not to enquire into the recipe. Local cops regard the death of the two high school youths as just another random violent incident associated with the weekend football game.

Hooper indirectly suggests that Enright wishes Stretch out of the way as much as the Sawyers. By contacting Enright, Stretch places herself in great danger. As she knocks on his hotel room, a drunken football spectator passes her. He wears a red jacket and red cap with horns on the top, the latter imagery having associations with an infernoesque Sawyer slaughterhouse conducted in an underground caverns. After Stretch falls into the tunnel, Enright prays significantly, "Help me beat this stranger who walks beside me and takes away my strength. Show me what to fear so I don't fear it anymore"—a reference to Stretch as much as to fear itself.

Enright is now Hooper's Leatherstocking, not Leatherface who is more of a mentally abused younger sibling than the earlier version. Enacting a morbid masculine "born-again" Christianity, Enright carries Leatherstocking's noble religious pantheism to pathologic extremes. Existing for fourteen years on a monomaniacal quest for his brother's killers, Enright enacts a twentieth-century western version of a gunfight between himself and Leatherface. This time it occurs with chainsaws in an underground tunnel. Emerging into battle, reminiscent of Robert Mitchum's deranged figure in *Night of the Hunter* (1955) singing "Bringing in the Sheaves," he carries Ford's duality between Ethan Edwards and Scar in *The Searchers* to its logical conclusions. Hero and monster now coexist in the same body.

As Robin Wood notes, Hooper's film "makes explicit . . . what was always implicit in the first film: the monstrous family as a metaphor for the ultimate debasement of American capitalist ideals."[35] The family is never a "haven from a heartless world." It produces and reproduces institutional structures. Keeping past memories alive with Grandpa and Grandma's mummified bodies, as well as Hitchhiker's corpse from the previous film, the Sawyer family furnishes products for American military imperialism. Younger brother Chop Top is the 1970s Hollywood cinematic version of a deranged Vietnam veteran.[36] Like the rest of the family, he is heavily into consumer capitalism.

Descending into the hellish pit beneath the sideshow, Stretch encounters the demonic nature of the family's capitalistic structure. The Sawyer family exists in a clearly defined hierarchical system. Chop Top and Leatherface jump to elder brother Drayton's admonishments. They are heavily involved in urban business entrepreneurship; they no longer supply plain barbecues but rather such delicacies as croissant sandwiches to Dallas's hungry weekend football spectators who are "blood crazy for a riot." Frenziedly moving in a dark Gothic parody of scenes in Arnold Wesker's *The Kitchen*, they rush to make up for lost time. For Drayton the family lost "valuable kill time" and money in dealing with Stretch and her partner. As Enright chainsaws the business foundations, Drayton complains over the economic disadvantages of a small businessman. "Never, never get a break. Damn property taxes fuck up everything! . . . Crooks don't pay taxes. Politicians don't pay taxes. Movie stars don't. . . . It's the little guy that can't make a dime that pays the taxes!"

Before Stretch can die at Grandpa's hands, replaying the earlier version's brutalization of Sally, Enright bursts into the family dining room. So caught up is Drayton within the capitalist ethos that he regards the chain saw-armed intruder as a rival competitor. Continuing corporate behavior he offers him money. "The old pressure game! . . . It's a dog-eat-dog world. . . . If you can't take the heat get out of the damn kitchen!" Enright refuses his deal. Drayton retreats, demolishing his business empire by exploding a grenade from Hitchhiker's pouch. "A man builds a good trade. Then the gods kick him in the balls. Not this time."

While Drayton's family business literally explodes, Stretch escapes to the top of the amusement park, successfully starting Grandmother's chainsaw to overpower Chop Top. As Chop Top's body falls back into the tunnel, Stretch remains alone, wielding the chainsaw and moving in a circular direction reminiscent of Leatherface's last appearance in the original film. Stretch's survival also occurs at the cost of her sanity. Although defeated, the Sawyer family exert one last victory.

◆　◆　◆

Jeff Burr's *Leatherface* returns the Sawyer family to its original rural environment. Designed as a *sequelitis* formula to cash in on the original's success, it does contain several new features. The family unit remains strong and hierarchical, but this time the leading member is matriarchal. Within its status quo alternative, Mrs. Sawyer (Miriam Byrd Netherby) rules over her aberrant male children exercising the same type of authority of Irene Dailey in *The Grissom Gang* and Shelley Winters in *Bloody Mama*.

Delivering an historic update, the spoken prologue surmises that Leatherface was the alternative personality of one of the Sawyers who died in the gas chamber in 1981. The original family is described as serial predators. This feature links the Sawyers to the contemporary cult status enjoyed by real examples such as Ted Bundy, Jeffrey Dahmer, John Wayne Gacy, and fictional counterparts such as Hannibal Lecter. However, unlike the preceding film's prologue, no firm assurance is given as to the Sawyers' nonexistence. *The Texas Chain Saw Massacre* is described as just the beginning.

 Although this version borrows heavily from its predecessors and Romero's zombie movies (especially with the presence of *Dawn of the Dead*'s Ken Foree), it contains several components that bring the series further within the "crisis" dimensions of apocalyptic cinema.

In this version the initial couple are not married. Traveling by car from Los Angeles to Florida, Ryan (William Butler) and Michelle (Kate Hodge) bicker like a married couple. Michelle asserts that she needs "some time on my own." Neither brother or sister nor married couple like their counterparts in *Night of the Living Dead*, the normal heterosexual couple is already in trouble.

As Ryan and Michelle argue, a sardonic radio commentary tells of the discovery of a mass grave; its significance is trivialized in tones reminiscent of the radio talk show commentary in Romero's *Martin*. The event is merely "entertainment." Reacting to the violence, Michelle believes that retaliation is no answer. Ryan asserts something she will soon learn, "Welcome to the real world, Michelle. One day you'll have to live in it, no matter where you run."

Passing a sign reading "Don't Mess with Texas," the couple later drive near the discovered burial pit. A worker garbed in a space-suit costume to avoid the contaminating affects of human decomposition remarks on the area's similarity to Vietnam's Dong Tre area. Links between family horror, Vietnam, and westerns develop. As in the previous films, the Sawyers carry the normal bourgeois family's mental cannibalism to logical conclusions. Organized in a strictly hierarchical structure, according to sexual repression and unquestioned obedience, they exemplify patterns within Romero's zombies. Ken Foree's Benny combines Ben of *Night* and Peter of *Day*. We know nothing about his occupation except that he has economic resources that enable him to attend weekend survival camps over the previous two years. His karate skills resemble Peter's S.W.A.T. training. Encountering Ryan and Michelle after their vehicle crashes, he initially dismisses their account of Leatherface's attack as the work of "militant lumberjacks. I see them all the time." Like Peter, he is fully aware of contemporary racism but has yet to see its family origins. He speaks of being in constant training because he is awaiting the "big blow-up." Benny will find his expected apocalypse within the American family. However, unlike the other *Chain Saw* films which contained some rationale for the Sawyers' activities, nothing is offered in *Leatherface*. Both Michelle and Peter ask "why" at different points of the film. Their assailants furnish no explanation. The apocalyptic dimensions contained in earlier films extend to logical, irrational conclusions. The Sawyer family appears as a nihilistic, violent unit outside society that preys on all who fall into their trap.

Despite his potential role as savior, Benny survives because of female aid. The solitary female survivor of an earlier attack and Michelle both help him at different points in the film. Like contemporary horror films, *Leatherface* stresses female resourcefulness and survival. Michelle emerges from the debacle in a much better situation than Stretch. Although lacking the richness and depth of *Dawn of the Dead*, *Leatherface* concludes with potential implications concerning the status of its survivors: an independent, resourceful female and a Black who owes his life to the former. However, Leatherface (R. D. Mihailoff) survives to watch them drive off into the distance. The threat still remains.

Now dominated by the mother with Grandpa in a subordinate role, this Sawyer family exists in a highly charged state of sexual repression; their only outlet is cannibalistic violence. Bereft of their former Dallas affluence, the family is now dependent on technology. Their crippled mother speaks with a voice-box while Leatherface (called "Junior" as the youngest family member) listens to a Walkman and tries to operate an educational computer given to him by elder brother Tink (Joe Unger) who wears an artificial hand. Attaching electronically operated hooks to Ryan's body prior to skinning it, Tink remarks to Tex, "That's progress, boy." Since the previous film validated Grandpa's aversion to modern technology, he now occupies a minor position in this version. The family remains as authoritarian and hierarchical as ever despite using modern advanced technology.

The gas attendant brother clips *Playboy* centerfolds into fragmented pieces symptomatic of Sawyer family dismemberment practices. This highly charged misogynistic brother relishes a physical future assault upon Michelle. Handsome elder brother "Tex" (Viggo Mortensen) reacts angrily when addressed by his actual name, Eddie, preferring the western masculine style he adopts. However, despite yearning for a now redundant ideal, the only way he enacts his illusions is by violent Indian assault on unwary travelers. Like his sexually repressed brother, he exists in a highly charged state. Refusing to answer Benny's question, "What the fuck is the matter with you people?" he sexually taunts him by equating violent desires with appetite. "Come on, sweetheart. Let's see what you've got. . . . I'm hungry. I like liver." Within the home he is mother's obedient son, a contradictory image depicted in his donning a domesticated frilly apron prior to skinning and carving up the family dinner. This process now occurs in the dining room before the guest's eyes (Michelle) and not in the kitchen.

The Sawyer family is a repressive institution that channels its desires into violence and cannibalism. Surviving into the conservative 1990s, its family structure has not fundamentally changed. Leatherface receives a present: it is a new chrome chainsaw inscribed with the caption, "The saw is family," reminiscent of Drayton Sawyer's line in *The Texas Chain Saw Massacre 2*. But, unlike the earlier film, there is no possibility of sublimated sexual liaison with the surviving female. As the group looks at Ryan's body as their future "sourbelly" banquet and Benny's prospective fate as "dark meat," Momma hints at Michelle's ensuing fate. "Junior likes them private parts. . . . We know what to do with them parts." Recalling male nightmares concerning "castrating" mothers, she further mentions, "I cut my own out years back. I did. Took care of Poppa's too."

Family values contaminate future generations. Fleeing into the Sawyer home, Michelle discovers a little girl weeping. However, this new addition to the slaughterhouse family proves just as treacherous as her older siblings. She catches Michelle off guard, stabbing her with a sharp bone after she displays her skull-headed doll. After Tex enters and carries Michelle away, an overhead camera shot reveals the little girl's "playroom" littered with human bones as she plays "house" with her tea set. Trapped within dominant family institutions, a younger generation is offered no alternative future. Rocked by Leatherface on his lap, she meekly responds to mother's command to wash up before dinner as Junior nods to affirm the suggestion before kissing her. The last aggressive action she performs is switching the house security lights on so her brothers can easily fight Benny.

◆ ◆ ◆

Apocalypticism thus explains how the genre developed in the eighties and nineties, leading to the *Friday the 13th*, *Halloween*, and *A Nightmare on Elm Street* films. But family motifs still exist within them.

The Return of Kronos

In *A Nightmare on Elm Street 5—The Dream Child* (1989), comic book devotee Mark attends a high school graduation swimming pool party with his friends. Seated beside Danny and Greta (the latter is forced to don an unwelcome glamour girl role by her ambitious mother), Mark contributes a significant insight into deep motivations structuring not just the Elm Street series but the vast majority of post-1970s horror films. He speaks of a classical figure, Melisares, who "killed his kids because he didn't like the way they were running his kingdom." The analogy applies to both 1980s cult figure Freddy Krueger and the various characters within series such as *Friday the 13th*, *Halloween*, *Poltergeist*, and *Nightmare on Elm Street*. The monster now represents the return of a patriarchy violently punishing the younger generation.

Whereas many 1970s horror films exhibit a productive crisis revealing tensions between sociohistorical chaos and bankrupt systems of meaning, their 1980s descendants attempt to assert patriarchal power by stifling the genre's relationship to its crisis-ridden cultural context. The poverty of meaning contained in many of the prolific slasher/stalker films echoes an era turning away toward conservative ideologies.

The reactionary nature of 1980s horror represents a culture in crisis attempting to deny social breakdown. Teen characters escape either into random sexual experiences or other avenues (drugs, comic books, rock music). Contemporary horror films attempt to inoculate the radical potentialities of the Gothic by abandoning the monster's identification with the return of the repressed. However, although these films try to remove the monster from its cultural context and identify characters with dominant social norms, they are never totally successful. In contrast to a commonly held belief, family horror films did not die in the 1980s. It took on a new form. Films such as *Grave of the Vampire* and *Black Christmas* (both 1974) anticipated motifs within the *Friday the 13th, Halloween, Poltergeist,* and *Nightmare on Elm Street* series.[1] The monster is now the patriarchal father.

This assumption separates most eighties works from their predecessors.[2] But not entirely. The eighties witnessed not just *The Stepfather* films but also significant exceptions such as *Day of the Dead, Flowers in the Attic* (1987), and *Parents* (1989). Most eighties horror films, however, reproduce the virulent conservative reaction of more mainstream productions such as *Fatal Attraction* (1987), *The Hand That Rocks the Cradle* (1991), *Basic Instinct, Single White Female* (both 1992), and *The Temp* (1993) whose unattached females threaten the family. The slasher/stalker corpus also contain various motifs of male insecurity.[3]

Disposable teenage characters of the 1980s represent particular changes. Living in a society that witnesses the decline of the nuclear family and traditional values (but hysterically affirming their bankrupt status), realizing the failure of the American Success Dream, fully knowledgeable of high school and college pressures concerning grades, suicides, and emotional problems (anorexia, bulimia, sexual and physical harassment), especially those arising from sexual and emotional abuse within dysfunctional families, contemporary teenagers face a dangerous world.

The specter of AIDS lurks over contemporary horror implicitly and explicitly. *Halloween 5: The Revenge of Michael Myers* (1989) and *Jason Goes to Hell: The Final Friday* (1993) insert safe sex messages into their narratives. But condoms do not save horny teenagers from punishment. The monster's fearful visage symbolizes the final stages of HIV positive. Throughout *The Friday the 13th* series Jason Voorhees's face progressively disintegrates from the mentally unbalanced rube of *Friday the 13th, Part II* (1981) to Kane Hodder's skull-faced Jason of *Friday the 13th Part VII, The New Blood* (1988); *Friday the 13th Part VIII, Jason Takes Manhattan* (1989); and *Jason Goes to Hell: The Final Friday* (1993). In *Jason Takes Manhattan,* two teenagers survive not just Jason but corporate capitalism's illegal dumping of toxic waste in Manhattan sewers.

The brutal slaughter and high body count within various slasher films articulate deep-seated fears of insecurity. In an era reacting against supposed permissiveness of earlier decades and lacking viable radical alternatives, there is *No Exit* for those hesitant to follow conformist patterns. Childhood experience no longer remains sheltered from a violent world as kids within the *Child's Play* series and Craven's *The People under the Stairs* (1991) discover. During a sequence played for laughs, but having disturbing consequences beyond the "in-joke" context *in Friday the 13th Part VI, Jason Lives* (1986), one sleeping eight-year-old has a copy of Sartre's *No Exit* on his bed. Cynically bemused at Megan's survival tactics, he sees himself as little more than "dead meat" for Jason. Before an expected sacrificial holocaust, his companion calmly responds, "What were you going to be when you grew up?"

Monsters now represent rage engendered within the nuclear family, an observation realized by demented Dr. Sam Loomis (Donald Pleasance) in *Halloween 5*.[4] But rather than finding positive channels, the rage directs itself against those who do not follow Nancy Reagan's advice to say "No!" Jason, Michael, and Freddy act in the service of punitive patriarchal values. If parents cannot discipline recalcitrant offspring, Jason, Michael, and Freddy will.

However, counterhegemonic features do occur in certain films. As Andrew Britton notes, we should never take "the fundamental thematic categories of the text completely for granted."[5] All filmic texts exhibit some degree of difference as well as repetition. This is particularly so even in the disparaged slasher films. Every *Friday/Halloween/Nightmare* teenager faces a cinematic gauntlet of survival. This becomes a key motif in mid-1980s horror films. To become distracted by anything—whether sexual union, comic book fantasies (*A Nightmare on Elm Street 5*), cyberpunk culture, or desired reunion with a resurrected father (*A Nightmare on Elm Street, Part 3: Dream Warriors*, 1987)—results in slaughter by patriarchal monsters. Surviving becomes the key motif for teenagers in contemporary horror. Chosen victims face a much more dangerous contest than predecessors in earlier decades.

Although Britton notes that institutionalizing the monster's indestructibility inoculates Gothic's radical potentialities[6] in the eighties, this is no new feature. The monster's continuing survival occurred in earlier films from Universal onward. Manifestations of the eighties result from a different cultural context. The monster's survival now symbolizes a dominant patriarchal hegemony ruthlessly attempting to deny viable counterhegemonic alternatives.[7]

Developments in special effects technology stimulate powerful sadistic-masochistic tendencies within contemporary audiences. Youthful audiences, cheering the ritual slaughter of their surrogate screen representatives, interact with the film similar to nineteenth-century audience responses toward theatrical performances.[8] Contemporary sadistic-masochistic cinematic reactions position audiences in split-subjective identification between killer and victim.[9] Although this theoretically might undermine rigid gender definitions (causing male masochistic identification with female victims), it is not progressive. These cinematic mechanisms symbolically position their viewers as participants within dominant-submissive roles owing their rationale to authoritarian principles. Associated with gratuitous displays of violence and special effects, they place audiences in spectacularly uncritical submissive positions by reproducing authoritarian patterns within the traditional family.

Naturally, a conservative era affects cinematic genres, especially horror, by developing regressive tendencies with excessive stylistic devices.

In *Halloween* (1978), Neale notes that Michael Myers's first attack actually recreates an aggressive fantasy specified by Ferenczi involving a "sexual attack by an adult who lives in a world of passion and guilt upon a supposedly innocent child."[10] After observing and misrecognizing his sister's lovemaking, Michael aggressively reenacts the situation by killing sister and boyfriend. He changes from an innocent child to an aggressor. A repetition-compulsion process develops throughout the film. Michael's act has family traumatic origins, but the film never investigates this. It chooses instead to neglect the social and demonize its monster.

Conservative motifs in the text contradict any supposedly progressive theories by Carol J. Clover that involve cinematic positioning of male audiences in "feminine" masochistic positions and identification with a "Final Girl" heroine.[11] A Final Woman may fight and sometimes defeat the monster. But her ultimate victory is undercut either by eventual death in a sequel (Adrienne King in *Friday the 13th, Part II*; Heather Langencamp in *A Nightmare on Elm Street III: Dream Warriors* [1987]) or insanity (the heroines in *The Texas Chain Saw Massacre I and II*; *Friday the 13th: Part II and III*; and *Hollowgate* [1988]). The mere fact of a woman directing a horror film such as *Slumber Party Massacre* (1982) never guarantees subversion of powerful conservative generic mechanisms. Gender alone does not ensure a progressive text.

Neale's Lacanian investigation of *Halloween* unveils such conservative mechanisms.[12] He shows the film's dependence upon a mother-child dyad containing both omnipotence and terror (the latter stemming from separation from the mother due to intervention within the father's symbolic terrain and the terrors he represents).[13] This also explains the unconscious terror motivating the punitive actions of Freddy, Michael, and the Voorhees family. As *The Texas Chain Saw Massacre* films state, "The family that stays together, slays together." But each text is not identical. For example every *Nightmare* episode contains differences resulting from several authors and production circumstances.[14]

Even if 1980s horror features female heroines with Clover's "visible adjustment in the terms of gender representations,"[15] the nature of such masochistic identifications necessitates qualification.[16] Case studies of masochism within Holocaust victims, Hiroshima survivors, Vietnam veterans, and family trauma victims reveal it as a powerful repressive device of psychic control. It may not result in oppositional modes of identification leading viewers toward greater awareness of horror's social and patriarchal roots.[17] Exclusive textual emphasis on sadistic or masochistic theories often ignores thematic contradictions. Male viewers may not masochistically identify with the woman, but sadistically enjoy her suffering. Clover's formal arguments often ignore textual complexity. Although Reverend Kane (Julien Beck) plays upon Steven's (Craig T. Nelson) male insecurities in *Poltergeist II—The Other Side* (1986),[18] the latter's "feminine" experience never makes him relinquish his position as head of the family. Steven's new patriarch represents President Bush's fantasy of a "kinder and gentler America." As Tania Modleski notes, textual moments involving gentle or alternative males may be more endemic of patriarchal accommodation to feminism.[19] Most 1980s horror films represent patriarchy's last stand.

◆ ◆ ◆

Family rage occurs in Brian De Palma's major horror films—*Sisters, Obsession, Carrie* (1976), *The Fury* (1978), and *Dressed to Kill* (1980). This group of films shares several common characteristics with successors. They feature troubled nuclear families that are unable to come to terms with early parental loss. Like their later counterparts, De Palma's "young adults are psychically devastated by the effects of a primitive, fused symbiotic relationship in interaction with a society that does not provide an adequate role for the developing person. Consequently, their attempt to psychologically move outside the family, which includes the maturation of their sexuality, results in the destruction of the family itself."[20]

Norman G. Gordon thus recognizes that De Palma's flawed families create raging, sexually repressed, destructive children such as Carrie, Dominique/Danielle, Gillian, and Robin.[21] The young survivors remain traumatized (Grace Collier, Danielle, Gillian, and Liz) after their experience. However, De Palma often drowns this important family motif in graphic displays of violence and voyeurism. Despite *Dressed to Kill*'s tentative narrative complexity, the film's visual structure depends too much on the operations of conservative sadistic-voyeuristic and masochistic mechanisms. As Gordon points out, "The means by which De Palma presents his dark view of human compromise and exploitation perhaps comes too close to the exploitation and traumatization of the audience itself."[22] Unlike George Romero or Larry Cohen, De Palma never maintains a dialectical balance between generic excess and social meaning. He overindulges in flamboyant stylistic rhetoric. Bobbi becomes a brutal monster. Although representing Dr. Elliot's aggressive male side, Bobbi refuses to accede to his feminized side's wish for a sex change operation. Like Mrs. Voorhees, Bobbi becomes a conservative nightmare phallic mother wielding revenge on helpless female victims with the razor/phallus. S/he is still a monster whose ambivalent gender associations can be safely disavowed. *Dressed to Kill*'s *Carrie*-influenced exploitative climax disavows recognition of the true nature of Liz's traumatic nightmare—realization of her threatened position within a society based on patriarchal power relationships.[23]

Such family power relationships dominate *The Fury.* Connections between state institutional power and the family occur throughout the film. Good father (Peter Sandza), good child (Gillian), and loyal female companion (Hester) balance darker counterparts—Childress, Robin, and Susan Charles. But, far from operating on a reductive level, *The Fury* subverts its dualities. Peter's (Kirk Douglas) efforts prove futile. Robin starts off as a good son before his eventual corruption. The film highlights individual vulnerability and corruption within a social system based upon manipulative family power. Susan (Fiona Lewis) seduces Robin like a scheming, incestuous mother. Childress (John Cassavetes) attempts the same ploy upon Gillian (Amy Irving). The children's telekinetic powers stem from family rage.[24] Training Robin and Gillian in the service of the state, Childress and Susan use manipulative techniques originating from the family. However, like the twins in *Scanners*, the children destroy their parental oppressors by exercising psychic powers derived from family rage. This destructive rage lies at the basis of the concealed influences motivating Jason, Michael, and Freddy in later slasher films.

Unfortunately, excessive special effects drown any form of family critique. Susan's spectacularly bloody death overwhelms audience recognition of it as Robin's reaction to incestuous-maternal manipulations. De Palma's cinema anticipates gratuitous fetishistic displays in 1980s horror. In *Dressed to Kill* he borrows heavily from Dario Argento's *The Bird with the Crystal Plumage* (1970). Argento's stylistic cinema stresses sadistic-voyeuristic onslaught against helpless females. *Dressed to Kill* is a split-text; the Argento elements overpower its social critiques.

◆ ◆ ◆

John Carpenter's *Halloween* (1978) cinematically disavows social factors for metaphysical explanation. Michael's final disappearance turns him into a supernaturally resurrected Universal monster. Michael's murder of his sister contains incestuous associations originating from a social taboo Wood notes as denying "sexual feeling precisely where the proximities of family life most encourage it."[25] Michael becomes a metaphysical bogeyman slaughtering promiscuous teenagers. But *Halloween*'s reductive ideologic project appears forced. Psychoanalyst Dr. Loomis hysterically designates Michael as evil. Confounded by his blank expression, irritated by a patient unresponsive to treatment who has "never spoken a word in fifteen years," he demonizes his quarry. Pursuing a figure wearing a white mask, a culturally significant color within American literature's regeneration through violence theme, Loomis's Ahab hunter figure (the associations are made explicit in *Halloween 4: The Return of Michael Myers* [1988]) acts within the service of a society seeking a convenient scapegoat to disavow contemporary social crisis. Despite his twenty-one-year-old physique, Michael is really a child in an adult's body who exerts a repressed child's rage not only against sexually promiscuous females (representing his own sister) but also against Laurie Strode. Although virginal and more aware than her girlfriends, Laurie embodies a family figure Michael reacts against—the elder sister who is usually given the mother's role in controlling and conforming the youngest member of the family.[26] Although fulfilling the ideologic role of patriarchal avenger, Michael is as disturbed as Lawrence Talbot of *The Wolf Man*. He acts as a mischievous child in a man's body and experiments with different forms of masquerade—a boy in clown's suit, a hospital patient, a sheet-clad bogeyman. He finally appears wearing a white mask in a garage mechanic's outfit.[27]

Halloween II also contains significant features.[28] Although commencing the usual stalking point-of-view movement when Michael enters Mrs. Elroyd's kitchen to pick up her knife, the camera shows Michael and follows him after Mrs. Elroyd screams. It then reveals his next victim, Alice, as she picks up the phone. Rather than being placed within the stalker's perspective, we objectively observe Michael in the shot. The audience can escape the stalker's *subjective* perspective and note the figure's *objective* relationship to events within the narrative. Alice explains Mrs. Elroyd's scream. "She's always picking on him. He probably got angry and decided to start beating her." Michael then slits her throat, murderously enacting patriarchal violence upon a surrogate female victim.

Michael's atrocities embody rage from the patriarchal unconscious. Mr. Elroyd sleeps before a television screen that is running the opening sequences of *Night of the Living Dead*. The soundtrack plays Johnny's taunt, "They're coming to get you, Barbara." The reference not only equates Michael with Romero's zombies, it also refers to the Haddonfield community's desperate need of a surrogate victim (Michael) to enact its repressed violence. As Rene Girard notes in *Violence and the Sacred*, community desire for violence usually projects itself onto a surrogate figure who is equally both victim and perpetrator. Michael Myers acts in the service of a community ignoring social contradictions. While Deputy Brackett (Charles Cyphers) irrationally blames Loomis for Michael's killings—"You let him out. His own goddam doctor!"— Loomis causes the death of an innocent teenager and nearly shoots another while obsessively denying Michael's humanity. "He was my patient for fifteen years, became an obsession with me when I realized that there was nothing within him, neither consequence nor reason that was remotely human." Michael becomes his convenient scapegoat. Haddonfield's hospital doctor (Ford Rainey) arrives in a condition oblivious to Laurie Strode's pleas. Before he puts her under sedation, a nurse remarks, "He's been in the country club. I think he's drunk." Institutional figures are morally bankrupt.

In a screenplay clearly indebted to British science fiction writer Nigel Kneale[29] (but also having links with the sacrificial concepts of Rene Girard), Carpenter recognizes community ritual thirst for blood. Watching the people throw stones at the old Myers home, Loomis comments, "The tribe! One of their number was horribly butchered. This is the Wake." Michael Myers becomes an apocalyptic figure removed from family roots, recreated according to the desires of a community in crisis. Haddonfield's fictional world represents a crisis-ridden America desperately seeking old answers to new dilemmas. Carpenter's original family monster becomes associated with the Old World Celtic Samhain sacrificial ritual. Michael's murders are ritual acts divorced from social origins. He performs the functions of Lord of the Dead as dark savior and surrogate victim whom the community may blame for enacting its own repressed desires. He punishes the younger generation for promiscuous sins, but he is also a convenient scapegoat. At *Halloween II*'s climax Dr. Loomis sacrifices his life to cleanse the community from its desired monster.

Based on an ill-fated collaboration with Nigel Kneale, *Halloween III: Season of the Witch* (1982) dropped Michael Myers to emphasize *Halloween II*'s sacrificial aspects and post-1960s ambivalent feelings toward childhood.[30] *Halloween III*'s ritual "monster" is Irish entrepreneur Conal Cochran (Dan O'Herlihy). He moves into a formerly rural Eastern community after World War II to establish his Silver Shamrock joke factory. Specializing in Halloween masks, Cochran plans to use Stonehenge's Blue Stone in the most macabre joke of all—destroying American children in a sacrificially technological ritual version of Samhain. Cochran is a patriarchal deity-figure, a Kronos/Melisares wishing to devour youthful progeny. They ruin his kingdom by overpopulation, making the adult world totally dependent upon their desires. As he tells Dr. Challis (Tom Atkins), Samhain was the old sacrificial way of "controlling our environment." Although ascribing his motivations to planetary conjunctions, Cochran sees parallels between primitive methods of dealing with overpopulation (he mentions children and animals) and society's need to discipline rebellious kids.

The film's "hero," Challis, parallels many weak parental figures in mid-1980s horror. Divorced, alcoholic, seeing his children weekends and dealing with an antagonistic ex-wife, Challis resembles *Halloween II*'s doctor who is characterized as "drinking and doctoring—a great combination!" He never relates to his children who sit perpetually fixed to the television screen as it beams out Silver Shamrock advertising jingles. Liasing with Ellie Grimbridge (Stacey Nelkin) to discover the reasons behind her father's death, he discovers that Grimbridge owned a declining business that is now totally dependent on children.

Halloween III's adult characters live in an alienated world dominated by corporate control and dehumanizing malls. Self-employed businesswoman Marge Gutman (Garn Stephens) remarks on her "problems in dealing with a large corporation like Silver Shamrock" selling children's toys. The Kupfer family, Cochran's first guinea pigs, admire him for achieving the great American Dream of financial success in a business full of obedient corporate yesmen. Although reticent about a future world without children, Cochran hints that his version of "an ancient sacrificial ceremony" will result in an ideal utopia containing his business-suited robots—"logical, obedient, unlike most human beings." *Halloween III* envisages the destruction of children and the victory of patriarchal corporate control.

Halloween 4: The Return of Michael Myers (1988) resurrects its monstrous agent of patriarchy; it also displays contradictions contesting reactionary elements within 1980s horror.[31] Having survived incineration at the climax of *Halloween II*, Michael fights Loomis in the saga's now-weary regeneration through violence formula. However, the film begins to question Loomis's and Michael's demonization, though not in a coherent manner.

In the opening sequence a doctor arrives to transfer Michael to another hospital. The dialogue presents an interesting balance of metaphysical and social factors absent from earlier versions. Responding to the doctor's exclamation on arrival, "Jesus!" an attendant answers, "Jesus has nothing to do with this place." To another's "Welcome to Hell" the answer is, "Yeah. This is where society drops its worst nightmares." *Halloween 4* develops *Halloween II*'s thesis of the American community's need for a surrogate victim. The opening sequence shows Dr. Hoffman (Michael Pataki) suspicious of Loomis's symbiotic relationship to Michael. "When Myers goes, I hope he will transfer, retire, or die." Encountering Loomis before Michael's transfer, Hoffman listens to the facially scarred, limping Captain Ahab's warnings. "You can't let them take it out of here . . . We are not talking about any Federal prisoner. We are talking about Evil on two legs." Hoffman responds knowingly, "I said this before. I think you are the one who needs mental help."

After her parents' death, Laurie Strode's daughter, Jaimie (Danielle Harris) now lives with her relatives in Haddonfield. Missing her mother, alienated by a generation gap from her teenage stepsister Rachel (Ellie Cornell), Jaimie doubts whether her adopted mother (Laurie's sister, Mary Jo) really loves her. After weeping over Laurie's photo, Jaimie passes a dressing table mirror that splits her reflected image in three parts. At the right of the mirror is a small replica of Michael in his Halloween mask. Victimized by the community because of her family history, Jaimie conjures a monster from her unconscious. He will not only take sacrificial vengeance on the community but also threaten her (for reasons *Halloween 5* reveals).[32] In the clothing store sequence, Jaimie chooses a Halloween costume identical to that worn by Michael in the original *Halloween* prologue. Viewing her reflection in the mirror, young Michael's image abruptly appears. Turning away she sees the adult Michael behind her. The concluding shot shows her monster is again inside Haddonfield. Michael's blank white-faced mask appears in a fragment of glass. A hand picks it up off-camera.

Loomis walks along the road after his vain attempt to offer himself as a sacrificial victim to appease Michael. A fellow traveler (obviously modeled on Graham Greene's "whisky priest") gives him a lift. Recognizing Loomis as a fellow hunter and pilgrim, he mentions the goal of his quest. "The apocalypse. The end of the world. Armageddon. It's always got a face and a name." Offering Loomis his whisky bottle, he begins singing Ford's favorite hymn "Shall We Gather at the River." This is the only time Loomis ever smiles in the entire series.

A paranoid Loomis later stirs up vigilantes who accidentally kill one of Haddonfield's citizens. He incites a Puritan witch-burning mob. One redneck exclaims, "We're going to fry his ass." Loomis still sees Michael as a metaphysical beast. But *Halloween 4*'s ending shows this interpretation is insufficient. At the climax Sheriff Meeker (Beau Starr) prevents the paranoid Loomis from shooting a new "monster": young Jaimie now wielding a knife, clad in young Michael's Halloween costume. Like her uncle she reacts murderously to social victimization.

Halloween 5: The Revenge of Michael Myers (1989) contains one sequence that recognizes the family origins of Michael's psychosis, which even Loomis admits. Michael believes his cure will result from killing Jaimie as the last member of the family that caused his original condition. Loomis attempts to reason with him by using language more social than metaphysical: "Michael. It will destroy you too, one day, Michael. This rage which drives you. You figure if you kill them all it will go away. It won't. You have to fight it in the place where it's strongest. Where it all began, if you want to get rid of this rage."

They return to the old Myers home where Loomis makes one final appeal. "You came back to us. Michael. I know why you came back here. Because the little girl can stop the rage. She knows how to do it if you let her.... You know how much better you used to be." Reacting to Jaimie, Michael removes his mask, revealing a shadowy, tear-stained eye. She recognizes the abused, hurt child beneath the mask and says, "You're just like me."

The revelation is temporary; Michael reverts to violence. The film cannot bear the fact that its monster is really an abused child victimized by the family and not possessed by Satan. An unsatisfactory metaphysical climax shows a demonic agent releasing Michael from jail. Loomis reveals his real nature throughout the film, aggressively bullying Jaimie, suggesting she has more to fear from a normal patriarchal avenger than from Michael. He brutally holds Jaimie up as bait—"You want her? Here she is. Come and get her. Come and get your little girl"—before he dies. Although flawed and incoherent, *Halloween 5* reveals a bankrupt patriarchal normality that needs a monster as its alter ego.

◆　◆　◆

Despite reductive formulas and gratuitous special effects, the *Friday the 13th* series contain family elements.[33] The basic conservative formula appears in Sean Cunningham's *Friday the 13th* (1980).[34] A stalker who ritually slaughters promiscuous teenagers proves to be Mrs. Voorhees (Betsy Palmer). She is avenging her deceased son, Jason. She is a phallic avenging mother, speaking with his voice ("Kill her, Mummy. Kill her"). Although Alice (Adrienne King) wins the battle, she loses the war. A nightmare epilogue shows Jason emerging from Camp Crystal Lake to drag her beneath the depths. In the prologue to Steve Miner's *Friday the 13th, Part II* (1981), Jason returns to slaughter a no-longer resourceful, terrified Alice. Before Alice dies, she answers a phone call from her dominating mother, an event hardly coincidental because Jason continues mother's disciplinary mission in the film.

Although Ginny (Amy Steel) recognizes Jason as a "child trapped in a man's body.... The only person he knew was his mother," she can only survive by masquerading as his deceased phallic mother. Any intuitive feminist sympathy with the monster's plight becomes lost. Jason's hut is a religious shrine with mother's decapitated head as a holy object. Although Ginny survives, she is in a state of "severe hysterical shock." *Friday the 13th, Part II* ends with a track-in shot to the real winner, Mrs. Voorhees. Although dead, her decapitated head displays an active malignant influence.

Miner's *Friday the 13th, Part III* (1982) continues Ginny's insights into Jason's violence which possibly results from child abuse. It initially identifies him with a future victim—inadequate, unloved teenager Shelley. Shelley plays scary practical jokes and wears masks (one of which is Jason's hockey mask!). In an early scene he actually staggers around with a fake axe in his head, anticipating Jason's demise. Although marginal in the film, these scenes suggest Jason's violent acts represent repressed family rage which originates from abuse and neglect. However, patriarchal violence still wins. Mrs. Voorhees assaults survivor Chris (Dawn Kimmel) in traumatic nightmares while Jason's executioner, young Tommy (Corey Feldman), takes on his role in the climax of Joseph Zito's *Friday the 13th: The Final Chapter* (1984).

A more critical attitude develops against parental authority in *Friday the 13th: A New Beginning* (1985). The real murderer is a medic, Roy, who abandoned his son Joey years ago. He disavows guilt over Joey's death by slaughtering teenage scapegoats. Was parental guilt for Jason's drowning really the reason for Mrs. Voorhees's pathologic activities? Tom McLaughlin's *Friday the 13th, Part VI: Jason Lives* (1986) resurrects Jason, who slaughters teenagers *and* adult authority figures. Megan (Jennifer Crew) also saves Tommy, finishes Jason off, and survives physically and mentally unscathed, unlike her predecessors. This change is significant. *Jason Lives* appeared when media attention focused upon parental inadequacy as well as scandals affecting a supposedly strong Reagan presidency. This film differs from its predecessors by having its teenagers survive the patriarchal avenger and breaking the usual ideologic closure.

Friday the 13th, Part VII: The New Blood (1988) developed critiques against the parental world's untrustworthiness. The opening shows Camp Crystal Lake at night, the camera tilting down to reveal Jason chained to a stone at the bottom, a repressed force awaiting release. The next shot shows young Tina looking at the lake from the jetty. She remains outside to escape parental marital strife. She hears her mother's pleas, "Please don't drink anymore." A violent blow follows her father's "Don't tell me what to do." The disturbed girl flees into a boat, starting the motor, to take her toward the lake's center. Her father calls her. Tina condemns him, "You hit Mom again. . . . I hate you. Go away. I hate you. I wish you were dead." The camera zooms into her face at these last lines. Her emotional rage produces a telekinetic ripple effect, resulting in the jetty's collapse and her father's death. Realizing the effect of her powers, Tina screams "No Daddy!" as her mother calls in vain to her husband. The scene changes to an older Tina (Lar Park Lincoln) awakening from her nightmare. She travels with her mother to get help from Dr. Crews (Terry Kiser). Tina exhibits reluctance to embark on this journey. She recognizes danger on two fronts—guilt feelings over her father's death and Dr. Crews's cynical manipulation of her insecurities. After looking at her father's photo, she complies with her mother's denial of domestic hell—"I miss him so much"—"I know. I miss him too." When Dr. Crews enters the room, Tina runs outside to the jetty area where her father died. Hearing her voice from the past, "I wish you were dead," and reexperiencing the trauma, she falls into a dangerous trap, one that restores not her father but a monster from the patriarchal id. As she utters the words, "I'm sorry, Daddy. I wish I could bring you back," a submerged Jason revives. A montage segment links his resurrection to Tina's past family trauma.

Doubted by her mother and Dr. Crews, Tina vainly asserts, "I know what you're thinking. The man was not my father." Angrily reacting against Crews, she rushes out after telekinetically fragmenting the glass that covers her father's photograph. Although Jason is not her literal father, he is a monster from the patriarchal unconscious. Crews manipulates Tina and her mother. He sees Tina as a guinea pig for medical research, threatening incarceration when her mother discovers his tape-recorded notes.

Although Jason is a patriarchal monster, he also attacks Crews as an uncontrollable avenging force. The only way Tina saves herself and Nick (Kevin Blair) from Jason's murderous rage is by causing her father's emergence from the depths to drag Jason under. At the climax an ambulance takes Tina and Nick away. When Nick enquires, "Where's Jason?" she replies, "We took care of him." Instead of the usual fade to white, *The New Blood* concludes with a fade to black as the ambulance drives away into the distance. Teenage survival now depends upon separation from family values in whatever forms it occurs—actual, psychic, or supernatural.

Set against scenes depicting New York's dangerous urban landscape, the opening song of *Friday the 13th, Part VIII: Jason Takes Manhattan* (1989) speaks about "surviving in the big city" in which there is "no escape" but "we've come to terms with it / Trying to survive on the darker side." This allegorically expresses the film's theme of adolescent survival and escape from family control. Uncle Charles (Peter Mark Richman) has caused Renee's (Jensen Daggett) emotional insecurity by forcing her to swim in the deep end of Lake Crystal when she was a little child. Recognizing his guilt the manipulative Charles attempts to divert Renee from discovering the origins of her trauma. Like Marge Thompson in *A Nightmare on Elm Street*, he conceals adult guilt behind a wall of silence. Sean Robertson (Scott Revere) suffers from an oppressive father who constantly humiliates him. Both youngsters end up pursued by Jason (Kane Hodder) in New York sewers. Jason now kills parental oppressors as well as arrogant teenagers.

Jason Takes Manhattan is highly flawed, but it contains interesting parallels between Renee's attempts to remember the traumatic origins of her insecurities and Jason's own memories. Like Ginny, Renee feels some affinity with

Jason. She is constantly haunted by nightmare images of the young Jason. The film links Renee's discovery of patriarchal violence generating her neurosis with Jason's own memory. As toxic waste in New York sewers consume Jason's adult body, an off-screen voice cries, "Mummy. Don't let me drown." This suggests a vulnerable being behind the monster's form. Throughout the film, nightmare images of young Jason haunt Renee. As she eventually remembers how Charles caused her trauma by a brutal action, so Jason remembers the time of his original drowning as his body disintegrates. Jason's call of "Mummy. Don't let me drown" presumes his mother's presence. The scene thus suggests that Jason's original death stemmed as much from parental neglect as teenage negligence. Compulsively repeating his mother's avenging role, Jason has repressed the real origins of a family trauma that made him a monster. Renee and Jason are both family victims.

Jason's face gradually dissolves. The final images reveal not Kane Hodder but a young boy. Jason's hockey mask flows away in the sewer. Like those brief moments in *Frankenstein, The Ghost of Frankenstein, Curse of the Cat People*, and *Halloween V*, a monstrous rage disappears, revealing a fragile child beneath the violent mask. Outside lightning strikes the Statue of Liberty. Sean and Renee emerge from the depths of the sewers into Times Square. The film ends with an overhead shot of the couple as they wander into the city. The final soundtrack theme, appropriately entitled "Wasted Life," plays. It is now clear what forces wasted their lives and Jason's, making everyone try to "survive on the darker side." Unfortunately, *Jason Goes to Hell: The Final Friday* (1993) never develops its flawed predecessor's insights. Like *Halloween 5*, it links Jason with surviving family members. But the younger generation's adherence to conservative family values destroy Jason, a disappointing factor after the tentative advances that suggest Jason's psychopathic murders are the result of obeying a patriarchally ordained revenge against promiscuous teenagers. Like Norman Bates and Michael Myers, Jason was a victim who became a victimizer. His condition originated from some undisclosed family trauma. Unfortunately, this motif never gains enough strength to make it a powerful antihegemonic factor combatting the dominant series structure of a patriarchal revenge fantasy.

Poltergeist and
Freddy's Nightmares

Although *Poltergeist* (1982) begins with a promising visual exploration of darkness within the family home, it soon degenerates into the infantile mind-set of typical Spielburbia, oppressing any of the differences Tobe Hooper intended.[1] Focusing on the closing logo of American television shutdown, the camera tracks away from the visual images of the Iwo Jima monument to reveal Steve's (Craig T. Nelson) feet asleep before the set. Cutting to separate images of other sleeping family members, the sequence presents a separation between Carol Anne (Heather O'Rourke) and the unseen monsters from an external televisual id who eventually threaten and consume her. Finally moving toward Spielberg's infantile epiphanic visions of adult faces beaming childlike wonder, *Poltergeist* safely projects family tensions onto the excremental demonic realm without interrogating potentially destabilizing images (Robbie's fascination with death, Ronald Reagan's image on a magazine cover, and Debbie's sexual experiences unknown to the family). Inserting its significantly named Freelings into a dark technological Disneyland, *Poltergeist* banally succeeds in its ideologic aim of reuniting the family and blaming convenient scapegoats.

Brian Gibson's *Poltergeist II: The Other Side* (1986) continues this smug ideological project, enlisting minority groups such as Native Americans to cure the ailments of a WASP family. *Poltergeist II aims* to soothe Steven's economic and personal insecurities and change him into a kinder and gentler patriarch. Unable to persuade the insurance company to indemnify him for the loss of his previous home, Steve now moves his family in with his mother-in-law (Geraldine Fitzgerald). Following Reverend Kane's (Julian Beck) first appearance at the shopping mall, grandmother dies, leaving a vulnerable Steve to face Kane's demonic onslaught. Presenting himself as representing a family crisis organization, Kane recognizes the same insecure fears in Steve that Grady discerns in Jack Torrance of *The Shining*. "You feel that you're not man enough to hold this family together."

Shaman Taylor (Will Sampson) recognizes Steve's dilemma in metaphysical, not social, terms. "That was him testing your power. He comes in many forms but that was him." Taylor operates as an institutional patriarchal agent seeking to turn Steve away from self-destructive paths. Offering him a feather as a substitute for the tequila bottle, Taylor wishes to make Steve a warrior in defense of the American family. Refusing Steve's offer of the bottle, he regards it as "a drain on your power" and urges spiritual preparation to overcome personal inadequacy. "I wanted to drink but I gave it up. Bad dreams. . . . You feel like a leaf at the mercy of the wind." Taylor counsels him against feeling sorry for himself and concludes with advice stemming from Reaganite ideology: "You should assume full responsibility for everything in your world."

Poltergeist II follows Spielberg's vision. It displays conservative directions within 1980s family horror. Taylor understands Kane as a dark patriarchal father. Advising Steve, he reveals Kane's goal. "He knows your strength is your love for your family. He has been trying to pull this family apart. If he succeeds he will possess Carol Anne and destroy your spirit."

No longer Regan's demonic child created by family tensions, Carol Anne is the divine healer not just for the Freeling family but also for those spirits tormented by Kane. As Taylor informs Steve, "He's fearful because they touched the Life Force represented by Carol." As the Beast, Kane's unacceptable brutal face of patriarchy needs a new gentler version. *Poltergeist II* feminizes its father-figure, but any radical gender implications collapse before the film's ideologic project of restoring the father. To protect his family from Kane's "Beast," Steve must recognize its potential unity. "Dianne and the kids are your power. And they are yours."

Ignoring Taylor's advice, Steve returns to the bottle after vainly trying to act a good father at the dinner table. Draining its contents, he swallows Kane's wormlike phallus and becomes a monstrous patriarch like Jack Torrance. However, Steve's demonically inspired assault on Dianne (Jo Beth Williams)—"You wish Carol Anne had never been born. You never wanted Carol Anne"—receives no firm anchorage within the film and is easily forgotten. This parallels Britton's observations concerning the Ronald Reagan reference in *Poltergeist*: "By at once adverting to the politics of an American present and refusing to define a discourse in terms of which the reference could make concrete sense, *Poltergeist* is able to draw on and disarticulate its audience's uncertainties at one and the same time."[2] Operating on an ideologically complicit contrast between bad father and quasi-feminized patriarch, *Poltergeist II* has its cake and eats it.

Like Keys in *E.T.* (1982), Steve becomes a father possessing and not possessing the phallus. He needs both family and resurrected spiritual mother-in-law's presence to succeed in rescuing Carol Anne. Steve then becomes a "kinder and gentler" patriarch in anticipation of the future title of Tania Modleski's book, *Feminism Without Women*. Unlike Kane, he will not dominate his congregation. But as the final shots reveal, Steve stands at the center of the reunited family. If the Freeling family does not "worship" their leader as Kane's did, they revere his new gentler model. The dialogue explicitly outlines the film's project; its banality echoes an impoverished structure. "Taylor said, 'We go back as a family.' We go back together. That's all of us." "The light of the family can defeat him. . . . This is the moment you've been moving towards all your life."

Set in the claustrophobic confines of a Chicago skyscraper, whose glass structure offers potential dualistic critiques of characters unthinkingly existing within a contemporary culture of narcissism, Gary Sherman's *Poltergeist III* (1987) offers much but delivers little.

Now staying with her aunt Patricia (Nancy Allen) and husband Bruce Gardiner (Tom Skerritt) within a glacial affluent consumerist ghetto encompassing mall, apartments, and art gallery, Carol Anne experiences another visitation from Reverend Kane (Nathan Davis). Although *Poltergeist III* never develops its mise-en-scene premises coherently, sinister visual imagery of mirrors, windows, and glacial interiors suggest deep personal insecurities lying within narcissistically inclined characters. Like Kubrick's Overlook Hotel, Gardiner's economically affluent glass temple proves a weak fortress against Kane's supernatural invasion.

Noting daughter Donna's excessive attention to her appearance, Bruce counsels her, "Better be careful honey. Remember what happened to Narcissus." The film develops imagery of cracked mirrors and broken thermostat glass meters, underlining the fragmentary nature of a culture based upon mere appearance. Feeling insecure about marriage to Bruce and her position as stepmother, Patricia regards Carol Anne as a convenient scapegoat. Knowledgeable about her niece's past, she, Bruce, and school psychiatrist Dr. Seaton all dismiss the reality of her previous history.

Dr. Seaton blames her for projecting mass hypnosis on to the Cuesta Verde neighborhood. Oblivious to his childless wife's obvious resentment of Carol Anne's presence and lack of enthusiasm in filling the traditional stepmother role with Donna, Bruce misses her facial grimace as he remarks to

Carol Anne, "If I had my way, I'd keep you here forever." Insecure at her niece's presence, Patricia reveals her true feelings. She regards Carol Anne as a little brat who plays "sick little jokes." Seeing Carol Anne as a symbol of a desired child, Bruce dismisses his "crazy brother-in-law," holding him responsible for using Carol Anne as the scapegoat for the failed Cuesta Verde real estate venture. Although insufficiently developed, these factors really make Kane's supernatural presence marginal.

Poltergeist III presents a superficial world denying unpalatable realities. Characteristically, Patricia runs an art gallery whose latest exhibit is "$26,000 worth of postmodern abstraction." This throwaway reference, having associations with a movement often supporting conservative discourses, aptly applies to *Poltergeist III's* ideologic project. Like its predecessors, it aims to restore a divided family while at the same time denying the tensions that make such a goal redundant. Its visually striking sequences of mirrored split personalities (Bruce, Donna, and boyfriend Mark) never sufficiently build up a coherent critique. Instead *Poltergeist's* miniature ideologic spokeswoman Tangina (Zelda Rubinstein) makes her last appearance in the cycle to attempt the affirmation of family values. "Your love. Your bond. Your caring for those two children is your most valuable weapon." Finally, Patricia becomes a caring mother who is reunited with both Carol Anne and her own family. Although affirming Tangina's ideologic fairy godmother role ("She did it. She saved us"), a lightning bolt strikes the skyscraper, accompanied by Kane's off-screen laughter, and underlines its (as well as the film's) shaky premises.

◆　◆　◆

Running from 1984–91, the Freddy Krueger saga reveals a similar pattern to *Friday the 13th* and *Halloween*. It charts a monster's rise to supernatural cult hero and then reveals his disturbing roots within a real-life situation.[3] Freddy's origins are clear. He is no longer a joke. He parallels the patriarchal, serial killer-cult figure of Hannibal Lecter[4] (now given the Hollywood seal of approval with Anthony Hopkins's Academy Award). Freddy's name derives from Wes Craven's earlier patriarchs, Krogh Stillo of *The Last House on the Left* and Freddy of *The Hills Have Eyes*. Although Freddy's dangerous essence as reincarnated child murderer does appear in the original *A Nightmare on Elm Street* (1984), Craven's reliance on manipulated suspense techniques and spectacular adolescent demises drowns the film's social implications. A *Nightmare on Elm Street* is a key exemplar of horror's relationship to Guy Debord's definition of "The Society of The Spectacle," a manufactured illusionary situation designed to deny any relationship to social reality in the 1980s. Despite this, the first film cannot entirely avoid some material facts.

A Nightmare on Elm Street (1984) introduces Freddy Krueger as a resurrected child murderer who avenges his incineration at the hands of an angry parental mob. He punishes their children in nightmares. The film uses classical generic archetypes such as the "Terrible House" that contains a hellish basement representing the Gothic within conservative terms. Freddy's returns as a 1980s Jehovah who seeks vengeance on the younger generation; he feasts on his young victims in a manner resembling Puritanical fears of a Satanic Eucharist. Unlike Elm Street parents, he can discipline and definitively punish his teenage victims. The Satanic implications within Freddy appear in Nancy's (Heather Langencamp) first confrontation with him. She exclaims, "Please, God!" Displaying his steel fingers, Freddy (Robert Englund) replies, "This is God." During one sequence Nancy falls asleep during a recital of Cicero's speech from *Julius Caesar* which foretells of omens that anticipate the demise of Rome's authoritarian figure. She falls victim to one of Freddy's dream attacks. The film makes no attempt to undercut Freddy's divine attributes, preferring instead to validate his position as bogeyman, especially when he attacks his first victims—sexually active teens Tina and Rod.

The film also indicts the adult world, presenting parents as weak, manipulative, and selfish. Nancy angrily reacts to her father, Sheriff John Thompson (John Saxon), who uses her as a decoy to capture Rod. He never responds to appeals for help against Freddy and puts her behind bars at home. Nancy's mother, Marge (Ronee Blakeley), withholds crucial information from her daughter until it is too late. She resorts to alcohol to conceal guilt feelings over her role in Freddy's murder, and she morbidly preserves his knives. *Nightmare on Elm Street* emphasizes the dangerous nature of parental silence. On many occasions it indirectly aids Freddy. Nancy attempts to warn Glen (Johnny Depp), but his father stubbornly refuses to pass on a phone message from "a crazy kid behind bars." Finally, Nancy's drunken mother admits her failings and recognizes her offspring's strength.

By recognizing her family's flawed nature, Nancy faces Freddy one last time, denies his psychic hold over her, and makes him disappear. However, the victory is temporary. An epilogue filmed in high-key light shows mother and daughter dressed in light costumes. The artificial brightness alerts us to an illusionary happy ending. Nancy remarks, "God. It's bright." Mrs. Thompson promises to turn over a new leaf. She says, "I'm going to stop drinking. I don't feel like it any more." Tina, Rob, and Glen wait for Nancy in the car. As she enters the car, the top (painted with Freddy's sweater colors) automatically covers them. The doors lock. Nancy calls in vain to her mother who clearly ignores what goes on as the car drives away. Freddy then drags Mrs. Thompson through the door. Nancy's victory is short-lived.

Jack Sholder's *A Nightmare on Elm Street 2: Freddy's Revenge* (1985) further links Freddy with a dysfunctional family situation.[5] Moving into Nancy's house, Jesse Walsh (Mark Patton) falls victim to nightmares and discovers that Freddy wants his body to continue attacking Elm Street kids. Freddy's choice is deliberate. Jesse has an antagonistic relationship with his father (Clu Gulager) that generates family trauma.[6] Walsh obtained their home in a special deal; he knows the house's dark history but conceals it from his family. Freddy's dream attacks on Jesse parallel Walsh's humiliating assaults against his son. Despite a 99-degree heat-wave and Mrs. Walsh's (Hope Lange) concerns about her son's health, Walsh refuses to switch on the air conditioning.

Jesse's second dream encounter begins when he sees Freddy stoking the basement furnace on a hot summer's evening. Believing his father to be in the basement, he discovers Freddy, who sardonically remarks, "Daddy can't help you now." Freddy also uses Jesse's body to avenge the latter's repressed rage against another patriarchal figure—Coach Snyder—before attempting to kill Jesse's kid sister, Kerry (Sydney Walsh).

The Walsh home contains repressed tensions associated with Freddy's dream world. Jesse's initial dream sequence ends with Freddy slashing a girl's stomach with his claw. This match-cuts with the next sequence that shows Mrs. Walsh slicing a tomato. Kerry gleefully flourishes a breakfast cereal gift of claws that resemble Freddy's. Walsh later refuses to sympathize with his son's disturbed condition and ascribes it to drug abuse.

Fearful for Lisa's (Kim Myers) safety, Jesse flees to hip friend Grady. But the room provides no sanctuary. However, Lisa (Jesse's girlfriend) understands Freddy Krueger's real nature. Reading Nancy's diary, Lisa understands that Freddy's power exists by virtue of the victim's unconscious complicity with the patriarchal unconscious.[7] "He is evil itself. We gave him all the energy he needed. I brought him into my world. We all did. We can fight him."

However, before she can save Jesse, Lisa sees Freddy functioning as the patriarchal unconscious. While her parents impotently complain about the noisy downstairs swimming pool party, Freddy reveals himself, Satanically shot in low-angle against a fiery background. He says, "You are all my children, now."

She awakens Jesse's dormant presence within Freddy's body and causes a schizophrenic reaction. Flames consume Freddy's body and Jesse reemerges from his Satanic father's charred flesh. But as the epilogue shows the victory is temporary. Freddy emerges from a girl's chest to continue terrorizing Elm Street teenagers on the school bus.

Chuck Russell's *A Nightmare on Elm Street III: Dream Warriors* (1987) contains further developments.[8] The kids are no longer in Elm Street with their parents but inside a mental institution; their condition is obviously the result of family trauma. They now act as a united force, attempting to find their own identities. Although there is never any move toward formulating radical alternatives, the film stresses combatting false ideas, particularly those concerning ideal family situations which no longer exist in an increasingly dysfunctional world.

Captions roll against images of Kristen Parker (Patricia Arquette) making a papier-maché house of the original Elm street dwelling. No. 1428 Elm Street metaphorically symbolizes any traumatic childhood. Her mother Elaine (Brooke Bundy) enters the house with her new boyfriend. Kristen hears his voice below—"Where do you keep the bourbon?" She turns on the radio to drown out the sounds before Elaine enters and sends her to bed. Kristen knows the real reason behind this supposed expression of care. "And as usual you don't want to keep him waiting." After dreaming of visiting the Terrible House, she awakes and goes to the bathroom. A momentary lapse allows Freddy to slash her wrists.

At the mental hospital Elaine describes the wound as self-inflicted— the result of Kristen's narcissistic desire for attention! Although intern Max (Larry Fishburne) later suggests to Dr. Gordon (Craig Wasson) that the kids' condition may result from "fucked up chromosomes" of the 1960s generation, that is, "Sex and Drugs and Rock and Roll," *Dream Warriors* never supports this. Instead it presents parents as unreliable flawed figures. Kids have to learn self-reliance and avoid escapist fantasies. They must be tougher and more resilient than their 1960s teen predecessors.

Dream Warriors describes its kids as "survivors." Although supposedly "traumatized" by group delusions over a bogeyman, Dr. Gordon's description of various symptoms (including sleep disorders, narcosis, and bed wetting) have obvious family origins. Official medical and psychoanalytic discourses are redundant. As one kid caustically states, "Great! Now it's my dick that's killing me."

Nancy is now a graduate student who uses her skills and sympathy to aid adolescents in their crucial rites of passage against Freddy. She stresses constant alertness against the demonic father. Recourse to narcissistic fantasy is dangerous. Freddy's first victims are puppet devotee Philip and television addict Jennifer. Freddy uses their fantasies as weapons against them. He kills Philip by using his veins as puppet strings before throwing him from a roof. While Jennifer watches a banal talk show, Freddy plunges her head through the screen. He always wins the final battle against those who avoid the reality of patriarchal oppression. Sexual fantasy (Joey), black macho toughness (Kincaid), sword and sorcery (Will), or cyberpunk (Taryn) all prove futile. As he tells Wizard Master Will in the dream world, "Sorry kid, I don't believe in fairy tales."

Although submerged within special effects and the conservative role of Sister Mary (Freddy's resurrected mother Amanda Krueger) who directs Dr. Gordon towards traditional religious methods, antifamily motifs still occur. Kristen tells Nancy about her family background, "If I had a nightmare I'd always bring my Dad in. Dreams would always get better. He used to tell me they were his dreams." Her father was always reassuring. She then exclaims, "The man in my dreams. He was real, wasn't he?" Definite connections exist between both men in her dreams. Nancy is also a traumatic family victim. After her mother died, her father turned to alcohol and self-pity. Facing Nancy after several years, he is guilt-ridden over his failure to protect his family from Freddy. Nancy confronts him with his responsibility toward her and other Elm Street kids. "You owe me."

Dream Warriors emphasizes family life as the source of danger. Kristen later dreams a replay of the film's opening scene, imagining Elaine as more caring and less selfish. However, Freddy brutally destroys the fantasy by appearing as the previously unseen boyfriend ("Where's the fucking bourbon?") and decapitating Elaine. Elaine's severed head verbally abuses Kristen. The dream expresses mother's real feelings toward her daughter. "You spoil everything when I bring a man home. You're just trying to get some fucking attention."

Nancy suffers from dangerous family illusions. After a temporary respite from Freddy's assault, the recently deceased Sheriff Thompson appears to make a last appeal to his daughter. "I've crossed over Princess . . . I love you so much. I'll always love you." Nancy allows her defenses to drop. Freddy appears in Daddy's place and rips her with his claws. Only Gordon's quick actions allow the survivors temporary respite.

Renny Harlin's *A Nightmare on Elm Street, Part 4: The Dream Master* (1988) develops these family motifs. Elm Street survivors Joey and Kincaid ignore Kristen's (Tuesday Knight) warnings about Freddy's revival. They die. Kristen's death results from Elaine's complicity. The disbelieving mother gives her daughter sleeping pills. Before reluctantly entering Freddy's dream world, Kristen condemns Elm Street parental responsibility for creating Freddy. "Sorry! That you and your tennis pals torched this guy and now he's after me! I'm his fucking banquet and I'm his last course." She becomes a sacrificial offering in a Satanic Eucharist unconsciously initiated by the parental world. As another Elm Street teenager remarks later, "If you took a look at our town history, it's not a safe place to be a teenager."

Kristen's successor Alice (Lisa Wilcox) has to learn self-reliance and overcome her family situation. Like John Thompson her father (Nick Mele) is an alcoholic and a parental failure. Alice has to avoid daydreaming as an escapist vehicle from a dysfunctional family. She tells Kristen she learned dreaming from her mother. "I love to dream. I hate the ones about my Dad." Kristen recognizes the similarity to her own plight. As psychic outlets from traumatic family situations, the dream world presents no real escape from the Dark Father. To defeat Freddy, Alice must divest herself of all dangerous illusions.

Falling into the dream world, Alice enters a cinema showing a 1940s college film titled *Burning Youth*. This film links vulnerable youthful generations victimized by patriarchal institutions. Alice penetrates the screen and becomes a participant in a hellish imaginary scenario. In a diner she encounters her aged, frustrated double, the figure embodies adolescent fears of entrapment in low-income service employment, a grim reality for most middle-class teenagers in the Reagan era. Freddy appears, orders a pizza, and devours an ingredient—the head of her deceased brother, Rick. Her announces her doomsday, "Your shift is over."

However, she finally sums up hidden reserves of strength by calling on the trapped souls of Freddy's victims to dismember his body. The final scene shows her with boyfriend Danny (Danny Hassel) in the real world, refusing his encouragement to make even a harmless birthday wish. Freddy's reflection appears in the pool; he is awaiting his next onslaught via some fantasy outlet.

Stephen Hopkins's A *Nightmare on Elm Street 5: The Dream Child* (1989) further emphasizes Freddy's role as Satanic avatar of the patriarchal family.[9] After sex with Danny, Alice descends into the dream world and becomes Amanda Krueger. Dressed in a nun's habit, she wanders down a mental hospital corridor and suffers rape by a hundred male patients (including an undisguised Robert Englund). Alice's nightmare ends with Danny turning into Freddy's father and attacking her.

The following high school graduation sequence reveals a dangerous world of uncaring parents and vulnerable children. Greta's (Erica Anderson) snobbish mother (Wendy Dobie) forces her into an unwanted fashion model career. Danny's father ignores his son's wish to take Alice on holiday and instead pushes him into the arms of his football coach buddy. Alice's father forms a marked contrast. Now reformed and attending Alcoholics Anonymous meetings, he is more of a gentle companion than a father—an exception to Elm Street parents, past and present.

Alice's next dream links these preceding sequences. Entering the mental asylum's Gothic terrains, she attends Freddy's birth. Dressed as a nun, she stands beside a medical staff that resembles parents and children in the previous scene. The parents are unsympathetic toward Amanda. A nun offers useless religious platitudes. "This is one of God's creatures. Take solace in that." Freddy's demonic baby escapes, rushing into a church, reemerging in adult form. He is shot in low-angle before a stained glass window, chuckling at his resurrection. Freddy returns as a supernatural embodiment of oppressive social forces—parental, religious, and medical.

Freddy chooses Danny as his first victim. In a scenario emphasizing Freddy's role as patriarchal avenger, Danny's car radio plays an imaginary talk show program. Danny's mother condemns Alice. "I'm calling about my wayward son Daniel. He's been like an unmanageable dickweed ever since he was seduced by that slut Alice." Freddy enacts appropriate vengeance, "If I was you lady, I'd kill that ungrateful piggy." After doing this Freddy speaks to Alice through Danny's charred body, "Hi Alice. Wanna make babies?" His grotesque use of Danny's body follows his similar use of Jesse in *Freddy's Revenge* and parallels Mrs. Anderson's plans for Greta. He intends returning through Alice's fetus.

Despite danger, Alice decides not to abort the child in memory of her gentle boyfriend. Freddy next acts in Mrs. Anderson's service, disciplining Greta for criticizing her mother's inhumanity and hypocrisy at a social dinner party. Appearing as a chef, he stuffs her with food emphasizing her mother's earlier injunctions concerning the social proprieties of public dining over private dieting. Freddy speaks paternally to his victim, "Don't talk with your mouth full!" Mark (Joe Seely) later discerns the real causes of Greta's death. "Maybe it was her mother that killed her with that Party Perfect Shit." As the surviving youngsters enter his apartment, a television set shows an aggressive, middle-aged talk show host who describes his adolescent guests as scumbags. They face danger both inside and outside Freddy's dream world.

Alice discovers how Freddy gains access to the adolescent world. He feeds the unborn Jacob his victim's souls like a drug-addicted parent hooking the next generation. Her recognition—"You're trying to make him like you so you can live through him"—is one applicable to Elm Street's real-life parents. Aided by Amanda Krueger she combats Freddy. But she faces one more challenge, one that Nancy lost. In her dream world she encounters Danny, who calls to his son, "Come to Poppa." But she recognizes Freddy beneath Danny's gentle presence and warns Jacob away. Danny responds with Freddy's voice, "Kids! Always a disappointment." Even a gentle teen father conceals a Freddy Krueger.

Alice wins the battle. The final sequence shows her with her father and newborn son, Jacob Daniel. But the war continues. As they walk away in the sunshine, a group of white-clad children (Freddy's former victims) play with a skipping rope, singing the dark nursery rhyme associated with their murderer. Freddy's laugh occurs on the soundtrack.

Rachel Talalay's *Freddy's Dead: The Final Nightmare* (1991) stressed family origins of its supernatural serial killer.[10] The kids are now outside the traditional family, suffering from parental abuse, and live in a Recovery House run by Maggie (Lisa Zane) and Doc (Yaphet Kotto), a single woman and a minority person who have no family ties. After the prologue an affluent father criticizes Maggie for his son Spencer's (Breckin Meyer) lack of improvement. Maggie angrily responds that her work does not echo corporate goals, "He isn't a Toyota!"

Like Nancy, Maggie sees her role in helping the kids develop "survival techniques" and face reality in healing family induced trauma. Spencer understands his father's desires. "All he wants me to be is for me to grow up to be like him, an exact copy." But Spencer seeks escapist avenues. Watching him hooked into a computer game, Maggie prophetically remarks, "One of these days, you'll have to face your father."

Tracey (Lezlie Deane) channels her violent rage into kick boxing practice. She refuses to speak of her deceased father, whose dream visitations ominously parallel Freddy's. Her father appears, "Every time I close my eyes." Carlos (Rickey Dean Logan) wears a hearing aid, enigmatically remarking, "I stopped talking back when it became hazardous to my health." New arrival John (Shon Greenblat) mistakenly believes Freddy is his real father. The group travel to Springwood to investigate.

Springwood is now a desolate town devoid of kids whose adult population cannot function without a younger generation to dominate. Tom and Roseanne Arnold appear in cameo roles as deranged parents desperate for children to smother. Teacher and orphanage director play imaginary games with unseen children. The school blackboard historically associates Freddy with another patriarchal bearer of genocide. Although the date is inaccurate, the associations are unmistakable. "In 1493 Freddy sailed over the sea. In 1494 Freddy came back to look for more."

Although all affirm a common oath, "We'll survive," Tracey and Maggie exhibit a self-awareness the others do not. John refuses Spencer's offer of dope. "I don't play that stuff. I need all the senses I can." Tracey sharpens her responses, reacting aggressively to Carlos. But not all escape the past. At the old Elm Street house, Carlos dreams himself back into his ghetto, masochistically submitting to a physically abusive mother. She turns into Freddy and tortures him to death. Spencer falls asleep before his videogame and becomes Freddy's manipulated computerized image. As Maggie foretold, he faces his computer-generated father, who hits him repeatedly, "Be like me! Be like me!" Freddy prevents Spencer's defense by making father's image bigger. John falls victim to filial love and finds out Freddy is not his real father. Only Maggie and Tracy survive these psychic traps; both are linked by a common family secret.

Returning to a world with no record of Freddy's victims, Maggie experiences John's dream. Missing elements fall into place. She sees a father chasing a little girl, calling, "Come to Daddy." Her mother emerges screaming, "I won't tell." Father (now revealed as Robert Englund minus makeup) goes to her, "We need to talk." As the parents argue, the little girl explores Daddy's basement and finds newspaper clippings of child murders and Freddy Krueger's claws. Now wearing the little girl's dress, resembling Judy Garland in *The Wizard of Oz* (an in-joke occurs in the prologue with Freddy as the Wicked Witch), Maggie confronts her real father, Freddy Krueger. He attempts to manipulate her, ascribing his revenge to separation from her. "You are my blood. They took you away from me but I made them pay. I took all their children away. But now, that's over." Maggie, like Tracey, is a possible incest victim.

Tracey reexperiences her father's incestuous assault in a dream, but she retreats in time, hitting "father" with a coffee pot, scalding her arms to reenter the real world. Before Maggie and Tracey temporarily escape Freddy's presence, they learn he is not alone. Some skull-headed "Dream People" saved him from death. Seen initially on a museum poster, these figures represent the Holy Trinity's Dark Side—demonic Father, Son, and Holy Spirit.

Entering father's domain, Maggie discovers his past history. She sees young Freddy taunted in a classroom by his peers after killing a mouse. Children mockingly chant "Son of a hundred maniacs" (a reference to his stated origins in *Dream Warriors* and *The Dream Child*). The sequence suggests more than a malicious child taunted by equally malicious children. Faces change to reveal senior citizens and middle-aged people repeating the chant, suggestive of an older generation molding impressionable minds. Where else would these children get the information concerning Freddy's origins? Young Freddy merely acts in an expected manner. Society needs scapegoats and finds one in Freddy Krueger.

Maggie then sees her adolescent father exhibiting symptoms of child abuse, masochistically slashing his chest with a razor in a basement—the scene of his future crimes. His drunken adoptive father (Alice Cooper) descends the stairs with a whip to perform a disciplinary function that is undoubtedly a normal part of family life. Experiencing the blows, Freddy responds, "Thank you, sir. May I have another?" He learns to bear pain and points the razor at his father. Thanks to family disciplinary procedures, a victimized masochist becomes a victimizing sadist.

Maggie drags Freddy into the world of reality, but she faces one last temptation. A tearful, unscarred, repentant figure pleads before her. "You saw what they did to me when I was a kid. I loved you and mother. I need so hard to be loved." However, she avoids the temptation, "Come to Daddy," and knocks away his razor-gloved hand. As Freddy's burnt face returns, Maggie bites her father's nose in a filial embrace that disavows the unequal power balance involved in such family relationships. "Oh Daddy. I didn't like it then. I don't like it now." Impaling him with an arrow, she pushes dynamite through his stomach, and kisses him, "Happy Father's Day." Freddy's body explodes, and the Dream People fly away in search of another vessel.[11]

◆　◆　◆

Friday the 13th, Halloween, Poltergeist, Nightmare on Elm Street all reveal the ugly operations of a patriarchal unconscious. Certain recurring features occur. Kids have to survive not just the monster but deep psychological scars arising from dysfunctional family situations. Although the films present stalemate situations, they show youthful audiences the importance of alertness, awareness, endurance, and a stubborn spirit of *survival*. S/he who *survives* lives to fight another day, one when Jason, Michael, Freddy, and their successors may not be as powerful.

Despite their impoverished nature, these texts have much to tell us about 1980s cultural attitudes. Similarly the horror films made from the writings of Stephen King are often testaments to the role of the family as the source of horror. Such features occur in his novels and, sometimes, emerge satisfactorily in particular film versions. As a best-selling author of his generation, King's works and films are also important evidence toward the different manifestations of fictional hearths of darkness.

The King Adaptations

Stephen King's movie adaptations show family horror's connections with the American cultural tradition.[1] King belongs to an era of the genre's finest achievements. He also chronicles certain historic influences on literature and cinema.[2] As he once said in reference to America's unjustly neglected naturalist tradition,[3] "Almost everything that we do has a history. No matter where you come in on any situation, you are not coming in at the beginning."[4] His fiction echoes many themes within horror cinema.[5] King's world shows believable, everyday Americans struggling to survive on a darker side, less fantastic than it appears.[6]

What strongly emerges in *The Shining* is not the Overlook Hotel's supernatural traps but Jack Torrance's failure in the American Dream, his past history as an abused child, and his alcoholic descent into a psychosis that is preferable to admitting personal failure and ideologic entrapment.[7] *The Shining* is King's *Death of a Salesman*. While Arthur Miller caustically penetrates Willie Loman's post–World War II delusions, King presents Jack Torrance as an equally tragic victim of a system that never guarantees fulfillment. A bleak future of minimum income awaits Jack, involving marital breakup, loneliness, and confinement in seedy hotels with other victims of the American Dream. The Overlook possession is his escape. As King's dark version of Thornton Wilder's *Our Town*, *Salem's Lot* presents vampirism as the logical consequence of rural isolation and emotional cannibalism. Ben Mears returns to a repressively conformist society that conceals physical and mental abuse. *Salem's Lot*'s associations attract Old World vampire Barlow. The novel *Christine* reveals another loser in the American Dream: Roland LeBay, who avenges his frustrations within a Plymouth Fury. Donna Trenton in *Cujo* fears marital breakup. Looking at the supermarket line, she envisages a degrading future of using food stamps for payment. *Carrie's* Sue Snell faces an equally bleak existence. Her material success within the American Dream of family life exacts the personal hell of a boring suburban future.[8]

The family is a crucial component in King's vision. His world depicts its dysfunctional and abusive nature.[9] Beginning with the White and Snell households in *Carrie*, the abused children of *Salem's Lot*, the Torrance family of *The Shining*, Randall Flagg's Charles Manson family of *The Stand*, Mrs. Dodd's *Psycho* home in *The Dead Zone*, the politically oppressed McGee family of *Firestarter*, the different class-structured (but equally economically insecure) Trenton and Camber families in *Cujo*, the "UnHappy Days" world of *Christine's* Arnie Cunningham, to the denying Creed family of *Pet Sematary*, King's fiction displays familiar family horror motifs.

King recognizes that dangerous institutional forces produce monsters such as the Moral Majority fundamentalism that motivates the "Children of the Corn" in his 1977 short story.[10] In *The Dead Zone*, Johnny Smith's mother insanely retreats into religious fundamentalism. Mrs. Dodd's sexually repressed Puritanism destroys her son. While Johnny seeks to save society, Frank enacts sacrificial patriarchal revenge against women. Like Jason Voorhees, he punishes single females—surrogate displacements for his mother.

The Mist complements George Romero's consumerist critiques. But while Romero sees the need for a new society, King never attempts alternatives. But he does recognize problems of closure. As he states, "the most difficult thing . . . is to end a book, because the story always goes on. And the story always does go on."[11] The same applies to his work's historical relationships and the possibility of future change.[12]

◆   ◆   ◆

Brian De Palma's *Carrie* (1976) still remains one of the best King adaptations. It has a more restrained visual style, as well as many of the original novel's social critiques.[13] Carrie is definitely a social victim.[14] In the opening shot Carrie fumbles a basketball. The dominating overhead camera views her as a Girardian "scapegoat."[15] Caught within a conformist world that stifles personal growth and alternative development, she is an easy target for frustrated peer group violence until she takes her telekinetic vengeance at the Senior Prom.

Carrie is an ironic film. Sue Snell (Amy Irving) genuinely attempts to make amends for humiliating Carrie in the shower room. But this leads to further disaster. Surviving Carrie's slaughter, she suffers psychological trauma, a condition that makes her as separate from the community as Carrie White. Even supposedly sympathetic teacher, Miss Collins (Betty Buckley) is culpable. Seen through Carrie's eyes as joining in the laughter, Miss Collins participates in a mob psychology she understands so well. Earlier she explains Carrie's plight to the high school principal. She revealingly states, "The thing is, I know how they feel." Her encouragement of Carrie to "open out" and deal with her appearance reveals her own social conditioning rather than genuine concern. Seeing Carrie with Tommy Ross (William Katz) at the prom, she nostalgically speaks of her earlier high school days. The high school prom is a rite of passage into adulthood, but the community decides who enters.

Initially Tommy Ross agrees to Sue's scheme and offers to take Carrie to the prom. He genuinely feels affection toward her. But De Palma's revolving camera emphasizes the illusory nature of their tentative relationship. Instead of winning his Cinderella, Prince Charming dies ignominiously from an empty bucket falling on his head.

Carrie emphasizes its heroine's supernatural powers without entirely ignoring social and familial factors.[16] Her actions express rage against a repressive society that has no positive roles for women.[17] Sue Snell's mother (Priscilla Pointer) presents no positive image. Before Margaret White (Piper Laurie) arrives, we see Mrs. Snell drinking and watching an afternoon soap opera on television. Although her humorous response to Mrs. White's "These are sinful times" always gains audience approval ("I'll drink to that!"), her solitary afternoon drinking and light-headed attitude reveal her to be an ineffectual parent.

Both women submit to patriarchy. Mrs. Snell is a bored housewife reduced to watching soap operas with alcoholic stimulus. The pathologic Mrs. White uses another drug—religious fundamentalism. King's work often displays patriarchal gender critiques. Observing similar features in *The Shining*, Greg Weller believes that King also recognizes patriarchal cooptation of female and bisexual forces. Noting the blurring of gender roles in *It*, Weller comments that "while It is ostensibly female, she presents herself as the same sort of patriarchal historical force as the Overlook. It is also significant to note that *It*'s avatar, Pennywise the clown, is male, in contrast to the Overlook, whose avatars are often female or bisexual."[18] Similarly, by complying with romantic fiction's conservative gender mechanisms, *Misery*'s author creates a female Frankenstein monster who terrorizes him once he becomes symbolically castrated.

Mrs. White is a monstrous creation of patriarchal fundamentalism. "Comforting" Carrie after her destructive revenge, she displays pathologic tendencies contradicting fundamentalism's antiabortion stance: "I should have killed myself when he put it in me....I liked it. I should have given you to God when you were born." She reenacts Abraham's attempted sacrifice of the firstborn by stabbing her daughter. Carrie ironically crucifies her, responding to mother's masochistic desires before telekinetically causing her Gothic home to collapse and burn.

But a dark legacy remains. As Sue awakes from a traumatic nightmare in *Carrie*'s climax, the camera cranes out to show Mrs. Snell comforting her daughter. Her words, "It's all right. I'm here" are ironic. Mrs. Snell was never a good mother. The final camera movement dwarfs mother and daughter into insignificance.

Shot for Warner Brothers television in miniseries format (but later released on video in a 110-minute version), Tobe Hooper's *Salem's Lot* (1979) is highly compromised. Although lacking many of the novel's interesting social features, *Salem's Lot* occasionally reveals family horror motifs. Inadequately realized on the television screen, the Marston House's decaying interior still aptly symbolized the community's dark side. Barlow's reasons for choosing Salem's Lot as a residence also remains. As Ben (David Soul) explains to Dr. Norton (Ed Flanders), the interbred nature of a closely-knit community with incestuously linked "warm blood" forms an obvious attraction for any monster.

◆ ◆ ◆

Lewis Teague's King adaptations intelligently realize the author's social vision.[19] Avoiding the original novel's supernatural elements, Teague's version of *Cujo* placed King's patriarchal critiques within a definite social context.[20] *Cujo* critiques masculinity and capitalism's sterile family life. Reacting against her husband's move to a rural location, Donna (Dee Wallace) drifts into an aimless affair with Steve (Christopher Stone). Discovering his wife's adultery, Vic (Daniel Hugh Kelly) departs on a business conference, leaving wife and young son vulnerable to attack by a rabid dog. The monstrous assault arises from definable social circumstances—tensions within the patriarchal family.[21]

Teague's *Cujo* depicts the monstrous assault of masculine violence against a heroine who defies husband and lover. Dominated by the Sharp Cereal Professor advertising account, Vic Trenton's desires to succeed within junk food consumer capitalism leave him little time to understand Donna's difficulties in adapting to rural life. Her unfulfilled yearnings lead to an extramarital affair. By abandoning her and Tad over the weekend, Vic unconsciously desires an avenging avatar to discipline his errant spouse. Piqued at Donna's decision to end their affair, Steve attempts to assault her at home. He eventually trashes the house, a violent action that parallels Cujo's assault on the family car near the Camber residence. When Steve attacks Donna, the camera moves 90 degrees rightward, its low angle point-of-view shot anticipating the position of Donna's future canine assailant.

Opening scenes begin with a zoom-out, leading to Cujo's chasing a rabbit across a field. They end with his head jammed in a tunnel—an action that makes him vulnerable to a bat's bite. The second sequence inverts the first. It begins with a zoom-in to Tad at his bedroom window suggesting psychic confinement within the home. Succeeding images reveal his fear of the closet door. The sequence concludes with a zoom-in to Tad. A parallel exists between Cujo's physical assault by a bat and Tad's imaginary fears of assault by unseen forces.

Rushing to Tad's room, Donna ascribes his nightmare as the result of "Too much junk food. Too much of the tube guys," an observation supported both by Vic's promotion of junk food cereal and the violent cartoons Tad watches on television. The Trenton family lives within a world of consumer culture. Dependent upon Vic's successful promotion of Sharp Cereal, the family begins to fall apart once a disastrous chemical error affects both advertising agency and Vic's career. His male ego affronted by discovery of Donna's infidelity, Vic drives away, leaving her vulnerable to monstrous assault.

Like Jason and Freddy, Cujo is contemporary horror's patriarchal monster. Although Donna is his main target, the dog also kills Joe Camber and drinking buddy Gary Pervier while leaving his human alter ego, Steve Kemp, unscathed. As Robin Wood cogently remarks, "masculinity, gone mad, turns upon itself."[22] Cujo punishes Joe and Gary for their respective failures to uphold patriarchal values, paralleling Jason's and Freddy's disciplining of weak father figures (*Friday the 13th, Part III; Jason Lives;* and *Dream Warriors*). Charity Camber wins five thousand dollars from the state lottery. She negotiates with her husband, offering him the money for the privilege of allowing her and son, Brett, to visit her sister in Connecticut. He takes the money, deciding to vacation with Gary. Teague obliquely suggests Charity tricks him. Before she leaves, Teague films her looking at a photo album before packing it. Although she might wish to show her sister a family album, she may also be taking a personal item with her on a permanent trip. If so, Cujo punishes a weak patriarch who is losing control of his family like Jack Torrance in *The Shining*.

Although Tad survives in the film (a freeze frame showing the Trenton family reunited), the climax is ironic. Despite Tad's survival, Donna suffers several bites from a rabid dog. Although she finally shoots Cujo, it is too late for her to receive medical treatment. Teague's final freeze frame suggests a deep irony within a typical Hollywood convention. Donna will eventually die a gruesome death—the result of Oedipal tensions and female transgression of repressive norms.

Commenting on the book, Douglas Winter notes features present in Teague's adaptation. He sees the dog as embodying fears of a material break-down in a once powerful American society.[23] One early scene in *Cujo* is significant. Visiting the Camber home, Donna sees Charity (Kaiulani Lee) outside. The two women look at each other. Donna recognizes her less affluent counterpart while Charity exhibits embarrassment before a "great lady." Probably thinking about the economic consequences of divorce, Donna's silent expression suggests cognizance of woman's unequal status within society.

◆　◆　◆

David Cronenberg's adaptation of *The Dead Zone* pertinently captures the essence of King's original novel. As Andrew Britton recognizes, the film version "engages directly with the thematics of Reaganite utopianism" and the various ways in which masculine dominance eventually points to "universal destruction as the logical outcome of this dominance."[24] *The Dead Zone* is a significant family horror film.

Emerging from a five-year coma, Johnny's greatest danger comes not from a society that regards him as a freak and uses him whenever it is convenient but from the family. Like his younger successors in mid-1980s horror, Johnny finds salvation outside the family. The first threat comes from his mother. Despite Dr. Sam Weizak's (Herbert Lom) solicitations, Mrs. Smith (Jackie Burroughs) reveals the duration of Johnny's long coma, ascribing dangerous messianic connotations to his condition. "Lost for five years and now reborn unto me." Her maternal manipulation anticipates Henrietta Dodd's (Colleen Dewhurst) dangerous parental role. The camera reveals Herb Smith's (Sean Sullivan) pained expression as he listens to his wife deliberately demolishing Johnny's future hopes, especially his expected marriage to Sarah (Brooke Adams). "She's turned her back on you. She cleaves to another man, a husband." The sequence ends with Johnny's emotional breakdown.

The Dead Zone reveals hidden institutional power structures behind family and religion. Mrs. Smith wishes to infantilize her son. When Johnny finally visits his dying mother, she refers to him as a "little boy." Johnny's first vision is highly significant. Touching his nurse's hand, he finds himself in her infant daughter's bed when her room catches fire. Physically debilitated due to his coma and "reborn" to a mother who wishes him to be a child again, Johnny, ironically, uses the visionary power resulting from his infantilized position to save a child from death. When his physical presence on a gazebo during another vision causes him to witness Frank Dodd's murder of a young girl,

Johnny becomes upset. Awakening from his vision, he cries, "I stood there. I did nothing." Johnny recognizes a dark affinity with Frank Dodd, his alter ego.

Like Mrs. Smith, whom Sheriff Bannerman (Tom Skerritt) describes as "a good woman, a Christian woman," Mrs. Dodd also infantilizes her offspring. However, she has successfully created a monster from the id expressing repressed sexuality by patriarchal violence. His victims are all surrogate displacements for his repressive fundamentalist mother. Reacting to Johnny's contact, she retreats regarding him not as Mrs. Smith's "reborn" Messiah, but as "the devil, sent from hell." Reacting to Johnny's touch, Mrs. Dodd encounters a different being outside the religiously inscribed patriarchal value system she subscribes to. To her, this feminized male visionary is clearly the devil.

The Dodd sequence ends in a visually striking manner. While Mrs. Smith emotionally wounds her son after the first hospital visit, Mrs. Dodd physically wounds Johnny as he leaves the scene of Frank's suicide. She falls on the stairs after Sheriff Bannerman shoots her. The closing overhead camera shot reveals Johnny holding her bloody hand as if realizing her affinity to his own mother. The final shot of Mrs. Smith as she dies from a stroke shows her hand touching Johnny's. Still believing him to be her "little boy," she gently orders him, "Leave your boots outside the door. . . . Don't go tracking snow all over the house. Good boy." Her injunctions concerning bourgeois cleanliness counterpoint Mrs. Dodd's more dangerous injunctions.

Separating from his family, Johnny leaves home to become a private tutor. But the outside world soon intrudes in the different, but related, personas of Roger Stuart (Anthony Zerbe) and Gregg Stillson (Martin Sheen). Although socially and politically apart, both men attempt to dominate others. Stuart's purpose in employing Johnny as tutor for his son Chris (Simon Craig) deviously echoes Gregg Stillson's methods in the Senate race. He wishes Johnny to bring Chris out of his shell. Roger intends to force his son into playing masculine team games. Chris recognizes his father's entrapment within gender roles. As he tells Johnny, "It's my Dad that lives in a shell, not me."

The Dead Zone reveals deep insecurities behind dominating male and females infected by patriarchal family values. Roger Stuart resorts to the same type of bullying Gregg Stillson uses against a newspaper editor. The final scenes of both men show them mentally debilitated after their self-aggrandizing dreams collapse. While Stuart retreats into mental apathy, Stillson commits suicide.

Apart from Johnny who remains outside the Law of the Father, others remain trapped within institutional structures (Sarah, Herb Smith, Weizak, Bannerman) or attempt violent domination. As *The Dead Zone*'s monster (whose personality combines John F. Kennedy's dubious charisma and

Reaganite "born again" politics), Gregg Stillson is within society, not outside Gothic's external parameters. Linking the diverse personas of Frank Dodd and Roger Stuart, he represents the logical culmination of patriarchal violence. Johnny sees the future president causing a nuclear holocaust. Stillson threatens a general in the same way he bullied a newspaper editor. Constantly associated with his male bodyguard Sonny (Geza Kovacs), Stillson is possibly a murderous gay, repressing sexuality in violence like Norman Bates and Frank Dodd. Sonny's leather jacket duplicates one worn by an aggressive reporter whose dark, incestuous secret (resulting in his sister's suicide) Johnny unveils during a press conference. Mrs. Smith suffers a stroke watching this on television, possibly realizing her actual feelings for Johnny. In the bathroom Frank's last act before suicide is in donning a leather overcoat over his naked body. *The Dead Zone* is replete with mirror associations suggesting diverse characters all belonging to the same dark family. Even at Camp David we never see any First Lady, only Sonny.

While Johnny conceals sensitive feelings from the outside world, other characters don deceptive social masks (whether deputy's badge or revered mother), veiling their true identities. Noticing Sarah and her family, Stillson invites them onto the platform, using their wholesome family values for his campaign. His attempt to use Sarah's child as a shield before Johnny's bullet ironically results in the end of his political masquerade.

◆　◆　◆

Lacking the original novel's social perspective, John Carpenter's *Christine* (1983) contains a reductive metaphysical conception of evil.[25] The precredits sequence presents Christine exclusively as a monstrous car. King's version is a more fascinating narrative and contains an allegory on the seductive culture of consumption.[26] The film version neglects these relevant features. Although *Firestarter* (1984) promised King's moving away from the Gothic toward more relevant social issues, it failed to develop promising motifs of political exploitation and telekinetic family rage. Bad direction and acting ruined the project.

◆　◆　◆

Based on a screenplay by King, Mary Lambert's *Pet Sematary* (1989) is one of the author's darkest visions of family life. But traditional Gothic motifs overwhelm promising dysfunctional family themes. Based upon King's own ambivalent feelings toward his family, *Pet Sematary* represents a step backward from the more social *The Dead Zone, Christine, Cujo,* and *Firestarter* toward the supernatural *Salem's Lot*. While "The Revenge of Lard Ass Hogan," depicted briefly in *Stand by Me* (1986), reveals relevant social factors within community scapegoating, *Pet Sematary* conceals themes of a father's desire to destroy his family by Gothic supernatural devices. *Pet Sematary* reveals a typical constraint affecting most contemporary horror films. As Britton points out,

> The Gothic no longer registers a hesitation at the surface of the text, but produces an esoteric sub-text which is directly at odds with the offered significance. Metaphor, in this instance, engenders and is engendered by misrecognition: the return of the repressed isn't cleanly distinguished from the return of repression, the very image which dramatizes the one enforcing the other.[27]

However, King's screenplay suggests disturbing tensions between family trauma and supernatural events.[28] Lewis (Dale Midkiff) and Rachel (Denise Crosby) exist in a tension-filled marital relationship worsened by her parents' refusal to accept Lewis. Both are neurotic products of a nuclear family trapped within designated parental roles. After their maid Missy commits suicide to avoid further pain from stomach cancer, Rachel tells Lewis about her personal demons. King's own trauma in looking after his dying grandmother (fictionalized in his short story "Gramma") forms the basis of this episode.

Suffering from severe spinal meningitis, Rachel's sister, Zelda, is her family's "dirty secret." As an abnormal child, her father and mother confined her in a back bedroom and hoped for eventual death. Avoiding their tormented offspring, Rachel's parents insisted on her feeding Zelda, a traumatic event worsened when Zelda chokes to death during parental absence. Psychologically affected, Rachel experienced guilt feelings induced by contradictions between repressed feelings of relief and the family's hypocritical masquerades. "I had to feed her rations. I hated it. I wanted her to die. We wished for her to be dead. It wasn't that we didn't want her to feel any more pain. It was so we wouldn't feel any pain." As Zelda dies in agony, Rachel encounters neighbors and their children watching. Feeling guilty, the little girl rushed outside with tormented emotions. "They say that I was crying. Do you know something? I think I was laughing."

Despite Lewis's correctly blaming her parents for leaving an "eight-year-old child in charge of her dying sister who was probably clinically insane by then," the incident psychologically continues to scar her. Rachel's father, Erwin, blames Lewis for Gage's death and assaults him at the funeral. Despite Judd Crandall's (Fred Gwynne) warnings concerning another bereaved father who restored his son to life during World War II, Lewis takes Gage's body to the sematary. His decision to recreate the past leads to disaster.

The real subject of *Pet Sematary* is parental guilt, involving families who deny unpleasant realities and refuse to accept death as natural. Family-generated guilt mechanisms result in Lewis masochistically blaming himself for circumstances beyond his control. In a society putting deep investment into family life and heavy social responsibility upon parental figures, trauma naturally results when things go wrong. Fleeing from her dying sister, Rachel experiences survivor guilt, blaming herself for her parents' failure. Feeling guilty over Gage's death, Lewis mistakenly attempts to recreate the past. Husband and wife become trapped within pathologic family situations.

Awaiting Lewis's call at her parents' Chicago home, Rachel reexperiences past guilt. She imagines her sister's dying image threatening her, "I'm coming for you Rachel and this time I'll get you. Gage and I will get you for letting us down." Returning home, Rachel first sees Zelda, then a demonic Gage wearing a child's costume that is worn by a figure in a portrait in her family home. Deceased sister and son become monsters from a family psychopathologic id. Gage murders Rachel and Lewis finally kills his son. But he does not learn from the past, and he resurrects his wife who returns as a violent monster. Despite Gothic overtones *Pet Sematary* contains an interesting subtext warning about the dangers of overemotional investment in the family.

◆ ◆ ◆

Stanley Kubrick's *The Shining* (1980) significantly locates the supernatural within relevant social and political boundaries. His version successfully conveys important features within King's fiction. As King's former university English professor Burton Hatlen states, "King's view of the world is, despite all the supernatural machinery, ultimately social and political rather than religious, and his novels, especially *The Shining*, present Good and Evil as born out of the social interrelations among people."[29] Focusing on King's debt to the naturalist tradition, Brian Kent notes the influence of Frank Norris's *McTeague*, especially "the primitive impulses that lie buried beneath the surface of conscious lives and in the influence of heredity and environment of individual destinies."[30]

In Kubrick's film social influences affect Jack and Wendy Torrance. Jack (Jack Nicholson) has an alcoholic past and fails in his goal of becoming the Great American Writer. His murderous rage against his family, supposedly directed by the Overlook, has social origins. Failing as writer and father, Jack overcompensates for masculine inadequacy by patriarchal violence toward his wife and child. His actions are reminiscent of Ed Avery's descent into paranoia in Nicholas Ray's melodrama *Bigger than Life* (1956). However, the role models are now neither the biblical Abraham nor Abraham Lincoln but American television cartoon violence and cultural banality ("Here's Johnny!"). Wendy's (Shelley Duvall) initially weak, supportive Raggedy Ann wife suggests insecurity over a socially proscribed maternal role that oppresses her real personality. This unstable family situation needs little external pressure to explode.

As the opening credit sequence reveals, the camera's surveillance of Jack Torrance's car to the Overlook is suggestive of evil traveling to a specific destination. It has human rather than supernatural associations. Obtaining a caretaker position, Jack takes his family to a hotel that embodies an American culture of consumption leisure ethos existing far beyond the historic period of its actual lifespan. Kubrick's Jazz Age ghosts are out of place in an era recovering from the 1970s recession. However, the 1920s was also a decade of the great American writer—Hemingway, Faulkner, Fitzgerald—an honor roll Jack obviously envies. But that time is past. Jack's incongruously scruffy appearance within the Overlook's Gold Room affirms Delbert Grady's classification of his status as always having been the caretaker. The death-affirming nature of a class structure American society denies will frustrate Jack's dreams of creativity and financial independence.

Far from promising personal liberation and freedom from want, the twentieth-century consumer world emanates a death-in-life sterility. Beginning as a writer before his Overlook possession, Jack succumbs to being a wordless, inarticulate cartoon character. Despite promising material advances, contemporary technology surrounding human beings reduces emotions and personality to banal ciphers. Like the Coyote in the *Roadrunner* cartoons watched by Danny (Danny Lloyd), Jack becomes a primeval Big Bad Wolf in a world that offers no opportunity for either family love or King's original happy ending for Halloran (Scatman Crothers), Wendy, and Danny. Everyone becomes psychically trapped within a culture of consumption that offers no easy escape.

The Overlook Hotel metaphorically embodies the ruthless violence behind an American society and chooses to conceal brutality beneath the veneer of affluence, cleanliness, and bland corporate relationships. Although more luxurious than either the Bates or Elm Street homes, the Overlook also manifests the return of a violent repressed. Frequent shots show the hotel corridor drowned in torrents of blood. This evokes Richard Slotkin's description of American culture as "A Pyramid of Skulls" and anticipates the gushing pile of entrails beneath the Alamo mural in *The Texas Chain Saw Massacre 2*. Like

Hitchcock's dark vision of anally excremental violence in *Psycho*, the image also resembles an overflowing toilet bowl discharging repressed forces within American life.

Living in a society based upon violence and genocide, the Torrance family falls victim to historic forces behind the American dream. Violence hides beneath a deceptive affluent exterior. Confronting inevitable bodily decay, Jack retreats from Room 237's decomposing female spirit to a Gold Room populated by ghosts from America's gilded era of post–World War I affluence. He meets his predecessor, Delbert Grady (Philip Stone), now an obsequious butler, in the spotlessly clean, but blood-red walls, of the Gold Room's restroom. To gain a position of responsibility, he must exercise discipline against his unruly family, a discipline whose violent overtones parallel other punitive epochs within American history. Jack goes off to exert responsibility. Discipline begins in the family. It then extends into society and history.[31] The 1920s were not only the Jazz Age of affluent luxury but of gangsterism, the rise of the Ku Klux Klan, the bigotry leading to the Scopes Trial, and the illegal aspects of the Sacco and Vanzetti and Scottsboro Boys trials.

Overcoming their respective subordinate positions within the family, Wendy and Danny survive. Jack regresses into incoherent atavism. Frozen within both time and space, Jack's body in the Overlook maze anticipates his place within a hotel photo of a 4 July ball during 1921. No longer dressed as a caretaker, he eagerly smiles at the audience joining in the Jazz Age celebration like his possible idol, F. Scott Fitzgerald, a fellow alcoholic and member of another dysfunctional family. Unlike Zelda, Wendy remains sane. Only her spouse regresses. Jack becomes successfully divorced from his family. But the photograph presents his illusionary entrapment. Jack is now within a world of his own, a false world of artifice and fakery that conceals violence and brutality.

As Frederic Jameson points out,

> The Jack Nicholson of *The Shining* is possessed neither by evil as such nor by the "devil" or some analogous occult force, but rather simply by History, by the American past as it has left its sedimented traces in the corridors and dismembered suites of this monumental rabbit warren, which oddly projects its empty formal after-image in the maze outside.[32]

He further notes another significant feature of *The Shining*. Demystifying the pastiche film and contemporary occult possession movies such as *The Exorcist*, Kubrick's work definitely reveals an ideologic project that characterizes much of the 1980s and 1990s—"the ideological project to return to the hard certainties of a more visible and rigid class structure, and this is a critical perspective which includes but transcends the more immediate appeal of even those occult films with which *The Shining* might momentarily have been confused."[33]

Jack Torrance yearns for past certainties, but Kubrick depicts this retreat as a monstrous regression. Despite the director's clinical style, his method is dispassionate but not cynical. Kubrick warns audiences about the human condition by revealing factors of historical entrapment and primeval regression that affect us today. In *The Shining* he unveils the dangerous psychic and material forces within family violence that are usually concealed within deceptive devices of supernatural Gothic.

Contrasting Jack Torrance's frozen stare with the Star Child's immobile stare at the climax of *2001*, Jameson notes both films illustrate the dangerous hold of "repetition, with all its overtones of traumatic fixation and the death wish." *The Shining* reveals the dangerous hold of the past and its stifling of human potential. As Torrance's frozen face finally changes into "a period photograph of his upper-class avatar in the bygone surroundings of a leisure class era," Kubrick's futuristic vision of *2001* changes to foreshadow "the dismal imprisonment in monuments of high culture (the regency room, the maze itself, classical music) which have become the jail cells of repetition and the space of thralldom to the past."[34]

◆　◆　◆

King's novels and occasional film adaptations have firm connections to a cultural tradition influencing family horror. Despite debates over their literary merits, King's works reveal similar associations with historical and cultural factors that also influence earlier family depictions in the fiction of Hawthorne, Poe, Melville, and Lovecraft. However, the challenges of the 1980s and 1990s reveal changing motifs within the family horror opus.

12

Into the Nineties

Far from being marginal to the genre, family horror still continues. Contemporary versions may be thematically unadventurous, but they never seriously suggest a return to family values. They all express lack of confidence in the institution. Even if radical alternatives never appear, the status quo is never entirely accepted in most films.

Although Steve Miner's campy *House* (1985) shakily attempts to reunite the family, other movies depict marginalized one-parent families or orphans attempting to survive on their own. In Tom Holland's *Child's Play* (1988), young Andy's widowed mother (Catherine Hicks) economically struggles to rear her two-year-old by working at a low-paying job at a Chicago department store. Threatened by the soul of a serial killer (Brad Douriff) that inhabits a child's doll, Andy survives Chucky's attempt to take over his body. The sequel reveals society's suppression of unpalatable facts. In John Lafia's *Child's Play* 2 (1990), the police department denies what has happened, separating mother and son. Andy's mother now undergoes psychological observation after trying to sue the corporation responsible for manufacturing the Good Guys dolls. Incarcerated in a Children's Custody Center, Andy becomes adopted by foster parents Philip (Gerrit Graham) and Joanna (Jenny Agutter) while his mother supposedly recovers. Joanna neurotically overcompensates for infertility by compulsively playing a maternal role. Andy's fellow adoptee Kyle (Christine Elise) discerns this. She teaches Andy about a hostile world, warning him of future peer group school treatment as the "new kid on the block." Lacking the family that abandoned her at the age of three, Kyle resourcefully decides to survive within successive foster families until she can gain independence. She tells Andy what to expect. "I've lived with dozens of different families and they always send me away when I get comfortable. Every time it happens, it just makes me stronger because it tells me all the more that the only one I can count on is myself."

Every surviving teenager at the end of any *Friday the 13th, Halloween,* or *Elm Street* film understands this. Kids know better than fathers who no longer know best. Kyle's final words to Andy affirms thus.

ANDY. Where are we going?
KYLE. Home.
ANDY. Where's home?
KYLE. I have no idea.

Jack Bender's *Child's Play 3* (1991) critiques allied patriarchal institutions of big business and military academy. During the opening scenes corporate executive Sullivan decides to relaunch the Good Guys dolls despite a subordinate's protests. Rejecting historical memory—"Andy Barclay is history. Nobody remembers him. Nobody cares"—he states capitalist goals and envisaged roles for children; "the hardest thing about this business is that it is a business.... What are children but consumer trainees?" Chucky searches for the nearest child's body. His desired object is now a young black dumped at a military academy by his career-orientated father.

Sixteen-year-old Andy arrives at this orphanage dominated by authoritarian macho figures such as an insensitive Vietnam veteran colonel and a sadistic haircutting sergeant (played by Andy Robinson, satirizing his *Dirty Harry* psycho performance). As cadet Tyler tells Andy, "They don't tolerate any form of individuality here. Even nothing so personal as a first name. Welcome to Hell, Barclay." Andy understands his particular social oppression— "They took me away from my mother. She's under special care"—as well as his past history. "I never felt anything with these people. They weren't family. They were strangers." Although managing to stop Chucky, the police arrest him. Andy understands the system will deny dangerous realities and continue to oppress him. "Don't worry. I've been here before."

◆   ◆   ◆

Horror themes are now within mainstream cinema. Martin Scorsese's *Cape Fear* (1992) presents monster figure Cady attacking a guilty yuppie family different from Gregory Peck's harmonious family in the 1962 version. One significant scene shows Cady (Robert DeNiro) playing on an adolescent girl's emerging sexuality like a dark, incestuous father. However, self-indulgent spectacular pyrotechnics and deliberately excessive overacting (DeNiro) suggest contempt for the project. Also mainstream productions usually trivialize motifs, as Tim Burton's postmodernist comic strip *Batman* films reveal.

Although no horror film monster, Michael Keaton's reclusive Bruce Wayne inhabits the same shadow world as compatriots in *Manhunter* (1986), *Psycho IV* (1991), and *Silence of the Lambs* (1991). Traumatic memories over his parents' deaths influence Wayne's obsessionally reclusive nature within a Gothic mansion. He wears a masculinized bodybuilding Bat costume rather than Mrs. Bates's feminine attire. His alter ego, Joker, engages in his own masquerade as he terrorizes Gotham City. Vicky (Kim Basinger) recognizes their common bond, "Some people think you're more dangerous than the Joker." Batman and Joker both play Dr. Frankenstein roles within a postmodernist homosocial paranoid fantasy. Joker asserts Wayne's responsibility for his creation—"You did it. You made me. You dropped me into that vat of chemicals." Remembering Joker's murder of his parents, Batman replies, "You made me first."

Batman Returns (1992) depicts the main characters as abused adult children. The Penguin (Danny DeVito) asserts Oedipal desires to know his parents, comparing his monstrosity to businessman Shreck (Christopher Walken), a "respected monster." Masquerading as an adult child produced by a dysfunctional family, the Penguin appeals to Gotham for recognition after rejection by parents who "could not deal with a son who was born a little different." The Penguin calls his androgynous killer clown associates an "extended family." Watching the television screen, Wayne initially approves of the Penguin's family odyssey. The Cat Woman is also a family victim. Reacting against family oppression, Selena (Michelle Pfeiffer) smashes family photos, a child's dollhouse, and an answering machine containing mother's nagging messages before she dons the Cat Woman costume. Tempted by Batman's offer to "go home," Selena realizes her schizophrenic condition prevents this. Instead she electrifies dark monstrous father Shreck and commits suicide. Gotham City cannot contain two dysfunctional family monsters.

Despite these motifs the *Batman* films (like most major studio productions) superficially exploit these ideas. Burton delivers glossy entertainment visual "quotes" for film buff aficionados. His movies are really conservative Gothic versions of Lucas-Spielberg films. Form dictates product. Mainstream productions can only venture so far. The *Batman* films are fashionable displays, consumerist postmodernist pastiche composite texts, culled from cinema history.[1] They trivialize family horror themes within a mega-budget Hollywood spectacle of excess.

◆ ◆ ◆

Many themes achieve better treatment in low-budget works free from studio interference. *Eyes of Fire* (1984), *It's Alive III—Island of the Alive* (1986), *Henry—Portrait of a Serial Killer* (1986), *Manhunter* (1986), *The Stepfather* (1987), *Stepfather 2* (1989), *Stepfather 3* (1992), *Parents* (1989), *Psycho IV* (1991), *Flowers in the Attic* (1987), and *Day of the Dead* (1986) illustrate this. Free from studio self-censorship of radical ideas to obtain general (non-R or X) ratings, these minor works often contain more radical treatments of family horror. Sometimes there are missed opportunities. Wes Craven's *The People under the Stairs* (1991) begins in a promising manner. Its opening vision of an impoverished Black family and a White incestuous couple kidnapping and abusing children suggests a revival of family horror's social dimensions. Unfortunately, it soon descends into trivial campish humor.[2]

Despite flaws, Avery Crouse's *Eyes of Fire* deserves better recognition. It is a rare American film dealing with the pre-Revolutionary era, tracing family horror to this historic era. Expelled from their homes in 1750, a mixed group of settlers attempt to find their Promised Land in the Allegheny Region. The family includes a mother living in adulterous liaison with a supposedly free-thinking preacher, and Leah, an adolescent girl with telepathic powers, who witnessed the Puritans burn her mother at the stake. Like Carrie White, her powers suggest adolescent rage against a reactionary adult world. This random group ventures into a forbidden zone that is shunned by the Indians. An androgynous "Queen of the Forest" tree spirit rules the area. The already fragile community find themselves under assault by naked ghosts of previous settlers.

These ghosts represent the divided community's repressed tensions and family antagonisms. One latter case involves the preacher and a hunter who returns to find his wife in another man's arms. After increasing attacks, only Leah and two adolescent girls survive. Choosing to become a "tree spirit" to save the others, Leah aids their escape. However, although the two girls reach a French military outpost, *Eyes of Fire* concludes ambiguously by suggesting the tree spirits will attack the French. Despite its supernatural framework, *Eyes of Fire* remarkably depicts a patriarchal family entrapment operating from the very beginning of American history.

Larry Cohen's *It's Alive III—Island of the Alive* develops further significant insights into the social origins of horror. As in the preceding films, the real threat comes from society rather than from mutant offspring. Managing to overcome fears about his mutant child, actor Stephen Jarvis (Michael Moriarty) convinces Judge Watson (McDonald Carey) to grant the babies a peaceful haven away from society. Pleading the case, Stephen protests, "How would you feel if you were born into a world which wants you dead? It's just a baby. There must be a place on earth where they can't hurt him and he won't harm them." Notably Stephen places the threat from society first. Ironically, the judge consigns all mutant children to an island previously used for radiation testing. The mutant children also face assault from pharmaceutical hit squads hired for the purpose of putting the original drugs back on the market after the evidence is destroyed.

His personal life destroyed by media publicity, legal bills, and popular designation as a freak, Stephen is forced into selling his autobiography for financial reasons. Divorced by his wife Ellen (Karen Black), Stephen becomes recruited by a scientific expedition eager to explore the island. The supposed reason is an investigation over the possibility of human survival after a nuclear attack. The state's earlier choice of the island as a haven is obvious. Eventually, Stephen discovers he is a grandfather. The dying mutants reunite him with Ellen; they entrust the newborn child into their care. Lacking home and finances, Stephen and Ellen drive off with their grandchild into an uncertain future.

Despite budget limitations and problems of depicting the mature mutants (who appear as unthreatening, overgrown babies), *It's Alive III* significantly recognizes capitalism as the real twentieth-century threat. Positioning his hero in the role of the monster, Cohen scrutinizes the arbitrary social judgments separating normal from abnormal. By placing another mutant baby in the arms of alienated human parents bereft of capitalist lifestyles, Cohen suggests an enigmatic positive future.

Henry—Portrait of a Serial Killer is not a horror film. But like so many nongeneric works, it is indispensable in understanding family horror motifs. John McNaughton's *Henry* is a quasi-documentary fictional exploration into the mind of a serial killer that is far more frightening than any generic treatment. It coalesces into a unified structure motif in *The Eyes of Laura Mars* (1978), *Don't Go into the House* (1979), and *The Boogeyman* (1980) by revealing the real source of family horror—child abuse. Michael Rooker's Henry is an emotionally numbed, traumatic victim of child assault who mechanically repeats past victimization on surrogate victims. Like the less accomplished *Confessions of a Serial Killer* (1989), *Henry* starkly reveals what special effects machinery within contemporary horror attempts to deny—pathologic family structures produce human monsters and victims. Both Henry and Tracey suffered child abuse. Tracey's mother ignored her father's incestuous assaults. Like her mother, she continues these denial mechanisms after discovering Henry's real nature. *Henry* elucidates past and contemporary patterns within family horror. Its protagonist resembles Alice Miller's description of a brutal serial killer of three hundred and sixty women in *Banished Knowledge*.

Abused by a mother who wished for a daughter, Henry's original murder of his victimizer results in the compulsive, repetitive, murderous reenactments on female surrogate victims. This psychic mechanism also occurs in *Psycho*, *The Eyes of Laura Mars*, *Don't Go into the House*, *The Boogeyman*, *Maniac* (1980), and *Pieces* (1983). The grim reality requires no distracting spectacular special effects. Like *Confessions of a Serial Killer*, *Henry's* low-key, quasi-naturalist style reveals what most horror films conceal: oppressive families produce vicious killers. As Alice Miller shows in *For Your Own Good*, normal and abnormal families often use socially approved disciplinary mechanisms against children that have been handed down throughout generations in a repetitive-compulsive manner.

Despite Academy Award recognition, Jonathan Demme's *The Silence of the Lambs* is a superficial reworking of themes better realized in Thomas Harris's original novel, *Red Dragon*, and its superior film version, *Manhunter* (1986). Michael Mann's script and direction appropriately link diverse worlds of normality and psychosis better than Demme's vague, redundant symbolism. Although *The Silence of The Lambs* revels in making its monster a serial-killer cult figure (unconvincingly drawing parallels between the heroine's family memories and the horrors she experiences),[3] *Manhunter* contains stronger affinities between killer and pursuer. *Silence of the Lambs* presents the viewer with a reactionary world of ugly people (including an FBI agent heroine!) by making its killer as aberrant as possible; *Manhunter* is far more subtle.

Despite the presence of several essays attempting to relate *The Silence of the Lambs* with the supposed sexual politics of its star, Jodie Foster, the film itself is a visually impoverished, thematically redundant text that lacks the radical insights contained in works such as *Day of the Dead*—a picture that contains far more sophisticated insights into an entire social and institutional order which makes monsters possible. Playing an FBI agent writing her dissertation on J. Edgar Hoover(!), Foster's heroine is an upwardly mobile bourgeois feminist. *Manhunter* explicitly depicts Crawford as ruthlessly exploiting Graham to trap a serial killer; *The Silence of the Lambs* is less critical of Crawford's tactics. Clarice Starling's odyssey results in certificated entry into the male-orientated FBI world, ideologically gaining Ross Perot's "piece of the pie." Despite use and abuse by both Crawford and Lecter, she never reaches Will Graham's self-knowledge and retreat from a corrupt system in *Manhunter*. The film's concluding images show her graduating from the FBI and receiving the appropriate patriarchal seals of approval from Crawford and Lecter.

Clarice cannot advance by her own efforts. She needs the guidance of dark father, Hannibal Lecter, to succeed. Demme's direction of Anthony Hopkins as Lecter parallels Leni Riefenstahl's depiction of Hitler in *Triumph of the Will.* Both glamorize their male subjects as all-powerful masculine forces. This contrasts with *Manhunter's* condemnation (as well as sympathetic understanding of) of Dollarhyde. Dollarhyde is victim as well as monster. His serial-killer activities have explicit family traumatic origins. But Demme depicts "Buffalo Bill" in obviously effeminate/gay stereotypical terms. He avoids the social roots of his condition to depict him as a convenient monster. By contrast *Manhunter* not only depicts Dollarhyde as a victim of society but also reveals his affinities with both Graham and Lecter, thereby undermining convenient barriers between monster and human counterparts. "Buffalo Bill" is always isolated from society and other characters. Despite acclaim, *The Silence of the Lambs* is a repugnant example of post-Reaganite cinema, narrowly opening patriarchal gates to allow ideologically conditioned post-feminists inside. Like all big budget productions, it appropriates, dilutes, and cheapens potentials inherent within the genre to gain Academy Award hype and approval.

Manhunter visually emphasizes fragile barriers between a normal family world and the hellish mental ghetto of Francis Dollarhyde (Tom Noonan). As Will Graham (William Peterson) recognizes, Dollarhyde's monstrous acts are basically pathetic. Explaining the motivations to his manipulative FBI superior Crawford (Dennis Farina), Graham states, "This started from an abused kid, a battered infant." When Crawford queries his motives—"Are you sympathizing with this guy?"—Graham replies, "Absolutely. My heart bleeds for him as a child. Someone took a kid and manufactured a monster. At the same time, as an adult, he's irredeemable. He butchers entire families to pursue trivial fantasies." Graham challenges Crawford with complex socially oriented explanations that negate any attempt to categorize Dollarhyde as an individual case.

Crawford avoids confronting the issue. He manipulates Will into returning to the FBI, though he is clearly aware of Will's earlier work-related psychological breakdown. Masquerading as a caring father figure in his opening appearance, Crawford plays upon Will's sensitivity to his family. He displays several graphic photos of murdered families. He places Will in a vulnerable position by using power mechanisms similar to those once used against Dollarhyde.

Physically assaulted by Hannibal Lecter (Brian Cox), Will suffered a psychological breakdown following his release from hospital. Recognizing his ability to identify imaginatively with his quarries, Lecter taunts Will about his affinities with family serial killers. Confessing his mental collapse to his son Kevin, Graham never describes the nature of his torment. Recognizing his father's ambiguous reply, "They're the ugliest thoughts in the world," Kevin changes the subject of their conversation. Moody, withdrawn, and introspective, William Peterson's performance aptly conveys an adult attempting to survive a past traumatic experience.

Early scenes show Will and Kevin erecting a barrier to save vulnerable turtle eggs from assault by crabs. Will tells his son that the fragile barrier should prevent crabs from getting at "the newborn." Following this dialogue, the scene changes to show Will and Kevin framed through a window as the camera zooms out to show Mollie Graham (Kim Griest) watching her family, and then Crawford. Her lines—"You were supposed to be his friend, Jack. Why don't you leave him alone?"—reveal other *crabs* threaten this family. A thin barrier separates Will from Hannibal Lecter and Francis Dollarhyde.

Michael Mann's strategic use of mirror imagery not only emphasizes the deep mental links between Graham and Dollarhyde but also succinctly underlines the screen memory behind the latter's psychological trauma. Graham's house faces the ocean; Dollarhyde's apartment is near a lake. These locations symbolize flowing maternal imagery. Recreating Dollarhyde's dark history with a violently abusive mother, Graham dreams of his wife on a plane journey. This scene significantly follows his traumatic encounter with Lecter and precedes his successful recreation of Dollarhyde stalking his family victims. "You watched them all goddamned day long. Didn't you, you son of a bitch." Falling asleep over graphic photographs of a murdered family, he dreams of Mollie. But his sleep is interrupted by the frightened screams of a passenger's young daughter accidentally seeing the photographs. As the stewardess hastily turns the photos over, passengers view Will as a serial killer.

Watching a home video of the Leeds family, Graham begins employing the same mental tactics he used in finding Lecter—"I tried to build feelings in my imagination that the killer had. So I would know why he did what he did and find him." Noting the killer smashed a mirror to select jagged pieces to use on Mrs. Leeds, he correctly intuits the killer took off rubber gloves to touch his victim's eyes. This scene follows his phone call to Mollie. In bed like Mrs. Leeds in *Manhunter*'s first scene, Mollie's visual identity with the murdered wife and mother triggers off Graham's empathy with the killer. Although he does not literally *see* his wife, participation in his act of imagining Mollie in bed leads viewers in understanding the special position of the mother for both men. For Graham she is the good object idealized in his dreams. With Dollarhyde the good object is something he attempts to recreate in his murderous acts, denying bad object associations from his actual mother. Supplying Dollarhyde's motives later to Crawford, Graham states, "It's in his dreams. His act fuels his fantasy." Looking at the Leeds family images on the television screen, Graham engages in dialogue with both Dollarhyde and his own dark self. "What are you dreaming? There's something you can't afford for me to know about, isn't there?" "She's lovely, isn't she?" He later tells Crawford that Dollarhyde took his gloves off, "Because Mrs. Leeds was a beautiful woman." After the FBI discovers a thumbnail print, Graham feels compelled to visit Lecter, who immediately perceives both his traumatic dreams and mental affinity. "The reason you caught me, Will, is we're just alike. Smell yourself!"

Manhunter develops psychic parallels between pursuer and pursued. For Graham his encounter with Lecter and obsessive pursuit of Dollarhyde represent the recognition of his fragile social identity. Dollarhyde's dark obsessions with mirrors and reflections parallel Graham's desires to see himself as a secure individual through the eyes of wife and family. Mollie first appears in a point-of-view shot through Graham's perspective as she approaches the camera. Relocating his family, following the discovery that Lecter passed his home phone number to the killer, Graham's last scene with Mollie shows them seated on the bench facing the ocean in the same alienated positions in which we earlier saw Graham and Crawford. The next shot shows him alone in a restaurant, obsessively gazing at his reflected image as the camera slowly zooms in. Deciding to go all the way in pursuing his quarry despite dangers to his mental health, Graham talks to himself, "Just you and me, sport. . . . I'm going to find you goddamit." Graham attempts to affirm the coherence of his reflected image realizing the necessity of externalizing his quarry. Only then can he return to his family. The scene inversely parallels Dollarhyde's own reflected construction of identity, as he obsessively recreates fantasies through his victim's eyes.

Dollarhyde becomes attracted to Reba (Joan Allen), a blind woman who also works at his photo, film, and video company. As Reba sits by Francis, he watches 16mm footage of one of his future victims, a bikini-clad mother by a swimming pool. Intercut shots show Reba's breast and legs before she initiates sex with him. Awakening in the morning Dollarhyde weeps and cuddles Reba like a little child with a "good" mother.

Following Lecter's explanation of the killer's sense of power, Graham finally experiences Dollarhyde's vision of his maternal victim. She looks at him with mirror eyes. "I see you there in the silver mirror of your eyes, desired by you and loved." Dollarhyde's condition pathologically reenacts Lacan's mirror stage. Sexually abused by his mother, Dollarhyde has not successfully entered the Oedipal stage. He cannot distinguish himself from mother's body and gaze to constitute himself as a separate being. Sharing in Lecter's definition of divine omnipotence, paralleling the infant's sense of imaginary plenitude before discovering his body as a separate entity in the mirror phase, Dollarhyde obsessively enacts a murderous pattern of rage induced by

early traumatic experiences. Sexually abused by a mother before his formative period of sexual identity, Dollarhyde recreates his desire for love by a
maternal "good object" while enacting rage against the "bad object," killing
and blinding with fragments from a mirror. Graham understands this family
key to his killer's identity. "He dreams about being wanted and desired. So he
changes people into beings who want and desire him ... killing and arranging
the people to imitate him. If our boy believes he is wanted and desired enough
he will become wanted and desired and accepted. It'll all come true."

Dollarhyde carries masculine divine omnipotence behind the Oedipal
trajectory to pathologic extremes. As Lecter finally reveals to Graham, "Why
does it feel good? It feels good because God is power and if one does it enough,
one becomes God. If one does what God does enough times one becomes
God." Lecter's speech also demonstrates the dark associations between religion and the serial killer. Both reflect the vicious nature of patriarchal society.
After listening to Lecter, Graham revisits the Leeds apartment and sees an
imaginary reconstruction of Mrs. Leeds's maternal presence through Dollarhyde's eyes. It counterpoints Graham's constant images of Mollie and his
desire to reassure his fragmented sense of identity through her eyes.

Recognizing pathologic wish-fulfillment imagery in the family home
movie, Graham eventually discerns Dollarhyde's motives. "He uses the mirrors to see it happen, but he doesn't take anything he needs such as souvenirs
and trophies to relive the event. Maybe he records it somehow over and over
again so he can be accepted over and over again. There's selection and design
in his choices." Looking again at the family video, Graham muses further,
"Everything you see is with you. Your primary sense of intake is seeing, reflections, mirrors, images. That makes your dream live—in seeing. You're *seeing*
these films!" The supposed cinema verite (but really artificial) family home
movie triggers off Dollarhyde's murderous rage, making him relive illusory
fantasies by repressing his ugly early life. Dollarhyde's employment within a
visual industry, where he creates illusions, is not coincidental.

Kidnapping Reba after psychotically imagining her betraying his new
feelings of affection, Dollarhyde sees her as another false mother figure whom
he will blind and slaughter. However, realizing that her sightless eyes cannot recreate his "mirror image" fantasies, Dollarhyde pauses and looks toward
his window. He sees, not his reflection, but Graham's running image. Breaking through the window into an apartment containing a television set's constantly fragmented wavy lines, Graham collapses on a glass strewn floor. As
Dollarhyde shoots policemen through the windows, Graham recovers and
kills his quarry.

Dawn breaks outside. Crawford wisely remains silent as Graham stands before Dollarhyde's lake. The scene changes to Graham back home. Looking at his rescue of the newborn turtles, he tells Kevin, "Most of them made it." The image freezes on a long shot of the vulnerable family looking at the ocean.

◆ ◆ ◆

Although made in a lighter vein, *The Stepfather* films show the continuing presence of family horror in the 1980s.[4] The films emphasize the family's role in creating patriarchal monsters. Joseph Rubin's *The Stepfather* begins with a tranquil opening crane shot. As a newsboy throws the local paper, the camera cranes right to a family residence. Inside a father cleans up in the bathroom before leaving a home littered with his family's bloody corpses.

Now remarried to young widow Susan (Shelly Hack), Jerry Blake (Terry O'Quinn) leads a normal suburban existence selling real estate for the American Eagle realty company. Blood, psychosis, and violence lie beneath the American Dream whose national symbol is a predatory bird. The film contains subtle hints that Jerry's own family life was by no means ideal. Like *Shadow of a Doubt*, *The Stepfather* displays a subtle, but highly revealing, ambiguity, leaving viewers to imagine the exact nature of the main character's early life.

Avoiding gratuitous special effects and excessive violence, *The Stepfather* presents its monster as an average guy seduced by tranquil images of 1950s family sitcoms. As he says at the dinner table, "Father Knows Best." Expecting ideologically imaginary happy, obedient families, Jerry murders those who do not live up to his ideals before starting anew elsewhere. *The Stepfather* illustrates the Law of the Father's inherent instability in Jerry's hysterical rage when things go wrong. Donald Westlake's intelligent script reveals patriarchy as an ideologic creation dependent on violence against women for its very existence.

Jeff Burr's *Stepfather 2* (1989) begins in Puget Sound mental hospital where Jerry is now a patient. His answers to psychiatrist Dr. Danvers reveal him as little different from other socialized males. Jerry is only more excessive in attempting to live a patriarchal American Dream. "An eternal optimist believes that you can fix what has been broken so you keep on trying." Terry O'Quinn's performance presents Jerry as no vicious monster but a pathetic individual seeking identity within illusionary worlds of the nonexistent family scenario documented by Stephanie Coontz in *The Way We Never Were*. Jerry escapes and uses Danvers's counseling skills to set up a family practice in a Los Angeles suburb. For him, "Everything begins and ends with the family in one way or another." He inflicts patriarchal rage against single, interfering women like Hattie (Caroline Williams) or reluctant brides-to-be such as his intended spouse Carol (Meg Ryan). *Stepfather 2* concludes its ironic treatment of the American Dream with Jerry's blood-spattered bride walking up the altar with her son. As she collapses, Jerry dies clutching an object from the wedding cake. Family ideology destroys everyone within this American Dream.

"Bad Daddy" returns in Guy Mager's *Stepfather 3* (1992). Physically changed by plastic surgery, stepfather Keith (Robert Wightman) floats like a plankton into the arms of socially indoctrinated widows who desire husbands for social acceptability. But the ideal husband and stepfather does not exist. Switching from literal wife to surrogate successor and back again, Keith finds himself pursued in a comic social scenario that makes him both victimizer and victimized quarry.

◆   ◆   ◆

Bob Balaban's black comedy *Parents* (1989) is set within the 1950s milieu that influences Jerry Blake. Opening with the family's arrival in a suburban Eden and concluding with the major actors stepping out before the audience in the manner of "The Adventures of Ozzie and Harriet," *Parents* explores family horror within the repressive world of Eisenhower's America. After showing the family's arrival in their new plastic paradise, *Parents* features a family photo image of Mom (Mary Beth Hurt) and Dad (Randy Quaid) at a barbecue, juxtaposed with their son Michael's (Bryan Modorsky) awakening from a nightmare. Despite his father's jovial description of nightmares as a "transitional process" leading toward "growing up to be a strong man like my Dad," Michael intuitively realizes these dreams suggest dark features within his family. As Mom and Dad attack the icebox for an unseen midnight feast, Michael experiences another dream. His bed becomes a raft floating on a sea of blood. The camera cranes upward into an overhead shot showing Michael clinging to his pillow before he sinks in the ocean. As the sequence concludes in the circular imagery of a bloody maelstrom, the following scene opens with a circular red dish in the family kitchen. Mother repressively warns Michael about his nightmares, "The only time you have nightmares is when you take your pajamas off." However, his nightmares are not sexual—his parents are predatory cannibals existing within Eisenhower-era images of normality.

Parents links the nuclear family with capitalist military aggression against the Third World. As Michael learns on his visit to father's company, the Toxico

Firm, the whole society rests upon exploitation. Witnessing the demonstration of an early "Agent Orange" defoliant on a model of a recognizable southeast Asian village, he also guesses that the family's continual meat supply may come from the company morgue. Dad works in the appropriately titled Division of Human Testing. The cannibalistic metaphor extends beyond the family into the Third World.

Aided by a social worker (Sandy Dennis), who later ends up as a family barbecue, Michael discovers his family's real nature. Taunted by father for his nonconformist, un-American feelings—"You are an outsider. You're not like us"—Michael refuses to partake in the family meal and escapes from a vengeful Dad who seeks to correct his offspring. "We'll have another one. . . . We'll bring him up right." After his parents die, Michael goes to live with his grandparents. The film concludes after they put Michael to bed, the camera tracking out to reveal a suspicious-looking sandwich at his bedside table.

◆ ◆ ◆

Despite the trivializing mediocrity of *Psycho II* (1983) and *Psycho III* (1986), the TV movie *Psycho IV: The Beginning* (1991) gave Norman Bates a decent burial. Joseph Stefano's teleplay investigated the origins of Norman's psychosis by showing him to be an abused child. Opening with a radio talk show on matricide conducted by Black host Fran Ambrose (C. C. H. Pounder), *Psycho IV* investigates the family dynamics determining Norman's character. Norman phones in to tell his own story using the pseudonym "Ed" (from the original real-life character inspiring *Psycho*—Wisconsin murderer Ed Gein). While Dr. Richman (Warren Frost) attempts to isolate male matricide as an aberrant phenomenon, claiming the same dynamics are inapplicable to girls, the streetwise Fran comments, "Maybe they're too smart to get caught." Originating from a probable ghetto background and knowledgeable about dark family relationships, Fran sympathizes with Norman.

Phoning from his kitchen, Norman reveals his past history and begins defending a mother who sexually and mentally abused him. His initial defense—"No. It wasn't her fault. She was the product of her time, the age of sexual repression"—does not match images of Mrs. Bates (Olivia Hussey), a woman in her late thirties or early forties. Her actions toward Norman are manipulative and destructive. Like a good child who cannot bear the thought of a bad parent, Norman displays denial mechanisms. Richman sneers at Norman's explanation—"Did all this happen in this century?"—by denying his evidence. Fran is more understanding. "Did she smother you in some way? The way some of us mothers do with our kids?"

As an only child Norman is a convenient scapegoat for mother's frustrations. We first see her with young Norman during his father's funeral. Norman's adult voice tells Fran, "I felt awful sad beside her. She looked so sorrowful." But Mrs. Bates's scornful expression and her deliberate tickling of Norman contradict this statement. Using Norman to express her scorn, she causes him to giggle, then abruptly slaps him, "as if it were my fault." Her response—"Don't you have any respect for the dead?"—foreshadows Norman's later schizophrenia. She speaks with Norman's adult masculine voice. This sequence reveals an abused child's divided self. He condemns himself via a parentally generated superego.

Successive flashbacks reveal Norman's tendencies to deny parental manipulations and his low self-esteem. Norman describes a lyrical afternoon picnic; he mentions his mother's "beautiful hair." But the visual evidence is more disturbing. Acting more like a lover, Mrs. Bates seductively plays with her son's emotions. Although Norman describes himself as "the master of the house," the images reveal who is actually dependent on whom. During a thunderstorm, Mrs. Bates calls the adolescent Norman (Henry Thomas) into bed to comfort her. Ignoring her son's sexual development, she deviously manipulates Norman into having an erection. Fleeing mother's bed, Norman runs into his own room. Discovering a semipornographic comic book, she falls into a furious rage and condemns him for feelings she arouses.

Richman suggests masochistic desires behind Norman's traumatic dependence. But Norman reacts against this conservative Freudian interpretation—"If the doctor is trying to turn this into some kind of incest tragedy, tell him to forget it." Norman mistakenly feels his problem is genetic, not social; he sees himself as a bad seed.

During the next memory sequence, Norman views his mother's insane behavior through a peephole in the Bates Motel office. We learn his father constructed this voyeuristic device. Norman is no genetic bad seed. A dysfunctional family created his monstrous persona. During a hot summer night. Mrs. Bates teasingly seduces her son, forcing him to apply ice water to her body with his fingertips. She falls upon Norman and rolls with him on the floor. Discovering Norman's erection, she disavows responsibility by emotional abuse. She destroys Norman's already fragmentary sense of gender identity, forcing him to wear her dress, smearing his face with lipstick, and locking him in a dark closet. The scene dissolves from young Norman's terrified expression as he peeps through the gap in a closet door to the older Norman collapsed on his kitchen floor.

Norman angrily rebuts Richman's conservative psychoanalytic explanation of a castration scenario. But he lacks the emotional distance to understand his mother's culpability. Like most adult children of abusive family situations, he cannot openly express his feelings. But Fran and Ellen understand Norman far better than the institutionally minded Dr. Richman.

Norman tells Fran about another traumatic memory. Learning of the state's intention to build a major highway elsewhere, Mrs. Bates expressed her anger by hitting Norman. She resents a son who supposedly caused her bodily damage during birth. "I can't hold my water. I was fine until I gave birth to you.... I should have gotten rid of you the day I found out I was going to have you. I should have killed you in my womb. You sure tried to kill me getting out of it."

She is also a victim of an abusive family situation. Moving from being past victim to present parental aggressor, Mrs. Bates follows a pathologic cyclical pattern. "You're just like my father, never a drop of sympathy." Confronted with these revelations, Norman consciously disavows them and blames himself. While Fran responds, "She sounds horrible," Norman exhibits denial. "But it wasn't always like that. You didn't know her. My mother was a remarkable woman."

The "last straw" for Norman is mother's acquisition of boyfriend Chet. Despite a supposedly Victorian upbringing, Mrs. Bates cruises local bars, hooking a bartender she intends to marry after his divorce. Physically and sexually humiliated by Chet during a boxing lesson, Norman poisons his oppressors. He removes mother's body from her coffin and preserves it. Disavowing matricide she will live on. Although he attempts denying mother's influence over his later murders, his defense is contradictory. "No. My mother has nothing to do with this. But she had always had, and always will have a strong effect on me. After all, I do have her seed in me." Rather than blame a dysfunctional parent, Norman sees himself as an aging bad seed. His motivations exhibit metaphysical tendencies similar to horror film rationalizations. Norman denies the material roots of a family trauma and adheres instead to conservative genetic theories. Learning of his wife's pregnancy, he decides to terminate any possibility of another Norman Bates whose "genes are the same ones I got from my mother."

At the Bates House, Norman's psychologist wife Connie dissuades him from pathologically repeating the past. "Your mother can't tell you what to do now." Deciding to "get rid of the past for good," Norman sets the Bates home alight. He encounters demons from his past, including a raging Mrs. Bates who repeats two sentences from his tormented memories—"I should have killed you in my womb!.... Don't you have any respect for the dead." Managing to escape the inferno, Norman and Connie stand outside the gutted Bates house. As Norman feels secure for the first time, "I'm free," the image changes to Mrs. Bates's rocking chair still swaying in the cellar. However, it then *stops* swaying. The camera quickly tracks out as the cellar doors slam shut. Mother's aged voice pleads, "Let me out of here." The image changes to darkness. A baby's cry is heard. Norman's firstborn emerges into an uncertain future. Escaping from past familial entrapment, Norman Bates's saga finally ends.

◆ ◆ ◆

Jeffrey Bloom's sensitively written and directed version of V. C. Andrews's *Flowers in the Attic* (1987) is one of the most significant testaments of family horror. Although the author's early life never paralleled the Dollanganger family's privations, the traumatic nature of her late adolescent arthritic ailment placed her in a dependent condition, subjecting her to family control.[5] Mediated through Cathy's (Kristy Swanson) voice-over, *Flowers in the Attic* depicts family misfortunes following father's death and their arrival at Foxworth Hall, the domain of their maternal grandparents. As the camera slowly tracks in to a stone lion's mouth leading to shots of the attic, Cathy's distanced melancholic narration sets the film in motion. Both visual style and narrative deliberately resemble female romantic literary discourse, a fictional mode now recognized as highly important in negotiating patriarchal oppression.[6] Speaking of Foxworth Hall as "grandfather's house," she recounts the domain's effect on her, "I always remember even my first impression was one of fear and wonder . . . lost childhood, innocence shattered and all our dreams destroyed by what we would find." Associated with grandmother's (Louise Fletcher) forbidding figure, European gentility, and a rigidly hierarchical class structure involving servants and masters, Foxworth Hall exemplifies dark traditional constraints upon American innocence.

As the camera conveys Cathy's romanticized images of her closely knit family, her voice-over continues, "My mother and father were the center of my universe when I was young. The whole family was really close. . . . I always wanted to grow up to be like mom." Bloom's depiction of father as a youthful Prince Charming only a few years removed from his daughter aptly conveys her idealized perspective of a fragile, idyllic family world. Clearly preferring Cathy to his other children (Christopher [Jeb Stuart Adams] and twins Corey [Ben Ganger] and Carey [Lindsey Docker]), father presents her with a musical ballerina. The sequence ends with a close-up of Connie Dollanganger (Victoria Tennant) enigmatically looking on as the musical box chimes.

Their fairy-tale world ends with father's death in an accident. Learning of their economically deprived condition, the family leaves home and travels by Greyhound coach to live with their maternal grandparents. Rudely awakened to the harsh realities now confronting them, Cathy's suspicions begin when she hears Corinne's narcissistic scheme to restore their fortunes by winning back her dying grandfather's love. Realizing the illusionary nature of her family life, she confides to the more trusting and naive Christopher, "Somebody should have told us that fathers die too, even if they're young and handsome and we need them." She has no desire for wealth.

Walking to the forbidding Foxworth Hall with its Alsatian guard dogs, sullen gamekeeper, and somber butler, Corey immediately recognizes it as a domain of witches and monsters. The young Dollangangers confront a nightmare situation rooted within the dark side of the family. Their stern black-clad, tightly coiffed grandmother immediately condemns them as a family sin. As products of their mother's seventeen-year incestuous liaison, the innocent fair-haired Dollanganger children are now "the devil's spawn, evil from the moment of conception," condemned to hidden incarceration.

Coping with Corinne's periodic absences, the children live in their own special attic world. While Christopher naively trusts mother, Catherine understands their bleak circumstances. As the children clean their attic world, the only light emanates from sunshine through a barred window. Catherine reflects that they are "all going to pay the price" for mother's return. Clinging to dreams of becoming a ballerina and Christopher's desires to enter the medical profession, they attempt to survive. As Corinne's visits gradually cease, the children find that they gradually weaken and become pale through lack of sunshine and exercise; close bonding enables them to exist day by day.

After Christopher's failed escape, Corinne visits her children and criticizes their wishes for freedom. While Cathy becomes more suspicious of her mother's reluctance to consider the ailing twins' need for fresh air and schooling, Christopher dutifully complies with his mother's plans to obtain future wealth. "If we leave now, we'll have nothing. If we stay we'll have more than we ever want."

While Christopher doubts that Corinne actually knows what is happening to them, a scene reveals her reading from the Bible to grandfather. As he strokes her head, she holds his hand. Grandmother watches in isolation. The scene contains several suggestions. Despite grandmother's stern authoritarian treatment of the youngsters, she has very little actual power in a patriarchal institution. She overcompensates for lack of power by brutalizing the most vulnerable members of her family. Corinne's motions toward her now-loving father have incestuous overtones—such a crime initially barred her from Foxworth Hall. Choosing to condemn the children as devil's spawn, grandmother enforces a brutal and hypocritical religiously ordained patriarchal family structure.

Managing to leave their prison one evening, Cathy and Christopher find Corinne's room, one whose lavish interior and wardrobe strongly contrasts with their own privations. Unknown to them, her parents have reintroduced Corinne back into society. While they wine and dine a prospective suitor, family lawyer Bart Winslow (Leonard Mann), the children slowly starve from lack of sunlight and food. "When grandmother stopped feeding us our bodies became thin." Young Corey gradually weakens.

Cathy and Christopher later discover an ailing grandfather. His sudden grasp of Cathy, mistaking her for Corinne, suggests mother's incestuous manipulations to write herself back into his will. They return to their prison. While Christopher naively defends Corinne, despite the sick twins, Cathy concludes, "All the money isn't worth the living that we've lost." Provoking Christopher to recognize the "truth," Cathy emphasizes the economic factors behind mother's neglect. "Can't you see what wanting all that money is doing to her?"

Gradually, the children discover who their real enemy is—a discovery anticipated by Cathy's nightmare in which grandmother's black-clad figure turns into a sinister Corinne. Eventually, her manipulative mother-love fails to seduce Christopher—"I make myself keep loving you every day despite what you do." The children gradually realize she not only plans to keep their existence a secret to inherit the family fortune, but she intends to remarry. Corinne envisages even more drastic measures.

Summoned to the children's room when Corey falls ill, Corinne initially refuses to get medical help. Challenged by Cathy—"What's wrong with you, mother? Are you going to stand there while Corey lies there and dies? Have you forgotten that you're his mother?"—she finds her daughter responding in kind to her chastising assault. As she reacts to this disobedient gesture, grandmother actually breaks the stalemate, ordering the butler to take Corey to the hospital. "My daughter is taking him to the hospital."

However, it is too late. As Corinne coldly announces Corey's death from pneumonia to the children, a tracking shot shows the gamekeeper digging a grave. As it moves right, it reveals three other dug graves. Using his rudimentary medical knowledge to conduct an autopsy on Corey's pet mouse, Christopher discovers arsenic in the crumbs. They finally realize that the threat does not come from grandmother.

Deciding to escape and risk an uncertain future in the outside world, Cathy discovers Corinne's wedding plans. After finding grandfather's will which stipulates any children from Corinne's first marriage will result in her disinheritance, the pale, emaciated children confront Corinne at the altar. Facing a mother who denies their existence, Cathy verbally and physically assaults her, offering an arsenic-coated cookie as a wedding present before the congregation. In an ending differing from the novel, Corinne falls to her death, hung by her wedding veil. The children then leave Foxworth Hall watched by grandmother's forbidding figure.

Flowers in the Attic is an extremely poignant and touching film. Shot in a Gothic romantic style, it beautifully articulates family horror dynamics without recourse to grotesque monsters, supernatural killers, or special effects. Using motifs such as the wicked witchlike grandmother and the dark castle, *Flowers in the Attic* manages subtly to subvert customary Gothic formations by lifting aside deceptive veils. The film reveals vulnerable youthful prisoners of an unjust, sadistic, religiously orientated patriarchal system based upon economic exploitation. Initially violating family taboos, Corinne returns to the fold, submitting herself to brutal physical punishment by playing the system according to its own rules and submitting to its power structures. Seduced by capitalist desire, she eventually plans to murder her own children and inherit Foxworth Hall. The film cleverly sets up grandmother as the traditional monster only to reveal that crimes result from ideologic imprisonment within the family. It is actually a supposedly, sympathetic mother, cruelly manipulating her offspring by artificially constructed family ties of dutiful love, who is the real threat.

By bonding together in a united, nonhierarchical family of their own, based upon genuine feelings of love and mutual sympathy, the Dollanganger children survive. As they walk away from Foxworth Hall, the camera records their departure in a fixed position that represents their former death-in-life family prison. Carrying her cherished ballerina doll, Cathy leaves with brother and infant sister. We hear her voice-over for the last time, disclosing the continuing nature of their family trauma.

> We finally got our real revenge. We managed to make it on our own. I finally got a job to put Chris through medical school.... Little Carey grew up but she was never totally healthy. We left the past behind us. All except the memories, of mother, of grandmother and the attic. I sometimes wonder if grandmother is still alive still presiding over Foxworth Hall and awaiting my return.

◆　◆　◆

Day of the Dead is justifiably one of the most important works within an aesthetically weak and conservative decade.[7] Centered upon its positive female character Sarah (Lori Cardille), it presents a dead world ruled by zombies. The last vestiges of capitalist civilization exist in military and scientific representatives who are confined to an underground shelter. Focusing upon a militaristic male hysterical unit and a complicit scientific establishment, the film strongly suggests that any attempt to save civilization (and related authoritarian family structures) is doomed to failure. The film's sympathies lie with outsiders Sarah (whose independent status parallels Romero's rewriting of Barbara in Tom Savini's *Night of the Living Dead* [1990]), West Indian helicopter pilot John, and Irish electronics expert Bill McDermott (two members of traditionally disparaged ethnic groups). At the climax this trio *may* have escaped to a desert island to begin a new society devoid of traditional class, racial, family, and gender structures. However, as with the ending of *Dawn of the Dead*, the future is tentative. On the other hand the ending's escapist nature resembles fantastic literary patterns described by Rosemary Jackson as suggestive of "compensatory, transcendental" dimensions substituting for frustration with a contemporary repressive order.[8]

Romero's director credit appears over a deserted Florida cinema, The Edison. It ironically comments on the cinematic institution's inability to present satisfactory answers to social problems. Accompanying scenes show insects crawling over a decomposing skeleton (the average horror film "consumer" consumed by special effects, perhaps?), useless money blowing in the wind, and consumer debris. The scene may parallel Godard's axiom at the climax of *Weekend* (1968)—"Fin du Cinema." The cinematic mechanism cannot change human behavior. Work must begin outside.

The family's role is pivotal in *Day of the Dead*. Its grotesque military and scientific figures represent the final result of techniques begun within the traditional family, a structure based upon hierarchical formations and behaviorally conditioned systems of reward and punishment.

Day of the Dead further develops *Dawn of the Dead*'s equation of humans and zombies. According to scientist Dr. Logan (Richard Liberty), zombies do not consume for basic nourishment. Some form of conditioning leads them to consume for the sake of consumption even though they gain no actual satisfaction. He wishes to discover the reasons and techniques behind such conditioning. Logan intends to educate the zombies so that "they can be conditioned to behave" and become civilized. Basic Pavlovian conditioning exercises occur with Logan's pet zombie "Bub" (Howard Sherman). In his former existence, Bub underwent military training. His salute before ultra-macho Captain Rhodes (Joseph Pilato) reveals this. Displaying Bub, Logan equates zombies with human beings. "They are us. They are the extensions of us." He wishes to train zombies into being "good little boys and girls."

Recognizing *Day of the Dead*'s conditioning thesis, Robin Wood comments that "all good capitalists are conditioned to 'live off' other people, and the zombies simply carry this to its logical and literal conclusion."[9] Because zombie residual (learned) instincts parallel those conditioned by capitalism, one may ask where these instincts first develop. *Day of the Dead* supplies the answer—the family. Sarah, Bill, and John investigate Logan's laboratory at night. They discover the real origins of civilized behavior Logan wishes his zombie subjects to achieve. The group finds the body of an infant zombie. Switching Logan's pocket tape recorder on, they listen to the doctor's notes, hearing the recording in a laboratory that resembles a slaughterhouse.

Logan's voice mimics traditional power-knowledge disciplinary structures within family training. He trains his zombies by a defined system of rewards and punishments similar to normal child-rearing practices.

CHILD'S VOICE. It's not father's stocking. It's my stocking!

MOTHER'S VOICE. OK. Put it away.

CHILD'S VOICE. I've put it away, mother. I've put it away.

LOGAN'S VOICE. Bastard! Be civilized! *(zombie growl in background.)* Take that! *(Logan hits zombie.)*

CHILD'S VOICE. Five minutes mother. Just five minutes. Father's stocking has a stripe. I wouldn't wear one of father's stockings.

MOTHER'S VOICE. Mother is very proud of you, very, very proud. You did quite nicely today.

Capitalist acquisitiveness conditions family disciplinary operations. Private property, parental obedience, rewards, and punishment motivate both military and scientific establishments and zombie guinea pigs. Logan mimics a nurturing mother acting in an ideologic oppressive role by conditioning individuals according to rigid, gender structures. As Ethel Spector, Person points out, the family often conditions infantile dependence according to a fixed system of rewards and punishments.[10]

Although this family revelation occupies a brief segment of *Day of the Dead*, it is crucially important. Alone of all the horror films made in the Reaganite era, Romero's film unveils key disciplinary and punitive mechanisms operating within families, which a death-affirming civilization depends upon for its very existence. Traditional family structures create human as well as supernatural monsters within a decaying institutional structure. Macrocosm and microcosm coexist in a tense and deadly relationship.

◆　◆　◆

Day of the Dead is an appropriate film to finish this study. Although not the most recent of family horror films, it is still the most important work of the past decade. Romero attempts to balance fetishistic aspects of horror with social motifs showing the latter's dialectical relationship to the former. The horror genre's formal nature often results in violent displays of special effects almost totally overwhelming its material aspects. Major works of family horror explore the social contradictions of dysfunctional families forced into rigid patterns by the dominant ideology producing victims and victimizers. Family horror films sometimes implicitly protest against this system. By use of generic codes, they depict human and supernatural monsters as material products of a society in need of radical change. The family represents the microcosmic component of a dominant macrocosm system. Family horror films enact social tensions occurring in different forms throughout the decades. The Universal Frankenstein monsters represented a return of a particular historical repressed for their era. Michael, Jason, and Freddy are reactionary patriarchal avatars for a conservative tendency much stronger than before. Recent works attempt rigidly externalizing monsters, but sometimes cracks appear. Michael Myers briefly appears as a vulnerable child in *Halloween 5*, linking him with other vulnerable monster figures in the Universal, Lewton series, and *It's Alive* before ideology reasserts itself again. Family horror films need to develop this theme, which shows monsters as the creation of a brutal patriarchal system and move toward new alternatives where monsters and horror films become obsolete.

Family horror films belong to a particular American cultural tradition, cinematically reflecting motifs appearing in other genres, and indirectly reflecting (and sometimes responding to) historic and social forces. They cinematically parallel the return of a material repressed. In some works repression succeeds, but others antihegemonically contest the dominant ideology. Family horror is an integral component of the entire horror genre. It voices particular discontents against a specific social order of things where families become agents of totalitarian forces and attempt molding vulnerable beings into conformity. Oppositional elements become conveniently coded as monstrous. Certain films see beyond the veil, expressing discontentment about having definable social roots. But until social changes occur, resulting in societies totally free from oppressive mechanisms, the family horror film will continue in its different forms to represent brutal negativity and, occasionally, suggestions for moving toward a better type of society. Despite featuring exploitative mechanisms within their forms, they have much to teach us concerning nihilistic aspects of human existence as well as providing a stimulus toward finally eradicating the problems they so bleakly depict.

Postscript

In his conclusion to *The American Horror Film: An Introduction*, Reynold Humphries begins his final chapter with the question, "Where do we go from here?" He repeats it at the end of his stimulating book. He begins his conclusion by noting that the "present state of things is not conducive to optimism, let alone enthusiasm" and ends by stating that it is "patent that we shall see no more films of the caliber of *The Texas Chain Saw Massacre* which represents for this writer everything that a horror movie can and should be."[1] As my previous chapter stated, for me the original *Texas Chain Saw Massacre* represented one of the great family horror films of the 1970s but its legacy has been tarnished by grotesque remakes emphasizing gore, violence, and spectacle, especially in its recent 3-D version using a once-obsolescent technique to attract younger audiences who have no intention of thinking inside and outside the cinema. "That's Entertainment!" as recent examples of corporate control and wasteful blockbusters reveal.[2] However, in the full version of a sentence I've abbreviated above, Humphries mentions that "with the exception of Shyamalan, no major talent has emerged in the last decade" or beyond. I do not regard Shyamalan as a major talent, as his recent decline reveals. What he has directed bears little resemblance to the iconoclastic talents of Larry Cohen (now engaging in writing rather than directing) and George A. Romero. The latter is still active but is isolated from the American film industry, making distinctive films on low budgets in Canada rather than the wasteful budgets lavished on inferior product in Hollywood.[3]

Cases of family dysfunction and child abuse increase daily and it is futile to supply statistics over a fact everybody knows about but which most people deny. Were there a responsible tradition of horror cinema free from commercial constraints and ideological taboos a very different renaissance of the genre could occur under very different circumstances than exist at the present time. Instead, very familiar gore manifestations appear making no attempt at relevance and doing nothing to suggest the possibility of positive change. It has to be a "scary movie" and nothing else. In terms of this malaise, I have Tarantino in mind generally and Eli Roth specifically. Films are still being made. Sometimes a promising work will emerge. But these are few and far between.

Yet repressed instances do exist within certain films and it is necessary to explore them as muted examples of lost potential that could be developed and explored in future works. The family horror film as such exists as a potential signifier of alternative meaning on the margins of mainstream generic films like *The Sixth Sense* (1999). These theatrically released and expensively promoted films promise much but deliver little due to the deficiencies of directors and hesitancy in exploring what are the really important aspects within the narrative. However, significant elements often exist in films that did not have a proper theatrical release and distribution at the time but went straight on to DVD. It is often the case that a random search sometimes unearths hidden treasures that develop themes common to the 1970s and 1980s in their own creative and particular ways.

It is only recently that I decided to return to look at certain films recommended to me by colleagues such as Reynold Humphries and Christopher Sharrett. Like many, I've despaired over the state of contemporary Hollywood and refrained from dutifully watching every contaminated remake that has appeared whether *Friday the 13th*, *Nightmare on Elm Street*, *The Last House on the Left*, *The Hills Have Eyes* and the interminable *Texas Chain Saw Massacre* series. It was an obligation insisted on by certain reviewers for the first edition of this book but I have no intention of any further painful confrontations in the future, especially as they appear to confirm what is already depressingly evident. Making such a statement rules me out in the eyes of certain people on the grounds of a spurious definition of objectivity that entails seeing everything no matter how bad it is. But my selectivity has a logical basis. A limit exists to how much I can watch of what is actually appalling dross, no matter what postmodernist critics and followers of other apolitical theories may say. The forthcoming book by David Roche admirably dismisses any claims concerning the quality of recent remakes and implicitly affirms the redundancy of the vast majority of new films. To paraphrase Howard Hawks, "They're just no good." Any justified celebration of a new work must be based upon its potential quality and meaningful contribution to issues affecting our present life no matter what style is used. But style must be related to some kind of substance and little of substance appears to me to have occurred in the past twenty years. As the title *What Lies Beneath* (2000) states, it is the suggestive potential of marginalized elements within a narrative that really counts when looking at certain mainstream examples.

When exploring films of the past and present it is often pleasurable when interesting discoveries sometimes come to the surface. One recently discovered classic Hollywood film appears superficially to have little relation to the family horror film. But it contains core elements that the family horror genre would later develop. *Saturday's Children* (1940) is a little-known Warner Brothers film starring John Garfield and directed by Vincent Sherman. Bobby Halevy (Anne Shirley) loves aspiring inventor Rims (Garfield), who dreams of going to the Philippines to make his fortune there. Inspired by her sister Florrie (Lee Patrick), she uses feminine wiles to trap him into marriage and remain in New York. It is not long before harsh economic realities and World War II (resulting in the loss of overseas markets affecting both their employment) begin to intrude into their dreams of domestic bliss. Rims begins to regret his loss of freedom. "Marriage is all right I guess but not for poor people." Noting tensions in the young couple's relationship Florrie suggests another devious female strategy to her sister. "Female Tactic # 1—a baby! There's nothing like that to tie a man down!" Unknown to her, Bobby is already pregnant. The last thirty-five minutes of the film reveal a devastating critique of marriage as an institutional trap, something affirmed by Bobby's father (Claude Rains) until censorship requirements demand that he retract this statement. "Marriage is no love affair. Dish pans, family quarrels. That's how the system gets you." When Rims complains about how marriage traps a man, Bobby responds (after revealing how she trapped him), "A girl also gives up a lot when she gets married." A dilemma occurs leaving the father, who has been in low-income employment for most of his life, to attempt suicide as a means of using his life insurance to keep the couple together. However, according to contemporary cultural conventions and the ideology of the Hollywood studio system, this does not happen. But it is enough to see this plan attempted despite the fact that "Father's Little Dividend" becomes nipped in the bud. Readers familiar with the works of the classical Hollywood system, a familiarity now becoming depressingly non-existent as this cultural heritage slowly disappears, will recognize my punning reference to the 1951 sequel to Vincente Minnelli's *Father of the Bride* (1950) and remember that nightmare dream sequence of Father's economic castration in the church. In *Saturday's Children*, a father attempts suicide for economic reasons while the Freudian-influenced dream sequence of *Father of the Bride* shows the title character about to be completely sexually and economically exposed due to the demands of the system.

This system of economic and ideological enslavement turns a happy couple into warring factions very much like the parents of *Jake's Closet* (2008). As a Warner Brothers film made under the studio system there are limits to such an explicit critique being made before the inevitable retraction occurs. It is not surprising that the film attempts to reverse direction at the end towards the usual happy ending, one which is unconvincing in terms of disturbing tensions that have been revealed throughout the narrative. These tensions will become manifest a generation later in a different way within a very different genre that will produce *It's Alive!*, *God Told Me To*, and *It Lives Again*, key works by one of the major talents of family horror—Larry Cohen. It takes no stretch of the imagination to see this happy Hollywood couple producing a monster child who represents further family contradictions produced by the system. *Saturday Children*'s scenarists Julius J. Epstein and Philip G. Epstein would later collaborate on *Casablanca* (1942). Their names would be supplied by Jack Warner to the House Un-American Activities Committee in 1952 but without any damaging effects to their careers. *Saturday's Children* could have easily become remade as a family horror film in the 1970s. The best examples of any Hollywood film genre have key roots within a society which influences them in one way or another.

The Sixth Sense appears to have little resemblance to the family horror films discussed in the first edition. On the surface it appears to be an average Hollywood ghost story with a surprise ending that any active viewer could have anticipated from the opening scenes (although very few did). It was an ideal Hollywood product, winning several awards at the Dream Factory's annual gathering to celebrate mediocre achievements. Workaholic Dr. Matthew Crowe (Bruce Willis) celebrates an award from Philadelphia concerning his achievements as a child psychologist with a loving wife (Olivia Williams) who gleefully accepts her status as secondary object in his life. Before a night of nuptial bliss occurs, traumatized failed patient Vincent Grey (Donnie Wahlberg) confronts them. He shoots Crowe and commits suicide in their presence. A year later, Crowe appears to have recovered from his wound and attempts to help a troubled boy, Cole Sear (Haley Joel Osment), from a single-parent family cope with psychological disability. Crowe eventually finds peace and resolution very much like the main character in *Ghost* (1990), which the film's narrative shamelessly reworks. Like *The Omen*, *The Sixth Sense* is a supernatural film for audiences who do not like horror or supernatural themes unless they become reworked in the most insipid manner. Unlike *The Omen*, which at least did have some element of threat, everything is satisfactorily resolved at the end very much in the manner of *Ghost*, Hollywood's version of *Casper, the Friendly Ghost* who does not threaten anyone. Like *Ghost*, *The Sixth Sense* is a Hollywood product designed to remove any threatening elements from the supernatural and reassure audiences. However, as Freud revealed, the repressed can return in ways beyond the constraints of censorship mechanisms and corporate Hollywood impositions.

What makes *The Sixth Sense* of interest is not its main narrative but subordinate elements existing within the text that at times threaten to destabilize it, question its premises, and move it in a very different direction. Like most films of the waning years of the last century and the beginning of the next, material affluence and its discontents, though denied, exists as a key element throughout the film. Crowe and his wife are successful products of the American Dream, the latter working in a jewelry shop selling very expensive rings. It is not accidental that the breaking of a window in the prologue has links to a later scene. In both cases, breaking glass alerts the couple to an intruder's entry. Grey's intrusion into the Crowe home represents both an economic and psychological return of the repressed. He is obviously from lower socioeconomic origins and resents Crowe's material success as much as the certificate he feels that his supposed successful mentor has unjustifiably earned. Crowe has gained his establishment success by failing to help others from a lower socioeconomic group than the ones to which he belongs. The film suggests that he gave Grey short shrift since poor people don't count in American society. When later in the film Crowe breaks the expensive jewelry-shop window, expressing resentment of his wife's supposed infidelity, this action operates as part of "the feared siege" derived from earlier films such as *Assault on Precinct* 13 (1976), remade in 2005, and *The Desperate Hours* (1955), remade in 1990. This element also occurs in twenty-first century films such as *Panic Room* (2002) and others that allegorically reflect paranoia on the part of affluent members of society against resentful losers outside a system supposedly guaranteeing marital and material stability to those who fulfill successfully capitalism's requirements of being fruitful and multiplying money. Cole is isolated from society psychologically and economically on the basis of class. Separated from her husband who has chosen to live with a toll-booth attendant elsewhere, Cole's mother works two jobs to keep her son at a private school to give him a "chance in life," one where he is looked down upon by his more affluent schoolmates. She also bears the strains of single parenthood in a changing society that still clings to traditional values. During Cole's supposed hallucination of ghostly presences, the boy witnesses another youth whose father has shot him in the head, a mother who is abusive due to family pressure and slashes her wrists, and a young girl who is dying from cancer. These represent the return of the repressed in his family situation. Cole feels abandoned, as if his own father had killed him, intuitively discerns the economic and psychological pressure affecting his own mother represented by the female ghost, and discerns other factors affecting the condition of the dying girl associated with his own state of ill-health. As Humphries notes in his discerning comments on the film, "the boy's hallucination of a female presence suggests a guilt complex over his close relationship to his mother, her conflict-ridden relationship with her husband and the child's place in this emotional struggle."[4]

The most remarkable aspect of the entire film is not Crowe's self-realization at the end, a realization any alert audience member could have made, but the significance of young female ghost Kyra, who supposedly died of cancer. It is revealed that her own mother poisoned her and is already beginning to work on her younger sister. In the film's terms, she is a bad mother since she wears a red dress at the funeral rather than the appropriate dark attire. Yet the film's banal symbolism cannot disguise the fact that other undisclosed issues operate in this sequence. Mother not only belongs to that dark mother tradition *of Flowers in the Attic* but she may also suffer from hidden social pressures influencing her decision to murder her own children.[5] Her ghostly alter ego who has slashed her wrists after blaming Cole for her entrapment within domesticity (another parallel to Cole's own mother?) is obviously working-class. She can thus appear as a bad ghost and a transference figure operating to deny any explicit acknowledgment of conformist pressures operating on Kyra's mother, who may also be deeply happy and traumatized by her role as wife and mother. Domestic pressures affect women of all classes. However, *The Sixth Sense* avoids this by making both mothers monstrous, one a mentally disturbed ghostly working-class woman and the other an evil Medea materialist figure who has benefitted from capitalism and appears to have no logical rationale for her actions other than the exercise of sheer malevolence. Kyra's mother thus becomes a convenient transference figure to distract viewer attention from the damaging nature of a socially imposed role that affects most women in society. These issues are far more important than whether Bruce Willis is a ghost or not. Who cares anyway? Since *The Sixth Sense* belongs to a more conservative era that has recuperated feminism for its own devices made by a director attracted by self-serving cinematic gimmickry, it is not surprising that subversive features remain undeveloped. *The Sixth Sense* could have been much more radical had its real potential attained better realization.[6]

Washington Irving's *The Legend of Sleepy Hollow* featured in the introduction to *Curse of the Cat People* (1944), a far more interesting film than Tim Burton's *Sleepy Hollow* (1999).[7] In the earlier film, the supernatural is clearly revealed to be a metaphorical device enabling exploration of tensions within the nuclear family. It does not exist for itself. Any attempt to understand it as merely a supernatural device of any major significance reveals its redundancy within the entire narrative. By contrast, in an era that deliberately engages in historical denial and displacing disturbing elements contradicting the worn-out ideological of America as a land of freedom and democracy on to convenient demonic figures such as the last ruler of Iraq or Islam in general, it is not surprising that one of America's major cinematic genres now indulges in deliberate mystifying spectacle rather than thematic interrogation. This is the way in which Martin Scorsese's disgraceful *Shutter Island* (2010) operates, a film which assigns the oppressive practices of the Cold War era to the psychosis of its investigative hero in a manner resembling the trite remake of *The Cabinet of Dr. Caligari* (1962), another historical Cold War product that lays the blame, if not on Mame, then on the errant individual. *Shutter Island* is a film where emphasis upon the supposedly aberrant individual overwhelms promising aspects of the text, revealing American Cold War totalitarian tactics that continue to operate today. The collective implications of the social become reduced to the limiting confines of an individual dilemma. *Shutter Island* is a dishonestly evasive film, ideologically influenced by the "war on terror" in which the director has chosen to be "with us" rather than "against us," as George W. Bush once eloquently stated. Although not a horror film, *Shutter Island* illustrates the same regressive tendencies within most recent examples of the genre by engaging in spectacle, denial and displacement rather than analyze key root causes within the narrative.

Beautifully photographed, anticipating the successful *Harry Potter* franchise in its combination of supernatural thrills and respectable British acting traditions, *Sleepy Hollow* pits Johnny Depp's rational detective against Christopher Walken's headless horseman terrorizing upstate New York village. Eventually, Depp's Ichabod Crane deduces what has actually caused the supernatural manifestation and returns successfully to New York with his bride-to-be and orphaned manservant who he treats little better than a slave. This is, after all, 1799, a world in which the supernatural still overpowers the prevailing rational premises of the Enlightenment philosophy Crane initially subscribes to.

However, despite the attempt of the film to tie threads together, the narrative is not as ideologically "elementary" as a later Dr. Watson would prefer. Like *The Sixth Sense*, subordinate elements make the film far more interesting rather than its main premise. As Humphries notes, "*Sleepy Hollow* is a film on patriarchal capitalism in the making: the hero restores the law by marrying the heroine and looking after the son of the man killed by the headless horseman."[8] He also notes that in one of the flashback scenes depicting the hero's troubled earlier family life, his own father is shot from behind in a manner evoking the headless horseman.[9] Yet, far from seeing the horseman as the bad symbolic father returning from the grave to claim a debt, it is far more important to discern the film as a disguised dysfunctional family horror film involving property relationships that will extend into the next century and later films such as *The Amityville Horror* (1979). The female villain of the piece becomes designated as such, not because she is a victim of patriarchal law attempting to gain a heritage denied to her but because she engages in unacceptable masculine acts "of decision and action"[10] by killing her hermit sister. *Sleepy Hollow* chooses to depict her as a monstrous witch-like figure and not as a woman appropriately reacting against the tenet of "Property as Theft." It is true that she murders her hermit sister but she is not the first monster in a horror film to engage in out of control acts of violence. Lady van Tassell (Miranda Richardson) is the surviving daughter of a family dispossessed by landowner Peter Van Garrett (Martin Landau). They are left to fend for themselves in the face of possible starvation. She marries into a wealthy family, related to the same family as the one responsible for her dispossession and aims at removing all obstacles to gaining the inheritance she feels is rightly due to her. Although Burton makes a humorous remark in the audio commentary about Lady Van Tassell being the first real-estate villain, he does not develop the implications of his remark. If Humphries sees the horseman as the symbolic return of the repressed of Ichabod's father who treats his wife in the way Puritan forefathers treated suspected witches, Lady Van Tassell is also the return of a repressed alternative mother figure. She avenges herself on a legal and patriarchal gender-biased system stipulating the exclusion of women from any role in owning property and becoming independent. Besides avenging her own wrongs, she also wreaks revenge on the patriarchal order for the way Ichabod's mother had been tortured to death by another bad father.[11] Rather than being a young maiden like her stepdaughter who will marry and lose property rights to her husband according to the law of that particular time, if she succeeds Lady Van Tassell will not only be a powerful woman of property but also a very Merry Widow who will continue her middle-aged sexual activities that offend the Law of the Father. As such, she must be designated as a monster who uses the supernatural for her own malevolent ends rather than a feminist heroine. Rather than grasp the implications of his past and present life, Johnny Depp's young Van Helsing chooses to destroy one monster and return to a capitalist civilization that will produce others in the future who will rebel against the unfair economic gender-biased Law of the Father. Like *The Sixth Sense*, radical implications occur in the film but they are heavily outweighed by the supernatural mystification the director chooses to develop instead of what really "lies beneath."

What Lies Beneath (2000) promises much but delivers little, as a second viewing reveals, to say nothing about the film geek DVD commentary. There, director Robert Zemeckis and his associates gleefully espouse their self-indulgent appropriation of Hitchcock without having any idea of the inherent redundancy of the supernatural elements they over-emphasize in the narrative. Like *Shutter Island*, mystification becomes the dominant aspect of the film.[12] Claire Spencer (Michelle Pfeiffer) has abandoned her promising career as a cellist to exchange her role as a single parent for domestic bliss with academic spouse Norman (the significance of whose first name will not be lost on even the dumbest audience member). When her daughter is about to leave home, Claire experiences the first of many supernatural experiences. She first sees herself briefly as a decaying corpse in the bath, a fate that has affected her predecessor, graduate student Madison (Amber Valetta).[13] The supernatural elements in the film distract the audience from recognizing far more significant social elements operating from beneath. Claire has chosen to give up her career and invest her whole personality in her daughter, an investment that ceases once she goes to college. Norman feels inferior to the achievements of his more successful father, and like his predecessor in *Psycho*, he chooses to live in the paternal (not maternal) home which he claims he is renovating. Faced with an Oedipal dilemma in his own personality and career, he also overinvests himself in work and overachievement wanting to maintain his sense of a powerful phallus in both work and sexuality. At one point in the film he accuses Claire of wanting to undermine his work and of marrying him to gain a more secure life than that of a single parent, accusations the film does not contradict. As a result, he indulges in quasi-incestuous desires in his sexual relationship with Madison and his envisaged one with Claire's daughter Caitlin. "When I see her, I see you." Before Claire dives into the lake, like Madeleine supposedly possessed by Carlotta Valdez in *Vertigo*, she blames Norman for her descent into banal domesticity. "I gave up everything. My life! My music!" Norman in turn accuses her of investing all her love in Caitlin. When he tears Claire away from Caitlin—now happily ensconced in a student dormitory—he tells her, "I'm excited. I expect my life back." Rather than understanding Norman's "seduction by the girl because he too is afraid of getting old,"[14] it is more important to see his affair with Madison as a substitution for the sexual relationship he has clearly been deprived of during most of his marriage. In many ways, Harrison Ford's Norman exhibits infantile behavior like his *Psycho* predecessor. He engages in an affair with Madison and envisages a future one with his own stepdaughter as a substitute for the "lack" he experiences in his relationship with Claire. Like Scotty in *Vertigo*, he moves from one substitute for the missing breast to another. He is obviously incapable of any relationship with a woman whose age equals his, such as Claire's divorced friend Jody (Diana Scarwid), who resembles the more down to earth Midge. "It's a beautiful thing, alimony. You lose a husband. You pick up a car."[15] When Madison becomes more assertive and threatens to report Norman to his dean (and thus ruin his chances of fulfilling the legal and academic legacy of his more illustrious father), it is the end for her. We also learn that she was preciously intelligent as a young girl whose mother considered enrolling her in a special school. Since Madison's father left her at the age of twelve, she may have looked on Norman as a substitute father figure until she found out that he had feet of clay and used her as a sexual substitute for his own wife. Elements such as these make *What Lies Beneath* interesting. The relationship between the academic Feur family initially promises to parallel that of the Spencers, with an insecure wife supposedly murdered by her academic husband. But it only functions as a distracting and irrelevant *Rear Window* appropriation before it is immediately discarded.

Far more imaginative is *Terror Tract* (2000). Co-directed by Lance W. Dresson and Clint Hutchison (who also wrote the screenplay), it is an example of an unjustly neglected film that tends to be marginalized in an era of over-publicized and over-promoted big-budget productions. Reynold Humphries acclaims it as "the only film that takes up that radical critical strain" that the horror film exemplifies. At its best, he sees it as an explicit attack on "life in suburbia and, crucially, its economic dimension via the representation of the pressures on real-estate agents to 'perform' according to instructions."[16] However, it is far more pertinent to see it as an American millennium version of that Ealing Studios anthology *Dead of Night* (1945) whose Gothic associations revealed national insecurities concerning the nature of British postwar society similar to American film noir hesitations expressed at the same time about the immediate future of postwar America. Following a black comedy montage of deadly sequences, real-estate agent Allan Doyle (John Ritter)) escorts a newly married couple interested in purchasing a home in suburbia and "helping people attain the American Dream." Seeing his clients eager to start a family, he fervently mentions "I'm a family man myself," more than over-enthusiastically emphasizing his adherence to American conformity. He then shows them the first of three houses, one owned by a married couple who have now moved away to that great subdivision in the sky. Doyle reveals the past history of the former occupants, a married couple whose relationship was built on deceit and violence. The second house was once owned by a family whose father loved his little daughter too possessively, while the third belonged to an affluent family whose neglected son shared a telepathic bond with a serial killer wearing a Granny mask. Following this last revelation, the enraged newlywed husband comments, "Is this your idea of the American Dream?" Since he refuses to help Doyle reach his quota and rescue his family held hostage in a life-threatening situation by his unseen boss, the young husband does not fulfill the American Dream of owning his own home but instead ends up on the real-estate agent's knife. His distraught wife rushes outside to witness a suburbia caught in the turmoil of uncontrollable violence, a climactic vision paralleling that of Mervyn Johns in the penultimate sequence of *Dead of Night*. As in *The Amityville Horror*, the American Dream of suburbia is a living hell that is as deadly for parents as it is for children.

Silent Hill (2006), *The Hole* (2009), and *Don't Be Afraid of the Dark* (2010) represent three different variations on family horror all linked in different ways with external factors that indirectly generate threatening events in each film. Derived from a Japanese action-computer game, *Silent Hill* begins with two parents concerned about the sleepwalking activities of their adopted daughter who mentions the location Silent Hill in West Virginia where she lived in an orphanage. Rose DaSilva (Radha Mitchell) decides to drive back to where her adopted daughter Sharon (Jodelle Ferland) once lived to discover the reason for her behavior. When she arrives, she discovers an abandoned town covered with white ash dust that drops from the sky. Although the disaster is supposedly the result of supernatural action, it also has key links to West Virginia's long history of mining disasters (the most recent being in 2010), as well as 9/11, since the ash falling from the sky parallels the immediate aftermath of the Twin Towers disaster.[17] Family trauma, capitalist instability, and archetypal American violence derived from the witch burning of the Puritan era are all intertwined in a film that goes far beyond its computer game original to reveal America as a geographical hearth of darkness. Sharon represents the manifestation of the remaining innocence of goodness that once belonged to abused child Alessa. As an illegitimate child, Alessa suffered verbal abuse from her classmates while the adult world did nothing to stop this vicious form of social scapegoating. When Aessa suffers rape by the school janitor, a religious cult led by Christabella (Alice Krige) promises Alessa's mother Dahlia (Deborah Kara Unger) that they will restore innocence and purity to her daughter. Excluded from the ceremony, Dahlia realizes that the cult intends to burn Alessa like a witch. She arrives too late with the police only to find her daughter badly burned. Alessa's fear and pain turns to hate and she vows vengeance against the townspeople who tortured her.

Although officer Thomas Gucci (Kim Coates) orders Sharon's adopted father Christopher (Sean Bean) out of town accusing him of bringing his "sick problems" to a supposedly unspoiled town, he and the authorities are engaging in the type of denial that West Virginia mine owners often did concerning mine disasters they were responsible for. The sheriff's comments also echo those made by relatives of the 9/11 disaster who demanded an official inquiry and were blamed for not accepting the official version. Alessa's revenge causes a coal seam fire leading to the town's abandonment. Screenwriter Roger Avery was very familiar with this type of local disaster. The mist and falling ash also resembles photographs of the aftermath of 9/11. Such coincidence cannot be entirely accidental. Although undeveloped, connections exists between depictions of tortured bodies in dark industrial infernoesque dungeons reminiscent of Abu Ghraib and rendition centers and the Inquisition practices of the fanatical cult now dominating Silent Hill. This cult celebrates traditional family values and American notions of conformity. *Silent Hill* depicts the latest manifestation of America's history of violence that began with the divinely ordained extermination of the Native American Indian population, encouraged by Cotton and Increase Mather, and the Salem witch trials. Anyone who falls outside paranoid definitions of normality, even though they are innocent rape victims like Alessa, becomes fair game for religious fundamentalist family violence. As a single mother, Dahlia becomes a community outcast. Under these circumstances, it is not surprising that the most dangerous elements in this film are not the monsters but the film's religious fundamentalists who evoke irrational right-wing Republicans and Tea Party supporters. They engage in an orgy of violence resembling witch burnings from the Puritan era. After Alessa achieves her revenge, leaving her own mother alive (the line "Mother is God in the eyes of a child" is strongly potent here), Rose and Sharon return home to Christopher. But they now exist in another dimension separate from that of father and the patriarchal violence that generated the darkness of Silent Hill. Sharon has also merged with Alessa. On one level, this suggests a positive resolution of the dilemma. It also intimates the future possibility of further female rage erupting against an American society responsible for the violence it has initiated against women and outcasts in the past and present as well as a probably future period.

Directed by Joe Dante, *The Hole* (2009) merges the typical contemporary Hollywood family movie represented by familiar examples such as *Parenthood* (1989) and *Cheaper by the Dozen* (2003). But it also evokes key elements of family horror, minus the obligatory gore. This does not debilitate the premises of the film, as one would expect from the director *of Gremlins* (1984) and *Gremlins 2* (1990). Instead of a father figure such as Steve Martin, *The Hole* supplies a single parent family headed by Susan Thompson (Teri Polo), the mother of two sons who have recently relocated from Brooklyn following a succession of moves. The hole in the basement manifests different types of fears held by the teenage characters, ranging from memories of an abusive, alcoholic father now in a New Jersey penitentiary (who manages to track his family's every move) to the girl next door who harbors guilt over the death of a friend years ago. Gradually, all the characters manage to confront their past with Dane (Chris Massoglia) eventually overcoming his father in a sur-realistic nightmare sequence as the murderous patriarch changes from a giant monstrous figure to normal size following his son's response, "I am nothing like you." Everything appears resolved at the end. However, Susan's mention of her own fear results in the trapdoor opening again. Family trauma can never be entirely resolved. Despite its lighthearted nature, *The Hole* has seri-ous elements revealing the family as a permanently flawed institution. Susan made a mistake in her life by marrying too young and leaving a bad relation-ship too late. Although her maternal role with her sons is positive, *The Hole* reveals that it is not possible to escape entirely the problems of the past and that family dysfunctional problems can never entirely disappear.

Directed by Jaume Collet-Serra, *Orphan* (2009) is one of the most remarkable family horror films of the new millennium. It could be described as *Rosemary's Adopted Baby* but it intuitively develops motifs inherent in the earlier film without having recourse to distracting supernatural elements. Following the stillbirth of her third baby Jessica, recovering alcoholic Kate Coleman (Vera Farmiga) and husband John (Peter Saarsgard)) decide to adopt nine-year-old Estonian Esther (Isabelle Fuhrman), whom they meet in an orphanage. Already experiencing tensions in their marriage due to an undisclosed incident in the past that led to their daughter Max (Aryana Engi-neer) experiencing deafness and Kate leaving a prestigious academic music teaching position at Yale, the new addition to the household seems an ideal solution to heal family divisions. Max welcomes her new sister while brother Daniel remains distant. Already exhibiting a maturity and sexual precious-ness beyond her years, Esther soon becomes a threatening presence in the family using threats and violence and undermining Kate's position to become closer to her adopted father. Still blaming Kate for causing Max's deafness by lack of care due to alcoholism, John begins to believe a psychologist who condemns Kate's personal inadequacies and resumed alcoholism for hinder-ing her relationship to Esther. The situation reaches such a crisis level that the husband, (not the wife!) expels Kate from their bed at night so that Esther can safely sleep with him. *Orphan's* screenplay by David Leslie Johnson not only depicts a nightmare Oedipal scenario where the female (not the male child) displaces the mother from the father's affection but also dark hidden incestu-ous feelings buried beneath the family relationship.

Despite the film's revelation that Esther is really a thirty-three-year men-tal patient whose growth has been affected by a hormone disorder known as hypopituitarism that results in her masquerading as a little girl, the real nuance lies in the fact that *Orphan* is a horror film depicting the violent unleashing of child sexuality in the family. The script provides what Freud would term the "manifest" level of the film's content by offering a supposedly realist scientific explanation for the dilemma. However, the visual style and acting in *Orphan* provide compelling evidence for the "latent" operation of this film according to the ideas expressed in Freud's classic text *The Interpretation of Dreams*. Freud emphasized penetrating the manifest level of the dream to discover a latent meaning that could not be directly expressed within the content of the actual dream. In a supposedly feminist and post-feminist era when the father's position seems less secure than it once was a century ago, *Orphan* reveals that Freud's same set of psychological conditions operates whatever changed family institution exists. Like John, Daniel is a weak link in this film. He exhibits no desire to sleep with the mother but (adopted) daughter Esther, a surrogate for the dead Jessica and her silent sister Alex, wants to displace the father as the male child once supposedly wanted, in Freud's classic Oedipal scenario. Esther wishes to sleep with the father without undergoing her own form of symbolic castration within the psychological demands of the Oedipal scenario. Esther will not turn to another male as a substitute for the actual father she cannot sleep with but will actively attempt to seduce him in a nightmare version of Freud's recognition of active childhood sexuality. When Esther appears to seduce John wearing make-up and adult dress he is horrified. Throughout the film, Esther succumbs to periodic fits of rage and violence whenever anything occurs that threatens her version of the "daughter's seduction." Certain shots show rapid intercutting of her normal drawings with violent flame-ridden scenes that suggest what really lays beneath these supposedly normal images drawn by a child. The final discovery of images of nude father and daughter represent "what really lies beneath" in no uncertain terms. Kate eventually learns from an East European hospital that her adopted daughter is an Oedipal sexual serial killer. When Esther failed to seduce the father, she killed the rest of the family and burned down the home before moving on to her next chosen victims. Esther is the female equivalent to the title character in *The Stepfather* films—only now the threat comes from the "stepdaughter" who plots destruction of the family by the eruption of repressed sexual violence. Rather than fulfilling the ideological goal of patriarchal conformity of the earlier *Stepfather* films, *The Orphan's* family monster directly aims to break the incest taboo by engaging in childhood sexuality with the father and take over the sexual role of the mother. *Orphan* deserves better recognition than it has so far received. It is one of the few twenty-first-century horror films having radical subversive qualities without needing Gothic and supernatural devices to hide its dark message.

Troy Nixey's *Don't Be Afraid of the Dark* (2010) is a remake of a 1973 TV movie that is far better in execution despite the depiction of the "little people." Co-produced by Guillermo Del Toro, it features another dysfunctional family. Young Sally (Bailee Madison) has been sent by her divorced mother, who lives in Los Angeles, to stay with her father Alex (Guy Pearce) and girlfriend Kim (Katie Holmes) as they renovate an old Rhode Island mansion, once owned by Emerson Blackwood, which they hope to sell at a huge profit. However, malignant forces in the house prevent Alex's dream of economic real-estate success and the bonding of Sally with Kim. Despite deriving the supernatural elements from writers such as Algernon Blackwood and Arthur Machen, it is clear that the monsters emerge due to Sally's resentment at Kim's taking on the role of substitute mother especially when Sally's own mother has dumped her on his ex-husband and girlfriend oblivious (or perhaps not) of traumatic consequences this may cause. Kim does not wish to be a surrogate mother since she is already recovering from her own problematic family background. She also does not want to rush into parenthood preferring to be Alex's partner in bed and business within an uncommitted relationship. During one scene, when Alex is on the phone arguing with his ex-wife, Sally listens to the conversation, like Regan does to the acrimonious phone call between her mother and father in *The Exorcist*. The supernatural elements distract from the real meaning of the film. During the climactic sequences, Kim performs the noble sacrifice leaving father and daughter once more in harmony. Afterwards, Sally embraces her father for the first time in the film: "I love you, Daddy." Although the final scene has the monsters whispering in Machen overtones, "They will forget us and others will come. We have all the time in the world," it is obvious that they will not have long to wait once another family occupies this particular hearth of darkness. When viewed in the light of the modest premises of the original version, the conservative values of the film become apparent especially as co-producer Del Toro seems to have a morbid fascination with conservative ideology especially in terms of disciplining and punishing single females in his films.

In John Newland's original 1973 version, Sally (Kim Darby) is the wife of Alex Farnham (Jim Hutton), who wants to work his way up the corporate ladder. He sees his wife as an asset in his careerism as she cannily recognizes. "You just married me because I'm the perfect hostess." Sally confides in her friend Joan (Barbara Anderson) about having workaholic husbands who focus on a "job and getting ahead." It is not surprising that monsters soon emerge who wish her to join them—especially when Alex's boss never sees her as a real person. "How's it feel to be the wife of a man with a great future?" Her breakdown during a business-related dinner may be due less to monsters from the closet but more to pressures exerted on her in an era of feminism when alternative models were available, models that she is aware of in this version. The teleplay alludes to this several times suggestively hinting that the monsters are actually redundant features and that Sally is reacting against her ideologically imposed role of "good wife." Nigel McKeand's teleplay contains several insightful observations as to what is the real dilemma in this haunted house. Rather than employing the Algernon Blackwood and Arthur Machen supernatural mystification, in the remake co-written by Del Toro, McKeand emphasizes instead patriarchal conformist pressures operating on Sally. A comparison of these two versions reveals significant differences between seventies' and contemporary horror films. Conservative elements often swamp promising meanings in later films while earlier ones allow for a more balanced interplay between different interpretations. Voices whisper to Sally, "It's your spirit we need." Despite their disturbing appearance, they appear more welcoming to Sally and may offer her the exit from domestic oppression she really needs. At the end of the film, the line "All the time in the world" is repeated but this time it is Sally's voice that speaks the lines unlike the later version where the lines come from one of the little people.

Directed by Andy Muscietti from a screenplay co-written with his sister Barbara and co-produced by Del Toro, *Mama* (2013) begins by promising much before it falls again into the supernatural conservative ideology characteristic of Del Toro. It opens in 2008 at the beginning of the economic crisis with corporate executive Jeffrey (Nicolaj Coster-Waldau) having murdered his business partner and estranged wife, fleeing into the woods with his two young daughters and about to kill them both before a shadowy presence intervenes. Five years later, the two girls are discovered by a search party funded by Jeffrey's twin brother Lucas. They inhabit the same log cabin of the prequel but have developed into feral children. The girls are adopted by illustrator Lucas and his punk rock bass guitarist girlfriend Annabelle (Jessica Chastain), who is by no means excited by her future role of surrogate mother. The film eventually moves towards its conservative ending by reconstituting the nuclear family as a result of the supernatural threat presented by a nineteenth-century mother separated from her child when earlier placed in a mental asylum and now seeking its remains. Visually proficient, the film wears its ideology on its sleeve with Lucas and Annabelle firmly molded into the world of family values at the climax as opposed to the alternative and independent lifestyles they once followed. One of the most repugnant scenes in *Mama* is a discussion Annabelle has with her friend Nina (Julia

Chanty), who is filmed in the most unflattering light since she suggests her friend would be better off single again. Annabelle confesses her reluctance to take on a maternal role since she is recovering from her own unhappy family life. Nina comments, "All families are messed up." Annabelle responds, "I don't have a chance to screw things up. They come like that." Naturally, this revealing comment is never developed in the film by a director who sees his heroine as a thirty-year-old still trapped in the world of adolescence. With Del Toro's preference for the supernatural over the material elements of everyday existence, problems within the family itself get swept away.

Fortunately, exceptions exist to this prevailing conservative tendency, as exhibited in Del Toro's *Pan's Labyrinth* (2006) where supernatural elements prove a distraction from the promising analysis of 1944 family and political fascism in Franco's Spain. Parallels between the historical and the supernatural were better handled in Victor Erice's *The Spirit of the Beehive* (1973). The Frankenstein monster more appropriately appears as a direct metaphorical embodiment of the Spanish Civil War trauma than the supernatural gimmickry of *Pan's Labyrinth*. If remnants of the family horror film remain alive and well in this present era, so does the influence of its reactionary counterpart. Del Toro now occupies the roles Robin Wood once assigned to Ridley Scott and David Cronenberg in the late 1970s—directors of the reactionary wing of horror film. By contrast, *Jake's Closet* is a refreshing response to this tendency.

Co-produced, written and directed by Shelli Ryan, *Jake's Closet* (2007) is one of those very rare exceptions to the current mediocre state of the horror film. It is also an important development of the seventies family horror tradition. Indebted to the work of George A. Romero as the references to *Night of the Living Dead* on the family television and an unseen "Mrs. Romero" in search of her missing cat, the film acknowledges a key past tradition without attempting to copy it or undermine it as the ignominious remake *of Dawn of the Dead* did. *Jake's Closet* works on many levels—the domestic melodrama, family horror, and a fictionalized case history of the traumatic effects of divorce on a young child. The film begins with Jake (Anthony De Marco) experiencing the anger shown by his father Peter (Sean Bridges) and mother Jules (Brooke Bloom) in their early stages of separation. Jake is manipulated by his mother and her friend Ruth (Monette McGrath) to take sides against his father and turn against him. Ruth immediately begins the first stage of a domestic psychological war campaign in which Jake will be the obvious loser. "I'm glad that you called. Us girls have got to stick together with things like that." However, the promising feminist element in this statement becomes undermined when it is revealed that Ruth is under the domination of her patriarchal husband who makes her life a misery. She vents her frustrations on others, especially Jake. In one scene she actually physically abuses him by doing the very thing that Jules accuses her husband of doing to Jake. Ruth's motivations are actually selfish since she sees her role in the family break-down as more of a displaced revenge against her husband than anything to do with sincere concern for her friend. Although the film has been criticized for its supposed anti-feminist attitude, it is important to understand that since Jake mostly lives with his mother, events are experienced from his perspective. However, Ryan does include one scene where Peter asks Jake about his wife's activities duplicating the very manner she manipulates her own son, "What's your Mom up to today?" In such a situation, Jake can only lose. He is a mere pawn in the war between a father and mother who show no concern for his psychological health.

Jake's Closet duplicates the emotional cannibalism within a dysfunctional family relationship paralleling Romero's own treatment of human tensions and dysfunctional operations in his films. It is only natural that Jake envisages a zombie in his closet that embodies on the supernatural level what is affecting his own family in daily life. In one scene, Jules exaggerates a minor incident that occurred between Peter and Jake, turning it into a child abuse allegation that bans him from contact with his own son. As family tensions rise to boiling point, the shadowy presence of the zombie created by Jake's imagination becomes more real. One of his fantasies involves a dinner table sequence where mother is the dish laid out before the zombie, Ruth, and Jules's lover Sam (Ben Bode), whom she has manipulated into a relationship. Eventually, Jake decides to take on the zombie in combat to the consternation of his warring parents who see nothing but a young boy running away from an invisible force. Jules blames Peter for Jake's condition. The zombie disappears and the film ends with Jake in the foreground of the shot with father and mother bitterly arguing and blaming each other for Jake's condition in the background. Jake no longer has any need to create monsters and indulge in the supernatural as a form of denial and escape. The monsters are within his family and he now realizes it. *Jake's Closet* is also a pessimistic counterpart to *Curse of the Cat People*. If the daughter's imaginary playmate embodying the image of her father's doomed first wife can now disappear since family tensions appear resolved, the same is not true for *Jake's Closet* as the final images reveal. Jake has to learn how to survive the warring relationship between two combative parents. In one sense he faces a bleak future but on another level the film ends with him becoming more mature than either parent. He no longer needs a manufactured emotional crutch such as a zombie on whom he can displace elements of denial. Jake sees the reality that is before him and will face his own version of family horror without recourse to the creation of monsters and the supernatural. Shelli's Ryan's first film is a much more mature example of the family horror film than anything that Del Toro and others can create. Supernatural elements are actually redundant and the real battle involves coming to terms with an institution that no longer works and damages everyone caught within its trap.[18]

What Lies Without

The horror film superficially appears to be an easily recognizable genre with scary moments, special effects, and prolific displays of gore, making it an easily recognizable style. However, as the earlier edition of this book mentioned, such features are marginal to the real achievements of the genre that has a distinct relationship to the outside world. It is not surprising that predominant mediocre prolific representations such as the *Scream* series, remakes of more radical 1970s films such as *The Texas Chain Saw Massacre*, *The Hills Have Eyes*, and *The Last House on the Left* emphasize special effects to the detriment of significant meaning—very much like *the Paranormal Activity* series (2009) made with an eye to the box-office economic franchise of the *Harry Potter* films. By their very nature they are all disposable products that say nothing new or relevant. Yet several films have appeared that eschew the supernatural in favor of unconsciously reproducing elements once common to family horror. We live in horrific times so it is not surprising that several different types of films echo our era by bringing what was once horrific into different categories of film.

Stimulated by 9/11, the home invasion horror film operates as a reflection of the increasing insecurity within America. But like the 1950s science fiction films, where the outside invader symbolically represented the Soviet Union, this current cycle of films often encompasses certain aspects of the family horror film tradition. The new invader represents both an internal threat and the embodiment of increasing economic insecurity affecting the American Dream, an insecurity stimulated by the economic meltdown of 2008 and still continuing today. It is not surprising that the supposedly secure home with its modern devices turns into a new hearth of darkness resembling the old Gothic house of the traditional horror film. In David Fincher's *Panic Room* (2002), filmed a year after 9/11, divorced mother Meg Altman (Jodie Foster) rents an affluent and spacious Manhattan apartment complete with "panic room," only to find herself under siege by outside forces representing dispossessed elements of society: an African-American (Forrest Whittaker), Hispanic (Jared Leto), and working-class redneck (Dwight Yoakum). Angered by the betrayal of her ex-husband, who has left her for a younger female, leaving her to care for her young daughter, Meg finds her supposedly secure spacious interior turned into a modern Gothic hearth of darkness at night, a realm reflecting both her anger at abandonment and a prey to the economic losers of American society that she and her class obviously feel insecurity concerning their very existence. The European Gothic overtones of the dark castle of Horace Walpole and Mrs. Radcliffe (and the dark house within the American Gothic equivalent) now becomes a spacious Manhattan apartment whose high-tech security room offers little protection against the modern version of outside forces. *Panic Room* also operates as a contemporary version of John Ford's *Drums Along the Mohawk* (1939), which contained earlier examples of home invasion where savage Indians invaded the 1776 hearth personified by Claudette Colbert's dutiful wife.

Panic Room at least supplies some motivation for the attack. Other films do not. They represent the assault as a product of random violence that has no rational explanation in today's contemporary American society. When facing their victimizers at the end of Bryan Bertino's *The Strangers* (2008), the young couple who have broken off their engagement at the beginning of the film ask their young assailants "Why us? Why do you want to kill us?" They receive just the enigmatic reply, "Because you're home." When the three assailants later encounter two Christian boys, one takes a religious tract from them. When asked, "Are you a sinner?" she replies "Sometimes." As they drive away, one of the group states, "It'll be easier next time." The circle of violence will continue. Inspired by the Manson Killings, *The Strangers* is an effective, understated horror film with its three assailants matching its three victims inside a house built in the 1970s revealing an American tradition of violence that is random and without any coherent explanation. Since the three victimized youngsters appear to come from an upwardly mobile social group and their assailants are young, working-class kids who seem unable to displace their rage except in random acts of violence, it again appears that economic resentment may be one cause of the assault. The deadly trio also represents repressed and unresolved tensions affecting the couple inside the house, who appear insecure about the marital institution. Michael Haneke's *Funny Games* (1997), remade by the director in an almost shot-for-shot American version in 2007, has been cited as another inspiration for *The Strangers*. Like the European version, the reasons for the intrusion into the Long Island holiday home of the couple appears unmotivated, yet unlike the original version, the affluent lifestyle and deep resentment existing in the family relationship is another possible reason for a home invasion that fits into a common generic pattern within American cinema.

Todd Field's *In the Bedroom* (2002) appears to be a well-made family tragedy and was acclaimed as such on its first theatrical release, earning many awards. Yet a closer look at its content reveals it to be a "realistic" version of Wes Craven's *Last House on the Left* (1972), without the grotesque and violent elements. Lacking the Stillos, *In the Bedroom* presents a supposedly normal family who suffer from the intrusion of an arbitrary intrusion of violence into their daily life. The only son, Frank (Nick Stahl), of a Camden, Maine, town doctor, Matt Fowler (Tom Wilkerson), and his wife, schoolteacher Ruth (Sissy Spacek), dies after estranged husband Richard Strout (William Mapother) breaks into the home of his wife Natalie (Marisa Tomei), with whom Frank is having an affair. The muted style of this film should not deceive viewers that strong tensions exist beneath the surface—as strong as those that lead the Collingwoods to take a bloody revenge on the Stillos for the rape and murder of their daughter in the original version of *Last House on the Left*. Frank was an only child. Ruth dominated him while Matt, as she saw it, was too gentle. After allowing their deeply repressed family tensions to erupt (tensions that also have their origins in the fact that economic circumstances could only allow them to have one child when Matt started his practice), they realize that Strout's affluent family connections, combined with the fact that the death was not witnessed, may result in a reduced sentence of manslaughter. Ruth's vicious slap to an apologetic Natalie also indicates repressed violence within the personality of this seemingly gentle woman who unjustifiably blames an unfortunate victim of this family tragedy. The passive-aggressive attitude that she has nurtured throughout her family life now becomes explicit. She also lies to her husband by saying that Richard smiled at her in a local store when he clearly did not. Like John Collingwood, Matt takes the law into his own hands by kidnapping and murdering Richard and later burying the body in the manner of a Mafia hit. When he returns home fatigued, Ruth asks him, "Did you do it?" Although she did not participate in the murder like Mrs. Collingwood in *Last House on the Left*, Ruth is clearly an accessory thus making her husband little better than the Richard Strout they have chosen to demonize. The film ends with the couple silent, repressing the implications of their joint activity in the same way that they buried their family tensions within the domain of acceptable family behavior for so many years. *In the Bedroom* is a more appropriate remake of *The Last House on the Left* than the 2009 version.

Before the Devil Knows You're Dead (2007) opens with a stylistically bleak scene and maintains a *mise-en-scène* evoking sterility throughout. Whether a corporate office, dehumanized shopping mall, palatial Manhattan drug-dealer apartment, or a home whose interior parallels the unfulfilling lives of a married couple without any satisfaction in their relationship, the film depicts the twenty-first century as a human wasteland. Although having little, if any, formal connection to the familiar style of the family horror film, like *In the Bedroom*, *Before the Devil Knows You're Dead* is indissolubly connected to this genre in all but name. Many critics have noted the family relationships as responsible for an implosion of violence, beginning with the fatal shooting of the mother in her jewelry store and continuing with the father's medical execution of his errant son whose development he bears responsibility for, as he admits following the funeral of his wife. Sidney Lumet's film is difficult and unpleasant to watch but those qualities derive from the fact that all family relationships in this film are perverted, spiritually bankrupt, and based on betrayal. Andy Hanson (Philip Seymour Hoffmann) betrays both his firm and family by planning to rob them both. Unknown to him, his wife Gina (Marisa Tomei) is having an affair with his weaker brother Hank (Ethan Hawke) whom he has drawn into his robbery scheme. Hank is divorced from his wife Martha and the only bond keeping them together is economic involving the alimony he is behind in paying. Martha exhibits muted feelings of antagonism towards her ex-husband, whom she clearly sees as nothing more than an economic convenience that she must tolerate. His daughter may be "Daddy's little girl" but when he cannot finance one of her school trips, he becomes a "loser" in her eyes. The brother of the assassin Hank has employed to do the robbery uses the plight of his sister-in-law to blackmail Hank. Lumet strongly implies that the expectations Charles Hanson (Albert Finney) had of Andy has turned him into a criminal. He cannot accept this and engages in murder at the end of the film to relieve frustrations and guilt feelings over his failure as a parent. This explains the deliberately grotesque facial expressions employed by Finney, who resembles a modern version of Colin Clive's scientist from *Frankenstein* (1931). One monster has created others: a corporate monster seduced by the American dream of financial success who becomes a criminal and the "baby" of the family who grows up into being an irresponsible adult. The whole world of *Before the Devil Knows You're Dead* is a twenty-first century nightmare version of T. S. Eliot's *The Wasteland*. It is a film that needs no monster since the characters and setting more than compensate for that convenient displacement figure in the traditional horror film. Capitalism and the family are clearly indicted in this film and its associated violence emerges from human beings, not horror film monsters. If *In the Bedroom* has several parallels to the original version *of Last House on the Left*, then *Before the Devil Knows You're Dead* functions as a realistic dramatic version *of It's Alive*, the one exception being that it is the father who kills the monstrous son whose very existence he is responsible for.

It may appear bizarre to conclude this postscript by mentioning a television series that, on the surface, appears to have little to do with the family horror film. But, on closer analysis, *The Sopranos* (1999–2006) is a series that has several indirect connections with the genre. It also reveals that elements common to the original family horror formation now infiltrate several other generic productions areas. Justifiably praised as one of the great television classics of our current era, as well as revealing that certain types of television are now much better than anything that Hollywood can produce, *The Sopranos* is a series that operates on many levels both stylistically and thematically blurring boundaries in several ways. The series does not engage in separating the domestic level from the world outside in the manner of Mike Lagana (Alexander Scourby) in *The Big Heat* (1953) who wishes to draw clear distinctions between his violent activities outside the home from the supposedly tranquil family life he has within. Instead, it shows how both are intrinsically connected. Capitalism corrupts on all levels, and it is no accident that advertising logos for the series stress Tony Soprano's involvement with two families, his own and his criminal organization. It has always been a characteristic of the gangster film to show connections between law enforcement and the Mob, as various examples such as *Underworld U.S.A.* (1960) and *Le Samourai* (1967) reveal. But no other series since *The Godfather* films has emphasized connections between the Mob and the family in such a manner that has close connections to family horror.

Tony Soprano (James Gandolfini) suffers from panic attacks, as does his son A. J. (Robert Iler). He begins therapy with Dr. Melfi (Lorraine Bracco) in an attempt to resolve his psychological problems, which are rooted in his own past relationship with his mobster father and mother. His widowed mother Livia (Nancy Marchand), whose name evokes the monstrous matriarch of Robert Graves's *I Claudius*, constantly attempts to undermine both himself and other members of the family whenever possible. Like *The Godfather's* Michael Corleone (Al Pacino), Tony cannot escape the demands of a controlling family whose existence is deeply rooted in violence. It is no accident that one flashback showing how the father puts meat on the table is shot in graphic colors reminiscent of a horror film. Neither are the very film noir stylistic features of the series accidental, especially since previous television series were characterized by high-contrast, brightly lit scenes. Developed by David Chase, who was very familiar with gangster films such as *Public Enemy* and noir-influenced television series such as *The Untouchables* (1959–63), *The Sopranos'* associations with film noir not only reveal a familiarity with the gangster film/television tradition but also intuitive connections between noir and horror, as in the Val Lewton films of the 1940s. Tony Soprano is a victim of his own family system that has made him a successful victimizer in the Mob world of New Jersey. His own family is dysfunctional on many levels. Carmela (Edie Falco) usually turns a blind eye to the source of her material wealth, while the children struggle with their own forms of identity crisis in one way or another. In the opening season, Tony's Uncle Junior (Dominic Chianese) and his mother actually conspire to murder him. After her death, sister Janice (Aida Turturro) attempts to force family members into delivering false tributes to her memory only to see her denial attempts collapse ignominiously.

Although Christopher Moltisanti (Michael Imperioli) may initially appear to be the heir apparent, like Vincent Mancini (Andy Garcia) in *Godfather III* (1990), this proves not to be the case. Christopher's yearnings for a normal family life lead him to betray his girlfriend who is also betraying him under pressure from a callous FBI who exhibit as little concern for their victims as the Mob does for those they brutalize and murder. His psychological deterioration and ultimate dependence on drugs may be as much due to his embrace of Soprano family values than anything else. During one episode, Christopher sees his former drug-addict friend out with his own family. Wishing to have a family of his own and realizing that his girlfriend Adrienne (Drea de Matteo) is infertile, this motivates him to become complicit in her execution as an FBI informant. It is one of the most chilling sequences in the entire series, as it again associates family life with violence. Several times in the series, Christopher disposes of bodies by using methods associated with the deranged family members of *The Texas Chain Saw Massacre* franchise films and those in the *Saw* series. It is not accidental that Christopher will later write and produce a gangster horror film *Cleaver*, financed by Mob money that represents a graphic return-of-the repressed elements from his own personal life. Ironically, the film attempts to be a money-making venture combining elements of *Saw* with the classic mobster film. *The Sopranos* has no real need to employ the supernatural elements of the traditional family horror film since it already indelibly belongs to that genre. Therapy sessions between Tony and Dr. Melfi emphasize the psychoanalytic roots also operating within family horror films. Blurring of boundaries between fantasy and reality throughout the series reveal features easily recognizable to those familiar with the genre. During Tony's last dream before he is about to recover from Junior's attempt on his life, he sees a figure entering a mansion. Seen only from the back and briefly, she resembles Mrs. Bates in *Psycho* leaving the scene of her crime during the famous shower sequence. Tony's near-death fantasy not only resembles his Catholic sense of limbo and purgatory but also his version of the Overlook Hotel from *The Shining* (1980).

References to 9/11, the wars in Iraq and Afghanistan, Dick Cheney's own accidental shooting of an associate on a hunting trip, and terrorism are not accidental. They also reveal connections between the series' internal and exterior worlds, which no longer need the familiar monsters from the traditional horror film. The monsters are now outside and inside us, especially within the family. That is the real genius of *The Sopranos*, another important chapter in the family horror saga that appears to have no end result in view unless it leads to the destruction of the human species. Thus, the final controversial scene does not show the death of Tony in the classic Robert Warshow "rise and fall of the gangster as tragic hero" thesis but the "death" of viewers who may have identified with this monster and face recognizing repressed affinities to a Father who certainly does not know Best but faces the darkness of oblivion in the final image concluding the series.[19]

The Sopranos is textually rich and may be viewed on many levels. Yet its affinity with the horror film is certainly not accidental. Before moving on to television series, Chase began his career by writing the screenplay for *Grave of the Vampire* (1972), a film mentioned in the first edition of this book that was based on his own novel *The Still Life*. Its central character James Eastman (William Smith) endures a grotesque deterministic existence as the result of being born the son of a vampire and the child of a mother who literally gives her own blood to keep him alive. Although Chase later became involved with the 1974–75 TV series *Kolchak: The Night Stalker*, he never directly approached the world of horror again until his creation of *The Sopranos* (originally known as *Family Man*), which approaches that generic realm in a subliminal manner and utilizes the world of psychoanalysis in Tony's sessions with Dr. Melfi. The panic attacks he suffers from seem to have no rational cause until he remembers a traumatic family episode when he was an eleven-year-old in the third episode of season three, "Fortunate Son" (2001). As Tony looks at the capicola he devours from his late mother's refrigerator, the image dissolves to the exterior of the Satriale butcher's shop, now taken over by the Mob. However, past and present are linked by the fact that a pig's head still remains dominating the front. In *Motel Hell* (1980), deranged patriarch Vincent (Rory Calhoun) runs a motel with his sister Ida (who resembles an early version of Aida Turturro's Janice Soprano). They plant body parts of their dismembered guests in a human garden. Towards the end of the film, Vincent engages in a chainsaw duel while wearing the head of a pig. Although told by his father Johnny Boy to wait in the car, young Tony sees Satriale beaten up by his father and Uncle Junior before his finger is cut off. At home Johnny Boy praises his son for watching the attack and not "running like a little girl." He tells him, "That's my livelihood—to put food on the table." Livia calls them to the table.

She sticks her finger in the meat's red juice and touches her husband's tongue. As he sings "All of Me" with the knowing line "Why not take all of me?" he seductively dances with his wife, grasping her rump while uttering suggestive lines such as "You like it with the bone standing in it" and "The lady likes her meat." During the first episode of the series, Tony walks into the kitchen bare-chested and slaps Carmela's rear in the presence of his children and Meadow's friend Hunter. Seen also by young Janice at the table, Livia interrupts Tony Sr.'s "invitation to the dance" and young Tony suffers the first of the panic attacks that will increase later in life. After the end of this flashback, Dr. Melfi draws the obvious conclusion. "Someday you'd be allowed to bring home the bacon like your father." In the pilot, Tony first collapses over a barbecue cel-ebrating his son's thirteenth birthday. Sexuality, meat, and violence are clearly associated throughout the series.

The flashback scene represents Tony's version of Freud's Primal Scene. Rather than secretly spying on father and mother having sex, he openly witnesses a suggestive dance combining sexuality with ritually celebrated violence near the dinner table after becoming fascinated by voyeuristically watching an act of brutal violence perpetuated by his father earlier that day. The Soprano family life is one of sexuality, violence, and capitalist values. As Maurice Yacowar notes, Livia's only good mood occurs on "the day of the meat delivery. Tony has since associated raw meat with violence, blood, his first intimations of sexuality, and his responsibility to 'bring home the bacon.'"[20] All this occurs within the family, and it is more than coincidental that *The Sopranos* contains numerous scenes of meals and food preparation. They often occur either with Tony and his own family or in association with his other Mob family. In many cases, they involve both families. Prior to Tony's flashback sequence, he is seen at one of his home barbecues with Christopher and Ralph (Joe Pantoliano). Ralph's body will later undergo the same type of dismemberment that Christopher employed on Richie (David Proval). That earlier action involved the aid of a chainsaw evoking the title of a well-known horror film. The lighting of this latter incident in "The Knight in White Satin," episode twelve of the second season (2000), contains unmistakable parallels to the horror genre.

As Mikita Brottman points out, the oral stage in childhood is particularly marked. "Psychologists have drawn attention to a fusion of complexes at this stage of childhood: the cutting of the child's teeth, the realization that teeth can inflict pain, and the (male) child's unconscious fear of castration. This infantile phase is never entirely forgotten, and sometimes is carried through into adult life. Indeed, many people have described the incorporation of the lover in penetrative sexual intercourse as a kind of symbolic and ritualized cannibalism."[21] Tony Soprano fulfills his voracious sexual appetite with many affairs with mistresses that parallel his huge appetite for food. Oral gratification exists on all levels. Although the residences in the film appear to bear little similarity to those terrible houses of *The Texas Chain Saw Massacre*, *The Hills have Eyes*, and *The People under the Stairs*, telling associations do exist.[22] Despite wanting to keep family and business matters apart, Tony frequently discusses "this thing of ours" with associates inside and outside his palatial mansion. By the time the series begins, Satriale is no longer around but his name and the pig's head dominate the gang's frequent meeting place similar to the Bada Bing Club, characterized by the "meat market" of the pole dancers and occasional acts of violence. We must not forget the blow jobs that the dancers at the Bada Bing always perform for clients and guests. Yet such practices are taboo for the male, as seen in episode nine from season one, "Boca," which marks the gangster as non-masculine and too close to the realm of the feminine, a stigma that can only result in violent reaction.

In the pilot, written and directed by Chase, Christopher's first kill occurs in an area where pig heads appear behind his left shoulder. In season one, episode eight, "Legend of Tennessee Moltisanti," Christopher gratuitously shoots the foot of a young bakery clerk for a supposed slight, in homage to a scene in *GoodFellas* (1990) where young Michael Imperioli incurred the undeserved displeasure of Joe Pesci in a restaurant. This evokes a particular type of Freudian repetition-compulsion both for Christopher, who may have been familiar with this scene, as well as audiences who also have knowledge of this intertextual reference to a Scorsese film. Although Christopher may appear to be, at times, Tony's natural successor, as Andy Garcia is for Al Pacino in the third *Godfather* film, he has also self-destructive features of Scorsese's Pesci character, whose loose-cannon behavioral traits mark him as dangerous to the Mob. This also explains Tony's murder of Christopher in the final season. All these characters exhibit repetition-compulsive behavioral disorders linked both to the family and its associated world of violence. Both are indelibly connected. These visual references in *The Sopranos* are subtly made and necessitate a high degree of observation and detection. They all suggestively contain subliminal links between family life, regressive violence, perverted sexuality, and murder.[23] Family horror film motifs have certainly moved into other generic areas as well as other fields of cinema, as Christopher Sharrett has demonstrated.

As the twenty-first century develops, the significant features that once dominated the family horror films of the 1970s and '80s now move into new areas, as *The Sopranos* shows. This does not mean the end of the genre itself but infiltration of its ideas into other genres and areas of human thought that will continue to raise important issues that need resolution. The way is always open to a solution that will lead us from the dead hand of the past, especially an institution that has caused harm for the most part and always will until more progressive directions are followed.

Notes

Introduction to New Edition

1. For an interesting comparison of the differences between the two versions of *Dawn of the Dead*, see David Roche, "'That's Real! That's What You Want!' Producing Fear in George A. Romero's *Dawn of the Dead* (1978) vs. Zack Snyder's remake (2004)," *Horror Studies* 2, no. 1 (2011): 75–87. Differences between the earlier 1970s versions of horror films and their later remakes is a subject Roche further explores in his book *Making and Remaking Horror in the 1970s and 2000s: Why Don't They Do It Like They Used To*, published by the University Press of Mississippi. It is an exemplary and rigorous study that puts to shame the academics who now deny this important tradition, choosing to hide within the corporate institutional world of academia and devoting their energies to postmodernism and Deleuze and Guattari's theories.

2. See Jason Middleton, "The Subject of Torture: Regarding the Pain of Americans in *Hostel*," *Cinema Journal* 49, no. 4 (2010): 1–24 for a weak attempt to argue for the supposed social relevancy of these films while ignoring the gratuitous self-indulgence of its director, an associate of Quentin Tarantino, one of the most appalling directors of this era. Similar problems affect Gregory A. Burris, "*Hostel* and the Spectacle of Self-Mutilation," *cineACTION* 80 (2010): 2–12, especially the vain hope expressed in the past page that Roth's work "might perhaps evolve in more progressive directions." (!) For a more intelligent and well-balanced argument concerning the real significance of these films see Christopher Sharrett, "The Problem of *Saw*: Torture Porn and the Conservatism of Contemporary Horror Films," *Cineaste* 35.1 (2009): 32–37.

3. For a very relevant obituary, see Christopher Sharrett, "For Robin Wood 1931–2009," *Cinema Journal* 50, no. 1 (2010): 121–25.

4. See Reynold Humphries, "The Semiotics of Horror: The Case of *Dracula's Daughter*," *Interdisciplinary Journal for German Linguistics and Semiotric Analysis*," 5, no. 2 (2000): 273–89; "On the Road Again: Rehearsing the Death Drive in Modern Realist Horror Cinema," *Postscript* 21, no. 3 (2002): 64–80; *The American Horror Film* (Edinburgh: Edinburgh University Press, 2002); *The Hollywood Horror Film 1931–1941: Madness in a Social Landscape* (Lanham, M.D.: Scarecrow Press, 2006); David Greven, *Representations of Femininity in American Genre Cinema: The Woman's Film, Film Noir and Modern Horror* (London: Palgrave MacMillan, 2011); *Psycho Sexual: Male Desire in Hitchcock, De Palma, Scorsese and*

Friedkin (Austin: University of Texas Press, 2012); Matt Wray and Annalee Newitz, *Pretend We're Dead: Capitalist Monsters in American Culture* (New York: Routledge, 1996); Linnie Blake, *The Wounds of Nations: Horror Cinema, National Identity, and Historical Trauma* (Manchester: Manchester University Press, 2008); and Brad Stevens, *Abel Ferrera: the Moral Vision* (Surrey, England: FAB Press, 2004).

5. For a partial translation in English, see Laurence G. Thompson, *Ta T'ung Shu: The One World Philosophy of K'ang You-wei* (London: George Allen and Unwin, Ltd., 1958). The figure of Kang and his philosophy is the subject of two essay documentaries by Evans Chan, *Datong: The Great Society* (2011) and *Two or Three Things about Kang Youwei* (2013). For further information, see the section on *Datong* in www.evanschan.com and Tony Williams, "Two or Three Things about Mao, Godard, and Kang Youwei," *Asian Cinema* 24, no. 1 (2013): 87–104.

6. Thompson, 38–39, 252. For a useful chart showing Kang's idea of Three Ages in the Development of Human Evolution, see Thompson, 105–28.

7. Ibid., 181.

8. Ibid., 186. Note also that Kang envisaged a free daily medical check-up for everyone in a world where hospitals would be empty except for those suffering from terminal old-age and having the opportunity of being "mercifully put out of their agony." See Ibid., 274.

9. Ibid., 51. In the section on the abolition of administrative boundaries, Kang emphasizes that everyone will be equal in the New Age and that all leaders and reverence of them, whether religious or secular, should be abolished, otherwise leading to an Age of Disorder and the return of force, the curbing of human rights, and the dissemination of ignorance. See Ibid., 255–57.

10. Ibid., 253.

Chapter 1. Introduction: Family Assault in the American Horror Film

1. Several works attempt a general overview to the horror film such as S. S. Prawer, *Caligari's Children: The Film as Tale of Terror* (Oxford: Oxford University Press, 1980); James B. Twitchell, *Dreadful Pleasures: An Anatomy of Modern Horror* (New York: Oxford University Press, 1985); Kim Newman, *Nightmare Movies* (New York: Harmony Books, 1989), and Noel Carroll, *The Philosophy of Horror: Paradoxes of the Heart* (New York: Routledge, 1990). Christopher Sharrett's comments on Prawer's work apply to most of them. "The pitfalls and digressions of this new book may themselves be areas for future investigations, and Prawer has certainly offered enough new perspectives *to clear the way for monographs rather than survey studies" (italics mine)*. "S. S. Prawer's *Caligari's Children*," *Film Quarterly* 33, no. 4 (1980): 39. Despite his recent cognitive approach, Noel Carroll's earlier essay on horror still remains more suggestive. See "Nightmare and the Horror Film: The Symbolic Biology of Fantastic Beings," *Film Quarterly* 36, no. 3 (1981): 51-81. For a good criticism of Carroll's recent totalizing approach, see Joan Morrison, "The Philosophy of Horror," *Film Criticism* 15, no. 3 (1991): 41–43. Harvey R. Greenberg presents a more appropriate perspective toward approaching the horror genre. "The best cruel cinema asserts a

formidable nihilistic view of the rampant greed and narcissism of the disintegrating capitalist ethos defying Prawer's easy moralizing." See "Germinal Dread," *Quarterly Review of Film Studies* 7, no. 2 (1982): 195. The relationship of contemporary horror films to social and political events occurs in various works such as Robin Wood, *Hollywood: From Vietnam to Reagan* (New York: Columbia University Press, 1986); Gregory Waller, "Introduction," in *American Horrors: Essays on the Modern American Horror Film*, ed. Gregory Waller (Urbana: University of Illinois Press, 1987), 12; Charles Derry, "More Dark Dreams: Some Notes on the Recent Horror Film," *American Horrors*, 163–74; Vivian Sobchack, "Bringing It All Back Home: Family Economy and Generic Exchange," *American Horrors*, 172–94; Kathy Merlock Jackson, *Images of Children in American Film: A Sociocultural Analysis* (Metuchen, N.J.: Scarecrow Press, 1986), 126–74; and Michael Ryan and Douglas Kellner, *Camera Politica: The Politics and Ideology of Contemporary Hollywood Film* (Bloomington: Indiana University Press, 1988), 168–93.

2. William Paul significantly makes these points in *Laughing Screaming: Modern Hollywood Horror and Comedy* (New York: Columbia University Press, 1994), 78, 445, n.2.

3. Michael Lerner, *Surplus Powerlessness* (Oakland, Calif: The Institute of Labor and Mental Health, 1986), 321.

4. For one such example stressing family influences Freud neglected, in one major case history, see Morton Schatzman, Soul Murder: Persecution in the *Family* (London: Penguin, 1976). Despite their differences from Freud's findings, the following works actually supplement traditional analysis by emphasizing the role of the family in causing trauma. See particularly Jeffrey Moussaieff Masson, *The Assault on Truth: Freud's Suppression of the Seduction Theory* (New York: Farrar, Straus and Giroux, 1984); *Against Therapy: Emotional Tyranny and the Myth of Psychological Healing* (New York: Atheneum, 1988); Alice Miller, *Banished Knowledge: Facing Childhood Injuries*, trans. Leila Vennewitz (New York: Doubleday, 1990), 37–81; *The Untouched Key: Tracing Childhood Trauma in Creativity and Destructiveness* (New York: Doubleday, 1990). For some insights into the Masson controversy, see Janet Malcolm, *In the Freud Archives* (New York: Alfred A. Knopf, 1984). Other relevant texts necessary to complement and complete Freud's work in revealing the role of abusive families as material factors in causing trauma are Robert Fliess, *Symbol, Dream and Psychosis* (New York: International Universities Press, 1973); *Child Abuse and Neglect: The Family and the Community*, ed. Ray E. Helfer and Ruth S. Kempe (Chicago: The University of Chicago Press, 1987); and Michael S. Roth, *Psychoanalysis as History: Negation and Freedom in Freud* (Ithaca: Cornell University Press, 1987). Many contemporary horror authors understand the family as an American nightmare cyclically generating patterns of violence. See especially Michael McDowell in *Faces of Fear: Encounters with the Creators of Modern Horror* (New York: Berkeley Books, 1985), 181.

5. In addition to *Rebecca, Suspicion, Shadow of a Doubt, Strangers on a Train*, and *Psycho* as revealing Hitchcock's understanding of kinship systems generating intense emotional conflict, Thomas Schatz also states that Norman Bates's chaos world is not too far removed from the family melodrama. He argues that *The Birds* "makes no sense whatever unless read as an Oedipal melodrama." See *Old Hollywood/New Hollywood: Ritual, Art and Ideology* (Ann Arbor, Mich.: UMI Research Press, 1983), 267.

6. Noted by Andrew Britton, *Katherine Hepburn: The Thirties and After* (Newcastle-upon-Tyne, England: Tyneside Cinema Publications, 1984), 32. He follows the arguments of Michel Schneider, *Neurosis and Civilization: A Marxist Freudian Synthesis* (New York: Seabury Press, 1975). Other arguments stressing relevant social factors influencing repression are as follows: Gad Horowitz, *Repression* (Toronto: University of Toronto Press, 1977); Herbert Marcuse, *Eros and Civilization* (Boston: Beacon Press, 1966); Wilhelm Reich, *The Mass Psychology of Fascism* (New York: Farrar, Straus & Giroux, 1970): 34–40; R. D. Laing, *The Divided Self* (London: Pelican 1965); *The Politics of Experience and the Bird of Paradise* (London: Pelican, 1967); *Self and Other* (London: Pelican, 1971); R. D. Laing and Aaron Esterson, *Sanity, Madness and the Family* (London: Pelican, 1970); and David Cooper, *The Death of the Family* (London: Penguin, 1971).

7. Wood, *Hollywood*, 78. Rosemary Jackson also suggests oppositional readings in her analysis of fantasy literature. See *Fantasy: The Literature of Subversion* (London: Methuen, 1981), 3. For an analysis of Jackson's arguments and an alternative argument concerning horror texts taking conservative directions, see Terry Lovell, *Consuming Fiction* (London: Verso, 1987), 61–64. Similar criticisms appear in Barbara Klinger, "Cinema/ Ideology/Criticism Revisited: the Progressive Text," *Screen* 25, no. 1 (1984): 30–44; and Dana Polan, "Eros and Syphilization: The Contemporary Horror Film," in *Planks of Reason: Essays on the Horror Film*, ed. Barry K. Grant (Metuchen, N.J.: Scarecrow Press, 1984), 210.

8. Christine Gledhill, "Horror," in Pam Cook, ed. *The Cinema Book* (London: British Film Institute, 1985), 104.

9. The concept of hegemony emerges from the work of Antonio Gramsci. See *Selections from the Prison Notebooks*, trans. and ed. Quintin Hoare and Geoffrey Nowell-Smith (New York: International Publishers, 1971), especially 321–472; and *Selections from Cultural Writings*, eds. David Forgacs and Geoffrey Nowell-Smith, trans. William Boelhower (London: Lawrence & Wishart, 1985).

10. For various insights into melodrama, see Griselda Pollack et al., "Dossier on Melodrama"; Geoffrey Nowell Smith, "Minelli and Melodrama," *Screen* 18, no. 2 (1977): 105–18; Laura Mulvey, "Notes on Sirk and Melodrama," *Movie* 25 (1977/78): 53–56; Michael Walker, "Melodrama and the American Cinema," *Movie* 29-30 (1982): 2-38; Robert Lang, *American Film Melodrama: Griffith, Vidor, Minnelli* (Princeton: Princeton University Press, 1989); Jackie Byars, *All That Hollywood Allows: Re-Reading Gender in 1950s Cinema* (Chapel Hill: University of North Carolina Press, 1991).

11. Andrew Tudor, *Monsters and Mad Scientists: A Cultural History of The Horror Movie* (Oxford: Basil Blackwell, 1989), 75.

12. Ibid., 128

13. Tony Williams, "Wes Craven: An Interview," *Journal of Popular Film & TV* 8, no. 3 (Fall 1980): 10–14; Wood, *Hollywood*, 125–29.

14. Christian Metz, "The Imaginary Signifier," *Screen* 16, no. 2 (1975): 18; Steve Neale, *Genre* (London: British Film Institute, 1980).

15. Neale, *Genre*, 21. For other examples of formal approaches, see Edward Lowry, "Genre and Enunciation: The Case of Horror," *Journal of Film and Video* 36, no. 2 (1984):

13–20; and Roger Dadoun, "Fetishism in the Horror Film," *Fantasy and the Cinema*, ed. James Donald (London: BFI Publishing, 1989), 39–62.

16. Laura Mulvey, "Some Thoughts on Theories of Fetishism in the Context of Contemporary Culture," *October* 65 (1993): 3–20.

17. Neale, *Genre*, 43–44. For an excellent analysis of the reactionary nature of David Lynch's films such *as Wild at Heart*, see Sharon Willis, "Special Effects: Sexual and Social Difference in *Wild At Heart*," *Camera Obscura* 25–26 (1991): 275–95. As well as instituting a traumatic look for the spectator, suggestively leading toward a more socially related identification, Tim Hunter's *River's Edge* combines devastating critiques of the family and a Reaganite-alienated youth culture. Note the mother's response to her children, "I'm nobody's mother. You're all mistakes anyway." See Vicky Lebeau, "'You're My Friend': *River's Edge* and Social Spectatorship," *Camera Obscura* 25–26 (1991): 251–72.

18. For examples of this school, see Wolfgang Iser, *The Act of Reading: A Theory of Aesthetic Response* (Baltimore, M.D.: Johns Hopkins University Press, 1978); Hans Robert Jauss, *Toward an Aesthetics of Response* (Minneapolis: University of Minnesota Press, 1982). A good introduction appears in Robert C. Holab, *Reception Theory: A Critical Introduction* (London: Methuen, 1984).

19. Neale, *Genre*, 45.

20. Pete Boss, "Vile Bodies and Bad Medicine," *Screen* 27, no. 1 (1986): 18.

21. Neale, *Genre*, 60–61. For an early argument of the horror film's ritual function as modern puberty rite, see Walter Evans, "Monster Movies and Rites of Initiation," *Journal of Popular Film* 4 (1975): 124–42.

22. Neale, *Genre*, 61. See also Christian Metz, *The Imaginary Signifier: Psychoanalysis and the Cinema* (Bloomington: Indigna University Press, 1982), 18. This reference also occurs in an extremely interesting article by Edward Baron Turk on 1930s Hollywood film musicals. It suggests the presence of similar psychological mechanisms existing in a wide number of diverse genres. See "Deriding the Voice of Jeanette MacDonald: Notes on Psychoanalysis and The American Film Musical," *Camera Obscura* 25–26 (1991): 225–51.

23. Linda Williams, "When the Woman Looks," in *Re-Vision: Essays in Feminist Film Criticism*, eds. Mary Ann Doane, Patricia Mellencamp, and Linda Williams (Frederick, M.D.: University Publications of America, AFI, 1984), 83–97.

24. Jacqueline Rose, "Paranoia and the Film System," *Screen* 17, no. 4 (1976–1977): 88–104.

25. Ibid., 97.

26. Barbara Creed, "Horror and the Monstrous Feminine: An Imaginary Abjection," *Screen* 27, no. 1 (1986): 44–70; Julia Kristeva, *Powers of Horror: An Essay on Abjection* (New York: Columbia University Press, 1982).

27. Creed, "Horror and the Monstrous Feminine," 45.

28. Neale, *Genre*, 45.

29. Raymond Williams, *Marxism and Literature*, quoted by Richard Slotkin, *The Fatal Environment: The Myth of The Frontier in the Age of Industrialization, 1800–1890* (New York: Atheneum, 1985), 21.

30. Robin Wood, "Ideology, Genre, Auteur," *Hitchcock's Films Revisited* (New York: Columbia University Press, 1989), 292. The material originally appeared in *Film Comment* 13, no. 1 (1977): 46–51.

31. Robin Wood, "Images of Childhood," *Personal Views: Explorations in Film* (London: Gordon Fraser, 1976), 163. For another study of children in the horror genre, see Sabine Bussing, *Aliens in the Home: The Child in Horror Fiction* (New York: Greenwood Press, 1987).

32. John G. Cawelti, *The Six-Gun Mystique* (Bowling Green, Ohio: The Popular Press. 1971), 82. Wes Craven aptly describes horror films as forming a "boot camp for the psyche." See Don Gire, "Bye Bye Freddy: Elm Street creator Wes Craven quits series," *Cinefantastique* 18, no. 5 (1988): 10.

33. See Janet Bergstrom, "Alternation, Segmentation, Hypnosis: Interview with Raymond Bellour," *Camera Obscura* 3/4 (1979): 88. However, as critics such as Robin Wood and Marion Keane note, Bellour's readings are often too rigid and do not discern important details within the relevant textual content. The same problem applies in any rigid application. See David Bordwell, "Happily Ever After: Part 2," *Velvet Light Trap* 19 (1982): 2–7. His application of the happy ending thesis to the conclusion of Anthony Mann's *Winchester 73* does not do justice to the complexities of James Stewart's performance. The actor's facial expression clearly denotes the film's complex conclusion. It is no happy ending.

34. Laura Mulvey, "Afterthoughts on 'Visual Pleasure and Narrative Cinema' Inspired by *Duel in the Sun*," *Framework* 15/16/17 (1981): 12–15. For different reactions to Mulvey's arguments, see the individual responses in "The Spectatrix" issue of *Camera Obscura* 20–21 (1989): 82–336.

35. Neale, *Genre*, 58–59. See also "Masculinity as Spectacle," *Screen* 24, no. 6 (1983): 2–11; "Sexual Difference in Cinema," *Oxford Literary Review* 8, nos. 1–2 (1986): 123–32; and Paul Willeman, "Anthony Mann: Looking at the Male," *Framework* 15/16/17 (1981): 16.

36. Carol J. Clover also emphasizes the importance of the western's relationship to the horror film. See *Men, Women, and Chainsaws: Gender in the Modern Horror Film* (Princeton, N.J.: Princeton University Press, 1992), 124–37, especially with its "demonizing tendencies." These arguments are familiar from Richard Slotkin's pioneering work as well as other critics such as Robin Wood.

37. Richard Slotkin, *Regeneration through Violence: The Mythology of The American Frontier 1600–1860* (Middletown, Conn.: Wesleyan University Press, 1973).

38. See John Hess, "*Godfather II*: A Deal Coppola Couldn't Refuse," in *Movies and Methods*, ed. Bill Nichols (Berkeley: University of California Press, 1976), 81–90.

39. As an excessive genre now increasingly directed toward the body, the contemporary horror film has much in common with other genres such as melodrama and pornography in terms of cultural coding of gender. For this connection, see Linda Williams, "Film Bodies: Gender, Genre, and Excess," *Film Quarterly* 44, no. 4 (1991): 2–13.

40. See Andrew Britton, "*Meet Me in St. Louis* or The Ambiguities," *Australian Journal of Screen Theory* 4 (1977): 7–25; Wood, *Personal Views*, 166.

41. See Richard Chase, *Herman Melville* (New York: Hafner, 1949), 159–63.

42. This is the major blind spot in Leslie A. Fiedler, *Love and Death in the American Novel* (New York: Stein & Day, 1966).

43. See Sandra M. Gilbert and Susan Gubar, *The Madwoman in the Attic: The Woman Writer and the Nineteenth Century Literary Imagination* (New Haven: Yale University Press, 1979), 581–650.

44. Robert Montgomery Bird, *Nick of the Woods*, ed. Curtis Dahl (New Haven, Conn.: College and University Press, 1967), 125.

45. For relevant borrowings, see Frank McConnell, "Rough Beasts Sloughing," *Kenyon Review* 32, no. 1 (1970): 109–20.

46. H. P. Lovecraft, "Supernatural Horror in Literature," *Dagon* (Sauk City, Wisc.: Arkham House, 1965), 380. See also Thomas E. Connolly, *The Scarlet Letter and Selected Tales* (London: Penguin Books, 1970), 7–8. "Hawthorne was extremely sensitive about the fanatical role played by his paternal ancestors in the early days of New England. A deep family guilt settled upon him and this guilt undoubtedly prompted him to critical attacks in his literary works on the rigors of Puritanism." For Lovecraft's own recognitions of associations between repressive Puritan behavior and the witch phobia, see his letter to Robert E. Howard in *Selected Letters III* (Sauk City, Wisc.: Arkham House, 1971), 175–84.

47. See Hugo McPherson, *Hawthorne as Myth Maker* (Toronto: University of Toronto Press, 1969), 187. "To the Puritans Pearl is an imp, a demonic child or a witch; she is outside the law; unrestrained, apparently, by any of the strictures which shape little Puritans."

48. See John Demos, "Underlying Themes in the Witchcraft of Seventeenth Century New England," *American Historical Review* 75, no. 5 (1970): 1311–26. For further information on the Salem incidents, see Perry Miller, *The New England Mind* (Cambridge: Harvard University Press, 1962), 191–208; and Paul Boyar and Stephen Nissbaum, *Salem Possessed* (Cambridge: Harvard University Press, 1974).

49. Cotton Mather, *Magnalia Christi Americana* 1712, Book VI (New York: Arno Press, 1972), 71–75

50. Cited by Demos, "Underlying Themes," 1319.

51. On the tale's revealing psychopathological aspects, see Frederick S. Crews, *The Sins of the Fathers* (New York: Oxford University Press, 1966), 51–52.

52. For various studies of Poe, see D. H. Lawrence, *Studies in Classic American Literature* (London: Heinemann, 1964), 61–77; Marie Bonaparte, *The Life and Works of Edgar Allan Poe: A Psychoanalytic Interpretation*, trans. John Hodder (London: Hogarth Press, 1949); Bernard Shanks, *Edgar Allan Poe* (London: Macmillan, 1937), 60, 99–100; Arthur Hobson Quinn, *Edgar Allan Poe: A Critical Biography* (New York: Appleton-Century Crofts, Inc., 1941), 255; N. Bryllion Fagan, *The Histrionic Mr. Poe* (Baltimore: Johns Hopkins Press, 1949), 195, 213; Vincent Buranelli, *Edgar Allan Poe* (New York: Wayne, 1961); Floyd Stovall, "The Conscious Art of Edgar Allan Poe," in *Poe: A Collection of Essays*, ed. Robert Regan (Englewood Cliffs, N.J.: Prentice-Hall, Inc. 1967), 172–79; and Daniel Hoffman, *Poe* (London: Hobson Books, 1973).

53. See Richard O'Connor, *Ambrose Bierce* (London: Gollanz, 1978), 9–22; Walter Neale, *The Life of Ambrose Bierce* (New York: Ams Press, 1929), 33–50.

54. See Lovecraft, *Selected Letters IV* (Sauk City, Wisc.: Arkham House, 1976); L. Sprague de Camp, *Lovecraft* (New York: Doubleday, 1975); and Frank Belknap Long, *Howard Phillips Lovecraft: Dreamer on the Nightside* (Sauk City, Wisc.: Arkham House, 1975), 5–7.

Chapter 2. Classical Shapes of Rage: Universal and Beyond

1. Ivan Butler, *Horror in the Cinema* (London: Zwemmer/A. S. Barnes. 1970), 48–49. Flight from the family into the scientific laboratory also features in *The Fly* (1958). For an exploration of this theme in terms of a fear of femininity, see Adam Knee, "The Metamorphosis of *The Fly*," *Wide Angle* 14, no. 1 (1992): 20–34.

2. *On Sexuality, Pelican Freud Library* 7, London: Penguin Books, 1977 116–20.

3. See Tony Williams, "*White Zombie:* Haitian Horror," *Jump Cut* 28 (1983): 18–20.

4. Sigmund Freud, "The Uncanny," *On Creativity and the Unconscious* (New York: Harper Books, 1979), 152–53.

5. Otto Rank, *The Double: A Psychoanalytic Study,* trans. and ed. Harry Tucker, Jr. (Chapel Hill: University of North Carolina Press, 1971), 76.

6. Freud, "The Uncanny," 142.

7. Rank, *The Double,* 85–86.

8. Ellen Moers, *Literary Women* (New York: Doubleday, 1976), 95–97.

9. Sandra M. Gilbert and Susan Gubar, *The Madwoman in the Attic* (New Haven: Yale University Press, 1979), 232. For an argument seeing the original text aiming to subvert unified character ideals and emphasizing repressed forms of subjectivity, see Rosemary Jackson, "Narcissism and Beyond: A Psychoanalytic Reading of *Frankenstein* and Fantasies of the Double," *Aspects of Fantasy: Selected Essays for the Second International Conference on the Fantastic in Literature and Film,* ed. William Coyle (Westport, Conn.: Greenwood Press, 1986), 43–53.

10. Ibid., 240.

12. Ibid., 241.

12. Ibid.

13. Ibid.

14. For Henry's continuing lines after his "It's Alive!" cry, cut from the soundtrack, see *Frankenstein,* ed. Philip J. Riley (Absecon, N.J.: Magic Image Film Books, 1989), 40. "In the name of God? Now I know what it feels like to BE GOD!" It anticipates Hannibal Lecter's feelings in *Manhunter* (1986).

15. See Paul Jensen, "Film Favorites," *Film Comment* 6, no. 3 (1970): 45; Richard J. Anobile, ed. *James Whale's Frankenstein. The Film Classics Library* (New York: Picador, 1974), 6; Butler, *Horror,* 46; and *Frankenstein,* ed. Philip J. Riley, 37–39.

16. See *Frankenstein,* 30–31, 40. Studio executives removed the happy ending in 1935 to coincide with the film's reissue on a double bill with *The Bride of Frankenstein.* After its rediscovery in Universal vaults in 1957, the conclusion was restored for television release.

17. Among the scenes removed by Universal following initial screenings was a subplot involving Karl (Dwight Frye) and his miserly family. During the creature's escape, he watches his uncle hide the family savings. Karl then strangles him and attaches blame to the creature. Deciding to dispose of his equally repulsive aunt, Karl exclaims, "I shouldn't be surprised if he visited Auntie, too." See *The Bride of Frankenstein,* ed. Philip J. Riley (Absecon, N.J.: Magic Image Film Books, 1989), 46.

18. According to the original screenplay, Minnie embodies society's bloodlust against the outsider, a trait extending into Haddonfield's pursuit of Michael in the *Halloween* series.

"Old Minnie has watched the gruesome disaster with a grim satisfaction: it is meat and drink to her—she has a lust for horror—her aged emotions are fed and glutted on violence, obscenity and death." See Riley, *Bride of Frankenstein*, A-10. Rachel Talalay's montage sequence revealing the older generation's effect on the younger during young Freddy's school persecution in *Freddy's Dead* (1991) forms an apt parallel.

19. Note also the identification of science and satanism in *Metropolis* (1926). Rotwang's house has an occult symbol above his door. Another appears over robot Maria during the creation sequence.

20. The film originally concluded with the destruction of all leading characters. See Riley, *Bride of Frankenstein*, 17, 27. Despite its Gothic overtones, the film also contains revealing insights into contemporary social anxieties concerning sexuality, gender, and race. For one such insightful reading, see Elizabeth Young, "Here Comes the Bride: Wedding Gender and Race in *Bride of Frankenstein*," *Feminist Studies* 17, no. 3 (1991): 403–37.

21. For Jack Otterson's intentions, see Denis Gifford, *A Pictorial History of Horror Movies* (London: Hamlyn, 1973), 126. See also *Son of Frankenstein*, ed. Philip J. Riley (Absecon, N.J.: Magic Image Film Books, 1990), 25–29.

22. *The Ghost of Frankenstein*, ed. Philip J. Riley (Absecon, N.J.: Magic Image Film Books, 1990).

23. For Bruce Kawin, "The Wolf Man is a transparently Oedipal nightmare, a full playing out of castration anxiety, whose heroine projects two sides of her sexuality on to wolf man and gamekeeper, and a clear example of how some horror films are analogous to one kind of dream." Despite this extremely interesting reading, Kawin does not sufficiently explore the role of both Sir John and the social order in making Larry a monster. See "The Mummy's Pool," *Planks of Reason* by Barry K. Grant, 9–10. Parental figures responsible for creating monsters feature in many horror films. In addition to well-known examples such as *Psycho*, *The Other* (1972) presents grandmother as responsible for her grandchild's possession by refusing to let him come to terms with his brother's death. Anthony Hopkins's demented parent in *Audrey Rose* (1977) causes the death of another child by his refusal to acknowledge the death of his own daughter.

24. For the original screenplay, see *Dracula*, ed. Philip J. Riley (Absecon, N.J.: Magic Image Filrnbooks, 1990), which also contains details of the simultaneously filmed Spanish language version.

25. See Frank McConnell "Rough Beasts Slouching," 111. For an excellent critique of the reactionary nature of Coppola's revisionist *Bram Stoker's Dracula* (1992), see Judith Halberstam, "On Vampires, Lesbians, and Coppola's *Dracula*," *Bright Lights* 11 (1993): 7–9.

26. See Franco Moretti, "Dialectic of Fear," *Signs Taken for Wonders* (London: Verso, 1983), 83–108, for a political reading of both *Frankenstein* and *Dracula*.

Chapter 3. Lewton or "The Ambiguities"

1. See here Joel Siegel, *Val Lewton: The Reality of Terror* (London: Secker & Warburg, 1972), 7–9; J. P. Telotte, *Dreams of Darkness: Fantasy and the Films of Val Lewton* (Urbana: University of Illinois Press, 1985), 7. The various films produced by the Lewton Group are

less authorial and more group collaborations exhibiting Val Lewton's major influence. See Siegel, *Val Lewton*, 23; Telotte, *Dreams of Darkness*, 8–11. They parallel New Line's role in producing the *Nightmare on Elm Street* series.

2. Note the presence of Albert D'Agostino as art director in *The Cat People*. He worked on significant RKO film noir productions during the forties such *as Murder My Sweet* (1944), *Born to Kill, Out of the Past* (1947), *Crossfire, Desperate* (1947), *The Set-Up, They Live By Night, I Married A Communist* (1949), and *On Dangerous Ground* (1950).

3. Using James Hillman's psychological concepts, Telotte believes the films reveal a vesperal journey into the psyche via processes of dreaming and fantasy usually leading to a positive catharsis. The various fantasies reflect a desire or need to gain access to an archetypal experience involving mythic patterns to gain salvation from the darker side of existence. See *Dreams of Darkness*, 4, 194, n. 11. However, analyzing the films and their frequent bleak endings raises doubt whether this therapeutic approach actually explains the major impressions these films contain. They definitely appear as "dreams of darkness," not salvation, often resisting positive conclusions.

4. Milton R. Stern, *The Fine Hammered Steel of Herman Melville* (Chicago and London: The University of Illinois Press, 1968), 153.

5. See Wood, 214–15, for the significance of this motif

6. As Telotte aptly illustrates, "The greatest threats that emerge from the Lewton films, after all, typically prove to be the most logical rational of people—especially the doctors, professors, and other authority figures who appear so frequently here—who simply interpret their world and others wrongly or harshly" (*Dreams of Darkness*, 17). *The Cat People* is a key text leading to feminist readings. Deborah Linderman discerns associations with medical discourses in the contemporary women's film, noting the film's particular mode of textual closure whereby "the cinema performs an *Aufhebung* on its own representation of psychoanalysis, negating it as impossibly domestic, Oedipal, and symptom-based, contravening it by the insistence of the cat transfiguration not as symptomatic but 'real'" (83). Karen Hollinger also notices the text's importance as a film based upon female threat to the male, a motif vulgarized in Paul Schrader's 1982 remake. See Deborah Linderman, "Cinematic Abreaction: Tourneur's *The Cat People*," in *Psychoanalysis and Cinema*, ed. E. Ann Kaplan (New York: Routledge, 1990), 7–97; and Karen Hollinger, "The Monster as Woman: Two Generations of Cat People," *Film Criticism* 13, no. 2 (1989): 36–45.

7. Wood, 217.

8. Elizabeth Russell dubbed Simone Simon's voice according to Siegel, 103.

9. Telotte notes that when Oliver turns to Alice it is like moving to "almost his mirror image" (*Dreams of Darkness*, 33).

10. See Siegel 54 and Clarens 169.

11. Schatzman, *Soul Murder*, 81–92. On the relation of *Curse of the Cat People* to Lewton's own life, see Telotte, *Dreams of Darkness*, 119.

12. Although resulting from studio intentions to inject some frightening components (Siegel, 56), the shot does have some relevance to the narrative.

13. Stern, 153.

14. The whole Farren sequence has unmistakable associations with Gothic melodrama especially in relation to the dark family motif, a relationship recognized by Mark Robson. In an interview he commented that when "dealing with melodrama, these mental aberrations or mental defects lend themselves very well to the situation." See Danny Peary, "Mark Robson Remembers RKO, Welles and Val Lewton," *Velvet Light Trap* 10 (1973): 3–7.

15. Oliver Reed has much in common with Lewton's other authority figures such as Captain Stone of *The Ghost Ship* and Sims of *Bedlam* (1945) who imprisons Nell because of her objections to his mental asylum. Nell suffers the fate Lewton's contemporary society plans for Irena of *The Cat People* and Jacqueline of *The Seventh Victim*. Telotte comments that "people like Mr. Sims are really more dangerous than caged inmates, precisely because they try hardest to maintain a sharp demarcation between themselves and the otherness of reason, to hold fast to their division of men into human and animal categories, to grant a soul to some and deny it to others" (*Dreams of Darkness*, 179).

16. For pertinent connections between Irena and Barbara, see Tom Milne, "Discovery: *The Curse of The Cat People*," *Focus on Film* 7 (1971): 55.

17. David Brion Davis, *Homicide in American Fiction 1798–1860* (Ithaca: Cornell University Press, 1957), 209.

18. For the associations with *Jane Eyre*, see Siegel, 25; Wood, 219; Telotte, *Dreams of Darkness*, 42.

19. Davis, 148.

20. Ibid.

21. Ibid., 155–56.

22. Ibid., 161–64.

23. Wood, 221.

24. Siegel, 108.

25. "Even Betsy, the least complex of the characters has some unusual kinks: her love for Paul is so great that she risks her life to restore Jessica's health through voodoo" (Wood, 223). I wish to acknowledge the stimulating discussions of this film by Andrew Britton and Robin Wood during seminar and class presentations at the Warwick University Department of Film Studies during 1976–77.

26. Siegel, 109; Wood, *Personal Views*, 219–20; Telotte, *Dreams of Darkness*, 51.

27. On the question of audience identification here, see Wood 221.

28. Note the costumes of Jessica and Betsy at different points of the film, Paul's breast pocket handkerchief, as well as Mrs. Rand's, echoes the voodoo "badges" both women wear to the meeting. See Wood, 222.

29. Telotte, *Dreams of Darkness*, 17.

30. For an account of this and other edited scenes, see Siegel, 127–28.

31. On the double motif see Telotte, *Dreams of Darkness*, 85–86.

32. Siegel, 127.

33. Ibid., 124.

34. Telotte, *Dreams of Darkness*, 111.

Chapter 4. To *Psycho* and Beyond: The Hitchcock Connection

1. See especially, William Rothman, *Hitchcock: The Murderous Gaze* (Cambridge: Harvard University Press, 1982); A *Hitchcock Reader*, eds. Marshall Deutelbaum & Leland Poague (Ames: Iowa State University Press, 1986); Tania Modleski, *The Women Who Knew too Much: Hitchcock and Feminist Theory* (New York: Methuen, 1988); Robin Wood, *Hitchcock's Films Revisited* (New York: Columbia University Press, 1989); and *Hitchcock's Rereleased Films: From Rope to Vertigo*, eds. Walter Raubichek and Walter Srebnick (Detroit: Wayne State University Press, 1991).

2. Wood, *Hitchcock's Films Revisited*, 336–57, 371–87.

3. See Bergstrom, 71–103.

4. See Wood, *Hitchcock's Films Revisited*, 336–57.

5. Charles Derry, *Dark Dreams: A Psychological History of the Modern Horror Film* (New York: A. S. Barnes, 1977).

6. Janet Bergstrom, "Enunciation and Sexual Difference (Part I)," *Camera Obscura* 3/4 (1979): 33–69.

7. Rose, "Paranoia and the Film System," *Screen* 17.4 (1976–1977): 85–194.

8. See Margaret M. Horwitz, "*The Birds*: A Mother's Love," *A Hitchcock Reader*, 279–87.

9. See Michelle Piso, "Mark's *Marnie*," *A Hitchcock Reader*, 288–305; Wood, *Hitchcock's Films Revisited*, 173–98.

10. Wood, *Hitchcock's Films Revisited*, 108–30; Laura Mulvey, "Visual Pleasure and Narrative Cinema," *Screen* 16, no. 3 (1975): 6–18.

11. Schneider, *Neurosis and Civilization: A Marxist Freudian Synthesis*, trans. by Michael Robeff (New York: Seabury Press, 1975.

12. See Nancy Chodorow, *The Reproduction of Mothering: Psychoanalysis and the Sociology of Gender* (Berkeley: University of California Press, 1978); *Feminism and Psychoanalysis* (New Haven: Yale University Press, 1989); Carol Gilligan, *In A Different Voice* (Cambridge: Harvard University Press, 1982).

13. *Feminism and Psychoanalysis*, 34–55.

14. Ibid., 227–28.

15. For various surveys of *Shadow of a Doubt*, see Ronnie Scheib, "Charlies Uncle," *Film Comment* 12, no. 2 (1976): 55–67; Framework Editorial Group, "The Family in *The Reckless Moment*," *Framework* 4 (1976): 21–22; James McLaughlin, "All in the Family: Alfred Hitchcock's *Shadow of a Doubt*," *A Hitchcock Reader*, 141–52; Wood, *Hitchcock's Films Revisited*, 288–302; Paul Gordon, "Sometimes a Cigar Is Not Just A Cigar: A Freudian Analysis of Uncle Charles in Hitchcock's *Shadow of a Doubt*," *Literature/Film Quarterly* 19, no. 4 (1991): 267–76.

16. Wood, *Hitchcock's Films Revisited*, 292.

17. *Framework* Editorial Group, "Family," 21.

18. Raymond Durgnat, *The Strange Case of Alfred Hitchcock* (London: Faber & Faber, 1974), 185.

19. Emmy mentions Philadelphia as Uncle Charles's last address. The poverty existing at the heart of a city whose name exemplifies brotherly love is an ironic comment by

Hitchcock. Its discordant presence parallels Santa Rosa's Till-2 club. For specific shot break-down, see Gordon 295, n. 1. He comments that Truffaut's analysis actually ignores the open-ing shot of Charles caressing his cigar.

20. The use of overlapping dialogue counterpoints family emotional isolation. Young Charlie's reference to the family's lack of communication foreshadows Donna Trenton's din-ner table comment in *Cujo* (1983).

21. "A marvelous inflection of the generic type of the smart, precocious tomboyish younger sister, produces in Anne Newton, a little girl characterized by a sustained autistic withdrawal from reality into movies (her ambition to look like Veronica Lake) and predomi-nantly, books,—she wants to become a librarian, and is introduced refusing, literally, to take her head out of 'Ivanhoe,' the classic novel of sublimated romantic dream by an author who epitomized, for Mark Twain, the rottenness of the European inheritance" (*Framework*, 2–22). She also foreshadows the Elm Street kid in *A Nightmare on Elm Street—Dream Warriors* (1987), who yearns to become a television actress and gazes in fascination at Zsa Zsa Gabor on *The Dick Cavett Show*.

22. *Framework*, 22.

23. For this connection, associated with Melanie Klein's theories, see Wood, *Hitchcock's Films Revisited*, 379–87.

24. Gordon, 270.

25. Ibid.

26. Wood, *Hitchcock's Films Revisited*, 301–302.

27. Ibid., 142.

28. "The walls are dirty, blank, a testimony to the impoverished unhappy nature of the love affair." So James Naremore aptly comments in *Filmguide to Psycho* (Bloomington: Indi-ana University Press, 1973), 28. The crucial importance of economic factors governing *Psycho* receive excellent recognition by Leland A Poague. See "Links in a Chain: *Psycho* and Film Classicism," *A Hitchcock Reader*, 340–50.

29. Wood, *Hitchcock's Films Revisited*, 144.

30. Naremore describes the "cuddly rabbit" as "no doubt one of Norman's first stuffed animals" (69).

31. Merlock Jackson, 112–14. For a recent examination of *The Bad Seed* recognizing Rhoda as the product of the nuclear family, see Paul, *Laughing Screaming*, 267–86.

Chapter 5. Return of the Native: The Satanic Assaults

1. *Rosemary's Baby* lends itself to readings concerning birth trauma. But this emphasis usually ignores important social and political meanings within the text. See Virginia Wright Wexman, "The Trauma of Infancy in Roman Polanski's *Rosemary's Baby*," *American Horrors*, 30–43; Lucy Fischer, "Birth Traumas: Parturition and Horror in *Rosemary's Baby*," *Cinema Journal* 31, no. 3 (1992): 3–18. A far more comprehensive and culturally orientated reading occurs in Christopher Sharrett, *Apocalypticism in the Contemporary Horror Film: A Typo-logical Survey of the Theme in the Fantastic Cinema, Its Relationship to Cultural Traditions*

and Current Filmic Expression (Ph.D. diss., New York University, 1983), 147–62. Sharrett also notes the film's ironic assault upon consumer capitalism. William Paul also notes significant contradictions in these films, many of which hint at child abuse. See *Laughing Screaming*, 288–350. He suggests Catherine in *The Omen* "does not really want her own child" (326).

2. For other relevant examples of Hollywood paranoia, see Paul Jensen, "The Return of Dr. Caligari: Paranoia in Hollywood," *Film Comment* 7. no. 4 (1971–72): 34–45.

3. See William Castle, *Step Right Up! I'm Gonna Scare the Pants Off America* (New York: G. P. Putnam's Sons, 1976). In addition to *Macabre* and *Homicidal*, Castle directed *The House on Haunted Hill* (1959), *Straitjacket* (1963), and *The Night Walker* (1964).

4. See especially Colin McArthur, "Polanski," *Sight and Sound* 38, no. 1 (1968–69): 14–17; Ivan Butler, *The Cinema of Roman Polanski* (London: Zwemmer. A. S. Barnes, 1970), 156–73.

5. See Butler, *Roman Polanski*, 161.

6. Ibid., 161. Jackie's suggestion that they tie Rosemary's legs down "in case of convulsions" is missing from the English print.

7. See Ralph Boas and Louise Boas, *Cotton Mather: Keeper of the Puritan Conscience* (1928; reprint, Hamden, Conn.: Archon Books, 1964), 99, 109, and especially p. 100 for associations between childish naughtiness and demonic possession. For some revealing nineteenth-century parallels to Regan's condition, emerging from a traumatic family situation, see Jeffrey Moussaieff Masson, *A Dark Science: Women, Sexuality and Psychiatry in the Nineteenth Century* (New York: Farrar, Straus and Giroux, 1986), 74.

8. Quoted from Peter Travers and Stephanie Rieff, *The Story Behind The Exorcist* (New York: Signet, 1974), 158–62. Majority opinion regards *The Exorcist* as a reactionary supernatural myth devoid of all social meaning. See Herbert J. Gans, "*The Exorcist*: A Devilish Attack on Women," *Social Policy* 5 (1974): 71–73; and Marsha Kinder and Beverle Houston, "Seeing Is Believing: *The Exorcist* and *Don't Look Now*," *American Horrors*, 44–52.

9. See R. D. Laing, *The Divided Self; The Politics of Experience and The Bird of Paradise; Self and Others* (London: Pelican, 1967). R. D. Laing and Aaron Esterson, *Sanity, Madness and The Family* (London: Heinemann, 1964); Aaron Esterson, *The Leaves of Spring: Schizophrenia, Family and Sacrifice* (London: Pelican, 1972); David Cooper, *The Death of the Family* (London: Penguin, 1971); Morton Schatzman, *Soul Murder* (London: Penguin, 1976). Despite Laing's supposedly dated significance, his works do lend themselves to appropriate literary and cinematic readings. For one example, see Sam B. Girgis, "R. D. Laing and Literature: Readings of Poe, Hawthorne, and Kate Chopin," *Psychological Perspectives on Literature: Freudian Dissidents and Non-Freudians*, ed. Joseph Natoli (Hamden, Conn.: Archon, 1984), 181–97. One critical reaction appears in Russell Jacoby, *Social Amnesia: A Critique of Conformist Psychology from Adler to Laing* (Boston: Beacon Press, 1975), 131–50. Although Jacoby correctly notes dangerous philosophic existentialist tendencies and asocial abstraction in this approach, Laing did perform a valuable service in directing attention toward the family's specific role as an oppressive institutional unit.

10. See Charles Foley, "The Teeny Shockers," *Observer Colour Supplement* (24 July 1977): 1–3.

11. See Carol J. Clover, 102–103.

12. See Dale Winogura, "Friedkin on *The Exorcist*," *Cinefantastique* 3, no. 4. (1974): 10.

13. *William Peter Blatty on The Exorcist* (New York: Bantam, 1974), 283, n. 20.

14. See Winogura, 17. Friedkin agrees with this interpretation. "I think that's very apt. What the shot is saying is that, and the fact that they're like minor canvas characters in a much larger canvas."

15. For a still, see Travers and Reiff, 53.

16. The film unfortunately omits this crucial information. "Chris was setting down the bird when she noticed the Ouija board. . . . She'd forgotten she had it. Almost as curious about it herself as she was about others, she'd originally bought it as a possible means of exposing clues to her subconscious. It hadn't worked, She'd used it at a time or two with Sharon, and once with Dennings, who had skillfully steered the plastic planchette ('Are you the one who's moving it, ducky?') so that all of the 'messages' were obscene, and then afterward blame it on the 'fucking spirits'" (Blatty, *The Exorcist*, 44). Both film and book associate the Ouija board with Regan's worry bird.

17. Quotes are from the transcript in *William Peter Blatty on The Exorcist*, 302, 304–305.

18. Ibid., 306.

19. Ibid., 347–48.

20. Jackson, 149.

21. Sigmund Freud, "On Narcissism," in *On Metapsychology: The Theory of Psychoanalysis. The Pelican Freud Library Volume II* (London: Penguin, 1984), 85.

22. *Exorcist II* has received little critical attention since its box office and critical failure in 1977. For supplementary information, see Barbara Pallenberg, *The Making of Exorcist II: The Heretic* (New York: Warner Books, 1977); Michel Ciment, *John Boorman*, trans. Gilbert Adair (London: Faber & Faber, 1986), 156–72.

Chapter 6. Far from Vietnam: The Family at War

1. Frederic Jameson, *The Political Unconscious: Narrative as a Socially Symbolic Act* (Ithaca: Cornell University Press, 1981).

2. Slotkin, *Regeneration*, 562–64; *Fatal Environment*, 16–18; Slotkin, "Gunfighters and Green Berets: *The Magnificent Seven* and the Myth of Counter Insurgency," *Radical History Review* 4 (1989): 65–90.

3. This film is treated in the concluding chapter. Many of Stephen King's novels and short stories refer to Vietnam's effect on American society. See, for example, "The Bogeyman" (1973) and "Children of The Corn" (1977) included in *Night Shift* (London: New English Library, 1979). The Vietnam motif also transcends several cinematic genres, again confirming Robin Wood's observations concerning Hollywood genres. See, recently, Renny Christopher, "Negotiating the Viet Nam War through Permeable Genre Borders: *Aliens* as Viet Nam War Film; *Platoon* as Horror Film," *Literature Interpretation Theory* 5 (1994): 53–66.

4. Tony Williams, "Oliver Stone: Less than Meets the Eye," *cineACTION* 29 (1992): 40–55.

5. See Tony Williams, "Wes Craven: An Interview," *Journal of Popular Film & Television* 8, no. 3 (1980): 10–14.

6. Pamela Cooper, "David Rabe's *Sticks and Bones*: The Adventures of Ozzie and Harriet," *Modern Drama* 29. no. 4 (1986): 615.

7. David Rabe, *The Basic Training of Pavlo Hummel and Sticks and Bones* (New York: Viking Press, 1973), 225.

8. Cooper 621. See also, David D. McDonald, "The Mystification of Vietnam: David Rabe's *Sticks and Bones*," *Cultural Critique* 3 (1986): 211–34; Weldon B. Durham, "Gone to Flowers: Theatre and Drama of the Vietnam War," in *America Rediscovered: Critical Essays on Literature and Films of the Vietnam War*, eds. Owen W. Gilman, Jr., and Lorie Smith (New York: Garland, 1990), 338–41; and Toby Silverman Zinman, *David Rabe: A Casebook* (New York: Garland, 1991).

9. Kim Newman, *Nightmare Movies* (New York: Harmony Books, 1981), 211.

10. Ibid., 211. For a critique of Vietnam Gothic, see Andrew Britton, "Sideshows: Hollywood in Vietnam," *Movie* 27/28 (1980–81): 2–23, especially 4–5.

11. Robin Wood, *American Nightmare*, 21.

12. Sumiko Higashi, "*Night of The Living Dead*: A Horror Film about the Horrors of the Vietnam Era," in *From Hanoi to Hollywood: The Vietnam War in American Film*, eds. Linda Dittmar and Gene Michaud (New Brunswick: Rutgers University Press, 1990), 179. Higashi's essay outlines specific reasons why the film "undercuts most of the cherished values of our whole civilization" as more traditionally minded critics note. See here, R. W. H. Dillard, "*Night of the Living Dead*: It's Not Like Just a Wind That's Passing Through," *American Horrors*, 28.

13. Higashi, "A Horror Film," 179–80.

14. See Barry K. Grant, "Taking Back *The Night of the Living Dead*: George Romero, Feminism & The Horror Film," *Wide Angle* 14, no. 1 (1992): 65–76.

15. Higashi, "A Horror Film," 189, in response to Vivian Sobchack, *Screening Space: The American Science Fiction Film* (New York: Ungar, 1984), 188–90.

16. Higashi notes that several commentators see Vietnam associations but do not develop them to their logical conclusions. "Although horror films readily lend themselves to different readings, downgrading political ones contributes to repression in the political unconscious" ("A Horror Film," 188). For such examples, see Dillard, 14–29; and Gregory A. Waller, *The Living and The Undead: From Stoker's Dracula to Romero's Dawn of the Dead* (Urbana: University of Illinois Press, 1986), 280–97, for a typical "English lit" discursive reading.

17. *Last House on the Left* contains several implicit Vietnam references mediated by cinematic style. Literally learning filmmaking on the set and dependent upon cinema-verite, hand-held camera style, Wes Craven comments, "We were trying to recapture a strong reality-based situation. I was very impressed with the footage that was coming out of Vietnam at the time which seemed to have much more immediacy and truth to it than anything I was aware of" (19). See David A Szulkin, "Keep Repeating 'It's Only a Classic!'" *Fangoria* 114 (1992): 16–21, 60–61. See also Dan Gire and Paul Mandell, "*Friday the 13th*: Horror's First Franchise," *Cinefantastique* 20, no. 1 (1989): 94, for producer Sean Cunningham's brief remarks concerning the film's Vietnam associations.

18. The preceding material originally appeared in Tony Williams, "Family Horror," *Movie* 27/28 (1980/1981): 122–26.

19. Wood, 93.

20. See Mark Walker, *Vietnam Veteran Films* (Metuchen, N.J.: Scarecrow Press, 1991), 90–93.

21. For some thematic observations, see D. N. Rodowick, "The Enemy Within: The Economy of Violence in *The Hills Have Eyes*," *Planks of Reason*, 321–30.

22. Wood, 95–97.

23. Robert C. Cumbow, "*Dawn of the Dead*," *Vietnam War Films*, eds. Jean-Jacques Malo and Tony Williams (Jefferson, N.C.: McFarland & Co, 1994), 104–105.

24. The following material is based on an article, "George A. Romero's *Zombies: Dawn of the Dead*," *Cinema Spectrum* 1 (1980): 14–19. I also wish to thank George A. Romero and his associates for the kind hospitality given during my Fall 1979 visit to Pittsburgh.

Chapter 7: Sacrificial Victims

1. Michel Foucault, *Discipline and Punish*, trans. Alan Sheridan (New York: Pantheon Books, 1977); *Power-Knowledge: Selected Interviews and Other Writings*, ed. and trans. Colin Gordon (New York: Pantheon, 1980); Herbert L. Dreyfuss and Paul Rabinow, *Michel Foucault: Beyond Structuralism and Hermeneutics* (Chicago: University of Chicago Press, 1983). Despite problems surrounding Foucault's "mandarin" tendencies and his dismissal of Marxism, his work does contain some significant insights into the operations of institutional discursive mechanisms inherent in family, school, and university.

2. As Andrew Britton recognizes, the horror genre shares several problems inherent in the Gothic format. "The gothic remains a progressive genre for as long as it can register a hesitation between conflicting systems of explanation (historical and existential) or functions as a means of evading a taboo" ("Sideshows," 4). Faced with the inevitable movement toward political and cultural expression, the genre's formal mechanisms of suspense and violence often intervene to blunt any positive meaning a particular film may have. Alternatively, films may take the direction Dana Polan notes: "At their political worst, the horror film can serve as a justification for vigilante violence. At their best, they can serve as a critique of the very ideological justifications by which contemporary society sustains itself." "Eros and Syphilization: The Contemporary Horror Film," in *Planks of Reason*, 209.

3. The original episode was "It's A Good Life," televised during the 1961–62 season. For the concept of "Reaganite entertainment," see Robin Wood, "80s Hollywood: Dominant Tendencies," *cineACTION!* 1 (1985): 2–5; Andrew Britton, "Blissing Out: The Politics of Reaganite Entertainment," *Movie* 31–32 (1986): 1–42; and Michael Rogin, *Ronald Reagan: The Movie and Other Episodes in Political Demonology* (Berkeley: The University of California Press, 1987).

4. See James B. Twitchell, 153–54. Rather than serving "to perpetuate a fatalistic, circular process" as Waller believes in *The Living and Undead*, 325, n. 41, *Grave of the Vampire* really allegorizes a particular familial process whose implications he ignores. It reveals a social repetition-compulsion process in which children from dysfunctional families usually repeat the past.

5. Relevant texts here include *Dressed to Kill* (1980), *Casualties of War* (1989), and *Bonfire of the Vanities* (1990). For criticisms of De Palma's alterations to David Rabe's original

screenplay of *Casualties of War*, see Martin Novelli, "Spiking the Vietnam Film 'Canon': David Rabe and *Casualties of War*," in *David Rabe: A Case Book*, 149–71.

6. Robin Wood makes an eloquent, but unconvincing, defense of *Dressed to Kill* in *Hollywood*, 147.

7. The following discussion owes much to Robin Wood's analysis *in Hollywood*, 150–55. See also Michael Bliss, *Brian De Palma* (Metuchen, N.J.: Scarecrow Press, 1983), 8–29.

8. Foster Hirsch sees it on one level as "an allegory of contemporary race relations . . . elemental hostilities between an oppressed minority and its white oppressors" ("*The Possession of Joel Delaney and The Other*," *Cinefantastique* 2, no. 3 [1973]: 27).

9. Carol J. Clover contests this reading Wood makes in "Gods and Monsters," *Film Comment* 14, no. 5 (1978): 23, believing that the film focuses on paternal acknowledgment, the infant becoming monstrous through apprehension of parental ambivalence toward its birth. She concludes that *It's Alive* is really pro-life and pro-family. See *Men, Women, and Chainsaws*, 76–77, n. 22. This is an extremely problematic interpretation that forces the text to bear the weight of an oppressive vaginal reading as well as ignoring the historical context of 1970s family horror. William Paul also astutely questions this overemphatic reading. See *Laughing Screaming*, 485–86. Clover also avoids certain features in the film that show the medical authorities demeaning Lenore's role in her own childbirthing process and attacking the baby at birth. The sequel makes this reading explicit. Clover's reading is too abstract, removing family horror from wider social relationships. Although her gender thesis is interesting, it tends to neglect intersecting social and political elements in the text. For a better recognition of the film's cultural (as well as birth) associations, see Bryan Bruce, "*It's Alive*," *Movie* 31/32 (1986): 115–17, an article absent from Clover's extremely selective and limited bibliography.

10. For information on the production of *Them!*, see Steve Rubin, "Retrospect: *Them!*," *Cinefantastique* 3, no. 4 (1974): 23–27.

11. Tom Milne, "*It's Alive*," *Monthly Film Bulletin* 42, no. 497 (1975): 137.

12. Slotkin, *Regeneration*, 389.

13. Wood, "Gods and Monsters," 23. For a recent reading, see Elayne Chaplin, "*Demon a.k.a. God Told Me To*," *Movie* 34/35 (1990): 103–107.

Chapter 8. Chain Saw Massacres: The Apocalyptic Dimension

1. See *Apocalypticism*; "The American Apocalypse: Scorsese's *Taxi Driver*," *Persistence of Vision* 1 (1984): 56–64; Lois P. Zamora, ed., *The Apocalyptic Vision in America: Interdisciplinary Essays on Myth and Culture* (Bowling Green, Ohio: The Popular Press, 1982).

2. *Apocalypticism*, 23.

3. Ibid.

4. Ibid., 13.

5. Ibid.

6. Pierre Machery, *A Theory of Literary Production*, trans. Geoffrey Wall (London: Routledge and Kegan Paul, 1978).

7. *Apocalypticism*, 14.

8. Ibid., 18; and *Crisis Cinema: The Apocalyptic Idea in Postmodern Narrative Film*, ed. Christopher Sharrett (Washington D.C.: Maisonneuve Press, 1992).

9. *Apocalypticism*, 22.

10. Slotkin, *Regeneration*, 57.

11. Ibid., 475.

12. Ibid., 136.

13. Ibid., 140–45.

14. Ibid., 157–58.

15. "Thorpe's 'Big Bear' gains the procreative power of the wilderness by merging his identity with that of its avatar, the bear; the result is a kind of elevation to heroic stature. Nor does Doggett lose his innocence as a result of the experience. On the contrary, he recovers lost innocence. Before the hunt he assumed himself to be powerful by virtue of the knowledge he had gained from worldly experience. After the hunt has proven the depth and strength of his power, he 'knows' less, is sure of less, then when he began. . . . He learns the limits of his power in the struggle, comes to respect and love the strength that nature's avatar embodies, and will play out his proper role with all the appropriate means at his disposal— not in contempt but in love and respect, not in the expectation of success but with resignation to failure" (483–84). Slotkin also notes Ahab's violation of the hunt's spirit in *Moby Dick* by seeking a union of Puritan hatred, not love, with his quarry.

16. See also 548.

17. Slotkin, 484. Filson and Cooper express the myth's romantic version. Daniel Boone follows the deer trail, entering a new plane of existence by sowing seeds and reaping the fruits of the earth. He thus avoids the Delaware creation myth's sexual violence and cannibalism. See also 269–311, especially 301. The relevance of Slotkin's findings to *The Texas Chain Saw Massacre* needs little emphasis.

18. Ibid., 412–13.

19. Ibid., 554–57.

20. Ibid., 558.

21. See also Christopher Sharrett, "The Idea of Apocalypse in the Texas Chainsaw Massacre," in *Planks of Reason*, 255–76.

22. For postmodernism's associations with the horror film, see Tania Modleski, "The Terror of Pleasure: The Contemporary Horror Film and Postmodern Theory," *Studies in Entertainment*, ed. Tania Modleski (Bloomington: Indiana University Press, 1986), 155–56. The postmodern movement needs special attention and analysis, not mere dismissal. However, her conclusion that "contemporary artists continue to be subversive by being non-adversorial in the modernist sense" (104) is certainly open to question because it justifies alienation and escapism.

23. Sharrett highlights Falk's role in "The Idea of Apocalypse," 262.

24. See Robin Wood, "Race with the Devil," *Movie* 23 (1977): 23.

25. See Leo Marx, *The Machine in the Garden* (New York: Oxford University Press, 1964), 5.

26. Christopher Sharrett, "Postmodern Narrative Cinema: Aeneas on a Stroll," *Canadian Journal of Political and Social Theory* 12, nos. 1–2 (1988): 78–103.

27. Frederic Jameson, "Postmodernism or the Cultural Logic of Late Capitalism," *New Left Review* 146 (1984): 71.

28. Sharrett, 81.

29. Christopher Sharrett, "Myth and Ritual in the Post-Industrial Landscape: The Horror Films of David Cronenberg," *Persistence of Vision* 3/4 (1986): 111–30.

30. Rene Girard, *Deceit, Desire and The Novel: Self and Others in Literary Structures*, trans. Yvonne Freccero (Baltimore: The Johns Hopkins University Press, 1965); *Violence and the Sacred*, trans. Patrick Gregory (Baltimore: The Johns Hopkins University Press, 1977); "Generative Scapegoating," in *Violent Origins*, ed. Robert G. Hammerton-Kelly (Stanford, Calif.: Stanford University Press, 1987), 73–148.

31. Sharrett, 31. I disagree with this particular interpretation. Despite some postmodernist associations, Cronenberg's films have more similarities with traditional motifs.

32. For further discussion on Cronenberg's significance, see *The Shape of Rage: The Films of David Cronenberg*, ed. Piers Handling (Toronto: General Publishing Company, 1983); *BFI Dossier 21: David Cronenberg* (London: British Film Institute, 1984).

33. Britton, "Blissing Out," 36.

34. Admiring the work's reflexive nature, Bruce Kawin sees the figure as a surrogate for Hooper. See "*The Funhouse* and *The Howling*," in *American Horrors*, 105.

35. Robin Wood, "Leavis, Marxism and Film Culture," *cineACTION* 8 (1987): 9. The film is a far better rendition of issues trivialized in Kevin Connor's *Motel Hell* and Charles Kaufman's *Mother's Day* (both 1980). Despite the latter film's emphasis on female resourcefulness and survival, the entire work is highly exploitative and weak.

36. Missing several significant social and cultural resonances, Carol J. Clover's factually inaccurate account also confuses Chop Top with his deceased brother, Hitchhiker, whom he carries around as a puppet. See Clover, 28.

Chapter 9: The Return of Kronos

1. Bob Clark's *Black Christmas* killer desperately wishes to submit to patriarchal norms of monogamy and family; he attacks any dissenting female. Although killed at the climax, an epilogue reveals another successor eager to continue this punitive mission.

2. See Robin Wood, "80s Hollywood: Dominant Tendencies," *cineACTION!* 1 (1985): 2–5; Britton, "Blissing Out." The decade saw the vigorous emergence of right-wing tendencies in American society. As an institution naturally responding to changes in the social structure, Hollywood tended to supply new consumer needs. For evidence of ideologic changes within this era and the tendencies leading to their emergence, the following works are relevant: William A. Rusher, *The Rise of the Right* (New York: William Morrow & Co, Inc., 1984); Mike Davis, *Prisoners of the American Dream* (London: Verso, 1984); Ruth Sidel, "The Family: A Dream Deferred"; Augustus F. Hawkins, "Minorities and Unemployment"; Lynn Hecht Schafram, "Women: Reversing the Decade of Progress"; and Ira Glasser, "The Coming Assault on Civil Liberties," in *What Reagan Is Doing to Us*, eds. Alan Gartner, Colin Greer, and Frank Riessman (New York: Harper & Row, 1982), 54–70, 125–40, 162–89, and 230–48;

Ronald Reagan, *A Time for Choosing: The Speeches of Ronald Reagan 1961–1980* (Chicago: Regnery Gateway Inc, 1983); Alan Crawford, *Thunder on the Right: The New Right and The Politics of Resentment* (New York: Pantheon Books, 1980), 144–58; Gillian Peele, *Revival and Reaction: The Right in Contemporary America* (Oxford: Clarendon Press, 1984); and Garry Wills, *Reagan's America: Innocents at Home* (New York: Doubleday & Co, 1987), 37–75. The infantile regressive works of George Lucas and Steven Spielberg are cinematic camp followers. For an analysis of conservative tendencies in one of the latter's works, see Tony Williams, "Close Encounters of the Authoritarian Kind," *Wide Angle* 5, no. 4 (1983): 22–29.

3. Carol J. Clover, *Men, Women and Chainsaws: Gender in the Modern Horror Film* (Princeton, N.J.: Princeton University Press, 1992).

4. From the mid-1980s, an abundance of material appeared in official and popular publications that dealt with dysfunctional families, child abuse, and trauma. This material infiltrated certain Hollywood representations, especially the horror genre. For relevant works, see Thomas J. Scheff and Suzanne M. Retzinger, *Emotions and Violence: Shame and Rage in Destructive Conflicts* (Lexington, Mass.: Lexington Books, 1991); Lucy Freeman, *Our Inner World of Rage* (New York: Continuum Publishing Company, 1990); and Willard Gaylin, *The Rage Within: Anger in Modern Life* (New York: Simon and Schuster, 1984).

5. Britton, 11. However, for a more diagnostic reading of contemporary cinema, see Douglas Kellner, "Film, Politics and Ideology: Reflections on Hollywood Film in the Age of Reagan," *Velvet Light Trap* 27 (1991): 9–24.

6. Britton, 11.

7. For Hollywood's mode of responding to changes in social ideology, see Richard Maltby, *Harmless Entertainment: Hollywood and the Ideology of Consensus* (Metuchen, N.J.: Scarecrow Press, 1983).

8. Britton, 2–3; Lawrence Levine, *Highbrow/Lowbrow: The Emergence of Cultural Hierarchy in America* (Cambridge: Harvard University Press, 1988). Clover misreads the particular perspective Andrew Britton takes in his observation, especially in the light of his critiques of Critical Theory. See Clover 9, n. 13.

9. Steve Neale, "Halloween," 341–42.

10. Quoted by Neale, "Halloween," 343.

11. The effectiveness of a supposedly progressive masochistic scenario in conservative mainstream narratives needs investigation. For various discussions, see Paul Smith, "Vas," *Camera Obscura* 17 (1988): 89–111; Kaja Silverman, *Male Subjectivity at the Margins* (New York: Routledge, 1992), 416, n. 48.

12. See Andrew Britton, "The Ideology of 'Screen,'" *Movie* 26 (1978/79): 1–28; Anthony Wilden, *System and Structure: Essays in Communication and Exchange*, 2nd ed. (London: Tavistock Publications, 1984), 474.

13. Neale, "Halloween," 344–45.

14. The auteur concept is inapplicable to these series, especially *Nightmare on Elm Street*, a product of New Line Cinema. See especially Frederick S. Clarke, "*Nightmare on Elm Street*: The Phenomenon," *Cinefantastique* 18, no. 5 (1988): 6–7, who focuses on the formative influence of producer Robert Shaye and line producer Rachel Talalay. Talalay began as a production accountant on the first film, eventually directing *Freddy's Dead* and working

her way toward being New Line's vice president in charge of production. See also Dan Scapperotti, "New Line Cinema: The House That Freddy Built," *Cinefantastique* 20, no. 1 (1989): 124–25. For Wes Craven's role, see Dan Gire, "Bye Bye *Freddy:* Elm Street creator Wes Craven quits series," *Cinefantastique* 18, no. 2 (1988) 8–10, and Steve Biodrowski, "Wes Craven: Alive and Shocking," *Cinefantastique* 22, no. 2 (1991): 11–12, as well as correspondence in succeeding issues. See also William Schoell and James Spencer, *The Nightmare Never Ends: The Official History of Freddy Krueger and the "Nightmare on Elm Street" Films* (New York: Citadel Press, 1992).

15. Clover, 64. For a different perspective, see Patricia Erens, "The Seduction: The Pornographic Impulse in Slasher Films," *Jump Cut* 32 (1987): 52–55.

16. Even supposedly progressive features usually read in Freud's "A Child Is Being Beaten" need scrutiny. Although certain critics believe this scenario reveals the potentially fluid nature of gender boundaries, a child is still being beaten, whatever the sex, under patriarchy. Concentration guards and contemporary sadists also delight in placing male victims into "feminized" positions.

17. See Wood, "80s Hollywood," 121–28; Peter Benson, "Identification and Slaughter," *cineACTION* 12 (1988): 12–18.

18. Clover, 94.

19. Tania Modleski, *Feminism without Women: Culture and Criticism in a "Postfeminist" Age* (New York: Routledge, 1991).

20. Norman G. Gordon, "Family Structure and Dynamics in De Palma's Horror Films," *Psychoanalytic Review* 70, no. 3 (1983): 441.

21. Gordon, 436.

22. Norman G. Gordon, "Controversial Issues in De Palma's *Dressed to Kill*," *Psychoanalytic Review* 69, no. 4 (1982): 566. Royal Brown sees *Dressed to Kill* and the *Friday the 13th* series as representing the return of a particularly American Judeo-Christian misogyny. He believes Robert/Bobbi represents a monstrous creation of Peter's Oedipal desires to punish both his mother, Kate, and the woman who will take her place (Liz). This reading is possible. However, Brown notes that although films such as *Dressed to Kill*, *Friday the 13th*, and *Halloween* may operate cathartically, they also revive dangerous mythic-religious stereotypes that the sixties unsuccessfully attempted to destroy. See "*Dressed to Kill*: Myth and Fantasy in the Horror/Suspense Genre," *Film/Psychology Review* 4 (1980): 169–82.

23. One wonders how many spectators, especially females, would arrive at this latter conclusion? For a defense of the film, see Wood, 147–49. A question remains as to whether De Palma deliberately exploits his audience, a tendency that may contradict the type of reading Allison Graham makes using James Hillman's psychological theories. See "'The Fallen Wonder of the World': Brian De Palma's Horror Films," *American Horrors*, 129–44.

24. Gordon, "Family Structure," 435–42.

25. Wood, *The American Nightmare*.

26. Vera Dika, *Games of Terror: Halloween, Friday the 13th and The Films of the Stalker Cycle* (London and Toronto: Fairleigh Dickinson University Press, 1990), 33–44. See also Robert C. Cumbow, *Order in the Universe: The Films of John Carpenter* (Metuchen, N.J.: Scarecrow Press, 1990), 49–67, for a different perspective.

See Modleski, "The Terror of Pleasure," 103. She notes that the baby-sitter is not only attractive but "represents familial authority." "The point needs to be stressed, since feminism has occasionally made common cause with the adversarial critics on the grounds that we too have been oppressed by the specious good. But this is to overlook the fact that in some profound sense we have also been historically and physically identified with it."

27. Danny Peary, *Cult Movies* (New York: Dell, 1981), 125–26.

28. See Cumbow, 68–70.

29. For Carpenter's interest in Nigel Kneale's work, see Cumbow, 70–74, 157–70, especially concerning the abortive collaboration over *Halloween III* (1982) and the influence on *Prince of Darkness* (1987).

30. Jackson, *Images of Children*, 126–74.

31. See Cumbow, 75–76.

32. Ibid., 75–76.

33. Vera Dika's work provides ample guidance to the formal structure of this cycle.

34. For an overview of this series, see Dan Gire and Paul Mandell, "*Friday the 13th:* Horror's First Franchise," *Cinefantastique* 20, no. 1 (1989): 91–94; Paul Mandell, "Jason Lives: The Birth of a Legend," *Cinefantastique* 20, no. 1 (1989): 92, 125.

Chapter 10. *Poltergeist* and Freddy's Nightmares

1. On Spielberg's influence in contemporary Hollywood, see Michael Ryan and Douglas Kellner, *Camera Politica*, 258–63.

2. Britton, 38.

3. For information concerning New Line's development of the series, see Steve Biodrowski, "*Freddy's Dead:* Post Mortem," *Cinefantastique* 22, no. 4 (1992): 56, 80.

4. The correct spelling is Lecter. *Manhunter* misreads it as "Lecktor" and *Silence of the Lambs* as "Lector." See Thomas Doherty, "Hannibal Lecter's Horror Pedigree," *Cinefantastique*, 22, no. 4 (1992) 36, 37.

5. Despite Craven's dismissal of the succeeding *Nightmare* films, they do contain his original idea of Freddy being a "paradigm of the threatening adult: the savage side of male adulthood, the ultimate bad father." See Dan Gire, "Bye Bye Freddy," *Cinefantastique* 18, no. 5 (1988): 10. For Freddy's emergence into popular culture, see Guy Johnson, "The Pleasure of Terror and 'All This Freddy Shit,'" *USC Spectator* 10, no. 1 (1989): 7–19.

6. In this sense the films represent Craven's idea of horror films being "boot camp for the psyche" (10). See Gire.

7. Robert Englund believes that Part II did not soft-pedal Freddy's child molester, dark father image. See Jim Clark, "A Nightmare on Elm Street—Part II," *Cinefantastique* 15, no. 5 (1986): 55.

8. See Jim Clark, "A Nightmare on Elm Street—Part III," *Cinefantastique* 17, no. 2 (1987): 6–7. In this version the kids are diagnosed as suicidal, a plot motif obviously influenced by contemporary reports of high school suicides. Wes Craven cowrote several drafts of the screenplay.

9. For New Line Cinema, this version was a "back to basis" approach. See Steve Biodrowski, "*Nightmare on Elm Street 5—The Dream Child,*" *Cinefantastique* 20, no. 1 (1989): 86–88.

10. Steve Biodrowski, "Freddy's Dead or Is He?" *Cinefantastique* 22, no. 2 (1991): 8–10, 60.

11. *Freddy's Dead* was supposedly to end with the Freddy concept still intact but not Freddy's character. The Dream Demons were to descend upon another abused child who would take Freddy's place. According to screenwriter and executive producer, Michael De Luca, "Originally, we had this idea about the cyclical nature of child abuse; then we came to the opinion that this is an inappropriate forum to bring up that issue, much less comment, and we cut it out." See Steve Biodrowski, "*Freddy's Dead:* Post Mortem," *Cinefantastique,* 60. However, De Luca's proposed ending would have duplicated that of *Don't Enter the House,* where Donny's schizophrenic voices befriend another child suffering maternal abuse.

Chapter 11. The King Adaptations

1. For information on King's college readings, see Douglas Winter, *Stephen King: The Art of Darkness* (New York: Signet, 1986), 23–24.

2. See especially, Stephen King, *Danse Macabre* (New York: Berkely, 1983).

3. For King's association with this tradition, see Jeanne Campbell Reesman, "Stephen King and the Tradition of American Naturalism in *The Shining*"; Brian Kent, "Canaries in a Gilded Cage: Mental and Marital Decline *in McTeague* and *The Shining,*" in *The Shining Reader,* ed. Anthony Magistrale (Washington: Starmont House, 1991), 121–38, 139–53. Reesman notes King's interest in this tradition while he was a student. See also Anthony Magistrale, *Landscape of Fear: Stephen King's American Gothic* (Bowling Green, Ohio: Popular Press, 1988); *The Moral Voyages of Stephen King* (Washington: Starmont, 1989).

4. Winter, *Art of Darkness,* 23.

5. For some astute observations concerning King's dialectical techniques usually missing from film versions, see Harlan Ellison, "Why the Children Don't Look Like Their Parents," in Jessie Horsting, *Stephen King at the Movies* (New York: Starlog Press, 1986), 100. Ellison comments on King's first success, *Carrie,* about "the everyday experience raised to the mythic level by the application of fantasy to a potent cultural trap." See also Douglas Winter, *Art of Darkness,* 9. See further Michael R. Collings, *The Films of Stephen King* (Washington: Starmont, 1986).

6. See the interview with King in Douglas Winter, *Faces of Fear, Encounters with the Creators of Modern Horror* (New York: Berkeley Books, 1985), especially 245, 252, 235–57. Note further Don Herron, "Horror Springs in the Fiction of Stephen King," in *Fear Itself: The Horror Fiction of Stephen King,* eds. Tim Underwood and Chuck Miller (California: Underwood/Miller, 1982), 76–89.

7. Winter, *Art of Darkness,* 53. This work is an expanded edition of his earlier work, *Stephen King* (Washington: Starmont, 1972).

8. Stephen King, *Carrie* (New York: Signet, 1974), 46. Note Carrie's fears of a similar fate on p. 124.

9. Herron notes that "child abuse, too, forms a connecting link of concern between King's stories" ("Horror Springs," 76). For relevant examples in *The Shining*, see Greg Weller, "The Redrum of Time: A Meditation on Francisco Goya's 'Saturn Destroying His Children' and Stephen King's *The Shining*"; and Burton Hatlen, "Good and Evil in Stephen King's *The Shining*," in *The Shining Reader*, 61–78, 81–104. For King's view of childhood, see Magistrale, "Inherited Haunts: Stephen King's Terrible Children," in *Landscape of Fear*, 73–89. King's fiction may even reveal evidence of early trauma. See Lenore C. Terr, "Terror Writing by the Formerly Terrified: A Look at Stephen King," *The Psychoanalytic Study of the Child. Volume 44* (New Haven: Yale University Press, 1989), 369–90.

10. "I think Jerry Falwell is a monster and I think Jimmy Swaggert is a monster," *Faces of Fear*, 242.

11. Winter, *Art of Darkness*, 101–103.

12. Ibid., 24.

13. Ellison, 101.

14. Winter, *Art of Darkness*, 35–36.

15. The term actually occurs in the original novel: "She looked the part of the sacrificial goat" (4).

16. For an argument seeing *Carrie as* a "masculine fantasy in which the feminine is constituted as horrific" (34), see Shelly Stamp Lindsey, "Horror Femininity, and Carrie's Monstrous Puberty," *Journal of Film and Video* 43, no. 4 (1991): 33–44. Although these elements certainly exist in the text, Sissy Spacek's sympathetic performance and the film's adoption of King's social elements do not make this reading exclusive.

17. For a recognition of poltergeist phenomena associations with disturbed adolescents, see Bob Warren, "The Movies and Mr. King," *Fear Itself*, 111.

18. Weller, 77.

19. See Robin Wood, "Cat and Dog: Lewis Teague's Stephen King Movies," *cineACTION!* 2 (1985): 39–45.

20. Winter, *Art of Darkness*, 109.

21. As Wood notes, the troll *in Cat's Eye* appears to assault the little girl as a result of family tensions ("Cat and Dog," 45).

22. Ibid., 44.

23. Winter, *Art of Darkness*, 110.

24. Britton, "Blissing Out," 19.

25. Cumbow, 123–32.

26. Winter, *Art of Darkness*, 136.

27. "The Devil Probably: The Symbolism of Evil," in *The American Nightmare*, 39, 41.

28. For King's aversion to this novel, see Winter, *Art of Darkness*, 145–54.

29. Hatlen, 81.

30. Kent, 140.

31. David Cook, "American Horror: *The Shining*," *Literature/Film Quarterly* 12, no. 1 (1984): 2. See also Christopher Hoile, "The Uncanny and the Fairy Tale in Kubrick's *The Shining*," 5–12, for a reading noting Kubrick's interest in Freud's "The Uncanny" and Bruno Bettelheim's *The Uses of Enchantment* while writing the script; and Stephen Snyder, "Family Life and Leisure Culture in *The Shining*," *Film Criticism* 6 (1982): 4–13.

32. Frederic Jameson, "*The Shining*," *Social Text* 4 (1981): 119-20.

33. Ibid., 123.

34. Ibid., 125.

Chapter 12. Into the Nineties

1. For a detailed overview of the Batman phenomena, see *The Many Lives of the Batman: Critical Approaches to a Superhero*, eds. Roberta E. Pearson and William Uricchio (New York: Routledge, 1990).

2. The script idea originally came from a newspaper report recording police investigation of a Santa Monica home and their discovery of a couple's children imprisoned there since birth. This twelve-year-old news item intrigued Craven into writing a screenplay based on the fact that beneath the surface of apparent normality may lie aberrant behavior. Everyday well-behaved adults may practice atrocities on their own children in private. See Steve Biodrowski, "Wes Craven's Elm Street Return," *Cinefantastique* 22, no. 3 (1991): 30–32. See also Biodrowski, "Wes Craven on the Politics of Horror," *Cinefantastique* 22, no. 6 (1992): 58. Craven attempted to make his film a strong, social statement concerning "oppression by adults against minorities and children." Unfortunately, his use of two actors from David Lynch's *Twin Peaks* added to the aura of trivialized camp, debilitating the seriousness of the entire theme, particularly in the film's second half.

3. For an argument hailing *The Silence of the Lambs* as a groundbreaking gender horror film, see Julie Tharp, "The Transvestite as Monster: Gender Horror in *The Silence of the Lambs*," *Journal of Popular Film & TV* 19, no. 3 (1991): 106–13. However, like similar theoretical orientations, it fails to consider how the acclaimed narrative devices actually represent both Hollywood ideologic recuperation as well as traditional sacrificial crises strategies operating in conservative directions. Far from representing a direction where the New Man (serial killer) and New Woman "will wreak vengeance on Traditional Males" (113) the real issue is a critical blinkered vision failing to consider as to who the joke is actually on. For a good analysis of contemporary cultural fascination with the serial killer, see Jane Caputi, "The New Founding Fathers: The Lure and Lore of the Serial Killer in Contemporary Culture," *Journal of American Culture* 13, no. 1 (1990): 1–12. Hailing *The Silence of The Lambs* as an uncomplicated breakthrough within the genre is extremely problematic as two essays in *Camera Obscura* reveal. See here Elizabeth Young, "*The Silence of The Lambs* and the Flaying of Feminist Theory," and Judith Halberstam, "Skin-Flick: Posthuman Gender in Jonathan Demme's *The Silence of the Lambs*," *Camera Obscura* 27 (1991): 5–36, 37–54. For a problematic folkloristic interpretation ignoring the film's repulsive ideology, see Harold Schechter, "Skin Deep: Folk Tales, Face Lifts, and *The Silence of the Lambs*," *Literature Interpretation Theory* 5 (1994): 10–27. Hopefully, a more critical attitude is now developing toward this overrated, repulsive, and reactionary film. See Mary Ellen Alea," A Feminist Look *at Silence of the Lambs*," *Society for the Philosophic Study of the Contemporary Arts Newsletter* 2, no. 2 (1993): 11–13; and Stephanie Wardrop, "They Don't Have a Name for It Yet: Patriarchy, Gender and Meat-Eating in Jonathan Demme's *The Silence of the Lambs*," *Literature Interpretation*

Theory, 5 (1994): 95–105. For an excellent critique of this film as well as contemporary horror, see Christopher Sharrett, "The Horror Film in Neoconservative Culture," *Journal of Popular Film & Television,* 21, no. 3 (1993): 100–110.

4. See also Patricia Brett Erens, "*The Stepfather,*" *Film Quarterly* 41, no. 2 (1987–88): 48–54. The whole *Stepfather* cycle of films operates effectively by removing supernatural dimensions. Unfortunately, this is not true of Patrick Rand's *Mom* (1989), which fails to develop the social critique of families as cannibalistic institutions (see *Parents*) due to over-reliance on supernatural overtones.

5. Winter, *Faces of Fear,* 169.

6. See particularly Janice Radway, *Reading the Romance: Women, Patriarchy, and Popular Literature* (Chapel Hill: University of North Carolina Press, 1984). This represents another example of how horror films cannot be separated from other literary and cinematic genres within American culture.

7. Robin Wood, "The Woman's Nightmare: Masculinity in *Day of the Dead,*" *cineAC-TION!* 6 (1986): 45–49.

8. Jackson, 180.

9. Wood, 47.

10. Ethel Spector Person, "Sexuality as a Mainstay of Identity," *Signs* 5, no. 4 (1980): 627.

Postscript

1. Humphries, 189, 195.

2. For an appalling example of contemporary practices see the tongue-in-cheek yet appalling article by Brooks Barnes, "Save my Blockbuster. . ." *New York Times,* June 23, 2013, 1, 12–13.

3. See Tony Williams, *George A. Romero: Interviews.* Jackson: University Press of Mississippi, 2011.

4. Humphries, 191.

5. The red outfit could be defended as part of the film's aesthetic choice to use red for upsetting elements within the *mise-en-scene.* Unfortunately, the color red appears in the film more as a trite (rather than a sophisticated) signifier of meaning, resembling the obvious-ness of most student films.

6. On the DVD feature, "Between Two Worlds," the director himself actually comments that in cases of supernatural visitations to children "they all come from broken homes." Family divorce and separation, not a death, usually inspire these events. However, he is too busy making a polished Hollywood production full of visual gimmicks to comprehend the material and social significance of this statement! By contrast, in the same feature William Peter Blatty recognizes that his son's own visitation followed the trauma of leaving maternal nurture behind. Unfortunately, Blatty does not go beyond the realm of the supernatural to develop the implications of his statement.

7. For some explorations of the film that appeared in *Literature/Film Quarterly* 31, no. 1 (2003), see Martin Kervokian, "You must never move the body: Burying Irving's Text

in *Sleepy Hollow*," 27–32; David L. G. Arnold, "Fearful Pleasures, or I am Twice the Man: The Re-Gendering of Ichabod Crane," 33–38; Susan M. Bernardo, "The Battle of the Sexes in Tim Burton's *Sleepy Hollow*," 39–43; and "A dark episode of *Bonanza*: Genre, Adaptation, and Historiography in *Sleepy Hollow*," 44–49. All provide insightful readings of the film in terms of its over-emphasis on the supernatural (Kervokian), the castration and remasculinization of the headless horseman in terms of castration anxiety (Arnold), the spider-woman role of Lady Van Tassell (Bernardo), and the anti-Enlightenment bias of the film (Orr).

8. Humphries, 192.

9. Although Burton refers to stylistic influences such as Hammer horror and the films of Mario Bava in his audio commentary, he is surprisingly silent on the implications of this particular shot.

10. Op. cit.

11. See especially David L. G. Arnold, op. cit.

12. Set during the Cold War period, *Shutter Island* disavows its implications into the dehumanizing nature of postwar American society into being merely a fantasy of its hero thus turning the historical into a MacGuffin technique. For an insightful reading of this film in terms of its ideological mechanisms of Scorsese's reactionary Catholicism and the scapegoat theory of Girard see Carl Myers, "Scapegoats and Redemption *on Shutter Island*," *Journal of Religion and Film* 16, no. 1 (2012): 1–20. The audio commentary discussion between Zemeckis and his associates evokes the type of superficial, know-it-all teen discussions in Wes Craven's tedious *Scream* (1996).

13. In his interesting reading of an unworthy film, Humphries (192–93) interprets this sequence as the heroine seeing herself as an old woman in a film dealing with the effects of aging in patriarchal culture. However, this vision again reoccurs to frighten Norman when he is about to dispose of his wife in the bath and parallels the decaying image of Madison that he finally sees towards the end of the film. The alternation of beautiful and grotesque images of the corpse in this penultimate sequence is a contradiction that defies any form of resolution. However, since Zemecks is a special-effects director and plagiarizes Hitchcock incessantly throughout this film (as the overdone references to *Rear Window*, *Rebecca*, *Vertigo*, and *Psycho* reveal), it is the "scary moments" that are important, rather than an accurate revelation of what actually "lies beneath." The scene where Claire wears a dark crimson dress, similar to that of Sister Ruth in *Black Narcissus* (1947), when Madison possesses her and makes her see her own repressed discovery of the affair through her own eyes, is another gratuitous appropriation. Scenes revealing Madison's decay are mere imitations of the appearance of Alice Krige in *Ghost Story* (1981). They have no meaningful function in the narrative.

14. Humphries, op. cit, 193.

15. Diana Scarwid also appeared *in Psycho III* (1986), in which she nearly managed to lay Norman Bates!

16. Op. cit, 194.

17. See the revealing list "WV Mine Disasters: 1884 to Present." West Virginia Office of Mine Safety and Training. 2002. http://www.wvminesafety.org/disaster.htm

18. *Jake's Closet* echoes the comments of Michael Haneke concerning the role of the family in *La Pianiste* (2002). "I always want to describe the world that I know, and for me

the family is the locus of the miniature war, the first site of all warfare. The larger political-economic site is what one usually associates with warfare, but the everyday site of war in the family is as murderous in its own way, whether between parents and children or wife and husband. If you start exploring the concept of family in Western society you can't avoid realizing that the family is the origin of all conflicts." Christopher Sharrett, "The World that is Known: Michael Haneke Interviewed." http://www.kinoeye.org/04/01/interview01.php. It is beyond the scope of this study to explore further critiques of the family in other areas of cinema but the following articles by Christopher Sharrett are highly recommended. "False Criticism: Cinema and the Conservative Critique of the Bourgeois Society," *Film International* 12 (2004): 26–41; "Michael Haneke and the Discontents of European Culture," *Framework* 47, no. 2 (2006): 6–16; and "Woman Run Amok: Two Films by Lars von Trier," *Film International* 60 (2012): 11–36.

19. The ending of the series was filmed in an oblique manner with Chase refusing to comment directly on its implications. "The way I see it is that Tony Soprano had been people's alter ego. They had gleefully watched him rob, kill, pillage, lie, and cheat. They had cheered him on. And then, all of a sudden, they wanted to see him punished for all that. They wanted 'justice'. They wanted to see his brains splattered on the wall. I thought that was disgusting, frankly." "*The Sopranos*: The Definitive Explanation of 'The End,'" http://masterofsopranos.wordpress.com/the-sopranos-definitive-explanation.com. Accessed 8/18/2013. This site provides a very detailed analysis of the final scene of the series.

20. Maurice Yacowar, *The Sopranos on the Couch: Analyzing Television's Greatest Series* (New York: Continuum, 2002), 134.

21. Mikita Brottman, *Meat is Murder: An Illustrated Guide to Cannibal Culture* (London: Creation Books, 1998), 22. For two insightful essays exploring relevant issues of capitalism, conspicuous consumption and food in the series see Avi Santo, "Fat Fuck! Why Don't You Take a Look in the Mirror?": Weight, Body Image, and Masculinity in *The Sopranos*" and Sara Lewis Dunne, "'The Brutality of Meat and the Abruptness of Seafood': Food, Violence and Family in *The Sopranos*," *This Thing of Ours: Investigating The Sopranos*," ed. David Lavery (New York: Columbia University Press, 2002), 72–94; 215–26, especially 92–94, which notes the significance of "Fortunate Son." "In this flashback, the cannibalistic metaphor is rendered nearly literal as the butcher shop that feeds the Soprano family becomes the spot where Satriale's own flesh is carved up by Tony's father who later explains to his son, "this is my livelihood. It's how I put food on the table." (93).

22. See Brottman, 120–29.

23. Despite the affirmation of male family values and attempted subordination of women, the world of the male Sopranos is one of "The Lost Boys" as suggested by Glen O. Gabbard. See *The Psychology of The Sopranos: Love, Death, Desire and Betrayal in America's Favorite Gangster Family* (New York: Perseus Books, 2002), 167–82. Male crises dominate the series. In the last season, two prominent father and son figures cannot live up to The Law of the Father, as the tragic demises of Vito (Joseph R. Gannascoli) and Christopher both illustrate.

Bibliography

Alea, Mary Ellen. "A Feminist Look *at Silence of the Lambs.*" *Society for the Philosophic Study of the Contemporary Visual Arts* 3, no. 2 (1993): 11–13.

Anobile, Richard J., ed. *James Whale's Frankenstein*. New York: Picador, 1974.

Bellour, Raymond. "Hitchcock: The Enunciator." *Camera Obscura* 2 (1977): 69–77.

———. "Psychosis, Neurosis, Perversion." *Camera Obscura* 3/4 (Summer 1979): 105–32.

Benson, Peter. "Ideology and Slaughter." *cineACTION!* 12 (April 1988): 12–18.

Bergstrom, Janet. "Enunciation and Sexual Difference (Part I)." *Camera Obscura* 3/4 (Summer 1979): 33-69.

———. "Alternation, Segmentation, Hypnosis: Interview with Raymond Bellour." *Camera Obscura* 3/4 (Summer 1979): 70–103.

Biodrowski, Steve. "*Nightmare on Elm Street 5—The Dream Child.*" *Cinefantastique* 20, no. 1 (1989): 86–88.

———. "*Freddy's Dead* or Is He?" *Cinefantastique* 22, no. 2 (1991): 8-10, 60.

———. "Wes Craven: Alive and Shocking." *Cinefantastique* 22, no. 2 (1991): 11–12.

———. "Wes Craven's Elm Street Detour." *Cinefantastique* 22, no. 3 (1991): 30–32.

———. "*Freddy's Dead*: Post Mortem." *Cinefantastique* 22, no. 4 (1992): 56, 60.

———. "Wes Craven on the Politics of Horror." *Cinefantastique* 22, no. 5 (1992): 58.

Bird, Robert Montgomery. *Nick of the Woods*. Edited by Curtis Dahl. New Haven, Conn.: College and University Press, 1976.

Blatty, William Peter. *The Exorcist*. London: Corgi Books, 1972.

———. *William Peter Blatty on The Exorcist*. New York: Bantam, 1974.

Bliss, Michael. *Brian De Palma*. Metuchen, N.J.: Scarecrow Press, 1983.

Blumenthal, Sidney. *The Rise of the Counter Establishment*. New York: Tunes Books, 1986.

Boas, Ralph, and Louise Boas. *Cotton Mather: Keeper of the Puritan Conscience*. Hamden, Conn.: Hamden Books, 1964.

Bonaparte, Marie. *The Life and Works of Edgar Allan Poe: A Psychoanalytic Interpretation*. Translated by John Rodder. London: Hogarth Press, 1949.

Bordwell, David. "Happily Ever After: Part Two." *Velvet Light Trap* 19 (1982): 2–7.

Borst, Ronald V. "*The Texas Chainsaw Massacre.*" *Photon* 26 (1975): 42–48.

Boss, Pete. "Vile Bodies and Bad Medicine." *Screen* 27, no. 1 (1986): 14–24.

Boyar, Paul, and Nissbaum, Stephen. *Salem Possessed*. Cambridge: Harvard University Press, 1974.

Britton, Andrew. "*The Exorcist*." *Movie* 25 (Winter 1977/78): 16–20.

———. "*Meet Me at St. Louis* or The Ambiguities." *Australian Journal of Screen Theory* 3 (1977): 7–25.

———. "The Devil. Probably: The Symbolism of Evil." In *The American Nightmare*, edited by Richard Lippe and Robin Wood, 34–42. Toronto: Festival of Festivals, 1979.

———. "Sideshows: Hollywood in Vietnam." *Movie* 27/28 (1980/81): 2–23.

———. *Katherine Hepburn: The Thirties and After*. Newcastle-upon-Tyne: Tyneside Cinema Publications, 1984.

———. "Missing Out: The Politics of Reaganite Entertainment." *Movie* 31/32 (1986): 1–42.

Brophy, Phil. "Horrality—The Textuality of Contemporary Horror Films." *Screen* 27, no. 1 (1986): 2–13.

Brown, Royal S. "*Dressed to Kill*: Myth and Fantasy in the Horror/Suspense Genre." *Film/ Psychology Review* 4 (1980): 169–82.

Bruce, Bryan. "*It's Alive*." *Movie* 31/32 (1986): 115–17.

Bussing, Sabine. *Aliens in the Home: The Child in Horror Fiction*. New York: Greenwood Press, 1987.

Butler, Ivan. *Horror in the Cinema*. London: Zwemmer Books, 1970.

———. *The Cinema of Roman Polanski*. London: Zwemmer Books, 1970.

Byars, Jackie. *All That Hollywood Allows: Re-Reading Gender in 1950s Cinema*. Chapel Hill: The University of North Carolina Press, 1991.

Caputi, Jane. "The New Founding Fathers: The Lore and Lure of the Serial Killer in Contemporary Culture." *Journal of American Culture* 13, no. 1 (1990), 1–12.

Carroll, Noel. "Nightmare and The Horror Film: The Symbolic Biology of Fantastic Beings." *Film Quarterly* 34, no. 3 (1981): 16–25.

———. *The Philosophy of Horror or Paradoxes of the Heart*. New York: Routledge, 1990.

Castle, William. *Step Right Up! I'm Gonna Scare the Pants Off America*. New York: Putnam, 1978.

Cawelti, John. *The Six-Gun Mystique*. Bowling Green, Ohio: Bowling Green University Press, 1971.

Chaplin, Elayne. "'*Demon*' a.k.a. *God Told Me To*." *Movie* 34/35 (1990): 103–107.

Chase, Richard. *Herman Melville*. New York: Hafner Books, 1949.

Chodorow, Nancy. *The Reproduction of Mothering: Psychoanalysis and The Sociology of Gender*. Berkeley: University of California Press, 1978.

———. *Feminism and Psychoanalytic Theory*. New Haven: Yale University Press, 1989.

Christopher, Renny. "Negotiating the Viet Nam War Through Permeable Genre Borders: *Aliens* as Viet Nam War Film; *Platoon* as Horror Film." *Literature Interpretation Theory* 5 (1994): 53–66.

Ciment, Michel. *John Boorman*. Translated by Gilbert Adair. London: Faber & Faber, 1986.

Clarens, Carlos. *Horror Movies*. London: Panther, 1971.

Clark, Jim. "*A Nightmare on Elm Street—Part II*." *Cinefantastique* 15, no. 5 (1986): 14, 55.

———. "*A Nightmare on Elm Street—Part III*." *Cinefantastique* 17, no. 2 (1987): 6–7.

Clarke, Frederick S. "Nightmare on Elm Street: The Phenomenom." *Cinefantastique* 18, no. 5 (1988): 6–7.

Clover, Carol, J. "Her Body, Himself: Gender in the Slasher Film." *Representations* 20 (1987): 187–228.

———. *Men, Women, and Chain Saws: Gender in the Modern Horror Film.* Princeton, N.J.: Princeton University Press, 1992.

Collings, Michael R. *The Films of Stephen King.* Washington: Starmont, 1986.

Connolly, Thomas F., ed. *The Scarlet Letter and Selected Tales.* London: Penguin, 1970.

Cook, David. "American Horror: *The Shining.*" *Literature/Film Quarterly* 12, no. 1 (1984): 2–4.

Cooper, David. *The Death of the Family.* London: Penguin, 1971.

Cooper, Pamela. "David Rabe's *Sticks and Bones:* The Adventures of Ozzie and Harriet." *Modern Drama* 29, no. 4 (1986): 613–25.

Crawford, Alan. *Thunder on the Right: The New Right and the Politics of Resentment.* New York: Pantheon Books, 1980.

Creed, Barbara. "Horror and the Monstrous Feminine: An Imaginary Abjection." *Screen* 27, no. 1 (1986): 44–70.

———. "Phallic Panic: Male Hysteria and *Dead Ringers.*" *Screen* 31 no. 2 (1990): 125–46.

Crews, Frederick S. *The Sins of the Fathers.* New York: Oxford University Press, 1966.

Crouch, William. "Friedkin on *The Exorcist.*" *Cinefantastique* 3 no. 3 (1974): 6–13.

Cumbow, Robert C. *Order in the Universe: The Films of John Carpenter.* Metuchen, N.J.: Scarecrow Press, 1990.

———. "*Dawn of the Dead.*" In *Vietnam War Films,* edited by Jean-Jacques Malo and Tony Williams, 104–105. Jefferson, North Carolina: McFarland & Co., 1994.

Dadoun, Roger. "Fetishism in the Horror Film." In *Fantasy and the Cinema,* edited by James Donald, translated by Annwyl Williams, 39–62. London: BFI Publishing, 1989.

Davis, David Brion. *Homicide in American Fiction 1798–1860.* Ithaca: Cornell University Press, 1957.

Davis, Mike. *Prisoners of the American Dream.* London: Verso, 1986.

De Camp, L. Sprague. *Lovecraft: A Biography.* New York: Doubleday, 1973.

Demos, John. "Underlying Themes in the Witchcraft of Seventeenth Century New England." *American Historical Review* 75, no. 5 (1970): 1311–26.

Derry, Charles. *Dark Dreams: A Psychological History of the Modern Horror Film.* London: Thomas Yoseloff, 1977.

———. "More Dark Dreams: Some Notes on the Recent Horror Film." In *American Horrors,* edited by Gregory A. Waller, 162–74. Urbana: University of Illinois Press, 1987.

Deutelbaum, Marshall, and Leland Poague, eds. *A Hitchcock Reader.* Ames: Iowa State University Press, 1986.

Dika, Vera. *Games of Terror: Halloween, Friday the 13th, and the Films of the Stalker Cycle.* Madison, N.J.: Fairleigh Dickinson University Press, 1990.

Dillard, R. W. H. "*Night of the Living Dead:* It's Not Just a Wind That's Passing Through." In *American Horrors,* edited by Gregory A. Waller, 14–29. Urbana: University of Illinois Press, 1986.

Doane, Mary Ann. *The Desire to Desire: The Woman's Film of the 1940's.* Bloomington: Indiana University Press, 1987.

Doherty, Thomas. "Hannibal Lecter's Horror Pedigree." *Cinefantastique* 22, no. 4 (1992): 36–37.

Dreyfuss, Herbert, and Paul Rabinow. *Michel Foucault: Beyond Structuralism and Hermeneutics.* Chicago: University of Chicago Press, 1983.

Drew, Wayne, ed. *BFI Dossier 21: David Cronenberg*. London: British Film Institute, 1984.

Durgnat, Raymond. *The Strange Case of Alfred Hitchcock*. London: Faber and Faber, 1974.

Durham, Weldon B. "Gone to Flowers: Theatre and Drama of the Vietnam War." In *America Rediscovered: Critical Essays on Literature and Film of the Vietnam War*, edited by Owen W. Gilman, Jr., and Lorrie Smith, 332–62. New York: Garland Publishing, Inc., 1990.

Ellison, Harlan. "Why the Children Don't Look Like Their Parents." In *Stephen King At the Movies*, edited by Jessie Horsting, 96–101. New York: Starlog, 1986.

Erens, Patricia Brett. "*The Seduction*: The Pornographic Impulse in Slasher Films." *Jump Cut* 32 (1987): 52–55.

———. "*The Stepfather*." *Film Quarterly* 41, no. 2: (1987–88): 48–54.

Esterson, Aaron. *The Leaves of Spring: Schizophrenia, Family and Sacrifice*. London: Pelican, 1972.

Evans, Walter. "Monster Movies and Rites of Initiation." *Journal of Popular Film* 4 (1975): 124–32.

Everson, William K. *Classics of the Horror Film*. Seacaucus, N.J.: Citadel Press, 1974.

———. *More Classics of the Horror Film*. Seacaucus, N.J.: Citadel Press, 1986.

Fagan, N. Bryllion. *The Histrionic Mr. Poe*. Baltimore: John Hopkins Press, 1949.

Fiedler, Leslie A. *Love and Death in the American Novel*. New York: Stein & Day, 1966.

———. *The Return of the Vanishing American*. London: Jonathan Cape, 1968.

Fischer, Lucy. "Birth Traumas: Parturition and Horror in *Rosemary's Baby*." *Cinema Journal* 31, no. 3 (1992): 3–18.

Fischer, Lucy, and Marcia Landy. "*Eyes of Laura Mars*: A Binocular Critique." *Screen* 23, nos. 3–4 (1982): 4–19.

Fliess, Robert. *Symbol, Dream and Psychosis*. New York: International Universities Press, 1973.

Foley, Charles. "The Teeny Shockers." *Observer Colour Supplement* (14 July 1977): 27–29.

Foucault, Michel. *Discipline and Punish*. Translated by Alan Sheridan. New York: Pantheon Books, 1977.

———. *Power-Knowledge: Selected Interviews and Other Writings*. Edited and translated by Colin Gordon. New York: Pantheon Books, 1980.

Framework Editorial Board. "The Family in *The Reckless Moment*." *Framework* 4 (1976): 21–24.

Freeman, Lucy. *Our Inner World of Rage: Understanding and Transforming the Power of Anger*. New York: Continuum Publishing Company, 1990.

Freud, Sigmund. "The Uncanny." In *On Creativity and the Unconscious*, edited by Benjamin Nelson, 122–61. New York: Harper & Row, 1958.

———. "A Neurosis of Demoniacal Possession in the Seventeenth Century." In *On Creativity and the Unconscious*, edited by Benjamin Nelson, 264–300. New York: Harper & Row, 1958.

———. *On Sexuality. Pelican Freud Library 7*. London: Penguin Books, 1977.

———. *On Metapsychology. Pelican Freud Library 11*. London: Penguin Books, 1984.

Gagne, Paul. *The Zombies That Ate Pittsburgh: The Films of George A. Romero*. New York: Dodd, Mead & Company, 1987.

Gans, Herbert. "*The Exorcist*: A Devilish Attack on Women." *Social Policy* 5 (1974): 71–73.

Gaylin, Willard. *The Rage Within: Anger in Modern Life.* New York: Simon and Schuster, 1984.

Gifford, Dennis. *A Pictorial History of Horror Movies.* London: Hamlyn, 1973.

Gilbert, Sandra M., and Susan Gubar. *The Madwoman in the Attic: The Woman Writer in the Nineteenth Century Literary Imagination.* New Haven: Yale University Press, 1979.

Gilligan, Carol. *In a Different Voice.* Cambridge: Harvard University Press, 1982.

Girard, Rene. *Deceit, Desire and The Novel: Self and Others in Literary Structure.* Translated by Yvonne Freccero. Baltimore: The John Hopkins University Press, 1965.

———. *Violence and The Sacred.* Translated by Patrick Gregory. Baltimore: The Johns Hopkins University Press, 1977.

———. "Generative Scapegoating." In *Violent Origins,* edited by Robert G. Hammerton-Kelly. Stanford, Calif.: Stanford University Press, 1987.

Gire, Dan. "Bye Bye Freddy." *Cinefantastique* 18, no. 2 (1988): 8–10.

Gire, Dan, and Paul Mandell. "*Friday the 13th*: Horror's First Franchise." *Cinefantastique* 20, no. 1 (1989): 91–94.

Girgis, Sam B. "R. D. Laing and Literature: Readings of Poe, Hawthorne, and Kate Chopin." In *Psychological Perspectives on Literature: Freudian Dissidents and Neo-Freudians,* edited by Joseph Natoli, 181–97. Hamden, Conn.: Archon, 1984.

Glasser, Ira. "The Coming Assault on Civil Liberties." In *What Reagan Is Doing to Us,* edited by Alan Gartner, Colin Greer, and Frank Riessman, 230–48. New York: Harper & Row, 1982.

Gledhill, Christine. "The Horror Film." In *The Cinema Book,* edited by Pam Cook, 99–106. London: British Film Institute, 1985.

———, ed. *Home Is Where the Heart Is: Studies in Melodrama and the Woman's Film.* London: British Film Institute, 1987.

Gordon, Norman G. "Family Structure and Dynamics in De Palma's Horror Films." *Psychoanalytic Review* 70 (1983): 435–42.

Gordon, Norman G., and Anaruth Gordon. "Controversial Issues in De Palma's *Dressed to Kill.*" *Psychoanalytic Review* 69 (1982): 559–66.

Gordon, Paul. "'Sometimes a Cigar Is Not Just a Cigar': A Freudian Analysis of Uncle Charles in Hitchcock's *Shadow of A Doubt.*" *Literature/Film Quarterly* 19, no. 4 (1991): 267–76.

Graham, Allison. "'The Fallen Wonder of the World': Brian De Palma's Horror Films." In *American Horrors,* 129–44.

Gramsci, Antonio. *Selections from the Prison Notebooks.* Translated and edited by Geoffrey Nowell Smith. New York: International Publishers, 1971.

———. *Selections from Cultural Writings.* Edited by David Forgacs and Geoffrey Nowell Smith. Translated by William Boelhower. London: Lawrence and Wishart, 1985.

Grant, Barry K., ed. *Planks of Reason: Essays on the Horror Film.* Metuchen. N.J.: Scarecrow Press, 1984.

———. "Taking Back *The Night of the Living Dead*: George Romero, Feminism and the Horror Film." *Wide Angle* 14, no. 1 (1992): 64–76.

Greenberg, Harvey. "Germinal Dread." *Quarterly Review of Film Studies* 7, no. 2 (1982): 191–96.

Grixti, Joseph. *Terrors of Uncertainty: The Cultural Context of Horror Fiction.* New York: Routledge, 1989.

Gross, Louis S. *Redefining the American Gothic: From Wieland to Day of the Dead.* Ann Arbor, Mich.: UMI Research Press, 1989.

Halberstam, Judith. "Skin-Flick: Posthuman Gender in Jonathan Demme's *The Silence of the Lambs.*" *Camera Obscura* 27 (1991): 37–54.

———. "On Lesbians, Vampires, and Coppola's *Dracula.*" *Bright Lights* 11 (1993): 7-9.

Handling, Piers, ed. *The Shape of Rage: The Films of David Cronenberg.* Toronto: Canada General Publishing Co., 1983.

Hatlen, Burton. "Good and Evil in Stephen King's *The Shining.*" In *The Shining Reader*, edited by Anthony Magistrale, 81–104. Washington: Starmont House, Inc., 1990.

Hawkins, Augustus F. "Minorities and Unemployment." In *What Reagan Is Doing to Us*, edited by Colin Grier Gastner and Frank Riessman, 125–40. New York: Harper & Row, 1982.

Helfer, Roy E., and C. Henry Kempe, eds. *Child Abuse and Neglect: The Family and the Community.* Cambridge, Mass.: Ballinger Publishing Company, 1976.

———, and Ruth S. Kempe, eds. *The Battered Child.* 4th ed. Chicago: The University of Chicago Press, 1987.

Herron, Don. "Horror Springs in the Fiction of Stephen King." In *Fear Itself: The Horror Fiction of Stephen King*, 57–84. San Francisco: Underwood-Miller, 1982.

Hess, John. "*Godfather II*: A Deal Coppola Couldn't Refuse." In *Movies and Methods I*, edited by Bill Nichols, 81–90. Berkeley: University of California Press, 1976.

Higashi, Sumiko. "*Night of the Living Dead*: A Horror Film about the Horrors of The Vietnam War." In *From Hanoi to Hollywood: The Vietnam War in American Film*, edited by Linda Dittmar and Gene Michaud, 175–88. New Brunswick: Rutgers University Press, 1990.

Hirsch, Foster. "*The Possession of Joel Delaney* and *The Other.*" *Cinefantastique* 2, no. 3 (1973): 27.

Hoffman, Daniel. *Poe.* London: Hobson Books, 1973.

Hoile, Christopher. "The Uncanny and the Fairy Tale in Kubrick's *The Shining.*" *Literature/Film Quarterly* 2, no. 1 (1984): 5–12.

Hollinger, Karen. "The Monster as Woman: 'No Generations of Cat People." *Film Criticism* 13, no. 2 (1989): 36–46.

Hollum, W. Eugene. *Frontier Violence.* New York: Oxford University Press, 1974.

Holub, Robert. *Reception-Theory: A Critical Introduction.* London: Methuen, 1984.

Horowitz, Gad. *Repression.* Toronto: University of Toronto Press, 1977.

Horsting, Jessie. *Stephen King at the Movies.* New York: Starlog, 1986.

Horwitz, Margaret M. "*The Birds*: A Mother's Love." In *A Hitchcock Reader*, edited by Marshall Dentelbaum and Leland Poggue, 279–87. Ames: Iowa State University Press.

Iser, Wolfgang. *The Act of Reading: A History of Aesthetic Response.* Baltimore, M.D.: The Johns Hopkins University Press, 1978.

Isherwood, Christopher, and Don Bachardy. *Frankenstein: The True Story.* New York: Avon, 1973.

Jackson, Kathy Merlock. *Images of Children in American Film: A Sociocultural Analysis.* Metuchen, N.J.: The Scarecrow Press, 1986.

Jackson, Rosemary. *Fantasy: The Literature of Subversion.* London, Methuen, 1981.

———. "Narcissism and Beyond: A Psychoanalytic Reading of *Frankenstein* and Fantasies of the Double." In *Aspects of Fantasy: Selected Essays for the Second International Conference on the Fantastic in Literature and Film,* 43–53. Westport, Conn.: Greenwood Press, 1986.

Jacoby, Russell. *Social Amnesia: A Critique of Conformist Psychology from Adler to Laing.* Boston: Beacon Press, 1975.

Jameson, Frederic. "The Shining." *Social Text* 4 (1981): 114–25.

———. *The Political Unconscious: Narrative as a Socially Symbolic Act.* Ithaca: Cornell University Press, 1981.

———. "Postmodernism or the Cultural Logic of Late Capitalism." *New Left Review* 146 (1984): 53–92.

Jauss, Hans Robert. *Towards an Aesthetic of Reception.* Minneapolis: University of Minnesota Press, 1982.

Jensen, Paul. "Film Favorites." *Film Comment* 6, no. 3 (1970): 42–46.

———. "The Return of Dr. Caligari." *Film Comment* 7, no. 4 (1971/72): 36–45.

Johnson, Guy. "The Pleasure of Terror and 'All This Freddy Shit,'" *USC Spectator* 10, no. 1 (1989): 6–19.

Jung, Carl Gustay. *Civilization in Transition.* London: Routledge, Kegan & Paul, 1964.

———. *Man and His Symbols.* London: Aldus Books, 1974.

Kawin, Bruce. "The Mummy's Pool." *Planks of Reason,* 3–20.

———. "*The Funhouse* and *The Howling.*" *American Horrors,* 102–13.

Kellner, Douglas. "Film, Politics, and Ideology: Reflections on Hollywood Film in the Age of Reagan." *Velvet Light Trap* 27 (1991): 9–24.

Kent, Brian. "Canaries in a Gilded Cage: Mental and Marital Decline in *McTeague* and *The Shining.*" *The Shining Reader,* 139–55.

Kinder, Marsha, and Beverle Houston. "Seeing Is Believing: *The Exorcist* and *Don't Look Now.*" *American Horrors,* 44–61.

King, Stephen. *Carrie.* New York: Signet, 1976.

———. *Night Shift.* London: New England Library, 1979.

———. *Danse Macabre.* New York: Berkeley, 1981.

Klinger, Barbara. "Cinema/Ideology/Criticism Revisited: The Progressive Text." *Screen* 25, no. 1 (1984): 30–44.

Knee, Adam. "The Metamorphosis of *The Fly.*" *Wide Angle* 14, no. 1 (1992): 21–34.

Kristeva, Julia. *Powers of Horror: An Essay in Abjection.* New York: Columbia University Press, 1982.

Laing, R. D. *The Divided Self.* London: Pelican, 1965.

———. *The Politics of Experience and The Bird of Paradise.* London: Pelican, 1967.

———. *Self and Others.* London: Pelican, 1971.

———, and Aaron Esterson. *Sanity, Madness and the Family.* London: Heinemann, 1964.

Lang, Robert. *American Film Melodrama: Griffith, Vidor, Minnelli.* Princeton, N.J.: Princeton University Press, 1989.

Laplanche, Jean, and J. B. Pontalis. *The Language of Psycho-Analysis.* Translated by Donald Nicholson-Smith. New York: Norton, 1973.

Lawrence, D. H. *Studies in Classic American Literature*. London: Heinemann, 1964.

Lebeau, Vicky. "'You're My Friend': *River's Edge* and Social Spectatorship." *Camera Obscura* 25–26 (1991): 251–72.

Lerner, Michael. *Surplus Powerlessness*. Oakland, Calif.: The Institute of Labor and Mental Health, 1986.

Levine, Lawrence W. *Highbrow/Lowbrow: The Emergence of Cultural Hierarchy in America*. Cambridge: Harvard University Press, 1988.

Linderman, Deborah. "Cinematic Abreaction: Tourneur's *Cat People*." In *Psychoanalysis & Cinema*, edited by E. Ann Kaplan, 73–97. New York: Routledge, 1990.

Lindsey, Shelley Stamp. "Horror, Femininity, and *Carrie's* Monstrous Puberty." *Journal of Film and Video* 43, no. 4 (1991): 33–44.

Long, Frank Belknap. *Howard Phillips Lovecraft: Dreamer on the Nightside*. Sauk City, Wisc.: Arkham House, 1975.

Lovecraft, Howard Phillips. *Dagon*. Sauk City, Wisc.: Arkham House, 1965.

———. *Selected Letters III*. Sauk City, Wisc.: Arkham House, 1971.

———. *Selected Letters IV*. Sauk City, Wisc.: Arkham House, 1976.

Lovell, Terry. *Consuming Fiction*. London: Verso, 1987.

Lowry, Edward. "Genre and Enunciation: The Case of Horror." *Journal of Film and Video* 36, no. 2 (1984): 13–20, 72.

Macherey, Pierre. *A Theory of Literary Production*. Translated by Geoffrey Wall. London: Routledge and Kegan Paul, 1978.

Magistrale, Anthony. *Landscape of Fear: Stephen King's American Gothic*. Bowling Green, Ohio: Popular Press, 1988.

———. *The Moral Voyages of Stephen King*. Washington: Starmont House, Inc., 1989.

———. *The Shining Reader*. Washington: Starmont House, 1990.

———, ed. *The Dark Descent: Essays Defining Stephen King's Horrorscape*. New York: Greenwood Press, 1992.

Malcolm, Janet. *In the Freud Archives*. New York: Alfred A. Knopf, 1984.

Maltby, Richard. *Harmless Entertainment: Hollywood and the Ideology of Consensus*. Metuchen, N.J.: The Scarecrow Press, 1983.

Mandell, Paul. "Jason Lives: The Birth of A Legend." *Cinefantastique* 20, no. 1 (1989): 92, 125.

Marcuse, Herbert. *Eros and Civilization*. Boston: Beacon Press, 1966.

Marx, Leo. *The Machine in the Garden*. New York: Oxford University Press, 1964.

Masson, Jeffrey Moussaieff. *The Assault on Truth: Freud's Suppression of the Seduction Theory*. New York: Farrar, Straus & Giroux, 1984.

———. *A Dark Science: Women, Sexuality and Science in the Nineteenth Century*. New York: Farrar, Straus and Giroux. 1986.

———. *Against Therapy: Emotional Tyranny and the Myth of Psychological Healing*. New York: Atheneum, 1988.

Mather, Cotton. *Magnalia Christi Americana*. New York: Arno Press, 1972.

McArthur, Colin. "Polanski." *Sight and Sound* 38, no. 1 (1968–69): 14–17.

McConnell, Frank. "Rough Beast Slouching: A Note on Horror Movies." *Kenyon Review* 32, no. 1 (1970): 109–20.

McDonald, David. "The Mystification of Vietnam: David Rabe's *Sticks and Bones*." *Cultural Critique* 3 (1986): 211–35.

McLaughlin, James. "All in the Family: Alfred Hitchcock's *Shadow of A Doubt*." In *A Hitchcock Reader*, edited by Marshall Deutelbaum and Leland A. Poague, 141–52. Ames: Iowa State University Press, 1986.

McPherson, Hugo. *Hawthorne as Myth Maker*. Toronto, Canada: University of Toronto Press, 1969.

Metz, Christian. *The Imaginary Signifier: Psychoanalysis and the Cinema*. Bloomington: Indiana University Press, 1982.

Miller, Alice. *Banished Knowledge: Facing Childhood Injuries*. Translated by Leila Vennewitz. New York: Doubleday, 1990.

———. *The Untouched Key: Tracing Childhood Trauma in Creativity and Destructiveness*. Translated by Hildegarde and Hunter Hannum. New York: Doubleday, 1990.

Miller, Perry. *The New England Mind*. Cambridge: Harvard University Press, 1962.

Milne, Tom. "Discovery: *Curse of The Cat People*." *Focus on Film* 7 (1971): 53–56.

———. "*It's Alive*." *Monthly Film Bulletin* 42, no. 497 (1975): 137.

Modleski, Tania. "The Terror of Pleasure: The Contemporary Horror Film and Postmodern Theory." In *Studies in Entertainment: Critical Approaches to Mass Culture*. Bloomington: Indiana University Press, 1986.

———. *The Women Who Knew Too Much: Hitchcock and Feminist Theory*. New York: Methuen, 1988.

———. *Feminism Without Women: Culture and Criticism in a "Postfeminist Age."* New York: Routledge, 1991.

Moers, Ellen. *Literary Women*. New York: Doubleday, 1976.

Moretti, Franco. "The Dialectic of Fear." In *Signs Taken for Wonders*, 83–108. London: Verso, 1983.

Morrison, Joan. "(Review of) *The Philosophy of Horror*." *Film Criticism* 15, no. 3 (1991): 41–43.

Mulvey, Laura. "Visual Pleasure and Narrative Cinema." *Screen* 16 no. 3 (1975): 6–18.

———. "Notes on Sirk and Melodrama." *Movie* 25 (1977/78): 53–56.

———. "Afterthoughts on 'Visual Pleasure and Narrative Cinema' inspired by *Duel in The Sun*." *Framework* 15/16/17 (1981): 12–15.

———. "Some Thoughts on Theories of Fetishism in the Context of Contemporary Culture." *October* 65 (1993): 3–20.

Naremore, James. *Filmguide to Psycho*. Bloomington: Indiana University Press, 1973.

Neale, Steve. *Genre*. London: British Film Institute. 1980.

———. "*Halloween*: Suspense, Aggression and The Look." In *Planks of Reason*, edited by Barry K. Grant, 331–45. Metuchen, N.J.: Scarecrow Press, 1984.

———. "Masculinity as Spectacle." *Screen* 24, no. 6 (1983): 2–11.

———. "Sexual Difference in Cinema." *Oxford Literary Review* 8, nos. 1–2 (1986): 123–32.

Neale, William. *The Life of Ambrose Bierce*. New York: AMS Press, 1929.

Newman, Kim. *Nightmare Movies*. New York: Harmony Books, 1989.

Novelli, Martin. "Spiking the Vietnam Film 'Canon': David Rabe & *Casualties of War*." In *David Rabe: A Casebook*, edited by Toby Silverman Zinman, 149–71. New York: Garland Press, 1991.

Nowell-Smith, Geoffrey. "Minelli and Melodrama." *Screen* 18, no. 2 (1977): 105–18.

O'Connor, Richard. *Ambrose Bierce*. London: Gollanz, 1968.

Pallenberg, Barbara. *The Making of Exorcist II: The Heretic*. New York: Warner Books, 1977.

Paul, William. *Laughing Screaming: Modern Hollywood Horror and Comedy*. New York: Columbia University Press, 1994.

Pearson, Robert E., and William Uricchio, eds. *The Many Lives of the Batman: Critical Approaches to a Superhero and His Media*. New York: Routledge, 1990.

Peary, Danny. "Mark Robson Remembers RKO, Welles and Val Lewton." *Velvet Light Trap* 10 (Fall 1973): 3–7.

———. *Cult Movies: The Classics, the Sleepers, the Weird, and the Wonderful*. New York: Dell, 1981.

———. *Cult Movies 2*. New York: Dell, 1983.

Peele, Gillian. *Revival and Reaction: The Right in Contemporary America*. Oxford: Clarendon Press, 1984.

Person, Ethel Spector. "Sexuality as a Mainstay of Identity." *Signs* 5, no. 4 (1980): 605–30.

Piso, Michelle. "Mark's *Marnie*." *A Hitchcock Reader*, 288–303.

Poague, Leland A. "Links in a Chain: *Psycho* and Film Classicism." In *A Hitchcock Reader*, edited by Marshall Deutelbaum and Leland S. Poague, 340–55. Ames: Iowa State University Press, 1988.

Polan, Dana. "Eros and Syphilization: The Contemporary Horror Film." In *Planks of Reason*, edited by Barry K. Grant, 201–14. Metuchen: The Scarecrow Press, 1984.

Pollack, Griselda, et al. "Dossier on Melodrama." *Screen* 18 no. 2 (1977): 105–18.

Poster, Mark. *Critical Theory of the Family*. New York: The Seabury Press, 1978.

Quinn, Arthur Hobson. *Edgar Allan Poe: A Critical Biography*. New York: Appleton & Century Crofts, Inc., 1941.

Rabe, David. *The Basic Training of Pavlo Hummel and Sticks and Bones*. New York: Viking Press, 1973.

Radway, Janice A. *Reading the Romance: Women, Patriarchy, and Popular Literature*. Chapel Hill: University of North Carolina Press, 1984.

Rank, Otto. *The Double: A Psychoanalytic Study*. Translated and edited by Henry Tucker, Jr. Chapel Hill: The University of North Carolina Press, 1971.

Raubicheck Walter, and Walter Srebnick, eds. *Hitchcock's Rereleased Films: From Rope to Vertigo*. Detroit: Wayne State University Press, 1991.

Reagan, Ronald. *A Time for Choosing: The Speeches of Ronald Reagan 1961–1980*. Chicago: Regnery Gateway, Inc., 1983.

Reesman, Jeanne Campbell. "Stephen King and the Tradition of American Naturalism in *The Shining*." In *The Shining Reader*, edited by Arlheny Magistade, 121–38. Washington: Stasmond House, Inc. 1990.

Reich, Wilhelm. *The Mass Psychology of Fascism*. New York: Farrar, Straus & Giroux, 1970.

Riley, Philip J., ed. *Frankenstein. Universal Film Scripts Series*. Absecon, N.J.: Magic Image Film Books, 1989.

———. *The Bride of Frankenstein. Universal Filmscripts Series*. Absecon, N.J.: Magic Image Film Books, 1989.

———. *Son of Frankenstein. Universal Filmscripts Series.* Absecon, N.J.: Magic Image Film Books, 1990.

———. *The Ghost of Frankenstein. Universal Filmscripts Series.* Absecon, N.J.: Magic Image Film Books, 1990.

———. *Frankenstein Meets The Wolf Man. Universal Filmscripts Series.* Absecon, N.J.: Magic Image Film Books, 1990.

———. *Dracula. Universal Filmscripts Series.* Absecon, N.J.: Magic Image Film Books, 1990.

Rodowick, D. N. "The Enemy Within: The Economy of Violence in *The Hills Have Eyes.*" In *Planks of Reason,* edited by Barry K. Grant, 321–30. Metuchen, N.J.: The Scarecrow Press, 1984.

Rogin, Michael. *Ronald Reagan: The Movie and Other Episodes in Political Demonology.* Berkeley: University of California Press, 1987.

Rose, Jacqueline. "Paranoia and the Film System." *Screen* 17, no. 4 (1976–77): 85–104.

Rothman, William. *Hitchcock: The Murderous Gaze.* Cambridge: Harvard University Press, 1982.

Rubin, Steve. "Retrospect: *Them!*" *Cinefantastique* 3, no. 4 (1974): 23–27.

Rusher, William A. *The Rise of the Right.* New York: William Morrow & Company, Inc., 1984.

Ryan, Michael, and Douglas Kellner. *Camera Politica: The Politics and Ideology of Contemporary Hollywood Film.* Bloomington: Indiana University Press, 1988.

Sayre, Nora. *Sixties Going on Seventies.* New York: Arbor House, 1973.

Scapperotti, Dan. "New Line Cinema: The House That Freddy Built." *Cinefantastique* 20 no. 1 (1989): 124–25.

Schafram, Lynn Hecht. "Reversing the Decade of Progress." In *What Reagan Is Doing To Us,* edited by Alan Gartner, Colin Greer, and Frank Riessman, 125–40. New York: Harper & Row, 1982.

———. "Women: Reversing The Decade of Progress." In *What Reagan Is Doing to Us,* 162–89.

Schatz, Thomas. *Old Hollywood/New Hollywood: Ritual, Art and Ideology.* Ann Arbor, Mich.: UMI Research Press, 1983.

Schatzman, Morton. *Soul Murder: Persecution in the Family.* London: Penguin, 1976.

Schechter, Harold. "Skin Deep: Folk Tales, Face Lifts, and *The Silence of the Lambs.*" *Literature Interpretation Theory* 5 (1994): 19–27.

Scheff, Thomas J, and Suzanne M. Retzinger. *Emotions and Violence.* Lexington: Mass.: Lexington Books, 1991.

Schneider, Michel. *Neurosis and Civilization: A Marxist/Freudian Synthesis.* Translated by Michael Roboff. New York: Seabury Press, 1975.

Scheib, Ronnie. "Charlie's Uncle." *Film Comment* 12, no. 2 (1976): 55–67.

Schoen, William, and James Spencer. *The Nightmare Never Ends: The Official History of Freddy Krueger and the 'Nightmare on Elm Street' Films.* New York: Citadel Press, 1992.

Shanks, Edward. *Edgar Allan Poe.* London: Macmillan, 1937.

Sharrett, Christopher. *Apocalypticism in the Contemporary Horror Film: A Typological Survey of the Theme in The Fantastic Cinema, Its Relationship to Cultural Tradition and Current Filmic Expression.* Doctoral dissertation, New York University, 1983.

———. "The Idea of Apocalypse in *The Texas Chainsaw Massacre.*" In *Planks of Reason,* edited by Barry K. Grant. Metuchen, N.J.: Scarecrow Press, 1984, 255–76.

———. "'Fairy Tales for The Apocalypse': Wes Craven on the Horror *Film.*" *Literature/Film Quarterly* 13, no. 3 (1985): 139–47.

———. "Myth and Ritual in the Post-Industrial Landscape: The Horror Films of David Cronenberg." *Persistence of Vision* 3/4 (1986): 111–30.

———. "Postmodern Narrative Cinema: Aeneas on a Stroll." *Canadian Journal of Political and Social Theory* 12, nos. 1–2 (1988): 78–104.

———, ed. *Crisis Cinema: The Apocalyptic Idea in Postmodern Narrative Film.* Washington, D.C: Maisonneuve Press, 1993.

———. "The Horror Film in Neoconservative Culture." *Journal of Popular Film and Television*, 21, no. 3 (1993): 100–10.

Shay, Dan. "Filming *The Omen.*" *Cinefantastique* 5, no. 3 (1976): 40–47.

Sidel, Ruth. "The Family: A Dream Deferred." In *What Reagan Is Doing to Us*, edited by Alan Gartner, Colin Greer and Frank Riesman, 54–70. New York: Harper & Row, 1982.

Siegel, Joel. *Val Lewton: The Reality of Terror.* London: Secker & Warburg, 1972.

Silverman, Kaja. *Male Subjectivity at the Margins.* New York: Routledge, 1992.

Slotkin, Richard. *Regeneration Through Violence: The Mythology of the American Frontier 1600–1860.* Middletown, Conn.: Wesleyan University Press, 1973.

———. *The Fatal Environment: The Myth of Frontier in the Age of Industrialization 1800–1890.* New York: Atheneum, 1985.

———. "Gunfighters and Green Berets: *The Magnificent Seven* and the Myth of Counter-Insurgency." *Radical History Review* 44 (1989): 65–90.

Smith, Henry Nash. *Virgin Land.* Cambridge: Harvard University Press, 1950.

Smith, Paul. "Vas." *Camera Obscura* 17 (1988): 89–111.

Snyder, Stephen. "Family Life and Leisure Culture *in The Shining.*" *Film Criticism* 6 (1982): 4–13.

Sobchack, Vivian. "Bringing It All Back Home: Family Economy and Generic Exchange." In *American Horrors*, edited by Gregory A. Waller, 175–94. Urbana: University of Illinois Press, 1986.

———. *Screening Space: The American Science Fiction Film.* New York: Ungar, 1984.

———. "Child/Alien/Father: Patriarchal Crisis and Generic Exchange." *Camera Obscura* 15 (1986): 7–34.

"Spectatrix, The." Special issue of *Camera Obscura* 20–21 (1989).

Stern, Milton R. *The Fine Hammered Steel of Herman Melville.* Chicago: University of Illinois Press, 1968.

Stovall, Floyd. "The Conscious Art of Edgar Allan Poe." In *Poe: A Collection of Essays*, edited by Robert Regan, 172–79. Englewood Cliffs, N.J.: Prentice-Hall, Inc., 1967.

Surmacz, Gary. "Anatomy of a Horror Film." *Cinefantastique* 4, no. 1 (1975): 14–27.

Szulkin, David A. "Keep Repeating 'It's Only a Classic,'" *Fangoria* 114 (1992): 16–21, 60–61.

Tarratt, Margaret. "Monsters from the Id." *Films and Filming* 17, no. 3 (1970): 38–42.

———. "Monsters from the Id." *Films and Filming* 17 no. 4 (1971): 40–42.

Telotte, J. P. "Val Lewton's Children: Horror, Innocence and Maturity." *Postscript* 1, no. 2 (1982): 46–61.

———. "Faith and Idolatry in the Horror Film." In *Planks of Reason*, edited by Barry K. Grant, 21–37. Metuchen, N.J.: Scarecrow Press, 1984.

———. "Through A Pumpkin's Eye: The Reflexive Nature of Horror." In *American Horrors*, edited by Gregory A. Waller, 114–28. Urbana: University of Illinois Press, 1986.

———. *Dreams of Darkness: Fantasy and the Films of Val Lewton*. Urbana: University of Illinois Press, 1985.

Terr, Lenore. "Terror Writing by the Formerly Terrified: A Look at Stephen King." In *The Psychoanalytic Study of the Child. Volume 44* (New Haven: Yale University Press, 1989), 369–90.

Tharp, Julie. "The Transvestite as Monster: Gender Horror in *The Silence of The Lambs*." *Journal of Popular Film & Television* 19 no. 3 (Fall 1991): 106–13.

Travers, Peter, and Stephanie Rieff. *The Story Behind The Exorcist*. New York: Signet Books, 1974.

Truffaut, Francois. *Hitchcock*. London: Panther, 1969.

Tudor, Andrew. *Image and Influence*. New York: St. Martin's Press, 1974.

———. *Monsters and Mad Scientists: A Cultural History of the Horror Movie*. Oxford: Blackwell, 1989.

Turk, Edward Baron. "Deriding the Voice of Jeanette MacDonald: Notes on Psychoanalysis and the American Film Musical." *Camera Obscura* 25–26 (1991): 225–50.

Twitchell, James B. *Dreadful Pleasures: An Anatomy of Modern Horror*. New York: Oxford University Press, 1985.

Underwood, Tim, and Chuck Miller, eds. *Fear Itself: The Horror Fiction of Stephen King*. San Francisco: Underwood-Miller, 1982.

Walker, Mark. *Vietnam Veteran Films*. Metuchen, N.J.: The Scarecrow Press, 1991.

Walker, Michael. "Melodrama and the American Cinema." *Movie* 29/30 (1982): 2–38.

Waller, Gregory. *The Living and the Undead: From Stoker's Dracula to Romero's Dawn of the Dead*. Urbana: University of Illinois Press, 1986.

Wardrop, Stephanie. "They Don't Have a Name for It Yet: Patriarchy, Gender and Meat-Eating in Jonathan Demme's *The Silence of the Lambs*." *Literature Interpretation Theory* 5 (1994): 95–105.

———, ed. *American Horrors: Essays on the Modern American Horror Film*. Urbana: University of Illinois Press, 1987.

Wilden, Anthony. *System and Structure: Essays in Communication and Exchange*. 2nd. ed. London: Tavistock Publications, 1984.

Willeman, Paul. "Looking at the Male." *Framework* 15/16/17 (1981): 16.

Williams, Linda. "When the Woman Looks." In *Re-Vision: Essays in Feminist Film Criticism*, edited by Mary Ann Doane, Patricia Mellancamp, and Linda Williams. American Film Institute Monograph Series 3. Frederick, M.D.: University Publications of America, 1984.

———. "Film Bodies: Gender, Genre, and Excess." *Film Quarterly* 44, no. 4 (1991): 2–13.

Williams, Tony. "*The Texas Chainsaw Massacre*." *Movie* 25 (1977/78): 12–16.

———. "George A. Romero's *Zombies: Dawn of the Dead*." *Cinema Spectrum* 1 (1980): 14–19.

———. "Horror in the Family." *Focus on Film* 36 (1980): 14–20.

———. "Wes Craven: An Interview." *Journal of Popular Film & Television* 8, no. 3 (1980): 10–14.

———. "Family Horror." *Movie* 27/28 (1980–81): 117–26.

———. "Close Encounters of the Authoritarian Kind." *Wide Angle* 5, no. 4 (1983): 22–27.

———. "*White Zombie*: Haitian Horror." *Jump Cut* 28 (1983): 18–20.

———. "Cohen on Cohen." *Sight and Sound* 53, no. 1 (1983/84): 21–25.

———. "Oliver Stone: Less than Meets the Eye." *cineACTION* 29 (1992): 40–55.

Willis, Sharon. "Special Effects: Sexual and Social Difference in *Wild at Heart*." *Camera Obscura* 25–26 (1992): 275–95.

Wills, Garry. *Reagan's America: Innocents at Home*. New York: Doubleday & Co, 1987.

Winogura, Dale. "Friedkin on *The Exorcist*." *Cinefantastique* 3, no. 4 (1974): 14–17.

Winter, Douglas E. *Stephen King*. Washington: Starmont House, 1982.

———, ed. *Faces of Fear: Encounters with the Creators of Modern Horror*. New York: Berkeley Books, 1985.

———. *Stephen King: The Art of Darkness*. New York: Signet, 1986.

Wood, Robin. "Images of Childhood." In *Personal Views: Explorations in Film*, 153–72. London: Gordon Fraser, 1976.

———. "*Race with the Devil*." *Movie* 23 (1977): 23–26.

———. "Ideology, Genre, Auteur." *Film Comment* 13, no. 1 (1977): 46–51.

———. "80s Hollywood: Dominant Tendencies." *cineACTION!* 1 (1985): 2–5.

———. "Cat and Dog: Lewis Teague's Stephen King Movies." *cineACTION!* 2 (1985): 39–46.

———. *Hollywood: From Vietnam to Reagan*. New York: Columbia University Press, 1986.

———. "The Woman's Nightmare: Masculinity in *Day of the Dead*." *cineACTION!* 6 (1986): 45–49.

———. *Hitchcock's Films Revisited*. New York: Columbia University Press, 1986.

———. "Leavis, Marxism and Film Culture." *cineACTION!* 8 (1987): 3–13.

Young, Elizabeth. "Here Comes the Bride: Wedding Gender and Race in *Bride of Frankenstein*." *Feminist Studies* 17, no. 3 (1991): 403–37.

———. "*The Silence of the Lambs* and the Flaying of Feminist Theory." *Camera Obscura* 27 (1991): 5–36.

Zamora, Lois, ed. *The Apocalyptic Vision in America*. Bowling Green, Ohio: Bowling Green University Press, 1982.

Zaretsky, Eli. *Capitalism, The Family and Personal Life*. Canada: New Dimension Pamphlet, 1975.

Zinman, Toby Silverman, ed. *David Rabe: A Casebook*. New York: Garland, 1991.

Index of Titles

Index of Names

CPSIA information can be obtained at www.ICGtesting.com
Printed in the USA
LVOW12s2133260215

428574LV00005B/374/P